THE COMPLEX LANDSCAPE OF
ASYLUM AND REFUGE IN EUROPE

THE COMPLEX LANDSCAPE OF
ASYLUM AND REFUGE IN EUROPE

Parihar Maninder

HOW
ACADEMICS
an imprint of Highlyy Publishing LLP

ISBN: 978-93-95522-92-2
First Published : 2024

Published by : HOW ACADEMICS

an imprint of Highlyy Publishing LLP

Correspondence Address : 4/30 A II Floor, Double Storey Buildings
Vijay Nagar, Delhi-110009
Editorial: +91 9811026449
Sales : +91 9999953412
Email: info@howacademics.com
Website: www.howacademics.com

Contents

List of Figures

List of Tables

Preface

In the tumultuous intersection of humanity's aspirations and geopolitical realities, the issue of asylum and refuge in Europe stands as a testament to our collective moral compass and the intricacies of policy-making in an ever-evolving world. "The Complex Landscape of Asylum and Refuge in Europe" aims to unravel the intricate tapestry of challenges, dilemmas, and possibilities surrounding this pivotal issue.

This book is a collaborative endeavor, a mosaic crafted by the insights, expertise, and dedication of scholars and experts committed to understanding and addressing the multifaceted dimensions of Europe's asylum landscape. Each chapter delves deep into a distinct facet, offering a comprehensive panorama that spans from pressing concerns to visionary solutions.

We commence our exploration by dissecting the amalgamation of Migration Pressures in Europe and the Rise of Terrorism Concerns. This sets the stage, highlighting the complex interplay between global migratory patterns and security apprehensions, grounding our understanding in the present-day reality.

From there, we embark on a journey through the nuanced trajectories of policy formulation for Asylum Seekers and Refugees, contemplating the intricate Future of Policy and grappling with the unpredictable Fate of Irregular Migration to Europe. Responding to Asylum Issues becomes paramount as we examine the Problems and Responses within the European landscape, punctuated by the complexities of Border Security Management and the dynamics of Mediterranean Migration.

As the narrative unfolds, we traverse the legal ramifications of Immigration between the European Union and Africa, pondering Factors Influencing Asylum Seeking and contemplating the far-reaching Effects of crises on security and defence expenditures.

Our journey takes a crucial turn toward envisioning a future built on Secure and Lawful Routes for Asylum Seekers, exploring Technology Solutions Centered on Migrants, and envisioning Migration Patterns and Advancements through the lens of the 2030 Blueprint. The Ukrainian Crisis becomes a poignant focal point, underscoring the pressing need for Improved Coordination in European Asylum Policy.

This compendium doesn't seek to offer absolute solutions. Instead, it serves as a beacon, illuminating the intricate pathways and complexities inherent in Europe's asylum and refuge landscape. It invites policymakers, scholars, activists, and global citizens to engage in an informed dialogue, fostering empathy, understanding, and collaboration to shape a future where the dignity and safety of those seeking asylum stand at the forefront of our collective conscience.

In essence, this book is an invitation—a call to navigate the complex terrain together, aspiring for a Europe where compassion, wisdom, and pragmatism converge to create a landscape where asylum and refuge are not just ideals but tangible realities for those in need.

Chapter 1
Migration Pressures in Europe and the Rise of Terrorism Concerns

Since 2015, when EU countries got more than 1.2 million requests for asylum, migration and terrorism have become more and more linked in Europe, both in public discussions and on government agendas. In particular, the fact that the terrorists who attacked Paris on November 13, 2015, used the eastern Mediterranean migration route to try to leave and return to Europe without being caught has moved counterterrorism debates towards looking at whether the threat of terrorism in Europe is linked to the number of people moving there. Here, a lot of worries about the refugee situation are based on two main assumptions: "refugees are vulnerable to radicalisation and recruitment" and "the refugee flow is a back door." Terrorists might try to get in touch with refugees on their way to or in protection centres. Are refugees more likely to become radicalised? Could terrorists sneak into Europe by pretending to be refugees? In conclusion, do the current migration flows to Europe make the threat that terrorist groups bring to Europe worse? Given how important these questions are to public and policy debates right now, this chapter thinks it's best to take an approach that neither cynically exaggerates nor totally ignores the risks that refugees and migrants from places where terrorist groups operate might pose.

This chapter starts by looking at the two key assumptions above to answer questions and address concerns about migration and terrorism. The chapter then talks about how a perceived link between the threat of terrorism and the ongoing refugee situation has led to new policy initiatives and legislative measures in the European Union (EU). This helps to figure out how important these assumptions are from a policy perspective. Among the new rules are the following:

- The extension of the role and capacity of Frontex (which in April 2016 was renamed the European Border and Coast Guard Agency)
- The extraordinary establishment of temporary national border controls by some member states

- The EU's March 2016 partnership agreement with Turkey
- The provisional establishment of a EU Passenger Name Record directive in April 2016
- The simultaneous creation in January 2016 of a European Counter Terrorism Centre and a European Migrant Smuggling Centre

Even though these measures were made to deal with not just terrorism but also migration as a whole, they still make the danger of terrorism through migration seem urgent, new, and high. But is the danger really so big that a lot of new steps need to be taken, or has it been blown out of proportion and can it really be handled by improving the steps that are already in place? Politicians rarely talk about these kinds of policy questions when they talk about security, because they are usually too busy talking about the nature of the threat. This DIIS report uses statistics, articles, reports, and a newly created database to question the two above-mentioned assumptions: "refugees as vulnerable to radicalisation and recruitment" and "the refugee flow as a back door." The goal is to talk about the policy changes that have come about because of these assumptions.

By questioning these two assumptions first, it's possible to understand the reasoning and evidence behind them and compare new policy measures to those that are already in place. Also, it gives us a chance to talk about how new and old measures are reacting to these logics and pieces of evidence. Instead of talking about why terrorist acts happen, which is how most debates on counterterrorism are set up, this chapter asks how terrorism has been done and what can be done to stop it.

There are three parts to the study. First, it talks about the idea that people coming into the EU through migration are more likely to become radicalised or join a terrorist group. Second, it looks into the idea that terrorists have used migrant flows as a way to sneak into the EU. Third, it looks at these assumptions in light of new and current EU policies and measures that are meant to deal with the idea that migration and terrorism are linked. In the end, the study says that the focus on new anti-terrorism initiatives in the EU risks making it hard to see the flaws in the measures that are already in place, which needs to be fixed if terror threats from migration are to be stopped. Since this particular threat has often happened because of flaws in measures that were already in place, it is not always necessary to find "new" methods to deal with it. Instead, it may be more important to invest in and strengthen measures that are already in place.

The Threat of Radicalization and Recruitment Among Refugees

In 2015, almost 1.3 million people from Iraq, Afghanistan, Nigeria, and Pakistan asked for refuge in the EU. Nearly half a million people from Syria also asked for asylum. Since almost three-quarters of all deaths from terrorism around the world in 2015 happened in these countries, there is already a clear link between the actions of terrorist groups and the situation of refugees in the EU. We don't know exactly why these migrants are seeking refuge in the EU, but it is clear that they are running away from places where terrorist groups are active. IS is trying to keep people from leaving their power, so they are trying to create this link, or disassociation. Since 2015, the group has used local media in Syria, Iraq, and Yemen to run large-scale propaganda campaigns that show people who leave the Caliphate as "infidels" who want to live in non-Islamic countries instead of protecting their Muslim friends.

The connection between IS and migration is an example of some of the complicated ways that terrorism and the refugee crisis in Europe are linked. But people have very different ideas about how this link should be understood and how it should affect policies. On the one hand, Islamic State's threats to use "migrants as a "psychological weapon"" have led far-right politicians across Europe, like the Czech Prime Minister Milos Zeman, to say that refugee flows are part of a "organised invasion" of radicalised Muslims into Europe, which means that borders need to be closed. On the other hand, international aid groups have pushed back against these claims by pointing out that refugees are running away from terrorism, not joining it. In a September 2016 report, the UN's Special Rapporteur on counter-terrorism and human rights said, "There is no evidence that migration leads to more terrorist activity." Instead, the chapter says that if people think that migration leads to a higher risk of terrorism, this could lead to "migration policies that are restrictive or that violate human rights" and "create conditions that are favourable to terrorism."

In the next part of the study, it looks at how much refugees and migrants have been radicalised or recruited to take part in recent terrorist attacks in Europe. The article then talks about how IS wants to use refugees to divide Europe.

The Hazard of Radicalization and Recruitment Amongst Refugees

In the December 2016 Europol report, Changes in Modus Operandi of IS revisited, it is called a "real and immediate danger" that unfriendly conditions in Europe could make some members of the Syrian diaspora more likely to become radicalised. The German government took this worry seriously because in 2016, they said they got about 300 reports of terrorists trying to attract refugees. No matter how much migrants hate the country that takes them in or how much they already hate the West, it is likely that Islamic extremist recruiters will try to get among asylum-seekers and asylum facilities, if not to try to get them to join, then at least to cause political division and polarisation. IS has known for a long time that it is in its best interest to make people suspicious of refugees and make the refugee situation worse. This is done to turn people in the EU against refugees seeking protection, creating an atmosphere of fear that could make it easier for people to become radicalised and join IS.

So far, the idea that IS is using the flow of refugees into Europe as a "weapon" has been greatly overstated. This doesn't mean that IS and other groups haven't tried to get refugees to join them in Europe, or that refugees haven't planned attacks in Europe on their own. Yet, when we only look at attacks in Europe that happened between January 2016 and April 2017, and only look at information from open sources, we find that out of four terrorist attacks in Europe, four asylum-seekers (three of whom had their asylum requests denied) were involved, but no refugees were. We started in 2016 because it was the first year after the large number of refugees arrived in 2015. Asylum seekers were engaged in attacks in Wurzburg, Ansbach, and the Berlin Christmas market in 2016, and in Stockholm in April 2017. Since a rejected asylum-seeker is technically a migrant, we could show the overview in a different way and come to the conclusion that no real refugees, one asylum-seeker, and three irregular migrants whose asylum requests were denied were involved in four terrorist attacks in Europe during this time.

Acts of Terrorism Perpetrated by Asylum Seekers

- Wurzburg train attack, 18 July 2016: Riaz Khan Ahmadzai (aka Muhammad Riyad). Pakistani asylum-seeker, arrived in Germany in 2015.
- Ansbach bombing, 24 July 2016: Mohammad Daleel. A Syrian asylum-seeker. Registered as a refugee in Bulgaria, but arrived in Germany in 2014, where he sought asylum. The German authorities rejected his asylum request on 2 December 2014 and sought to deport him back to Bulgaria. The deportation could not be carried out due to his psychiatric condition, which had led him to attempt suicide.
- The Berlin Christmas market attack in December 2016: Anis Amri, Tunisian citizen, came to Italy in 2011 to escape a prison sentence in Tunisia. In July 2015, after spending years in an Italian prison, he traveled to Germany. In April 2016, he applied for asylum under a false name. The request was rejected, and the German authorities tried to deport him back to Tunisia.

- Stockholm attack, 7 April 2017: Rakhmat Akilov. Uzbek citizen. Arrived in Sweden April 2014. His asylum request was rejected.

As the above story shows, it can be very important to tell the difference between refugees, asylum-seekers, and migrants when trying to figure out how dangerous the claimed link between refugees and terrorists is. It's important not to mix up the different types of people and to be very clear about whether someone is a refugee, an asylum seeker, a migrant, or a foreign soldier. Asylum-seeker is a very broad and inclusive term, since anyone who is not a member of the EU can, in theory, ask for asylum. 'Refugee' is a much smaller group. In this study, "refugee" is used as a legal term. The appropriate authorities of the country that is taking in the asylum seeker decide whether or not the person can become a refugee.

We think that four people seeking refuge were involved in the attacks that happened during the time we are looking at. Since "asylum-seeker" is a very broad term that, in theory, lets any non-EU person ask for asylum, the cases that fall into it need to be broken down and clarified. In the next section, we'll also say if the killings had any direct link to IS.

The attack in Wurzburg is the first time in 2016 that an asylum-seeker has done something terroristic in Europe. Riaz Ahmed Khan Ahmadzai, who was from Pakistan, struck several people in a train in Wurzburg on July 18, 2016. He hurt four people before he was shot and killed. Ahmedzai asked for asylum as a minor from Afghanistan in Germany in 2015, but it turned out that he was possibly from Pakistan, which isn't usually thought of as a refugee country. Shortly before the attack, he talked to an IS member in Saudi Arabia, and IS was quick to take credit for it afterwards.

On July 24, 2016, a Syrian man looking for refuge, Mohammad Daleel, blew himself up in front of a wine bar in Ansbach. He killed himself and hurt several other people. Daleel tried to get protection in Germany, but his request was denied because he had already done so in Bulgaria in 2013. Later, it came out that Daleel had also talked to a member of IS in Saudi Arabia, and IS later took credit for the attack. Daleel's case is different from the attack in Wurzburg because he had mental illness and had tried to kill himself more than once. The German government tried to send him back to Bulgaria, but because of his health, the move was put off.

Rakhmat Akilov, who was from Uzbekistan, drove a truck into a department store in Stockholm in April 2017, killing four people. Akilov came to Sweden in 2014 and asked to be let stay there. His request was turned down, and he went away before he could carry out the attack. Even though he swore allegiance to IS, there is no proof that he is directly connected to this group.

Lastly, Anis Amri, who attacked a Christmas market in Berlin in December 2016, had also asked for refuge, but it was denied because he didn't have a good reason. Amri went to Europe in 2011 to avoid going to jail in Tunisia. He ended up on the island of Lampedusa, where he took part in a violent riot at a temporary shelter for migrants. He was then given a jail sentence of four years. When he was freed in July 2015, he went to Germany without permission and applied for shelter there in April 2016. He had sworn loyalty to IS, so the German security services kept an eye on him for a while. Amri is an example of an illegal immigrant with a serious criminal record who chose to apply for asylum under a fake name after living in Europe for five years. At the time of the attack, Germany was trying to send him back to his home country of Tunisia. Amri's situation shows how broad the term "asylum-seeker" can be. Even though he was officially a refugee seeker, he had been in Europe for five years before he asked for asylum under a fake name. So, we think of him as a borderline case.

Two of the people mentioned came to Europe before 2015, which is when the official start of the refugee crisis in Europe is believed to be. This means that the Wurzberg attack was the only act of terrorism in Europe that was carried out by an asylum-seeker from 2015.

Refugees as a Ground for Fostering Polarization

Even though there have been cases of asylum-seekers being involved in terrorist attacks in Europe, the idea that refugees are a "Trojan horse" of potential terrorists seems overblown, if not totally false. Also, there is evidence that asylum-seekers and migrants who come to the EU from places where terrorist groups operate are not only open to becoming radicalised but also willing to report attempts to join them or cases where they think they are becoming radicalised. Under any circumstances, the rise in the number of terrorist acts in 2015 and 2016 cannot be linked to the rise in the number of refugees and asylum seekers. Instead, most of the attacks and most of the deaths in Europe in 2015 and 2016 were done by European citizens, some of whom were "returnees" who had joined IS or al Qaeda in Syria or elsewhere to fight. In fact, the same thing happened in the last ten years.

But we shouldn't forget that terrorist groups like IS can make money off of the mere idea that refugees are being radicalised and turned into weapons. This kind of suspicion helps these groups achieve their larger goals of causing political and social changes instead of real physical harm. Also, we shouldn't forget that IS had and still has a reason to want to use the ongoing refugee situation in Europe and how it is handled by European officials to increase fear, deepen political and social divisions, and make it easier for people to join IS and become violent extremists.

IS's claim in January 2015 that they had sent 4,000 fighters to Europe through Turkey is a clear example of how they want Europeans to think wrongly about refugees. Even though this amount is too high, just talking about it makes refugees seem more dangerous and creates environments that aren't friendly to refugees, which could make them easier to recruit and radicalise. So, Europe's so-called "refugee crisis" gives IS a lot of ways to make people fight with each other. Even though it turned out to be false, the idea that asylum-seekers were behind the attacks in Paris on November 13, 2015, caused political disagreements about refugees in Europe and may have been a factor in the attacks on refugee camps in Germany, France, and Sweden that happened afterwards. IS gets political power from these violent and divided responses, and the group hopes to use fear and division to get more people to join and become more extreme.

Even though one asylum-seeker, three irregular migrants, and no refugees were involved in terrorist attacks in Europe from January 2016 to April 2017, IS has a clear interest in portraying refugees, asylum-seekers, and migrants as terrorists in order to spark polarisation and create a base for recruitment and radicalisation.

Backdoor Entry of Refugees into Europe

In September 2015, the influx of refugees put a lot of pressure on the EU's external borders. There were also fears that terrorists from IS-controlled areas outside the EU could "infiltrate" refugee flows to sneak into the EU without being caught. Later, it was found that a large number of the Paris attackers in November 2015 and the Brussels attackers in March 2016 had gotten into the EU by using fake papers and Syrian passports to register as asylum seekers or travel through migration flows to Hungary and then to Belgium. The danger of terrorists entering the EU through migration flows raises the question of how much extra steps need to be taken to control migrants and borders.

Migration

Recent news that IS has been putting together teams of foreign fighters in Syria since 2014 to carry out "revenge" attacks "back" in Europe has helped shed light on how European foreign fighters who were on watch lists in Europe used illegal migration routes to get back to Europe without being caught. The Soufan Group says that about 27,000 foreign rebels have gone to Syria and Iraq. About 6,000 of them are thought to be Europeans. Most of them are from France, Germany, and the UK. Foreign soldiers leave their home countries and cross borders. Because of this, they are migrants. If European foreign fighters use illegal migration routes on purpose to get back into the EU and then do things related to terrorism, this suggests a link between migration trends and terrorism.

Frontex's 2016 annual risk report says, "The Paris attacks in November 2015 made it clear that terrorists could use irregular migration flows to get into the EU." Former French Interior Minister Bernard Cazeneuve also said that IS had turned making fake travel papers and using passports stolen in Iraq, Syria, and Libya into a whole "industry." Since then, such comments have become part of a trend towards making migrant controls and border policies more like airport security. In August 2016, for example, Europol sent a team to Greece to look for possible jihadists among the 60,000 refugees living in the country's migrant camps. Still, the fear of terrorists getting into the EU through migration flows raises the question of how much extra steps need to be taken to control migrants and borders. Exploring how migration routes can be attractive to terrorists, like how the Paris attackers were able to get back into the EU without being caught, is a good way to start figuring out how likely it is that terrorists will use migration flows as a back door to get into Europe and how policy could be changed to make that less likely.

For European foreign fighters, who are often already known to the authorities and being watched, migration routes and the position of asylum-seeker may be good ways to get back into Europe to carry out attacks. Foreign fighters and people suspected of being terrorists can sneak back into Europe without being caught if the refugee process is confusing or border guards don't have the tools to check identity papers when they arrive. By using fake names and connections they made in Europe, they can escape being arrested when they get back to the United States. IS is getting a lot of pressure in Syria and Iraq right now, but Europeans who have returned home could still try to sneak into migration paths. In a press release from December 2016, Europol said that the coalition's work to weaken IS's strongholds in Syria and Iraq could cause more foreign fighters to try to join the EU. In May 2017, the head of the U.N. Security Council's counterterrorism office, Jean-Paul Laborde, warned that European countries think the number of foreign fighters coming back has gone up and that these people could be "more dangerous." So, we can see that there is a clear link between migration trends and terrorism. Again, it's important not to underestimate IS's political desire to show that they can use migration paths and that they are doing so. But it doesn't look like the main threat is one in which more refugees coming into the EU increases the risk of terrorism. The threat seems to come from the fact that foreign fighters who are European citizens or residents are coming back to Europe and that officials don't know how to find them.

The French-Belgian Foreign Fighter Nexus and its Intersection with Migration Pathways

The French-Belgian foreign-fighter network, which was behind the Belgian Verviers plot in January 2015, the Paris attacks on November 13, 2015, and two attacks in Brussels in March 2016, is a good example of how migration flows to Europe can be used as a back door for foreign fighters and terrorist suspects. Except for the two suicide bombs at the Stade de France and the explosives expert Ahmad Alkhald, all of the accomplices in Paris and all five of the attackers in Belgium were European citizens. Many of them had gone to Syria to fight as foreign fighters and then come back to the EU to do attacks. None of them was a refugee. As of June 2015 and onward, European foreign fighters with European passports, many of which were flagged as suspicious in EU information sharing databases, were using migration routes to get back to Europe without being caught by the French-Belgian network.

Fig. 1.1 - Popular Migration Routes

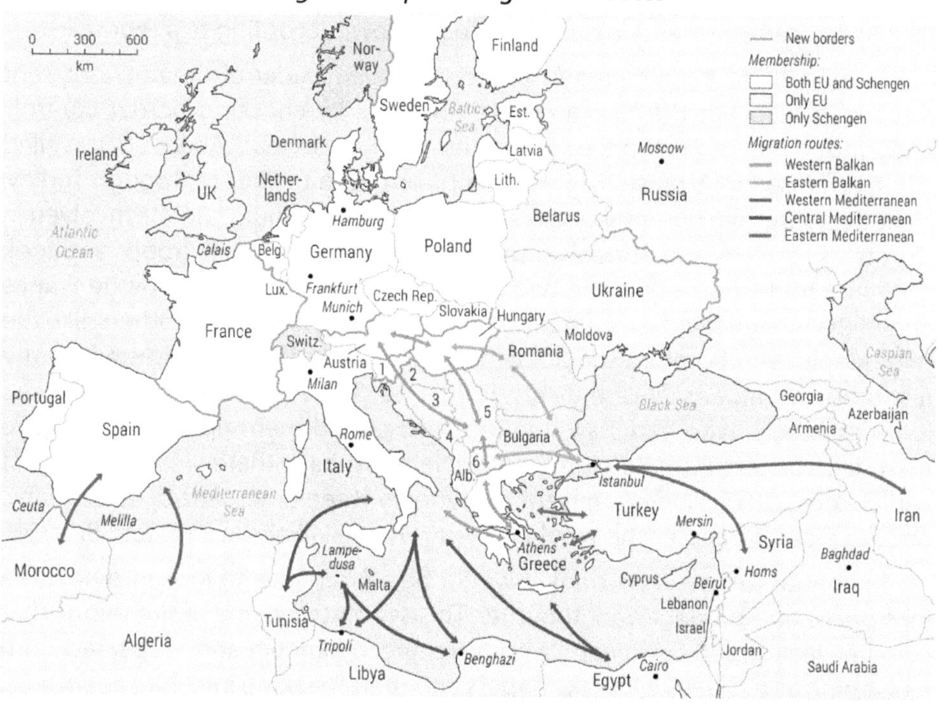

Source: Europol, ICMPD, IGM, UNHCR.

Note: 1) Slovenia - 2) Croatia - 3) Bosnia Herzegovina - 4) Montenegro - 5) Serbia - 6) Macedonia.

IS set up a branch for outside operations in the second half of 2014 to plan and carry out strikes in Europe. Foreign fighters who spoke French in the Syrian town of Raqqa were especially busy in this way. The Verviers plot, which was stopped in Belgium in January 2015, was the first large-scale attack in Europe that this group had planned. Most of the people who had come back from IS and were involved in this plot came back to Europe through Turkey and Greece, possibly using fake Belgian passports. Only one of the people who planned the attack in Verviers, a Frenchman named Walid Hamam, is known to have pretended to be a Syrian refugee in Greece before going to Belgium.

In June 2015, Macedonia agreed to give people going from Greece to Serbia a 72-hour transit pass. The opening of this "Balkan route" was a turning point that made it possible for the francophone IS network to use the migration paths in a planned way to get back into Europe. Using fake Syrian IDs, the network was able to send back into Europe experienced foreign fighters whose names were already on European watch lists. This was done without being caught. Because of this, "almost all of the Paris and Brussels attackers came back to Europe with fake Syrian passports and joined the refugee flow," according to a report.

In June 2015, Abdelhamid Abaaoud, the main leader of the network, sent a scout to map out the "Balkan route" in detail by checking border controls and smuggling opportunities. Once the path was clear, Abaaoud travelled along it himself in August 2015. He went from Syria to Greece through Turkey, Macedonia, Serbia, Hungary, and Austria. Others who would later be involved in the attacks in Paris and Brussels came back to Europe in small groups and took the same route. Some, like the two people who bombed the Stade de France and Alkhald, registered as refugees on the Greek island of Leros. Others, like the two people who bombed the Stade de France and Alkhald, registered for the first time in Hungary. Once they got to Europe, Salah Abdeslam, the network's logistics expert, who had stayed in Brussels, picked them up. Abdeslam gave them fake papers from Belgium and drove them back there. Between August and October 2015, Abdeslam went to Hungary three times and Ulm, Germany, once to pick up people who would take part in the killings in Paris and Brussels.

In light of this case, we think it would be a good idea to look into how the EU's police and borders work together. This seems to be one of the things that could have stopped Europeans who were already known and suspected from registering as refugees with fake papers and then sneaking into Europe without being caught.

Failure of EU Border Control

The Paris killings were a wake-up call for Europe about what needs to be done to stop terrorists from moving there. Eight of the Paris suspects were already on monitoring lists and EU databases as radicalised or suspects. Two of the people who attacked the Stade de France, for example, had stolen Syrian IDs and fake papers that matched their registrations at a refugee centre on the Greek island of Leros. But none of these checks or applications showed that the passports were on Interpol's list of stolen items or that they were fake. In a similar way, after the Paris attacks, French gendarmes stopped Salah Abdeslam's car at the Belgian border and held him for 30 minutes before letting him go. In the EU's shared information database, the Schengen Information System (SIS), the Belgian government had only put information about his criminal past, not his ties to radical Islamism.

In the February 2015 issue of IS's magazine Dabiq, the main planner of the Paris attacks, Abdelhamid Abaaoud, bragged about how he had made several trips between Syria and Belgium without being caught, even though both French and Belgian intelligence services were looking for him as a possible terrorist. Abaaoud was wanted for arrest in both Europe and the rest of the world, but he was able to get from Belgium to Syria via Egypt in March 2013 and then back to Europe. Even though there is no proof that he made it all the way back to Belgium before August 2015, the fact that he was able to watch the Verviers plot from an apartment in Athens shows that he had no trouble getting into the Schengen area. When he went back to Belgium in August 2015, it turned out that he had also gone to the UK, possibly by ferry to Dover.

Lapses of SIS (Schengen Information System)

SIS is the most common way for people in Europe to share information about border control and security. It has information about people who are not allowed to enter or stay in the Schengen area, people who are wanted, and lost or stolen property. It also has the documents and information needed to find people and prove their identities. One of the good things about the SIS database is that it can be used in real time, like when a police officer or border guard checks the IDs of people who want to cross an EU border. SIS was changed to SIS II in 2017. SIS II should get more and better info than SIS I. But SIS II still doesn't take into account the different laws in each country about how data can be used or how well each police officer or border guard can use the database.

Issues with Border Management System

Foreign fighters who were already known to authorities and flagged in international databases for sharing information were able to travel without being caught, even though they registered at EU asylum facilities and border crossings. This shows that border management has a role to play at the intersection of migration and terrorism. This study says that border policies and management are in a special place when it comes to dealing with the problems caused by this nexus. As the study says, terrorists rarely work from "one place." Instead, they need to be able to cross borders or "migrate" between the strongholds of terrorist organisations outside of Europe and networks that already exist in Europe that can help with logistics and organisation.

The fact that foreign fighters and possible terrorists move across lines could be used to link the risk of terrorism not only with migrants but also with freedom of movement in general. But making these kinds of links would be oversimplifying things and could lead to extra steps that put too much faith in how well border controls work. As everyone knows, most terrorists are born or raised in the country or are legal residents. This means that closing or tightening borders can only do so much. Also, closing borders can make organised international crime worse and force foreign fighters who want to come back to use more illegal entryways that are harder to control. But the fact that terrorists often cross borders and are often under monitoring and known to national security services does make law enforcement, police, and border cooperation and processing unique ways to find and identify terrorists.

The strikes in Paris in 2015 show how weak the EU's borders are and how they can be used against it. One of the Paris terrorists was able to get past Greek front-line staff with a passport that had already been marked as stolen in Interpol's database. This may be the best example of how weak these systems are. Another example is how Abdelslam was able to pass checks at the French-Belgian border right after the Paris attacks, even though he was known, suspected, and in the EU's SIS database.

When put together, these cases show two major problems. The first problem is that there isn't enough operational staff and frontline technology to handle and find things like stolen passports in the flow of migrants at the EU's external borders. The second example, about Abdelslam, shows that national police and security forces don't have the same access to international information or don't have access to it at all. In conclusion, one of the biggest problems with returning foreign fighters and terrorist suspects seems to be a lack of or limited operational and technological capability to use and cross-check suspects with already existing and available information-sharing resources within the EU. This weakness is important for evaluating and improving both the front-line staff at the EU's external borders and the police and national security forces inside Schengen.

The Risk of Introducing New Solutions to New Problems

In recent years, the EU has taken a number of steps to recognise the important role that sharing information and managing borders play in the fight against terrorism. Yet, the speed and newness with which these anti-terrorism measures are introduced run the risk of overshadowing the need to spend in aligning and improving already existing measures like SIS at the EU's external borders and in Schengen.

Since the attacks in Paris and Brussels in 2015 and 2016, security and law enforcement cooperation are two of the places in the EU that have gotten the most money and changed the most. The EU's spending budget for 2017 includes a total of six billion euros, which is 11,3% more than in 2016. This money will be used to deal with migration and strengthen security and anti-terrorism actions at EU borders. Several policy initiatives have been set in motion with the goal of improving and expanding information-sharing databases. These include the temporary creation of a Passenger Name Record in April 2016, a new version of the Schengen Information System (SIS II), and the creation of a Europol terrorist centre with "updated powers."

Passenger Name Record (PNR): PNR, which was adopted in April 2016, facilitates the use of passenger data for the prevention, detection, investigation and prosecution of terrorist offences. It obliges airlines to hand over passenger data on passengers who enter or depart from EU countries. This is supposed to enhance the control of travel flows at the external borders of the Schengen area.

European Travel Information And Authorization System (ETIAS): ETIAS was founded in order to strengthen security checks and information-gathering on visa-free travelers coming to Europe. Visa-free travel has been the most common way for criminals, including terrorists, to travel into the EU from the outside. ETIAS is supposed to contribute to the more efficient management of the EU's external borders.

In April 2016, the EU passed the Passenger Name Record (PNR) rule. This is one of the most important steps towards controlling travel into and out of the EU in recent years. The ruling makes it easier to use passenger information to stop, find, investigate, and prosecute terrorist crimes. It makes it so that airlines have to give EU countries the information they have on passengers who join or leave the EU. Also, in November 2016, the European Travel Information and Authorisation System (ETIAS) was set up to improve security checks and information gathering for people who don't need visas. Since April 2017, all people crossing the outside borders of the Schengen area, including EU members, are checked against the SIS II database. These are important steps, as visa-free travel has been one of the most common ways for criminals, including people suspected of being terrorists, to get into the EU from outside the country. The EU has also made it harder for refugees and migrants who don't have visas to move within its borders. This is happening at the main entry points, which are currently in Greece, Italy, and eastern Europe. In this case, the EU has put money into making FRONTEX, the European border institution, stronger by improving its operational skills and powers, especially by working with national border and coastguard staff.

By 2017, the Schengen Information System (SIS) was finally changed to SIS II. SIS II lets police, border guards, and customs officials, on the one hand, and European institutions like Europol and Eurojust, on the other, record information about wanted people and things, like criminals and terrorists, stolen ID papers and cars, and get real-time information and alarms when needed. This system is important for increasing and coordinating the sharing of information and making sure that it can be used right away. It does this by sending data put into SIS in one country right away to the central system, which can then alert searches in other countries that are relevant. By being able to find stolen passports or suspicious people in real time, SIS II could help EU countries stop known terrorists and possibly dangerous people from travelling without being caught.

But it's still not clear if these new and updated efforts will be able to get rid of the big technical and human problems that made it hard to use information-sharing databases until recently. There is a chance that the EU's problem with finding terrorist suspects isn't just a lack of data or data that isn't aligned. It could also be that member states, especially Italy and Greece, don't have the operational and technological skills or don't have the same skills to act on data that is already available in real time. It's one thing to have the technology, but it's a whole other thing to know how to use it.

Julian King, the EU security commissioner, told reporters in Brussels on December 21, 2016, after a meeting of three EU commissioners, "We are only as strong as our weakest database." He later added, "SIS is only as good as the data that is registered in it." Dimitris Avramopoulos, the Commissioner for Migration, Home Affairs, and Citizenship, said the same thing on September 14, 2016: "Improving the way we share information will help us fight terrorism better." But it might have been better to say, "We are only as strong as the ability of our weakest member state to use databases that share information." Or, to be more exact, "the EU's borders are only as strong as those of Italy and Greece, which are both in the Mediterranean." Many of the Paris attackers were listed in international databases, but national border guards at the EU's external borders did not notice them or their fake or stolen IDs. So, there were files, and they were updated. During the large influx of refugees in 2015, however, EU member states with an external border had a hard time getting the technology and people they needed to use these databases to process and track migration flows and asylum requests.

When it comes to countries like Greece and Italy, it doesn't seem like a good policy answer to give them more data without also giving them the people and tools they need to use that data. New and more data-sharing programmes don't automatically fix more basic problems with the way the EU manages its borders. Aside from the fact that some countries don't have enough money, these weaknesses also include the fact that law enforcement, spy services, and border controls in different member states have different practises, skills, and abilities.

EU Legislative Initiatives Post-2015

- End of 2015 to early 2016: Several EU countries introduced extraordinary internal EU border controls
- January 2016: Creation of European Counter Terrorism Centre and European Migrant Smuggling Centre
- March 2016: Partnership agreement with Turkey
- Early March 2016: The so-called Balkan route was declared shut when Macedonia, Croatia and Slovenia closed their borders
- April 2016: Provisional establishment of an EU Passenger Name Record directive (PNR)
- October 2016: Extension of the role and capacity of Frontex, renamed the European Border and Coast Guard
- April 2017: An amendment to the Schengen border code comes into force that introduces systematic database checks on all persons, including Schengen citizens, when they cross external borders

International Problems

There are many and complicated reasons why the EU's external borders don't have joint investments in their operational parts. One of the most obvious is probably that law enforcement and border management have been seen as the job of national security agencies and laws for a long time. This point is backed up by the fact that different border states have had different ways of managing, registering, and screening, which has sometimes led to information uploaded to foreign databases that isn't aligned and isn't the same as what was uploaded to other databases. This is made worse by the fact that the EU does not have a single method for checking documents. In this way, the EU's new focus on improving cooperation around sharing information could be seen as a simple way to avoid uncomfortable questions about how national law enforcement and border control work differently, what they are allowed to do, and how well they can do it in each member state.

So, you could say that the EU's focus on information sharing between states, joint capacity-building of internal security providers, and cross-border operational cooperation are all about national autonomy. This challenge is shown by the fact that EU member states are increasingly turning to national frameworks to improve their own security and border management. For example, Brexit, the re-imposition of temporary national border controls by member states, and the general unwillingness of national security services to share data are all examples of this. These examples of a return to national frameworks are attempts to protect national security through the autonomous management of national borders and to put national law enforcement ahead of the joint efforts of the EU and agencies like Europol and Eurojust. This trend doesn't fix the problems that let the Paris attackers get around without being caught. Those problems are the different, mismatched, and often nonexistent abilities of EU member states, especially EU border states and their national border staff, to process, register, and use the information-sharing databases at border crossings.

In relation to this, the claim that the Paris attacks show how terrorists can "sneak" into Europe by posing as refugees and that this attack makes it necessary to make refugees more secure, rely more on national security frameworks, and turn away from EU initiatives and agreements is not backed up by evidence. Most likely, member states won't be able to stop terrorism as well if they focus more on national security measures. Since terrorism is often international, it must also be stopped by people from different countries working together. As a result, along with new initiatives to share data, the most effective response would be to provide more operational, technological, and administrative support to the EU's external borders. This would include ensuring electronic connections to relevant Interpol and Europol databases and efficient processing of migrants at all external border crossings.

Bigger Picture

Terrorist groups like Islamic State and al Qaeda pose a threat to the EU in many ways. The problems that come up when the work of these organisations and the constant flow of people into Europe come together are mostly new and have never been seen before. Terrorist groups like IS depend on being able to change how they do things in response to weaknesses and changes in their surroundings. In this way, worries about a dangerous link between terrorism and the EU's continued flow of refugees are valid, and so is the effort to keep changing policies to address these worries.

This study looked at how terrorists can use migration flows by focusing on two main ideas: "refugees as likely to be radicalised and recruited" and "the refugee flow as a back door." It found that most people involved in terrorist acts in Europe were EU citizens or residents. It also found that Europeans who had joined IS in Syria used migration routes to sneak back into Europe without being caught. From January 2016 to April 2017, acts in Europe were done by neither refugees nor asylum-seekers, of whom three were turned away. In the short term, the terrorist danger in Europe does not come directly from refugees. Instead, it comes from EU citizens, residents, and to some extent, asylum seekers. However, in the long term, it is impossible to rule out less direct effects of mass immigration and possible ties to terrorism. Disenfranchisement and a real or perceived lack of opportunities and fairness make it possible for refugees and asylum-seekers to be recruited. When we think about the long run, we also have to ask if and how much radicalisation is a problem for the second generation of migrants. This question needs to be looked into more.

As the chapter moved on to talk about possible solutions, it looked at how our two main assumptions have been used to make EU policies and measures to stop terrorist groups from using migrant routes and flows. In this chapter, it was claimed that policies and measures related to border management have a unique chance of stopping some of the ways that terrorists have sometimes been able to use migration flows to their advantage.

The study also says that new international and national policies and laws about borders and cross-border cooperation run the risk of making it hard to see how much capacity needs to be built up in the way borders are normally managed. These weaknesses, which were in some ways used by the Paris attackers, are caused by differences in how, why, and how well member states share and use international information-exchange systems for border management and law enforcement in their own countries.

If these weaknesses get worse, they can't just be fixed by sharing more info or taking new steps, like making borders stricter. Instead, they require that the EU spend in people and technology to help with the normal and operational management of external borders as a joint project instead of a national one. Such an investment would not only help find terrorist suspects who are often already known, but it would also make it easier to process asylum claims. The security of refugees in need should never be put at risk by efforts to find potential terrorists or foreign fighters who are coming back home.

Chapter 2
The Future of Policy for Asylum Seekers and Refugees

The Syrian refugees' flight from their country caused a crisis that has thrown Europe's protection system into disarray and led to a growing divide over quick solutions. It has made it clear that the system isn't working well and that it needs to be changed. The current asylum system pushes people to make dangerous sea or land crossings to get to a place where they might be able to get refugee status. This system is inefficient, doesn't target people well, and doesn't have public support. In this chapter, I talk about some important facts about how refugee applications and policies have changed over time. I also talk about some economic results about what causes people to ask for asylum and how asylum policies affect how many people ask for asylum in countries where they end up. I look at several important aspects of public opinion in Europe and how it has changed over the last ten years to show why policy changes might be possible. This shows that the main focus of changes should be on three key areas. These are policies for controlling the borders, programs for resettling refugees who need safety the most, and better cooperation and sharing of the load among European countries.

From this chapter, there are a number of things we can say. One is that, contrary to what some people think, refugee policies, especially those that have to do with border control, have had a big effect on the number of asylum applications. Second, people are getting more and more supportive of real refugees, but they are very against illegal aliens. This suggests that people won't support an asylum policy that encourages migrants to take dangerous sea or land crossings to get into the country illegally so they can claim protection. This is especially true because a lot of people who ask for refuge don't get it and end up staying in the country illegally. Existing policies are also not well-targeted. They choose people who are willing to risk dying at sea or falling into the hands of shady people smugglers, not necessarily those who need humanitarian protection the most.

Direct resettlement of refugees from what are often very bad situations in their first countries of protection would be better, but it would require a big increase in the number of resettlement places. That would mean that host countries would have to work on sharing the load more. Even though some governments are against it, there is surprisingly strong popular support at the EU level for policies that are made together. Lastly, the current crisis has led to a quick change in policy, but the ongoing pressures of movement have made it harder to increase the number of people who can resettle. Still, the long-term goal should be to move away from'spontaneous' refuge seekers and toward a full resettlement program.

Refugees and Asylum Seekers

Ongoing Trends

In the last few years, Europe has been going through a migration problem, which has brought more attention to the situation of refugees. It's not a new thing. Every year, hundreds of thousands of people leave their home country or country of birth to find a safer place to live. The 1951 Refugee Convention says that refugees are people who have left their home country because they have a "well-founded fear of persecution." From 1982 to the present, the United Nations High Commissioner for Refugees (UNHCR) has kept track of the number of refugees around the world. This is shown in Figure 2.1. The most was 18 million in 1992, and then the number went down until 2005. In the last 10 years, it has grown slowly at first and then more quickly, reaching 16 million in 2015. It's important to remember that refugees are only a small part of the 65.3 million people who were violently displaced around the world at the end of 2015. This number also includes people who are looking for protection, don't have a nationality, are returned refugees, and, most importantly, the 37.5 million people who are displaced within their own country.

Asylum seekers are people who are trying to get refugee status in a different country. Figure 1 shows the number of asylum requests filed each year in 38 "industrialized" countries. This is a much smaller number (right scale) than the number of asylum requests filed all at once. Most of these are made up of people who got to their target country on their own and then applied for asylum on their own. Because of this, they are sometimes called "spontaneous" refuge seekers and just "migrants" when they are on the way or when they arrive. In 1992, there were more than 800,000 asylum requests. In the early 2000s, there were fewer, but still a lot. In 2015, there was a sharp rise to double the previous peak. The number shows that most of the applications are from Europe, which makes up 78% of the total over the whole time period, and especially from the EU-15, which makes up 71% of the total of 38 countries.

Fig 2.1 - Refugees and Asylum Seekers, 1982-2015

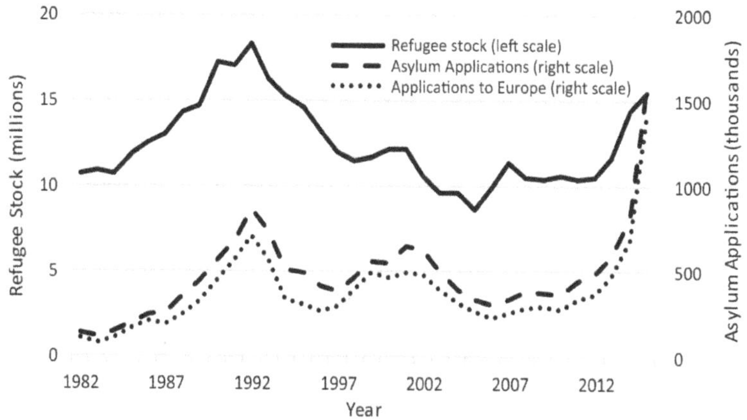

Sources: Refugee stock: 1982—99 from UNHCR (2000), Annex 3; 2000—15, UNHCR Statistical Yearbook, 2007 Annex Table 20, and 2014 Annex Table 25, and UNHCR Global Trends, 2015 Annex Table 1. Asylum applications to 'industrialized countries': 1982-2000 from UNHCR Statistical Yearbook, 2001, Table C1; 2001-15 from UNHCR Asylum Trends: Levels and Trends in Industrialized Countries, 2005, 2009, 2013 and 2015, Table 1.

Table 2.1 Top 20 origin countries for asylum applications to the EU

Annual applications 2006-10				**Annual applications 2011-15**			
Iraq	23,491	Bangladesh	5,713	Syria	112,093	Iran	13,874
Serbia	16,670	Sri Lanka	5,439	Afghanistan	58,331	Bangladesh	9,727
Russia	16,650	Eritrea	5,403	Serbia	43,619	Georgia	7,777
Afghani-stan	13,748	China	5,251	Iraq	34,168	Ukraine	7,392
Somalia	13,169	D R Congo	4,494	Pakistan	24,431	Macedonia	7,285
Pakistan	10,030	Armenia	4,335	Russia	21,461	D R Congo	6,753
Nigeria	7,851	Syria	4,228	Albania	20,491	Mali	6,690
Iran	7,337	Zimbabwe	3,834	Eritrea	19,023	Gambia	5,924
Turkey	6,244	Guinea	3,167	Nigeria	15,653	Algeria	5,854
Georgia	5,722	India	3,117	Somalia	15,379	Bosnia	5,382

Sources: UNHCR, Asylum Levels and Trends in Industrialized Countries, Table 4 or 5 for 2006-14; Eurostat, 'First time asylum applicants' for 2015. Notes: Serbia includes Kosovo and Montenegro; 'stateless' accounts for 1,878 applications p.a. in 2006-10 and 9,951 in 2011-15.

Since the fall of the Berlin Wall and the end of the Soviet Union in the mid-1980s, the number of asylum requests has gone up very quickly. This is because the fall of the Berlin Wall and the end of the Soviet Union opened the borders between Eastern and Western Europe. This made it easier for people to get asylum from these countries and for people from farther away to get to Europe. Even though there was some pushback in the form of stricter refugee policies, it is important to note that the number of people seeking asylum never went back to what it was in the early 1980s. The last few years have seen a very steep rise (but from a higher starting point), with the number reaching 1.6 million in 2015, which is much higher than the 1992 peak. With the current rise in asylum seekers and the partial breakdown of border controls, it's hard not to think of what happened 20 years ago. This could be seen as another "paradigm shift," but it's not clear yet if this small step up will lead to a higher level of asylum applications in the long run.

Origin of Refugees and Asylum Seekers

Most people who ask for refuge come from poor and middle-income countries where human rights are often violated or where minorities are often persecuted. Many of these countries are also in the middle of civil wars or international conflicts. Table 2.1 shows the 20 countries from which the most people moved to EU countries from 2006 to 2010 and from 2011 to 2015. In 2006–10 and 2011–15, these made up 72% of all bids to the EU. There are big source countries in Asia, Africa, and Europe, but some are more talked about in the news and in public debate than others. As you might expect, the Middle East is a big source, with countries like Iraq, Iran, Syria, and Turkey. However, Russia, Serbia, and Georgia are also important sources throughout the decade. Eritrea, Nigeria, the Democratic Republic of the Congo, and Somalia are the most important source countries in Africa. Afghanistan, Pakistan, Bangladesh, and Sri Lanka are the most important source countries in Asia. India and China, which have a lot of people, are also on the list for 2006–10, even though they have a small number of applications compared to the source population.

It is also important to note that the causes of asylum claims have stayed the same over time. From 2011 to 2015, 13 of the top 20 countries of origin also made the list from 2006 to 2010. In fact, 17 of the top 20 songs from 2011 to 2015 were also in the top 30 in 1995 to 1999. This is mostly because of long-lasting conflicts, government instability, and differences between different groups of people. So, changes in the number of applications over time are mostly caused by changes in the number of applications from a set of about 50 source countries, not by countries joining or leaving the list. From 2011 to 2015,

Syria had the most applications from the top 10 countries. In 2015, the number of applications from Syria hit an all-time high of 433,500. But the number of applications from Afghanistan, Eritrea, and Serbia, as well as to a smaller extent Iran, Pakistan, Nigeria, and Albania, has gone up sharply. Even though it is clear that the rise in refugee seekers from the Middle East and Eritrea is due to the rise in violence, it is less clear that this is the case for some of the other countries.

In the past few years, most of the focus has been on illegal immigrants who travel by sea. Many of them, but not all, planned to ask for refuge. In 2015, 1.8 million people crossed the Mediterranean and Aegean Seas, which was six times as many as the year before and twelve times as many as in 2008. Up until recently, the most common way to get in was by air with a legal visitor visa. However, as visa restrictions have spread and electronic tracking has become more common, these options have become less likely. People smugglers often help people travel by land and sea to get into the country where a refugee claim has been filed. Many people who are looking for asylum journey in stages, often through a number of transit countries. As we'll see below, the most common ways to get into the country have changed. This is partly because the origins of refugees are changing and partly because of new security measures at the border. The fact that there are more dangers on the way may be one reason why the number of asylum seekers with kids has dropped sharply since the 1990s. In 2014, two-thirds of the people who asked for protection in the EU were men. 54% were between the ages of 18 and 34, and of those, nearly 80% were men. More than a quarter of them were under 18 years old, and about a fifth of those were alone.

Choice of Country for Refuge

Different places have different numbers of people applying for asylum. Table 2.2 shows how many people have asked for refuge in EU countries, Norway, and Switzerland on average every year since 2001. The total from 30 countries shows that applications dropped to about a quarter of a million at the end of the 2000s, but rose to over 650,000 per year from 2011 to 2015. The EU-15 plus Norway and Switzerland make up about 90% of applications. From 2011 to 2015, nearly two-thirds of all applications went to the top five target countries, with Germany alone getting 27%. Most of the big destinations saw a drop in applications between 2001 and 2005 and 2006 and 2010, but applications to Italy, Greece, and Sweden went up. And while most countries grew over the last five years, some grew less, and a few even went down. Some of the Eastern European countries where people asked for refuge in the 1980s and 1990s later became places where people went.

Table 2.2 Annual Average Refuge Applications

	2001-05	2006-10	2011-15		2001-05	2006-10	2011-15
Austria	29,790	12,990	34,308	Latvia	16	40	295
Belgium	18,324	14,418	26,331	Lithuania	204	214	453
Bulgaria	1,764	850	8,218	Luxembourg	1,132	528	1,830
Cyprus	4,952	4,264	2,349	Malta	642	1,560	1,848
Czech R.	9,490	1,686	826	Netherlands	17,356	12,642	22,765
Den-mark	5,734	2,984	11,634	Norway	12,314	10,714	16,993
Estonia	10	20	131	Poland	6,026	7,194	10,087
Finland	3,146	3,542	9,743	Portugal	158	162	513
France	56,326	37,090	69,022	Romania	1,182	798	1,871
Germa-ny	54,900	26,252	175,212	Slovakia	8,618	1,556	438
Greece	6,572	16,692	11,638	Slovenia	1,238	316	335
Hungary	4,314	3,160	48,062	Spain	6,504	4,646	6,746
Iceland	84	50	176	Sweden	25,716	28,210	78,166
Ireland	7,790	3,360	1,966	Switzerland	18,376	13,326	27,705
Italy	11,664	16,102	48,075	UK	65,162	28,140	35,692
				Total	379,504	253,506	653,431

Sources: UNHCR, Asylum Levels and Trends in Industrialized Countries (various years), Table 1 for 2001 — 14; Eurostat, 'First time asylum applicants' for 2015.

The 1951 Refugee Convention is the basis for the rule on asylum in countries where people want to go. It has three main parts. First, Article 1 says that a refugee is someone who lives outside of their normal country and has a "well-founded fear of persecution" because of certain things. So, the status of a refugee must be decided on a case-by-case basis based on the evidence that is provided. The second is the non-refoulement clause (Article 33.1), which says that a person who wants refuge can't be sent back to the border of a country where his or her life or freedom would be in danger. In reality, this means that some applicants can't be sent back even if they don't meet the requirements for refugee status. This is one reason why there are other types of protection besides refugee status. Article 31 says that being in or entering the country illegally doesn't stop someone from going through the process to see if they are a refugee or change the result of that process. In theory, a state doesn't have a cap on how many applications it has to accept, and each one has to go through the proper steps. But the Convention was made in a time when things were very different than they are now, and it didn't include a specific set of rules for how to deal with a large number of asylum seekers coming to the territory at once. So, it gave receiving countries a lot of options for what they could do to stop people from asking for protection. The most important of these are stricter controls at the border and stricter ways to figure out someone's standing.

Fig. 2.2 - Convention and total recognition rates, 20 European countries, 1982-2015

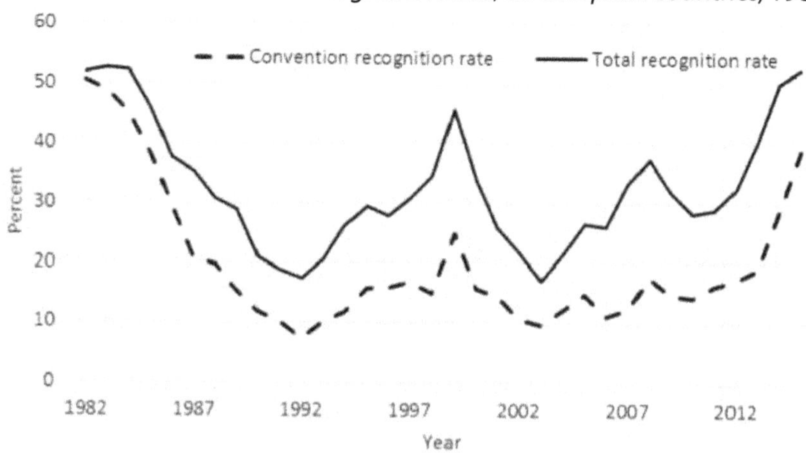

Asylum claims are put through a process to see if the person can be recognized as a refugee according to the Convention's meaning or is given protection for other humanitarian reasons. A lot of people who try to get asylum fail to get some kind of respect. From 1982 to 2015, Figure 2.2 shows the general recognition rate for 20 European countries. The number of countries that recognized the Convention fell from more than half in 1982 to just 7% in 1992. The number of countries that recognized both the Convention and humanitarian needs also fell to 17%. In the 1990s, acceptance rates went up quickly, and by the time of the Kosovo crisis, they had reached a peak of 45%. Then, recognition rates went down until the middle of the 2000s, but by 2014, they were back up to 50%. One reason is that the EU recognized 95% of Syrians in 2014, which is a lot more than in the past. But since 1982, the overall rate of recognition has been less than one-third on average. Since these are first-instance decisions, they don't take into account successful appeals, which would add about 10 percentage points to the number of people who get some kind of acceptance. Those who don't get the visa must leave the country, either on their own or with help from the government. Still, an unknown but large number of illegal aliens are still in the country.

In the countries that get the most applications, the number of refugees who are given some kind of safety is rising. Table 2.3 shows that in 2015, more than 100,000 refugees were living in each of seven wealthy countries. With 17.5 per thousand people, Sweden has the most people than any other country. This is followed by Norway, Switzerland, and Austria. The UNHCR says that 1.8 million refugees, or about 12% of all refugees in the world, come from the 15 countries on the left. On the other hand, 70% of the total is made up of the countries on the list on the right. In fact, 86% of all refugees live in their first place of asylum, which is often just across the border from their home country. About 30% of people in these countries live in refugee camps, which are often very bad places.

Table 2.3 Refugees in host countries in 2015

Country	Refugees	Refs/ Pop	Refs/ GDP	Country	Refugees	Refs/ Pop	Refs/ GDP
Germany	316,115	3.92	0.10	Turkey	2,541,352	32.79	3.70
USA	273,202	0.86	0.02	Pakistan	1,561,162	8.44	10.37
France	273,126	4.26	0.12	Lebanon	1,070,854	190.82	26.30
Sweden	169,520	17.48	0.38	Iran	979,437	12.54	3.54
Canada	135,888	3.82	0.10	Ethiopia	736,086	7.59	24.04
UK	123,067	1.91	0.05	Jordan	664,118	89.56	31.11
Italy	118,047	1.98	0.07	Kenya	553,912	12.35	18.74
Netherlands	88,536	5.25	0.12	Uganda	477,187	12.63	28.99
Switzerland	73,336	8.94	0.15	D R Congo	383,095	5.12	18.06
Austria	72,216	8.48	0.21	Chad	369,540	27.20	35.49
Norway	50,389	9.79	0.15	Cameroon	327,121	16.75	16.36
Australia	36,917	1.57	0.04	Russia	314,506	2.19	0.32
Belgium	35,314	3.15	0.08	Sudan	309,639	8.94	9.19
Denmark	27,326	4.84	0.10	China	301,052	0.22	0.06
Greece	18,489	2.38	0.13	Iraq	277,701	7.88	3.23

Source: UNHCR, Global Trends, 2015, Table 1; Real GDP in $US (2010) and population from the World Bank at: http://data.worldbank.org/indicator/NY.GDP.PCAP.KD.

In 2015, Turkey had the most refugees, with 2.5 million, even though a lot of them had moved to Europe. But Lebanon and Jordan have more refugees per person than any other country, and 12 of the 15 have more than 7 refugees per 1000 people. Even more surprising are the numbers in the last column, which show refugees per million dollars of total GDP (in US 2010 dollars). There are more than ten refugees per million dollars in nine of the countries, and there are more than twenty refugees per million dollars in Lebanon, Ethiopia, Jordan, Uganda, and Chad. On the other hand, the left panel shows that Sweden is the only wealthy country that takes in more than a third of a refugee for every million dollars. These numbers just show what everyone already knows: that some of the poorer countries take in the most refugees.

Applicants of Asylum

Recent events in the Mediterranean and Aegean Seas have brought up the question of whether people seeking protection in the West are real refugees or just "economic migrants" from poor countries looking for a better life. On the one hand, it is said that most refugee seekers come from countries with civil wars and abuse of human rights, so they probably do have a right to asylum. On the other hand, it is said that less than half of all applicants are accepted as refugees or as people who are in need of safety for humanitarian reasons. So, it seems likely that the main reason they are moving is for business reasons. Here, I look at the main reasons why people ask for protection.

Several studies have looked at how people move around the world, focused on the number of refugees or how that number changes. One of the main ideas of these studies is that the number of refugees who leave their homes depends on how the costs and benefits of leaving compare to those of staying. Early cross-sectional studies found that genocide, civil war, dissident battles, and changes in political regimes were the main causes of people being forced to move . More study has been done on this theme since then. Moore and Shellman found that civil war, terror by dissidents, and violence by the government raise the number of refugees compared to the number of people who are moved within their own country. In line with this, Melander and Oberg (2007) find that the more violence there is, the more likely it is that it will cause people to leave their homes. Moore and Shellman (2007) looked at where refugees go and found that they go to places where there are no wars, where the incomes are better, and where the costs of getting there are less. Melander and Oberg (2006) looked at how long displacements last and said that flows tend to slow down when the people who are most able or willing to move have already done so. They also found that when a country's government changes, outflows go down, but when the government falls, outflows go up.

Several studies have looked at the effects of asylum policies by looking at panel data on the flow of asylum claims to the developed world. Neumayer (2004) and Thielemann (2006) looked at how many people from each country of origin applied to each target country in the 1980s and 1990s. This method nets out effects that come from the same source country. Controlling for things like the number of immigrants from the origin who were already in the destination country, as well as economic and political conditions in the destination country, these studies found some evidence that tougher procedures for deciding who is a refugee cut down on asylum claims. When I looked at applications to EU countries from 1981 to 1999, I found that an index of policy had a strong deterrent effect when factors about conditions in both the country of origin and the country of destination were present. In a later study, I looked at the effects of policy on panel data from 1997 to 2006 about refugee applications from 48 countries to 19 countries. Overall, the tightening of policies from 2001 to 2006 cut the number of refugee requests to 19 countries by 108,000 per year, or about one-third of the total drop.

An Analysis

Here, I look at how many people from 48 different countries asked for refuge in 19 different countries every year from 1997 to 2014. There are 16 European countries on the list, as well as Australia, Canada, and the United States. Together, these four countries have received 91% of all asylum claims to industrialized countries in the last 20 years. Since 2000, the countries of origin are the ones where the most people have asked for refuge. About four-fifths of the flow to all developed countries comes from these countries. The information on asylum requests comes from the UNHCR's yearly reports and online database. This study looks at pairs of origins and destinations for which at least 300 applications were made between 1997 and 2012. This keeps from having a lot of dyad-years with no applications, and it leaves 626 pairs of destination-source countries out of a total of 48 x 19 = 912 dyads. Some observations are also lost because of missing data, especially for the years 1997–1999. The average number of observations per pair is therefore 17.4.

The factors used to explain things are ones that have been used a lot in other studies. The Political Terror Scale is a measure that goes from 1 (no terror) to 5 (high terror) to show how bad terror and abuse of human rights are. The Freedom House indexes of civil freedoms and political rights are also included. These range from 1 (complete freedom) to 7 (freedom is very limited). Even though these factors are often linked to different kinds of violence I also include a measure of full-on war: the number of battle deaths on the origin country's land as a percentage of its population, which I got from the Uppsala Conflict Data Program. The real GDP per capita from the Penn World Tables (updated with IMF figures to 2014) shows how well people live in both the country of origin and the country of destination. The OECD's harmonized unemployment rate for all workers shows how many jobs are available in target countries. I use the number of migrants from each starting country who lived in each destination country in 2001 to measure the "friends and relatives effect," which is well known in the literature on migration. This is from the most latest version of the data set put together by Docquier and Marfouk (2006), which includes adults over the age of 25.

To figure out how policies affect the number of asylum requests, we need an index of refugee policy. Asylum policy is a mix of different things like rewards and rationing. This is different from, say, international trade, where the most obvious policy tool, a tariff, is a single index with a clear value. As with immigration policy, we have to use rough stand-ins to try to understand the different parts of refugee policy. Here, I use an index of policies from Hatton and Moloney (2015) that is up to date to 2014. It has measurements for 15 different parts of asylum policy, which can be put into three groups of five parts each. The first is policies that, in some way, stop or discourage asylum seekers from getting to a country's border, making it harder for them to use that country's asylum processes. The second tries to figure out how likely it is that a candidate will get some kind of notice. And the third part has different rules about the person's well-being during and right after processing.

Table 2.4 Components of the policy index

Access policies	Processing polices	Welfare policies
• Visa requirements • Border control/security • Trafficking regulations • Carrier sanctions • Application outside country	• Definition of a refugee • Humanitarian category • Manifestly unfounded claims • Expedited procedures • Scope for appeals	• Permission to work • Access to welfare benefits • Detention policy • Deportation policy • Family reunification

Source: Author calculations

Table 2.4 shows the 15 parts that make up the index. Starting at zero in the first quarter of 1997, each component goes up by one if a policy change is likely to hurt an asylum candidate and down by one if the change is likely to help them. The index is meant to measure "major" changes in policy, or changes that have a big effect on the lives of a large number of refugee seekers. These kinds of decisions are always subjective, but they are based on summaries of laws and secondary reports by experts, not on how people in general feel about how tough refugee policies are. One of their strengths is that they are based on reports that were made public at the time that a law was passed or when new rules were put in place, rather than on reviews made after the fact based on how things turned out. And, as much as possible, the change in policy is put in the quarter of the year when it took effect. I also look at three other factors that have to do with policy. One is the total recognition rate, which shows how many applications are accepted as refugees or for other humanitarian reasons. Another is a dummy variable for whether or not a destination country and a country of origin have a readmission deal. This is called a bilateral variable. And the third is an index of the target country's policy on immigration for work, which is used to see if migration routes can be replaced by each other.

Econometric Results

Table 2.5 shows the main reasons why people ask for protection. The dependent variable is the log of the ratio of the number of applications from an origin to a destination (plus one for zeros) to the population of the origin country. In the first column, there are fixed effects for the start and dummy variables for each destination, but the coefficients are not shown. There is some proof that people are applying for asylum at a rate of about 5% per year more than the other variables in the model can explain. In the second column, there is a "dummy" variable for each year. This variable takes into account general trends but doesn't change the other coefficients very much. In the first two columns, the coefficient on the log of the ratio of the number of migrants from a certain origin to the population of that origin (in 2000/1) is very important. This shows how strong the "friends and family effect" is, which is found in most studies of what makes people move. It's generally taken to mean the effect of cultural and historical ties, as well as the appeal of joining expatriate communities and getting information and help from them. The coefficient shows that a 10% rise in the number of immigrants would make 2.3% more people ask for refuge. Even with the migrant stock, the effect of the log of the distance between the capital cities of the country of origin and the country of destination is negative and important. So, the cost and difficulty of getting to a destination go up with its distance, but this isn't fully represented in the number of people who have moved to the same place in the past. The slope is very steep, which may represent how dangerous it is to move across long distances without being seen.

The effects of the migrant stock and distance, which only have one number for each origin-destination pair, are fully taken into account in columns (3) through (5). The R-squared is smaller in these equations because the migrant stock and distance explain a lot of the total variation. But there isn't much change to the coefficients on origin country factors. The Political Terror Scale is one of the most important. If the scale goes up by one point, the number of applications goes up by about 20%. The Freedom House index for human liberties is the better and more important one. Based on the coefficient, one point on the scale means that about 25% more people apply for protection. The lack of importance for political rights may be because political suppression can make people want to leave but also make it harder for them to do so. When these things are taken into account, the effect of civil war, as measured by the number of fight deaths per thousand people, is not important. This could be because running away from a civil war does not automatically make someone a refugee. The coefficient on GDP per capita in the country of origin gives some support to the idea that bad economic conditions at home cause people to seek refuge, even though poverty may also make it hard to move. When the GDP per person goes up by 10%, the number of applications goes down by about 6%.

Table 2.5 Asylum applications by origin and destination, 1997-2014

Explanatory variable	**(1)**	**(2)**	**(3)**	**(4)**	**(5)**
Political terror scale in origin country	0.197 (3.72)***	0.231 (4.32)***	0.238 (4.32)***	0.221 (4.45)***	0.237 (3.91)***
Civil liberties in origin country	0.243 (4.04)***	0.249 (4.08)***	0.247 (3.94)***	0.255 (4.33)***	0.289 (3.91)***
Political rights in origin country	-0.028 (0.57)	-0.030 (0.68)	-0.028 (0.62)	-0.028 (0.63)	-0.022 (0.39)
Civil war battle deaths/origin population	0.180 (0.95)	0.196 (0.99)	0.173 (0.81)	-0.181 (1.99)*	0.163 (0.77)
Log origin country real GDP per capita	-0.797 (3.26)***	-0.619 (2.48)**	-0.605 (2.32)**	-0.427 (1.92)*	-0.665 (2.34)**
Log migrant stock in destination/ origin population	0.227 (8.69)***	0.227 (8.68)***			
Log distance from origin to destination	-0.826 (4.27)***	-0.827 (4.27)***			
Log destination GDP per capita	-0.329 (0.92)	-0.036 (0.07)	-0.110 (0.22)	-0.251 (0.52)	-0.512 (1.01)
Unemployment rate at destination	-0.043*** (4.36)	-0.030*** (2.84)	-0.032 (3.05)***	-0.032 (3.08)***	-0.042 (3.75)***
Policy index in destination	-0.059 (5.18)***	-0.065 (5.56)***	-0.058 (5.10)***	-0.057 (4.99)***	-0.054 (4.43)***
Year	0.054 (2.88)**			-0.015 (1.53)	

Distance X year					
Battle deaths/origin population X year				0.061*** (8.07)	
Fixed effects (number of FE)	Origin (48)	Origin (48)	Orig X Dest (626)	Orig X Dest (626)	Orig X Dest (503)
Destination dummies	Yes	Yes	No	No	No
Year dummies	No	Yes	Yes	Yes	Yes
R^2 within	0.397	0.414	0.130	0.145	0.129
No. of observations	10,875	10,875	10,875	10,875	8,760

******Note: The dependent variable is the log of the ratio of asylum applications from an origin to a destination over the origin population. 'z' statistics in parentheses from standard errors clustered by origin country; significance at 1, 5 and 10% denoted by ***, ** and *, respectively. Constant terms and coefficients on destination dummies and year dummies are not reported.*

There are a few different ways to explain why Column (1) is going up. One theory is that it's because communication has gotten better and more people are able to move because of the growth of migrant smuggling networks. This would make the distance between the places where conflicts start and the places where they end up smaller. But in Column 4, the relationship between distance and year is negative and doesn't mean much. Another idea is that wars have become a bigger reason why people ask for refuge. This idea is backed up by the fact that the interaction between fight deaths and year has a positive and highly significant coefficient. But this is all because of the time since the Arab Spring. If the last three years are taken out of the data, the z-statistic of the interaction coefficient is only 0.41. The unemployment rate is one of the variables for the target country, and it gives a significant negative coefficient. The GDP per capita, on the other hand, is not significant. The policy index gives a strong negative value, which suggests that stricter rules make people less likely to apply. Lastly, the analysis in Column 5 leaves out the three countries that are not in Europe. This is done to see if the results change if these three countries are included. Since the size and importance of the factors doesn't change much, it's clear that they don't.

Scrutinizing Policy Outcomes

Table 2.6 goes into more depth about how asylum laws affect people. One thing that could be a worry is that policy is organic. If an increase in asylum requests leads to stricter rules, policy factors would be biased against finding bad effects. But because the political process takes a long time, this is likely to work slowly.

In Table 2.6, there are fixed effects for each country of origin by each year. These effects take up all of the origin-country factors from Table 2.5 and any differences in their effects. Under some conditions, using origin-by-year fixed effects also takes into account any deflection effects of policy in one destination on applications in other destinations. Compared to Column (2) of Table 2.5, the first column of Table 2.6 shows that the choice of fixed effects has little effect on the coefficients on the bilateral variables and the target country variables, especially the policy index.

Table 2.6 Asylum applications and policy, 1997-2014

Explanatory variable	(1)	(2)	(3)	(4)	(5)
Log migrant stock in destination/ origin population	0.227 (8.67)***	0.228 (8.68)***	0.228 (8.68)***	0.223 (8.33)***	0.223 (8.33)***
Log distance from origin to destination	—0.819 (4.21)***	—0.819 (4.21)***	—0.819 (4.21)***	—0.790 (4.23)***	—0.790 (4.23)***
Log destination GDP per capita	—0.121 (0.26)	—0.310 (0.68)	—0.336 (0.74)	—0.354 (0.79)	—0.206 (0.43)
Unemployment rate at destination	—0.034 (3.31)***	—0.032 (3.23)***	—0.031 (3.04)***	—0.031 (3.05)***	—0.032 (3.23)***
Policy index overall in destination	—0.064 (5.59)***				
Policy on access in destination		—0.160 (4.98)***	—0.159 (4.93)***	—0.153 (4.81)***	—0.148 (4.68)***
Policy on processing in destination		—0.115 (7.98)***	—0.115 (7.96)***	—0.119 (8.25)***	—0.122 (8.55)***
Policy on welfare in destination		0.041 (1.56)	0.046 (1.77)*	0.046 (1.77)*	0.036 (1.24)
Lagged recognition rate in destination			0.219 (2.56)**	0.201 (2.23)**	0.181 (2.00)**
Readmission agreement origin-destination				0.356 (1.85)*	0.364 (1.89)*
Lagged immigration policy in destination					0.022 (2.12)**
Fixed effects (number of FE)	Origin X Year (862)	Origin X Year (862)	Origin X Year (862)	Origin X Year (862)	Origin X Year (862)
Dest. dummies	Yes	Yes	Yes	Yes	Yes

Year dummies	No	No	No	No	No
R2 within	0.413	0.416	0.417	0.419	0.420
No. of observations	10,875	10,875	10,875	10,875	10,875

*Note. The dependent variable is the log of the ratio of asylum applications from an origin to a destination over the origin population. 'z' statistics in parentheses from standard errors clustered by origin country; significance at 1, 5 and 10% percent denoted by ***, ** and *, respectively. Constant terms and coefficients on destination dummies are not reported.*

In Table 2.6, the three main parts of the policy index are written out independently in the second column. Both the policy on entry to the territory and the policy on how asylum claims are handled have coefficients that are significantly negative. If either of these measures goes up by one point, the number of applications goes down by 17% and 12%, respectively. But the coefficient on the measure that shows how well asylum seekers are doing is not important. One way to look at these results is that they show that the chance of getting lasting residency is the most important thing to asylum seekers. Asylum seekers are already willing to go through a lot to get where they want to go, so it may not be strange that the thought of more hardships doesn't bother them much.

Some studies use the rate of recognition to measure how hard it is to decide if someone is a refugee. In Table 2.6, column 3 shows the general acceptance rate for asylum claims to each destination country, not just for each country of origin. To account for potential endogeneity, it is delayed by one year. The coefficient is positive and significant, but the coefficient on asylum processing, to which it is linked, doesn't change all that much, which is surprising. One reason for the independent effect could be that it shows changes in the way things are done in administration that aren't picked up by the policy index. But the effect is small: a 2% rise in asylum requests for every 10% increase in the rate of acceptance. In column 4, a dummy is added to show if there was a readmission deal between the country of origin and the country of destination. There are many different kinds of these deals, but they all include a promise by the country of origin to take back a person from that country who has been told to leave the country of destination. The coefficient is positive, which means that readmission agreements are linked to more applications, but this is only important at the 10% level. One reason could be that these agreements are often part of a package of measures that give incentives to the country that agrees to work with the other country, such as letting its people travel without a visa. Another reason is that the bilateral dummy would not be able to measure any drop in movement from other countries to transit countries.

Lastly, some people say that strict immigration policies have made people more likely to use refuge as an alternative way to get into the job markets of developed countries. In order to test this theory, the last column of Table 2.6 has an index of how restricted employment-based immigration policies are in destination countries, where higher values mean more restrictive policies. This variable is added with a one-year delay. It has a positive, but not very important, coefficient. From 1997 to 2014, employment-based immigration policies got less strict on average, so they didn't increase the number of refugee requests. In fact, the average number of applications will go down by 9% as a result.

What did the major changes in refugee policy mean for the number of asylum requests? Figure 2.3 shows how the (unweighted) average of the whole policy score has changed over time. This goes from 0 in 1997 to 3.5 in the middle of the 2000s. After that, there is no further tightening until the end of the time. The first time policies got stricter was after the Kosovo crisis and the September 11, 2001, strikes, when a lot of people asked for asylum. Figure 2.3 also shows that each of the index's three parts followed the same pattern: a sharp tightening up to the middle of the 2000s, followed by little change. But at the country level, policy changes vary a lot in how big they are and when they happen.

Table 2.7 Predicted percentage change in asylum applications due to policy

Country	1997-2005	2005-14	Country	1997-2005	2005-14
Australia	—48.6	— 18.5	Italy	—28.3	20.0
Austria	—42.3	— 10.9	Netherlands	—48.6	— 10.9
Belgium	— 14.8	—20.5	Norway	—32.3	—20.5
Canada	— 18.2	—32.3	Poland	— 14.8	— 14.8
Czech Rep.	—4.4	— 10.9	Spain	—29.4	— 12.7
Denmark	—39.6	0.0	Sweden	0.0	73.3
France	—27.4	17.4	Switzerland	—29.2	—38.3
Germany	—7.1	2.9	UK	—59.1	— 19.5
Hungary	0.0	— 10.9	USA	—27.4	—21.3
Ireland	—42.3	0.0	Total	—28.7	— 1.1

Source: Author calculations based on coefficients from Column (2) of Table 6.

Table 2.7 shows how policy affects refugee requests, which shows how true this is. Here, I use the coefficients in Column (2) of Table 2.6 for entry policy and processing policy to figure out the percentage effect of policy on asylum requests from 1997 to 2005 and from 2005 to 2014. From 1997 to 2005, many countries made it much harder for people to get refuge. As a result, the number of asylum requests dropped by more than 25% in 12 of the 19 countries and by more than 40% in 5 of them. The sum of all the percentage changes adds up to almost 30% less. If these percentage changes are applied to the average number of asylum requests for each destination country (not just the 48 starting countries used in the regressions), this means that between 1997 and 2005, there were 133,072 fewer asylum requests each year. From 2005 to 2014, policy changes were more mixed, with only two countries lowering applications by more than 25%. On the other hand, policy was loosened in four countries, especially in Sweden, where policy was loosened a lot. This is the major reason why the weighted average policy effect is positive, and the overall effect for all 19 countries is just a decrease of 4,378 annual applications.

Fig - 2.3 Trends in policy and its components

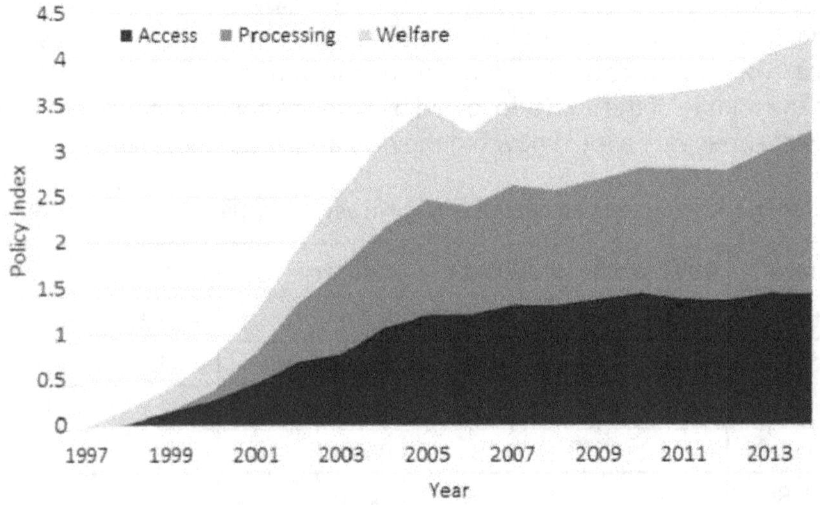

Source: Author calculations. These are averages of policy components for 19 countries equally weighted and stacked up to form the total index.

Public Opinion

Refugee policy and immigration policy in general have been hotly debated because of the current migration crisis. When making decisions about asylum, governments have to pay attention to what the people who voted for them think. Here, I look at four different parts of European public thought.

Opinion on Immigrants and Refugees

People often think that people are getting more and more against immigration. The rise of far-right populist groups and negative news coverage of immigration-related events seem to point in that direction. Recent evidence suggests that public opinion changed in a bad way during the recession that followed the global financial crisis, but that these changes have not been very big in the long run. It's important to tell the difference between how people feel about refugees and how they feel about newcomers in general. Even though there are a lot of surveys about how people feel about immigration in general, there is much less information about refugees. But the European Social Survey (ESS) can be used to compare things over a longer period of time.

Table 2.8 Public opinion (percent) against refugees and immigrants 2002 and 2014

Country	**Immigration of different ethnic group**		**Immigration from poor countries**		**Be generous in judging refugee claims**	
	% few or none		% few or none		% disagree	
	2014	Change	2014	Change	2014	Change
Austria	49.0	-17.3	55.9	-9.0	36.8	-6.1
Belgium	41.2	-3.6	47.6	3.9	44.4	-15.1
Czech Rep.	72.3	19.2	72.4	23.6	44.5	-18.2
Denmark	38.7	-12.8	55.2	1.4	29.0	-21.2
Finland	53.1	-9.5	64.8	4.8	21.8	-11.3
France	38.3	-7.1	48.0	-0.9	18.0	-0.3
Germany	23.4	-18.7	33.7	-7.2	32.4	-26.9
Hungary	80.7	-5.5	87.3	-0.7	39.0	-25.8
Ireland	47.4	12.4	57.3	21.2	20.9	0.0
Netherlands	32.7	-9.5	46.7	2.8	47.0	-27.9
Norway	23.5	-20.0	32.0	-6.4	18.4	-27.8
Poland	42.7	-2.6	47.5	4.2	8.5	-4.5
Portugal	47.2	-14.2	52.9	-9.5	7.7	-3.6
Slovenia	35.9	-7.9	47.8	4.3	24.2	-25.3
Spain	44.7	-3.6	47.5	-3.5	16.2	-2.3
Sweden	7.6	-9.3	12.6	-2.8	9.8	-13.3
Switzerland	37.1	3.5	44.5	13.2	34.9	-15.5
UK	43.2	-6.6	57.4	5.9	27.7	-19.4
Country average	42.1	-6.3	50.6	2.5	26.7	-14.7

Source: European Social Survey, rounds 1 and 7.

In 2002 and again in 2014, the ESS included a module on opinion towards immigration. Unfortunately, most of the questions differ between the two modules but one of the questions on refugees is the same. With the lead-in line that 'Some people come to this country and apply for refugee status on the grounds that they fear persecution in their own country', respondents were asked:

- Please say how much you agree or disagree that: 'the government should be generous in judging people's applications for refugee status' (agree strongly/agree/neither agree nor disagree/disagree/ disagree strongly).

  ESS respondents were also asked their opinions on government policy on different types of immigrants. For comparison, I examine the questions on immigrants from minority ethnic backgrounds and from poorer countries as these seem to be the most relevant comparisons for refugees. Prefaced by 'Now some questions about people from other countries coming to live in [country]', the questions are:

- To what extent do you think [country] should allow. . .. people of a different race or ethnic group from most [country] people? (many/ some/a few/none).
- How about people from the poorer countries outside Europe? (many/ some/a few/none).

The number of people who answered "a few" or "none" to the last two questions and the number of people who disagreed or strongly disagreed with the statement about how refugees should be treated show how many people are against immigration.

Table 2.8 shows the number of people who said they were against immigrants in 2014 and how that number changed from 2002 to 2014. For the 14 countries in the table, people have a lot of different ideas about letting in immigrants from different ethnic groups than the rest of the country. Changes in opinion are also very different. In the Czech Republic, the number of people who are against immigration went up by 19.2 percentage points, while in Norway, it went down by 20.0 percentage points. The average number of people who don't like immigrants in the 18 countries is down by 6.3%. Changes in how people feel about immigrants from poor countries outside of Europe are also very different. In the Czech Republic, Ireland, and Switzerland, attitudes have become more negative by more than ten percentage points. The average rise in people who don't like immigration is 2.5 percentage points per country. Even though there are some differences, the cross-country correlation coefficient of changes in opinion between these two questions (18 observations) is strong at 0.92.

Countries also have very different public attitudes about how they should treat people who want to become refugees. On this measure, more than 40% of people in Belgium, the Czech Republic, and the Netherlands are against refugees, while less than 10% of people in Poland, Portugal, and Sweden feel this way. Anti-refugee feelings have gone down in all 18 countries, though to different degrees. The average drop in these 18 countries is 14.7%. As a result, there are now fewer people in every country who don't like refugees than people who don't like newcomers from different ethnic groups or from poor countries. There is a 0.27 correlation between how people feel about refugees and how they feel about different racial groups (columns 2 and 6), and a 0.35 correlation between how people feel about refugees and how they feel about immigrants from poor countries (columns 4 and 6). These links aren't as strong as the one between how people feel about the two types of immigrants.

Table 2.2 shows that different European countries have had very different experiences with refugee seekers. This is one reason why people's opinions change so much. The correlation coefficient between the change in opinions from 2002 to 2014 and the change in refugee requests from 1997 to 2001 to 2009 to 2013 shows this. The number of refugee requests changes in a way that is linked to how people feel about immigrants from minority ethnic groups or poor countries (r = 0.36, 0.48). On the other hand, there is a weak negative association (r = —0.17) between the number of asylum requests and how people feel about refugees changing. Regression analysis on individual-level data, which takes into account social factors that have been shown to affect opinion, backs up these results. Even though a rise in asylum requests is linked to a hardening of views toward immigrants from ethnic minorities and poor countries, it doesn't seem to have changed much about how people feel about real refugees. But it's important to remember that this is only one part of how people feel about something. There are other things to think about.

Importance of Immigration

It's important to tell the difference between what people think about how much immigration is good and how much immigration is seen as an important policy problem. Almost all of the economic study of how people feel about immigration has been based on "more or less" (sometimes called a "Likert scale") questions, or what you might call "preference." This doesn't take into account how important or important to the respondent immigration is as a policy problem. The link between salience and policy is important. Voters who want more or less immigration won't be able to get their way unless the issue is important enough to make it a political priority.

The Eurobarometer polls of popular opinion in EU countries are one way to measure how important something is. The poll is done twice a year, in the spring and fall of each year. There are about 1,800 cases in each country each year. Countries outside of the EU are not included, but as the EU has grown, more countries have been added. Since 2002, the Eurobarometer polls have asked a question about how important a problem is. This is the question: "What do you think are (our country's) two most important problems right now?" The respondent is given a list of 14 political topics, including immigration, and asked to choose two. Crime, the business, health, and education are some of the other topics. The respondent may also choose one or two other topics that are not on the list. Because each person can only choose two, this measure shows how important immigration is compared to other policy-related issues. If the person says that immigration is one of the two most important problems, the salience variable is coded as 1, and if not, it is coded as 0.

Table 2.9 shows how many people said immigration was one of the two most important problems facing the country in 2003, 2007, 2011, 2015, and 2019. Most of the time, the number isn't very high, but it tends to rise sharply when immigration problems are in the news or when politicians argue about them. There are also big differences from one country to the next. Even before the current refugee crisis, Austria, Belgium, Denmark, and the UK paid more attention to immigration than other places. In these countries, it is often thought that people are against immigration more than their views for more or less immigration would indicate. This helps explain why people often think the UK (and its government) are more against immigrants than other countries. Even though UK opinions are only slightly more negative than average, salience is always much higher than average.

After the global financial crisis, there was a recession. As economic problems became more important, immigrants became less important. As Table 2.9 shows, it went down in all countries except Finland and Greece, and it stayed low throughout the long Euro crisis. A multilevel analysis of annual data shows that this trend changed as the Euro crisis ended, immigration picked back up, and the effects of the Arab Spring played out. As the Syrian situation got worse and more people tried to get to Europe by sea and land, the topic of immigration became much more important. As column 5 shows, by May 2015, when the most recent Eurobarometer poll was done (at the time of writing), immigration was more important than ever. People often say that the migration problem has changed people's minds a lot about immigration. But this is mostly a change in how important immigration is, not a change in whether people want more or less immigration.

Table 2.9 Salience of immigration as a policy issue 2003-15 (percent)

Country	2003	2007	2009	2011	2013	2015
Austria	10.4	23.1	13.7	16.2	12.7	31.2
Belgium	16.9	19.4	14.1	20.6	15.1	23.0
Czech Rep		4.6	3.9	3.5	2.4	18.0
Denmark	23.4	21.8	11.8	9.5	13.7	35.4
Estonia		2.4	0.3	1.4	2.8	24.3
Finland	5.0	5.3	8.7	7.4	4.6	5.9
France	10.0	12.2	5.0	10.2	10.3	12.3
Germany	5.7	6.7	3.9	7.0	15.5	46.8
Greece	6.6	5.0	9.0	5.4	5.9	10.5
Hungary		1.6	0.7	0.5	1.6	13.1
Ireland	7.8	12.9	3.0	5.6	8.0	7.3
Italy	13.6	14.6	12.4	13.9	5.9	31.3
Luxembourg	12.2	10.9	8.1	20.6	12.0	15.1
Netherlands	8.2	14.1	6.6	10.8	3.9	22.9
Poland		8.8	1.9	1.1	3.1	9.0
Portugal	2.6	2.0	1.2	0.6	0.9	2.6
Slovenia		2.7	1.2	0.5	0.8	3.9
Slovakia		2.5	1.0	0.7	0.5	1.2
Spain	19.5	30.1	7.8	5.6	1.8	5.9
Sweden	8.8	11.1	7.1	8.2	12.8	27.8
UK	25.9	32.7	22.5	20.3	29.6	35.8
Country average	11.8	11.6	6.9	8.1	7.8	18.3

Source: Eurobarometer. Each year includes the autumn and spring rounds except the last, which is for May 2015. The rounds used are: 57.2 and 60.1 (2003), 66.1 and 67.2 (2007), 70.1 and 71.3 (2009), 74.2 and 75.3 (2011), 78.1 and 79.3 (2013), and 83.3 (2015).

When high salience and negative underlying views about immigration come together, it can lead to political debate and sometimes even action. So, a rise in salience makes biases that were already there even stronger. As one writer in the UK says, "public opinion becomes important when the mood is very negative and the issue is important to voters and the media, forcing policy responses from both the government and the opposition parties." The rise in salience may also cause views to become more divided because it makes both positive and negative preferences stand out more. But, as shown in Table 2.8, if people's feelings about immigration (and especially about refugees) are not overwhelmingly bad, then there shouldn't be a political and social backlash. But there is one thing that people strongly dislike, and that is illegal immigration. Obviously, this is important for refugee policy, since a lot of people who recently asked for asylum did so without permission.

Table 2.10 Public concerns about legal and illegal immigration (percent)

Country	Worried about legal immigration			Worried about illegal immigration		
	2009	2011	2013	2009	2011	2013
France	20.5	21.6	32.2	57.3	59.1	70.9
Germany	30.4	24.9	29.4	63.9	55.6	72.1
Italy	20.7	22.5	27.2	80.5	79.9	86.2
Netherlands	31.2	-	31.9	58.0	-	69.1
Spain	22.2	23.5	23.9	71.4	73.8	73.9
UK	36.3	37.6	40.6	68.0	70.9	80.2

Source: Transatlantic Trends — Immigration 2009 and 2011; Transatlantic Trends 2013. The survey is based on telephone interviews with an average of a thousand respondents in each country; the figures here are calculated using the socio-demographic weights. Data kindly supplied by Inter-University Consortium for Political and Social Research.

Illicit Immigration

As we've seen, the current crisis has been caused in large part by people getting in without permission. The results of the survey show that most people don't like the idea of illegal immigrants. In 2009, 2011, and 2013, the Transatlantic Trends poll asked people about their worries about legal and illegal immigration. Table 2.10 shows how these worries compare. "Can you tell me if you are worried or not worried about legal immigration?" is the question, and the same question is asked again about illegal immigration. In general, people worry more about illegal immigration than about regular immigration, which is more than twice as much. Even more surprising is that these worries grew quickly from 2009 to 2013, especially those about illegal immigrants, which went up by about 10 percentage points. Unfortunately, the same question wasn't asked in the most recent survey in 2014, but it seems possible that the number of people who said they were worried would have grown as the migration crisis got worse. The UK had the most worries about legal immigration, but Italy and Spain had the most worries about illegal immigration. In these countries, which saw the most people crossing the Mediterranean, worries about illegal immigration didn't grow as much because they were already high in 2009. In 2013, Transatlantic Trends looked at a wider range of countries. In Portugal, 88.9% of people were worried about illegal immigrants, but the numbers were lower in transit countries like Poland (46.2%), Romania (46.2%), Slovakia (59.4%), and Sweden (59.4%).

Concerns about both legal and illegal immigration are linked to the idea that there are too many immigrants and that immigration is more of a problem for the country than a chance. Several studies have shown that anti-immigration views are linked to economic and personal insecurity as well as other defensive tendencies. People with these traits tend not to trust public institutions and government policies. But, according to Transatlantic Trends, there isn't a strong link between worrying about illegal immigration and thinking the government is doing a poor or very poor job with immigration policy: 0.06 in 2009 and 0.16 in 2013.

Core Decision-Making on Immigration Policy

Anti-immigration views are often linked to nationalism and a focus on one's own country. Because of this, you might think that most people would want their national government, which they can directly affect, to be in charge of immigration policy instead of a supranational body like the EU. Even more so because trust in the EU has dropped since the global financial crisis of 2007. People might think that this will slow down the work on the Common European Asylum System. There are signs that support for the EU has dropped sharply during the slump, even though it was already weakening. Even so, there is a surprising amount of support for an EU-wide policy on immigration and refugees, even though there are some bad signs.

At the beginning of the 2000s, studies of public opinion showed that there was a lot of support, but not a lot of overwhelming support, for immigration policy to be set at the EU level instead of at the national level. Luedtke (2005) said that 43% of Eurobarometer respondents in 2000 were in favor of a single EU strategy. He found that people who only identified with their own country and not with Europe or with a shared identity were very against EU-wide immigration policy. He thought that this effect might lose some of its power over time. When I looked at a similar question from the ESS 2002, I found that support for a joint policy on immigration and asylum was linked to trust in both the national and the European parliaments, but not to the idea that the respondent's country had more asylum requests than it should have.

But these cross-sectional studies don't tell us much about how people's views on immigration policy at the EU level have changed over time. Unfortunately, these numbers aren't very good. Since 2000, Eurobarometer has done polls every five years. Table 2.11 shows some of the results. These are the answers to the question, "In each of the following areas, do you think decisions should be made by the (national) government or by the European Union as a whole?" In 2000, a lot of people thought that decisions about refugee policy should be made at the EU level. This is shown in the first column. In one-third of the EU-15 countries, these were the majority, but the numbers varied a lot, from less than a quarter in Austria and the UK to more than a third in Italy and the Netherlands. In the same wave, the answers in the next column are about immigration policy, not asylum policy. The country-to-country correlation is 0.98, which shows that the overall means are very close. Unfortunately, polls that came after this one only talked about immigration policy and not asylum. Still, it seems that people in any given country have very similar ideas about how immigration and refugee decisions should be made.

Table 2.11 Percentage supporting EU-level decision-making on asylum and immigration policy

Country	Asylum Spring 2000	Immigration Spring 2000	Immigration Autumn 2005	Immigration Autumn 2010	Immig. Policy Spring 2015
Austria	24.0	21.6	40.5	39.4	57.8
Belgium	55.8	55.0	64.9	72.0	74.9
Bulgaria			59.1	77.9	78.3
Cyprus			62.0	67.5	75.2
Czech Rep			56.1	56.4	51.7
Denmark	32.0	30.0	45.4	47.0	61.8
Estonia			46.5	51.9	52.7
Finland	25.6	13.3	17.6	30.0	56.6
France	53.5	53.1	68.4	72.4	71.1
Germany	43.1	41.2	55.9	64.2	83.5
Greece	39.5	37.1	53.5	51.5	71.5
Hungary			65.8	65.8	68.5
Ireland	33.8	31.3	54.6	56.8	74.6
Italy	68.0	67.7	64.7	71.8	73.2
Latvia			62.6	69.0	64.6
Lithuania			63.3	67.7	82.0

Luxem-bourg	42.6	43.1	54.9	62.7	82.4
Malta			70.6	80.9	84.3
Netherlands	72.4	68.9	53.2	62.3	84.3
Poland			66.9	66.8	66.0
Portugal	31.3	32.2	58.3	68.7	71.4
Romania			64.6	67.6	77.5
Slovakia			64.3	69.4	65.4
Slovenia			63.1	66.4	69.1
Spain	54.2	55.6	65.5	66.8	80.9
Sweden	33.9	30.7	30.6	45.3	77.4
UK	21.6	22.9	40.2	39.2	61.0
EU-15	42.1	40.3	51.2	56.7	72.2
EU-27			56.0	61.4	71.0

Source: Eurobarometer rounds 53 (2000), 64.2 (2005), 74.2 (2010) and 83.3 (2015).

Table 2.12 Ratio Supporting Added Initiatives against Illegal Immigration

Country	**(1) At national level**	**(2) At EU level**	**(3) At EU and national level**	**(4) Total**	**(5) Change since 2014**
Austria	29.1	17.4	42.7	89.2	10.2
Belgium	18.6	43.3	28.6	90.5	1.1
Bulgaria	21.5	22.1	45.9	89.4	3.4
Cyprus	26.0	17.3	50.7	94.0	0.8
Czech Rep.	32.3	33.6	27.3	93.3	3.0
Denmark	13.9	41.8	34.8	90.4	4.7
Estonia	12.8	16.3	62.9	91.9	6.2
Finland	16.1	37.2	34.4	87.7	0.6
France	15.1	32.4	32.0	79.6	0.8
Germany	10.4	29.1	46.7	86.1	4.1
Greece	34.4	26.1	37.9	98.4	1.7
Hungary	25.4	20.2	45.5	91.1	4.6
Ireland	23.8	21.9	42.9	88.6	2.9
Italy	22.5	30.8	40.1	93.4	2.7

Latvia	15.0	24.7	41.9	81.7	1.5
Lithuania	20.0	31.0	35.6	86.5	8.3
Luxem-bourg	7.2	35.0	47.7	89.9	2.6
Malta	11.6	27.0	57.3	95.9	0.3
Nether-lands	7.3	37.3	43.2	87.8	3.1
Poland	22.5	24.4	34.2	81.0	14.4
Portugal	23.9	31.4	36.6	91.9	9.0
Romania	20.9	27.3	24.0	72.1	0.2
Slovakia	30.1	23.7	32.4	86.1	-1.2
Slovenia	17.8	27.4	31.8	77.0	2.4
Spain	16.8	37.5	30.3	84.5	-0.8
Sweden	8.1	32.6	35.0	75.8	7.1
UK	24.7	18.8	38.7	82.2	-3.5
EU15	18.1	31.5	38.1	87.7	3.1
EU27	19.5	28.4	39.3	87.3	3.3

Source: Eurobarometer 83.3 (2015) and 82.3 (2014).

In later runs of Eurobarometer, the answers to questions about immigration policy (Columns 3 and 4) show that support for EU-level decision-making and, by extension, a joint EU policy on asylum has grown by a large amount. Focusing on the EU-15, the average country score went up by 16 percentage points and the number of countries where a majority of people chose EU-level policy went from one-third to two-thirds over the course of a decade. There are also more supporters than opponents in all of the countries that joined the EU in 2004 and 2008. After a while, Eurobarometer stopped asking the same question and started asking a different one instead. This is even clearer: "Please tell me if you support or oppose a common European policy on migration." The number of people who agree is even higher than it was in 2010 when the same question was asked. Part of the reason for this could be that respondents were not given the option of a national strategy. Still, the answer to this question is that most people in every country back EU-level policies.

So why has there been such a big jump in support for EU policies when Euroskepticism is on the rise? One option is that the people who answered the question thought it meant that their country would have less immigrants if policies were decided at the EU level. Transatlantic Trends shows that the relationship between liking how the EU makes policy and thinking that there are "too many" immigrants or that immigration is "more of a problem than an opportunity" is only slightly negative at the individual level. There is also no link between liking the way the EU makes policy and thinking that the national government has done a bad or very bad job of handling immigration. It seems more possible that the public has realized that at least some parts of policy would work better if they were handled at the EU level.

This is clearest when people talk about taking steps to stop illegal immigrants. Eurobarometer asked people in 2015, "Do you think more should be done to stop illegal immigration from outside the EU?" If so, people were asked at what level these kinds of steps should be taken. As was said above, the vast majority of people who answered the survey want more steps. As Table 2.12 shows, the numbers are very high in countries like Cyprus, Greece, and Malta. However, more than three quarters of people in every country except Romania support taking more steps to stop illegal immigration. As shown in Table 2.12, people have different ideas about what the government, the EU, or both should do. This may not be surprising because some measures, like employer punishments, are inherently national while others are not. What stands out is the strong support for actions to be taken either just at the EU level or both at the EU level and at the state level. In every single country, more than half of the people who answered the survey want stricter policies, either from the EU alone or from the EU and the national government together.

Ongoing Events and The Future of Asylum Policy

Future policies should be thought about in light of the study above and the events of the past few years. For policies to make sense, they need to take into account how and why people are applying for shelter. But its political viability is just as important for making policy. In a democracy, suggestions for policy changes that go against what most people want will not get very far. It is much better to work with what people want than against what they want. This points to three important places where policy should be made.

- Border controls need to be tightened and enforced. This would limit the policy backlash arising from public concerns about unauthorized entry together with increased salience of immigration as a policy issue. The fact that more than half of asylum applicants fail to qualify suggests that existing policy fails to select those most in need of humanitarian protection. But enhanced border controls will also restrict access for genuine refugees.

- Asylum policies must be refocused away from spontaneous asylum-seeking towards a comprehensive resettlement programme that targets those in countries of first asylum with the most urgent protection needs. Greater support is also needed for those that remain in the camps and shanty towns.
- Capacity to host resettled refugees must be expanded through enhanced cooperation between European countries. This would require agreement on a distribution of resettlement quotas that is more even across countries than that which is produced by the existing system.

Border Control

Recent events show that attempts to control the EU's border with other countries have failed horribly. It would be easy to think, as many people do, that these policies will fail because the more hurdles are put up, the more desperate migrants will find ways to get around them. Studies of illegal border crossings from Mexico to the U.S. show that when enforcement is tighter at one crossing point, traders help move migrants to another crossing point, which has a small effect on the flow as a whole. Recent events in Europe seem to show that point perfectly. Yet, the results of the regression analysis in Table 2.6 show that policies on entry to the territory do have some effect, at least on the level of each country. This is also shown by the case of Australia, where the number of illegal immigrants who came to the country by boat was cut almost to zero twice after a policy change.

Recent events also show that EU border control could do a much better job of stopping the flow of illegal immigrants. As in the case of Mexico and the US, the policy has been to block some routes while keeping others open (and in the case of the EU, even to encourage them). Before 2011, there weren't many people coming across the Mediterranean, mostly from North Africa. One reason is that EU governments made deals with countries of origin and transit to stop the flow. These deals included steps to be taken on land and at sea. In one case, Spain made deals with countries in North and West Africa with the help of Frontex. In another case, Italy made a deal with Libya. These steps worked to cut down on illegal migration, but when the Arab Spring ended, it left a political gap that made it easier for people to cross the western and central Mediterranean. Frontex estimates that the number of people crossing borders without permission is going up, as shown in Table 2.13. From just over 150,000 in 2008 to more than 1.8 million in 2015, the number went up. Changes in how people move from the West to the East are also interesting. In 2015, 90% of all illegal border crossings into the EU happened through the Western Balkan and Eastern Mediterranean paths.

Table 2.13 Unauthorized border crossings by migratory route 2006-15

Year	West Africa	West Med	Central Med	Albania-Greece	West Balkans	Eastern Med	Eastern Borders	Total
2006	31,600							
2007	12,500							
2008	9,200	6,500	39,800	42,000		52,300	1,335	151,135
2009	2,250	6,650	11,000	40,000	3,090	40,000	1,050	104,040
2010	200	5,000	4,500	35,300	2,370	55,700	1,050	104,120
2011	340	8,450	64,300	5,300	4,650	57,000	1,050	141,090
2012	170	6,400	15,900	5,500	6,390	37,200	1,600	73,160
2013	250	6,800	40,000	8,700	19,950	24,800	1,300	101,800
2014	275	7,840	170,760	8,840	43,360	50,830	1,270	283,175
2015	874	7,164	153,946	8,932	764,038	885,386	1,920	1,822,260

Source: Frontex at: http://frontex.europa.eu/trends-and-routes/migratory-routes-map/.

These changes were clearly affected by policies that have gone back and forth between being limiting and letting people do what they want. As the number of crossings increased, especially to Lampedusa, Italy started operation Mare Nostrum in October 2013 to save people who might die. As the number of people increased, the policy was changed a year later. It was replaced by the Frontex-led operation Triton, which focused less on search and rescue and more on protecting the borders. Over time, the lines have changed because of both changes in transit countries and changes in how the EU protects its borders. After Gadaffi's government fell, a lot of people from the Middle East and Sub-Saharan Africa used Libya as a way to get to other places. But as Libya fell into chaos and the West Mediterranean became more heavily policed, the main route across the Mediterranean moved east, with Egypt as the hub. As the number of Syrian migrants grew, the path through Turkey and across the Aegean Sea became more popular (and not just for Syrians). This was because migrants took advantage of the weak border controls in the Balkans.

As the war in Syria got worse and the Islamic Caliphate of ISIS said it would go to war against the West, the pressure grew. Since then, the number of people moving to Turkey, Lebanon, and Jordan has gone up, and more people are moving through Turkey to get to Greece and other EU countries. In response to these pressures, borders were closed and limits were put in place, first on the land border between Greece and Turkey and then on the borders between Hungary and Serbia and Bulgaria and Turkey. Angela Merkel, the German Chancellor, said in August 2015 that Germany would accept refugee seekers from Syria, Iraq, and Afghanistan. This caused more people to come to Germany. Frontex found that the number of illegal border crossings on the road through the western Balkans went up from 34,559 in the second quarter of 2015 to 229,746 in the third quarter. Under pressure from a growing number of migrants who wanted to go to the EU's interior, the Dublin system stopped working in Mediterranean countries, and Mrs. Merkel's welcome news caused it to fall apart completely. So, Greece and other EU countries on the EU's southern and eastern borders became stopover countries where migrants often didn't even get registered. As a result, border controls were put back in place in northern Schengen countries like Denmark, Sweden, and Belgium. As the system fell apart, border controls moved closer to the countries themselves. By March 2016, six of the 22 countries in the Schengen area had put controls back on at least one of their borders.

The EU finally realized that the only way to stop the flow of refugees is to remove or at least lessen the reasons why people want to move. On March 18, 2016, it worked out a deal with Turkey that gave money to refugees living there in exchange for restarting the process of Turkey joining the EU. In exchange for taking back the migrants, the Turkish government promised that the same number of refugees would be resettled directly from the camps in the EU. In the first three months of 2016, fewer people crossed through the Western Balkans. This was because Greece made it harder for people to move on. After the EU and Turkey deal, the numbers went down even more, and by July 2016, there were only 3% as many as there were in July 2015. Even though some people may have taken different paths, the effects seem to have been small. About the same number of people crossed the Central Mediterranean route in the first half of 2016 as in the first half of 2015.

Recent events show that strict policies can work to stop people from entering the country illegally, especially on maritime routes and in partnership with transit countries. The shifts between different routes are caused in part by changes in where refugees come from and in part by the weakness of Frontex, whose job has been to advise and coordinate with national agencies rather than to set up an independent border control system for the whole EU. But it also shows a number of policy changes and, in 2015, the end of all controls at the EU's border in the south-east. Tighter border controls are possible in the real world, and they are also an important way for the refugee system to win back public support. As we've seen, the public is very in favor of tightening border controls and very against illegal immigration. Because of this, cutting down on illegal entry is a top concern. Even so, there is going to be pressure on the EU's outside border for the foreseeable future. But if the strategy is successful and people can't get into Europe, it will affect both "economic migrants" and real refugees. This shows that there needs to be more than one way to help refugees.

Support for refugees and their resettlement

If we really want to help real refugees, this is where relief efforts should be focused. This work should be done in two ways. The first is to put money toward helping people who are stuck in camps close to their home country. Many of these people are women and children, and they face great hardship, disease, insecurity, and often violence. The second option is to start a large-scale resettlement program that would focus on refugees who have been accepted and whose applications have been handled in a country of first asylum. These refugees would then be sent straight to Europe. This would help protect the people who need it the most, not those who have enough money and are willing to risk their lives on dangerous illegal land and/or sea trips. Unlike the current system, where people just show up and ask for protection, this would make sure that these people really are refugees.

Not surprisingly, the homeless people in Turkey have been in the news a lot lately. Even though the first conditions in camps like Kilis and Kahramanmaras were better than in many first-asylum countries, the number of refugees has far exceeded the capacity of the 22 camps (about 220,000). Food, medicine, housing, and social services, especially education, as well as facilities for living space and social services, like education, all require a lot of money. In Lebanon, where a fifth of the people are refugees, things are worse. On the outskirts of Beirut, many Syrians live in slums like Sabra and Shatila, where the damp, overcrowded shelters and open sewers pose major health risks. And even though most of the recent attention has been on refugees in the Middle East, we shouldn't forget about long-term refugee situations in other parts of the world, where conditions are often worse. One example is the Dadaab camp in northern Kenya, which is the largest in the world and was home to 330,000 people (mostly Somalis) in 2015. There are serious threats to safety there, and people can barely meet their basic needs. Since the Garissa University College shooting, the camp has been threatened with closure. Refugees in Turkey need help, and the recent donation of €6 billion to help them is a good step in the right direction. However, resources are also badly needed in other places. The UNHCR says that it only gets 60% of the money it needs to provide the least amount of help.

The UNHCR says that there are three long-term solutions for refugees: going back to their home country, becoming a part of the community where they first found shelter, or moving to a third country. Over the years, these parts have been a part of a number of large-scale projects. Aside from the time right after the war, the International Conference on Central American Refugees (CIREFCA, 1987–1994) and the Comprehensive Plan of Action for Indochinese Refugees (CPA, 1988–1996) were the two most successful programs. Both of these had to do with multilateral deals between countries of origin, countries of first asylum, and countries of resettlement. The first one worked on getting about 2 million El Salvadorans, Guatemalans, and Nicaraguans who had been forced to leave their homes to go back and find a place to live. The second one was mostly about getting people back home, especially helping more than half a million Vietnamese and Laotians find new homes. There are many things to learn from these shows. One is that they weren't just one-time deals, but instead involved ongoing ways of working together. Another reason is that they needed resources from the west and, most importantly, leadership, either to bring the strategic interests of different countries closer together or to help solve the collective action problem.

Aside from these special programs, there has been a steady stream of resettlements every year, most of which have been made possible by the UNHCR. Under this method, people who have been moved are registered in their first country of asylum and their claim to be a refugee is decided. Case-by-case, the people who need to be resettled are those who can't find any other long-term answer. The refugees who are thought to be the most fragile or in the most need are then sent to the countries that have agreed to a resettlement program for a certain number of refugees. Even though there have been shared meetings and agreements, very few refugees have been resettled in developed countries. From about 150,000 at the beginning of the 1990s to about 90,000 per year in the last five years. One reason why the number of relocation places hasn't grown is that resettlement countries are worried about how refugees are chosen after the attacks of September 11, 2001. More than half of the 73,331 resettlements that the UNHCR helped with in 2014 went to the United States alone. Just under 10,000 went to 18 European countries, with more than a third going to Germany. Even though the number of countries that take refugees went from 14 in 2005 to 28 in 2015, most of them have very small limits. On the other hand, the UNHCR estimated that 1.15 million refugees needed to be resettled at the end of 2014.

In 2012, the EU agreed on a joint resettlement program for refugees chosen for resettlement by the UNHCR. The program focused on refugees in countries or areas where working together would have a "significant impact in addressing protection needs." Member states were asked to take part in the resettlement program on a voluntary basis. To encourage them, the European person Fund gave them €4,000 for each person they resettled. Even with this incentive, the effects have been very small so far. One possible reason is that countries that get a fluctuating and possibly large number of asylum requests on their own don't want to commit to resettling large numbers of people. Still, the fact that 18 European countries have started some kind of resettlement, most of them not too long ago, shows that this is seen as a worthwhile part of the humanitarian effort. In reaction to the crisis in Syria, European countries promised to give 72,500 people a new home. Even though only a few people have been moved so far, this is a big improvement over what had been done before and could be built on in the future. But a required first step would be to set up border controls that make it harder for people to get in without permission and limit the number of people who ask for asylum on their own.

Hosting Ability for Refugees and Fair Burden-sharing

A big resettlement program would need a big increase in the number of places that can house refugees. This could be done if European countries worked together to share the load. It's important to explain quickly why countries that take in refugees should share the load. Several writers have said that, for one reason or another, taking in refugees could be seen as a public good. That means that these kinds of policies should be run by a group that is bigger than a single country, like the EU. But from these stories, it's not clear at all what the mechanism is and, by extension, what the policy consequences are.

A good way to show why this is important is to compare it to immigration policy. Immigration policies are often looked at from the point of view of how well they serve the interests of the people who live in the country where the immigrants will be living. This could be specific people, like the supporters of those coming through family reunification, or the economy as a whole, as in the case of skill-selective labor migration. Refugees, on the other hand, are let in because it's good for them, not because it's good for the host society or certain people in it. In fact, the only requirement is that the refugee has a "well-founded fear of persecution." This has nothing to do with the refugee's "value" to the host country. Instead, the reason for the host society to give refugees a safe place to live is to help people in need. So, the benefit to one person from the host country does not lower the benefit to other people from the host country, who cannot be effectively excluded. Hosting refugees can be seen as a public good because this gain is good for everyone and can't be taken away.

If a country gives refuge to people who are running away from danger, people in another country gain from knowing that these people have found safety. But the only country that has to pay the economic and social costs is the one that takes in refugees. If each country makes its own rules about refuge, those rules won't take into account the benefits that come to people who live in other countries. In this case, the general good won't be given enough attention. A good social manager would make rules that take into account the externality.

Under the current system of unplanned asylum-seeking, each country makes its own rules without taking the effects on other countries into account. The main goal of the EU's Common European Asylum System, which has been changing since 1999, has been to make policies and processes for receiving, processing, and integrating people who apply for asylum on their own. Even though these policies are still not the same in all member states, they are getting closer together. And there is proof that when policy was tightened (Fig. 2.3) from 2001 to 2006, it caused a difference in the number of asylum applications. Plans to set up a distribution key for putting refugee seekers in different EU countries have been made many times, but they haven't gone anywhere until very recently.

In August 2015, a "deal" was made, led by Germany, to move 160,000 people from Italy and Greece to other EU countries. Several member states, especially those in Eastern Europe, fought back hard against this. Viktor Orban, the prime minister of Hungary, said on state radio, "This is not solidarity." We can't agree to this plan because it is unfair, wrong, and dishonorable. It is a crazy plan for someone to let refugees into their own country, not protect their borders, and then say, "Now I will give them to you, who didn't want to let anyone in." (Associated Press 5/8/15). It is important to note, though, that this comment is about people who got in because other countries didn't control their borders well enough. Even more important, Hungary got 174,000 refugee requests in 2015, which is more than four times the number from the year before and 13 times the average from 2010 to 2014. When you look at it this way, the Hungarian response doesn't seem so strange. Even so, not enough people showed up to the vote on October 2, 2015, for the EU plan to be turned down.

Any strategy that tries to spread asylum seekers out more evenly among European countries is likely to face political opposition. This is how public goods are supposed to work, so the EU has to act as the social manager. But it's important to point out that a more even distribution has a lot of general support. In September 2015, at the height of the crisis, Eurobarometer asked if refugee seekers should be spread out more evenly among EU member states. The average number of people in each country who fully or mostly agreed with the statement was 73.3%, with 84.8% in the EU-15 and 58.9% in the other 12 countries. Even in Hungary, 63.8% of people who answered said yes. Still more surprising is that an average of 72.6% of those who wanted a better distribution agreed or were leaning toward agreeing that the distribution of asylum seekers should be chosen at the EU level using binding quotas. Even among countries that are not in the EU-15, the average is 66.8%, and Hungary has a very high rate of 73.3%.

Still, it's important to keep in mind how strongly people feel about illegal entry and to make a clear difference between redistributing asylum seekers who are already in EU countries and resettling refugees directly from their first country of asylum. Taking into account what the public thinks about real refugees and how they feel about a distribution plan, it is likely that governments would feel better about a placement program for refugees in which they had a say. One way to make this process easier would be to create a market for tradable refugee limits that takes into account the political and economic costs that each government has to pay. This could be combined with a matching system that takes into account refugees' and host countries' tastes for different kinds of refugees. But it seems unlikely that a large-scale, ongoing resettlement program could be agreed upon as long as more than a million people apply for refuge on their own every year.

An Overview

An asylum policy that requires a person to risk his or her life and safety on a dangerous sea journey on a leaky boat, at the mercy of people smugglers, and is often followed by a long walk in the cold and wet while avoiding fences and border guards seems like a very unsatisfactory policy. One that chooses for the trip many people who don't qualify for refugee status once they get to their chosen destination, who are often hard to send back, and who end up in the limbo of the informal sector, seems to be very poorly targeted. And one that leaves many of the people who need protection the most behind and doesn't do much to help them in the camps and slum towns where they are left makes it look even worse. In fact, it's completely insane.

In the last three years, a huge event has happened that has scared people more than ever before. As the Syrian tragedy has gone on, each week the media has reported on the struggles of refugees and travelers. The EU and individual countries have been slow to act, which has been criticized by many people. As we've seen, stricter border controls can stop the flow of migrants, especially those who arrive by boat, and the EU is moving steadily toward an approach like Australia's, which makes it less appealing to move by boat. This shouldn't be a surprise, given how many people worry about illegal immigrants. The package that the EU and Turkey decided on in March 2016 has helped stop the flow of migrants by making it less appealing to leave and giving one refugee a home for every migrant sent back to Turkey. This model or the one that worked well in the western Mediterranean could be used to make more deals. When these kinds of plans don't work, like in Libya, tougher steps are needed, even if that means sending back migrant boats. Such policies would be easier to carry out now that Frontex has been turned into the European Border and Coastguard Agency, which has much more power to step in and put border defence policies into action directly.

The problem has pushed the EU to take some steps to change from a system in which people just show up and ask for asylum to one in which refugees are resettled in Europe. In April 2016, the EU Commission and Council put out a statement that said:

> The overall objective is to move from a system which by design or poor implementation places a disproportionate responsibility on certain Member States and encourages uncontrolled and irregular migratory flows to a fairer system which provides orderly and safe pathways to the EU for third country nationals in need of protection or who can contribute to the EU's economic development. The EU needs a robust and effective system for sustainable migration management for the future that is fair for host societies and EU citizens as well as for third country nationals and countries of origin and transit. For it to work, this system must be comprehensive, and grounded on the principles of responsibility and solidarity .

This agenda focuses on possible ways to change the Dublin regulation, such as by using a distribution key. It also talks about more harmonization, border control, limited secondary movements, and making the European Asylum Support Office's job more important. Even though there is a commitment to resettlement to "ensure that the EU takes its fair share of global responsibility," the details have not yet been worked out. Recent events have clearly placed resettlement on the agenda, but the size of the crisis is making it hard to create the resettlement places that are so desperately needed. But moving people to new homes should be the long-term goal. Over time, a large relocation program could also make it much less appealing for people to move on their own, which comes with risks and traumas. Formal plans to share the load are now taken more seriously, but their ability to increase the total number of places that can take in refugees has not been used. If this were used for a resettlement scheme, it would get much more public support. In fact, one important reason to switch to a different system for refugees is that it would work with public opinion instead of against it, which is what the current system does.

Chapter 3
The Fate of Irregular Migration to Europe

Since the beginning of migration studies, people have tried to make models that can predict how big groups of people will move. Scholars have tried to predict the size of migration flows by thinking of large-scale human mobility as the combination of bad reasons for people to leave their home country (such as economic hardship, war, violations of human rights, etc.) and good reasons to go to a certain place. Most of the time, these are called the "push" and "pull" causes of migration. Newer studies, on the other hand, have questioned whether it's even possible to predict migration with deterministic models, saying that the idea of push and pull forces is too simple.

The study of migration across the Mediterranean is a good place to use these tips. In the last few decades, economic migrants and refugees from sub-Saharan Africa, the Maghreb, and the Middle East have used the sea to move between Africa and southern Europe. The complexity of these mixed flows not only makes it hard to tell the difference between economic migration and forced removal, but it also makes it harder for European policymakers to figure out what to do. The many different reasons why people come to Europe illegally by sea, where they come from, and what their legal status is, along with the political and economic complexity of the Mediterranean area as a whole, make it hard to predict the future of illegal seaborne migration to Europe.

Even with these caveats, this chapter will try to figure out some of the most important trends in illegal movement by boat across the Mediterranean Sea. It will focus on the Central Mediterranean route, which goes from Libya and Tunisia to Italy. Even though it's impossible to know exactly what will happen in the future with seaborne migration, a review of the available literature and a look at how people have moved across the Mediterranean over the last thirty years may help find some plausible future scenarios. This chapter is broken up into the following parts. The first part gives an outline of migration across the Mediterranean Sea by boat, pointing out some of the most important factors that have changed irregular maritime over the past few decades. In the wake of the Arab Spring, the second part focuses on sea migration and looks more closely at the Central Mediterranean corridor between 2013 and 2019. In the last part and the conclusions that follow, we'll look at all the evidence we've seen so far and try to figure out what might happen in the future that might affect migration across the Mediterranean.

Illicit Maritime Migration to Italy

The history of the Mediterranean area can't be separated from the movement of people by sea. At least since the middle of the 20th century, people have not only moved north across the Mediterranean area, as shown by the Spanish, French, and Italian settlements in Morocco, Algeria, Tunisia, and Libya. Since the 1970s, illegal maritime travel from North Africa and the Middle East has become more important. This is because tightening visa limits have made it much harder for temporary migrant workers to enter legally. Before 2001, the Adriatic Sea was the most common way for people to sneak into Italy. When the Communist government fell in 1991 and a new wave of unrest broke out in Albania and Kosovo in 1997–98, tens of thousands of people moved to Italy by boat through the Otranto Channel. On March 7, 1991, more than 27,000 people arrived in one day. This caused the Italian government to start a naval blockade to stop the ships bringing illegal immigrants. At the end of the 1990s, the southern coast of Sicily became the most popular place for people to go by boat. Most of these people came from Tunisia and crossed the Strait of Sicily to get there. As Tunis started making it a crime to leave the country illegally, Libya became a stopover country as well as a place to go. Between 1997 and 2008, between 30,000 and 15,000 people moved by sea from Libya and Tunisia each year.

Italy tried to cut down on illegal crossings by working with both North African countries on return and border control. Tripoli's terrible record on human rights and lack of democratic credentials make it hard to reach deals with Libya about outsourcing. The 2008 Treaty on Friendship, Partnership, and Cooperation was signed by the authoritarian leader of Libya, Muammar Gaddafi, and the Italian Prime Minister at the time, Silvio Berlusconi. In order to make it easier for the two countries to work together, Italy decided to pay up to five billion euros and help build infrastructure in Libya. Most of the Treaty is about how the two countries will work together to deal with illegal migration. For example, the two countries agreed to patrol the shores of Libya with boats from Italy and workers from both countries. Rome's cooperation with Gaddafi was bad from a humanitarian point of view, but it helped cut down on irregular departures and stayed in place until the start of Libya's civil war in 2011. After that, Italy joined other NATO members in supporting the rebels through the Unified Protector bombing mission.

Fig. 3.1 - Irregular sea arrivals in Italy, 1998-2010

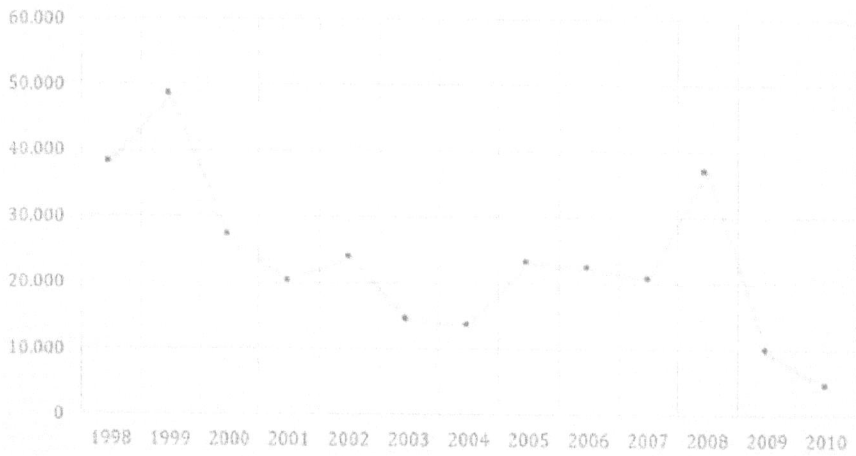

Source: International Organization for Migrationand the Italian Ministry of the Interior

Irregular Sea-based Migration since the Arab Uprisings

Policymakers and researchers who study migration across the Mediterranean have found three main routes to Europe: the Eastern Mediterranean route, which goes from Turkey to Greece and Cyprus; the Central Mediterranean route, which goes from Libya and Tunisia to Italy; and the Western Mediterranean route, which goes from Morocco to Spain. Even though there are other routes, such as the Eastern Atlantic route from West Africa to the Canary Islands or the longer journeys directly across the Mediterranean from Algeria to Sardinia and the Balearic islands and from Turkey and Egypt to southern Italy, most crossings have taken place along the three corridors listed above.

Figure 3.2 shows that Italy hasn't always been the main way people got into Europe. In 2015, the Eastern Mediterranean route was by far the biggest path for illegal migration. This sudden rise in illegal crossings across the Aegean was caused by a sudden increase in the number of people fleeing Syria's civil war. It was also caused by tighter controls and a border fence at the land border between Turkey and Greece, which made migrants and people-smuggling groups choose to cross the sea illegally. The March 2016 deal between the European Union and Turkey, on the other hand, made it much harder to cross from Turkey to Greece, but it didn't make it impossible.

Fig. 3.2 - Migrant arrivals along the Western, Central and Eastern Mediterranean Maritime Routes after the Arab Uprisings

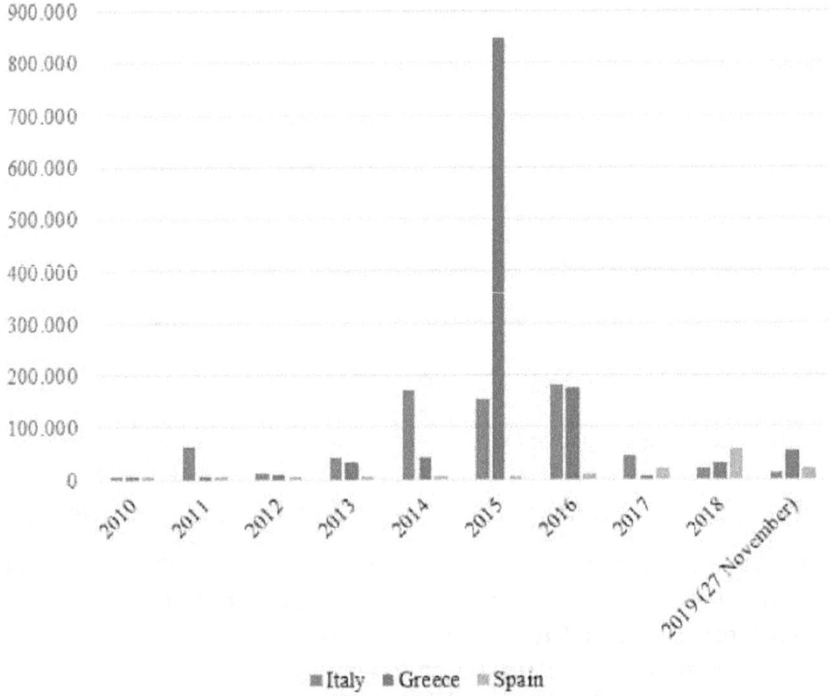

Source: International Organization for Migration

Fig. 3.3 - Casualties along the Western, Central and Eastern Mediterranean Routes

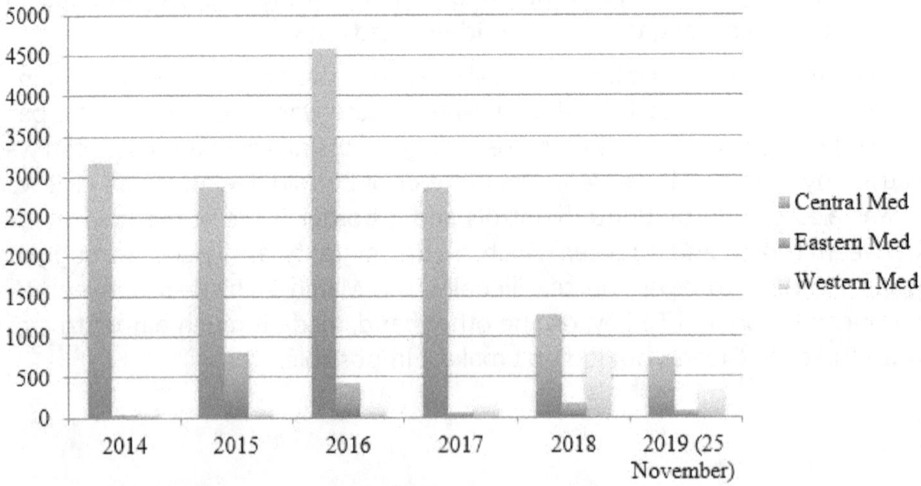

Source: International Organization for Migration Missing Migrants Project

Contrary to what was thought, the fact that the Eastern route was almost shut down did not cause a significant rise in illegal movement from Libya. Since the summer of 2017, when Libyan militias started holding refugees for longer instead of sending them out to sea, the Central Mediterranean has lost some of its importance as a route for illegal migration. It is now less used than both the Eastern and Western routes. But the Central Mediterranean corridor has stayed the most dangerous way to get to Europe and other places around the world. From 2014 to 2019, more than 15,000 people were believed to have died off the coast of Libya. Even though the number of deaths has gone down a lot since 2016, when more than 4,500 people died, the crossing is now so dangerous that one person dies for every five people who leave. As of November 25, 740 people have been claimed to have died off the coast of Libya.

Irregular Coastal Migration in the Central Mediterranean Region

Gaddafi tried to stop Italy and other NATO countries from helping by saying he would "turn Europe black." However, after the uprisings and NATO's military involvement, the number of illegal migrants crossing the Central Mediterranean did not immediately skyrocket. Even though there was a first, smaller spike in irregular departures in 2011, when 62,000 people came to Italy by sea from Libya and Tunisia, it wasn't until late 2013 that irregular departures rose dramatically. In the middle of the civil war, when state structures fell apart, Libya became a great place for people to get to Europe without going through the proper channels.

In the meantime, Gaddafi's government had fallen, and the European Court of Human Rights (ECHR) had challenged the legality of Italy's methods for enforcing its borders to stop people from coming to the country illegally. In the landmark Hirsi case from 2012, the European Court of Human Rights (ECHR) found that the Italian Navy was wrong to send Eritrean asylum seekers who had been saved at sea in 2009 back to Libya. This sending back was against the non-refoulement principle, which says that refugees can't be sent back to places where their basic rights would be threatened.

The Italian government then chose to change how it controls its borders by letting all the migrants saved at sea get off the boats on its own land. After two well-known shipwrecks near the island of Lampedusa at the end of 2013, Italy started operation Mare Nostrum. This involved 34 Navy boats that worked in shifts off the coast of Libya. Italy was frustrated by how much the operation cost, so it wanted to use its upcoming role as president of the European Council to get help from the rest of the European Union. Other EU Member States, on the other hand, didn't help Italy at all. Instead, they criticized the Italian Navy action as a reason for illegal immigration and "a bridge to Europe." The European Council made a deal that led to the suspension of Mare Nostrum and the start of Triton, a smaller mission run by Frontex. So, Triton was designed as a border guard instead of a rescue mission, and it patrolled an area much smaller than Mare Nostrum at first. Under the Common Security and Defence Policy (CSDP), the EUNAVFOR MED operation "Sophia" began in the spring of 2015. EUNAVFOR MED, which is also focused on "disrupting smugglers' networks," does not say in its mission statement that it will carry out maritime search and rescue activities. Figure 3.3 shows that Triton and EUNAVFOR MED did what they were morally and legally required to do to save lives, which was to help more than 138,000 people. Fear of becoming a pull factor, on the other hand, kept European assets from getting involved in rescue operations. This left a gap in SAR skills that had to be filled by civil society groups.

Fig. 3.4 - Rescues in the Central Mediterranean per organisation in absolute terms, 2014-2018

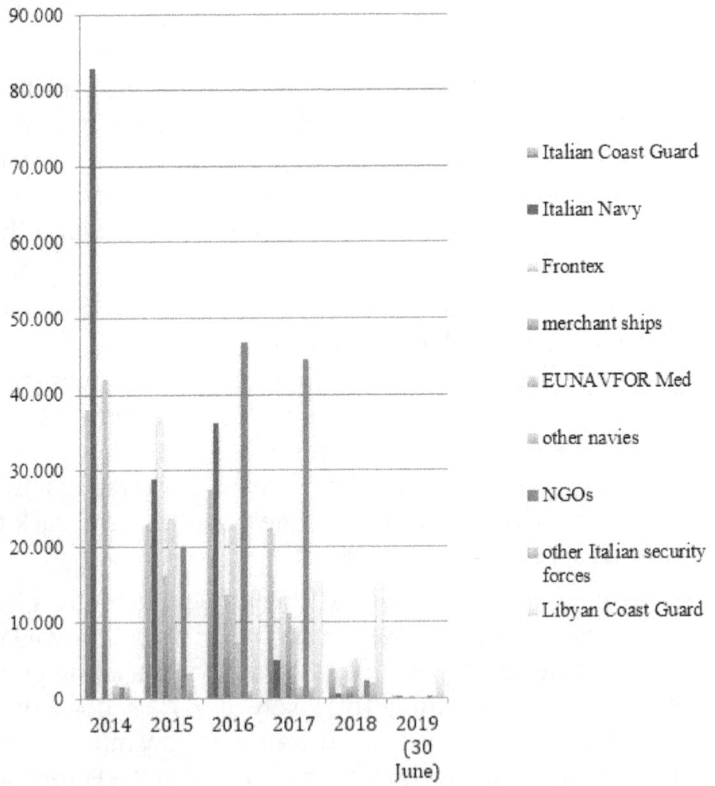

Source: author's elaborations on Italian Coast Guard and UNHCR data.

After the Migrant Offshore Aid Station was set up in the summer of 2014, non-government rescuing operations picked up speed in the years that followed. In 2016 and 2017, ten different non-government organizations (NGOs) worked in the Central Mediterranean and sent between 12 and 14 ships to the area off the coast of Libya. Even though most organizations don't have a lot of resources, NGOs have become the biggest source of maritime rescue, helping over 115,000 migrants in total.

But since the beginning of 2017, NGOs' work has been getting more and more criticism. Italian lawmakers and prosecutors used Frontex's claim that NGOs were acting as a "pull factor" as a way to get people to come to Italy. In 2017, NGOs were asked to sign a Code of Conduct that limited their actions. In 2018, it was made clear that they couldn't let saved migrants off in Italian ports. A 2019 security order also says that ships that enter Italian territorial waters without permission can be fined a lot and have their boats taken away. During the same time period, Italian judges looked into several NGOs and seized three ships.

Late in 2019, a new government was put in place, and Italy, Malta, France, and Germany came to a tentative deal in Valletta about how to share out migrants who were rescued at sea. This made Rome's position a little bit more flexible. But Italy and other European states did not change much in how they dealt with NGOs. The willingness to help the Libyan Coast Guard do its job and the worry that SAR operations might be a pull factor have led to a continued readiness to stop NGOs from doing their jobs. In fact, the draft of the September 2017 Valletta summit's conclusions says again that the 2017 Code of Conduct puts limits on what NGOs can do, indirectly repeating the criticism that unregulated rescue operations encourage people to leave.

Because of this ongoing process of criminalization, the number of NGOs involved in SAR has dropped by a lot. As of this writing, the only organizations working off the coast of Libya are MSF and SOS-Mediterranee, which work together on the Ocean Viking, and Open Arms and Aita Mari, which are both from Spain. Critics have used the fact that the number of people leaving Libya is going down, the number of deaths is going down, and the number of NGOs is going down to show that policies meant to discourage marine rescue are working. Recent study, on the other hand, shows that the work of NGOs did not have a big impact on migration from 2014 to November 2019. Migration flows from Libya were not changed by the pull effect of NGOs and other rescue resources. Instead, weather and events on land were the main factors.

The attempts of Libyan institutions and tribes to stop people from leaving the country illegally were especially important. In 2017, Marco Minniti, who was then Interior Minister, started a new way to handle migration. He offered financial help to Libyan tribes and militias in return for their help stopping people from leaving the country illegally across the Mediterranean. Since 2016, the Libyan Government of National Accord (GNA) Navy and Coast Guard, which was trained by Operation Sofia and the Italian Navy and Coast Guard, has also started to do its own rescue work by stopping migrant boats and taking the people on them back to Libya. From 2016 to November 2019, more than 50,000 people who had left Libya were taken back there. But this newly formed force wasn't ready for the job, and many migrants didn't want to be taken back. This led to a number of problems, including the bullying of NGOs and the use of violence and leaving migrants at sea during rescue operations.

Emerging Patterns in Irregular Waterborne Migration to Europe

Even though it's hard to predict irregular migration to Europe because there are so many things that push, pull, and stop people from moving across the Mediterranean, there are some important trends that can be seen.

First, population growth in sub-Saharan Africa and the Middle East, as well as geopolitical and environmental factors, make it likely that people will continue to move across the Mediterranean and that the number of people doing so will likely rise. Predictions that there will be a big rise in migrant exits, on the other hand, are too negative. Contrary to what most people think, most migration happens along south-to-south routes, not north-to-south ones, and most migrants and refugees stay in countries nearby. In the near future, these factors will continue to affect how people move around in sub-Saharan Africa and the Middle East, which will indirectly make it harder for people to move to Europe.

Long-term, there may be more people moving to Europe, but the big number of people who moved there after the Arab uprisings in 2011 is unlikely to be matched in the short to medium term. Since 2017, illegal migration has slowly gone down, and in 2018, it went down by 27%. Even though there have been small increases in landings along the main migration routes in the second half of 2019, this hasn't stopped the trend of arrivals going down. As of November 21, 2019, 90,744 people had crossed the Mediterranean. In the first 11 months of 2018, 108,146 people did so illegally. Such paths are not likely to change drastically in the near future. Unrest in countries where people leave and, to a lesser extent, in transit states that are currently working with the EU to stop migrant flows could still cause new spikes in migration to the north.

Also, the number of people traveling by sea from Libya to Italy is expected to stay much lower than during the peak years of 2013 to 2017. Academic study has shown over and over again that most migrants don't go to Libya with the goal of getting to Europe. Libya is still a popular place to visit because it has a strong currency and a lot of low-skilled work. This situation is not likely to change, and if the country gets more steady, it may get even worse. Certainly, as shown by the small rise in crossings after Haftar's attack against Tripoli in April 2019, new outbreaks of hostilities could make migrants want to leave Libya, which would affect irregular departures. Higher local instability and EU initiatives at the borders of Mali and Niger may both make it less likely for people to journey to Libya in the first place. In fact, it looks like the number of people crossing the border illegally from Niger to Libya has gone down a lot in 2018 and 2019. Lastly, the fact that the number of illegal crossings has been going down steadily since July 2017 shows that coordinated action by the EU has worked to stop crossings. This is unlikely to change much, even though there is more and more proof of widespread human rights violations. If nothing unexpected happens, like a major war breaking out or the GNA in Tripoli falling apart, irregular crossings will be lower in the next few years than they were in 2014–2017. This is because fewer people will be arriving and the Libyan government will be working hard to stop the flow.

The main things that will drive migration across the Mediterranean will continue to be push factors rather than pull factors. Existing research has already downplayed the importance of "pull factors," showing clearly that the things that make migrants want to leave their home country are much more important than the benefits of the countries where they end up or the "incentive" that NGOs say they provide by rescuing people at sea. This is especially true for people moving to Europe, where there will continue to be a mix of economic and forced migration, which will make refugee and humanitarian protection policies in Europe more difficult. Extreme poverty, war, and unrest in sub-Saharan Africa and the Middle East, as well as population growth and environmental damage in most of the countries in these areas, will continue to be the major reasons why people move north. As European leaders have admitted, climate change is likely to cause more people to move than anything else. On the other hand, the refugee and border control policies that Italy and other European countries have made are likely to have only a small and, in the end, no effect on the flow.

Only activities that physically stop migrants from reaching Europe's shores will continue to play a big role in slowing down the flow along a particular route. But international law, as shown by the Hirsi case, says that European security forces can't send refugee seekers back to most countries at the southern end of the Mediterranean basin. Demands from the public to stop illegal migration will keep pushing European governments to use externalization policies to get around these legal restrictions. They will use bilateral agreements and European instruments like the European Neighbourhood and European development policy to convince transit countries to stop migrants from getting to the EU's external borders.

Such plans are likely to hold up in the face of major human rights worries. Policies about outsourcing, on the other hand, are not a magic bullet. Not only are these measures unethical and open to review by the European Court of Human Rights, but they are also weakened by the weak institutions and widespread corruption in countries of transit and departure, which could make local authorities suddenly unwilling or unable to help. Also, countries in the EU's Southern Neighbourhood are likely to take advantage of the EU's increased willingness to stop migration flows. These countries will use their ability to stop or help migration flows as a bargaining chip to get financial aid and other concessions. Repatriation deals that make it easier to send illegal immigrants back to where they came from will also be strengthened. The effectiveness of these measures, however, is likely to stay low because of legal and practical limitations, as well as the fact that countries of return aren't very willing to work together, since migrants' remittances are often a bigger source of income than development aid. Arrangements that make it possible to immediately and forcibly send refugees back home when they arrive, like partnerships between Italy and Europe and Tunisia, have played and will continue to play an important role. As the recent rise in the number of people crossing from Tunisia to Italy in 2018 and 2019 shows, however, these kinds of steps also have their limits and may not be enough to stop people from leaving illegally when there is trouble in their home countries.

Europe's policies for controlling its ocean borders will continue to be a balancing act between the moral and legal need to save lives and the fear of making it easier for people to cross illegally. Recent research has called into question how much rescue operations are pull factors, but these kinds of policy tales tend to be very strong even when the evidence doesn't back them up. So, it's not likely that there will be any more state-led rescue missions in the near future. Even though they don't have a big impact on the size of migration flows, maritime border enforcement and rescue efforts like Mare Nostrum can save lives and direct migration flows. This helps find irregular arrivals that could be used by criminals or terrorists to get into a country. Fear of creating a "pull factor" and being seen as "soft" on migration by the public is likely to keep EU governments from starting border control missions with a large maritime rescue component. Even when news of migrants drowning is widely reported and causes anger and calls for action, European maritime border control policies will continue to be hampered by the fact that they have to deal with both humanitarian needs and strategies to keep people from coming. Between 2014 and 2017, civil society helped fill at least some of the gap left by the withdrawal of EU military forces from the southern Mediterranean. This helped reduce the number of people who died at sea. Even though criminalizing NGOs hasn't worked very well so far, they won't be doing as much maritime rescuing as they did in the past. As I showed in my earlier research, the large number of NGOs off the coast of Libya between 2014 and 2016 was caused by a number of factors coming together at the same time. These factors included how legitimate, possible, and financially viable non-government migrant rescue was seen to be. It's not possible that these things will happen in the near future. Even though the charges of helping illegal immigration against several organizations are likely to be dropped because of the organizations' humanitarian goals, this criminalization campaign has hurt the public's view of the legitimacy of these organizations, which has led to a drop in donations and strong opposition from the media. A higher risk of being prosecuted for helping illegal immigration, delays in giving NGOs a place to disembark, the fact that the Italian MRCC is no longer a source of information about the situation, and the tense relationship with Libyan coast guards, who have often threatened violence against humanitarian workers, have all made it harder for NGOs to do rescue work and make it less effective when they do. Even though the EU has been criticized, it is likely that it will not do proactive rescue efforts in international waters and will try to stop people from doing them on their own. In fact, rescue operations will still be given to the security forces of third countries like the GNA Coast Guard and Navy, which can combine rescue and interdiction by taking migrants back to the beaches of the southern Mediterranean.

Without organized efforts to deal with the root causes of migration, measures like "externalization" and "immediate repatriation" may continue to give smugglers and traffickers a reason to move people to more dangerous routes and strategies to avoid being caught. Migration routes to Europe are not directly linked, as shown by the fact that the number of people crossing the main Mediterranean paths has changed over the years. So, sudden changes in how open some European borders are won't cause quick, large-scale rerouting across the Western, Central, and Eastern routes. But migration flows along certain paths will continue to change in response to certain measures of externalization and border control. Eastern Mediterranean flows are changing from land to sea, and migrants are trying to get to Spain by taking longer paths that go to places like the Canary and Balearic islands, which are further away.

In a similar way, externalization policies will continue to hurt people in very bad ways. The Central Mediterranean is a good example of this. The fact that Libyan marine forces aren't well-trained, that the state institutions they answer to are weak, and that their operations are more like arrests than rescues, so migrants often fight them, will keep causing serious humanitarian problems. Because of this, there will continue to be a lot of deaths at the EU's coastal borders in the south. The lack of European law enforcement, the criminalization of NGOs, and an over-reliance on the Libyan Coast Guard have all made it easier for people to cross the border without permission. Since none of these things are likely to change soon, the Central Mediterranean road will continue to have a high number of deaths. Since the number of crossings is expected to stay lower than in previous years, there won't be as many deaths at sea as there were in 2016. The relative timeliness of the route is not likely to change much in the near future, though.

Future arrangements for the redistribution of migrants saved at sea could help Italy and other Southern European countries get over their tiredness of the migration crisis and be more willing to take the lead in rescue operations. The perceived lack of solidarity from the rest of the EU has been a major factor in pitting Italian authorities against rescue operations and the people who run them. This is best shown by Rome's growing tendency to only let NGO ships rescue migrants after an agreement has been made with other European partners about where they will go. Such agreements, on the other hand, are hard to make and are unlikely to work well. The September 2019 Valletta summit is a good example. Only France and Germany agreed to help Italy and Malta move some of the refugees who were saved off the coast of Libya. In the end, effective redistribution of migrants would require a full overhaul of the Dublin regulations, which say that asylum applications must be processed in the country of first entry. Even though the Von der Leyen panel promised to change the European asylum system, EU Member States are unlikely to agree on enough changes.

The very different origins, reasons, and legal status of seaborne migrants heading to Europe, the geopolitical complexity of the Mediterranean region, and the fragility of the current border externalisation arrangements made by the EU and its Member States make it hard to predict migration across the Mediterranean. Keeping these limits in mind, this study looked at irregular migration along the Central Mediterranean route over the last twenty years to find some long-term trends and likely future scenarios.

Based on the population and economy of sub-Saharan Africa and the Middle East, it seems likely that illegal migration to Europe from the south will continue. On the short term, however, the large-scale migrations caused by the Arab uprisings won't be matched until there's a major conflict in the area. Even though there are legal and moral issues, policies of onshore containment that try to stop migrants from physically getting to Europe's borders will remain important tools in the European Union and Italy's toolkits for managing migration. Migration flows that don't stop and policies that try to stop them will continue to kill people at sea. This hurts the EU's marine borders in the South in a big way from a humanitarian point of view.

Chapter 4
Responding to Asylum Issues
Bolstering and Simplifying Strategies in Western Europe

A record number of people have to leave their homes and look for shelter right now. By the end of 2015, the UNHCR reported that there were 65,3 million refugees, people who had been forced to leave their homes, and people who were looking for asylum. This was the biggest number of refugees reported since the end of the Second World War. This number went up by 12,4 million in a year. In 2015, about 1.65 million people asked for refuge in OECD countries, which are mostly in the Western part of the world. Most of the applications were made in Europe, where it was hard for countries to register, house, and figure out the status of nearly 1.1 million refugee seekers in 2016. The so-called "refugee crisis" that is putting pressure on European governments right now is caused not only by a large number of people looking for asylum, but also by the inability of European governments to work together to find political answers to this humanitarian crisis.

Migration scholars say that over the last few decades, industrialised countries have relied more and more on tightening policies to deal with the growing number of asylum seekers. These policies either limit who can apply for asylum or try to make the country less appealing as a place to seek asylum. But some new studies that compare the two show a more complicated picture.

We think that this traditional, one-dimensional view should be paired with the idea that policymakers are depending more and more on so-called "streamlining" policies. Efficiency-boosting policies like these aim to speed up the asylum process and reorganise the roles and responsibilities of people working in national refugee systems. The trend towards streamlining hasn't been talked about much in the academic literature, but the fact that asylum policies are getting stricter is well known. Recent policy surveys, on the other hand, have put a lot of stress on how widespread these reforms are. Most notably, the OECD (2013) said in the title of the asylum policy part of its 2013 International Migration Outlook that "humanitarian policies are being streamlined and there is a general trend towards deterrence." So, we think it's important to look at both tightening and streamlining policies to get a full picture of how Europe's asylum changes are going right now.

We look at the conflict structure of asylum changes in terms of both making policies stricter and making them simpler. In order to do this, we focus on the roles of actors in written rules. We think that elite actors disagree about both making rules stricter and making them easier to understand. By making two hypotheses, we also say that political organisations react to these two types of policies in systematically different ways. As for tightening, we think that actor preferences will be based on the new culture conflict dimension that pits authoritarian and nationalist values against libertarian and cosmopolitan ones. So, our first theory says that the more to the ideological right a political actor is, the more support there will be for making rules stricter. Our second theory says that the amount of extremeness on the left-right axis will lead to less support for policies that make things easier. In other words, we think that there is a cross-cutting split between the left-right divide and the need to simplify policies. The reason for this is that more extreme actors tend to criticise the asylum systems that are currently in place in Western Europe on a basic level. Because of this, more radical groups on either end of the political spectrum are less likely to back policies that aim to make national asylum systems work better in a practical way.

The empirical study is based on structured interviews with elites about the so-called changes to the federal asylum law that were passed by both houses of the Swiss Parliament in September 2012. From a logical point of view, this bill has two very important benefits. First, it can be seen as a balanced reform plan because it had the same number of policies that tightened and policies that simplified. Second, this bill turned out to be very political, since it led to a push for a referendum. When it comes to streamlining, the fact that it is so important makes it much more possible that groups of people from different political backgrounds have already made up their minds about these policies. The facts tend to back up the two theories we've already talked about.

Here's how the rest of this piece is put together. In the "Theoretical framework" section, we sum up the "tightening" approach to refuge and explain how we see "streamlining" policies. In the "Conflict structures over tightening and streamlining reforms" section, we explain how we came up with our two theories about how these two different policies affect the conflict structure. The research design is the topic of the next part. After we've thought about how to choose the cases, we'll talk about how we'll get the data and how the key factors will be used. In the 'Empirical results' section, the theories are tested statistically. In the "Conclusion" section, we look at the results of the quantitative analysis and talk about what they mean and where they fall short.

Concept

In OECD countries, there have been some big changes in how refugee policies are made and carried out over the past few decades. Since the beginning of the 21st century, the process of standardisation has been one of the most important things going on in Europe. Europeanization led to national asylum policies becoming more similar, asylum institutions in Southern and Eastern European countries becoming more official, and security standards getting better. Still, most experts think that asylum policies at the national level are still very important.

So far, the academic literature has tended to look at state asylum policies through the lens of a single policy approach. Many writers say that industrialised countries have become more strict about their policies, which means that they are slowly giving up their more open policies towards refugees from after the Second World War. Recent studies that use different sets of data to compare migration policies have found some more complex trends.

We suggest that, in recent years, policies that focus on making things easier have become more popular. Over the last few decades, these kinds of changes have been made by asylum officials all over Western Europe. After the London Resolution of 1992, national efforts at the start of the 2000s followed a logic of rejection by focusing on asylum seekers whose claims were "manifestly unfounded." Since the 2010s, attempts to streamline have gotten bigger. This is because most of these changes were made to make the national asylum systems work better.

Bolstering

During the Cold War, Western countries were kind to refugees because they were thought to be against communism, the political philosophy of the enemy. Since the fall of the Soviet Union, this sympathy has turned into general disdain and a lot of noise. Demands from the public to cut down on the number of asylum applications have mostly come from extreme right parties, but sometimes from moderate ones as well. This has led to a policy reaction, which has led to a tightening of rules in all industrialised countries.

Basically, there are two kinds of rules that make things tighter. The first way is to make it harder for people to get protection, either by making it harder for them to get into a country where they want to go or by making it harder for them to find out if they are refugees. The second method focuses on making asylum places less appealing. Some examples of bad incentives are making it harder to decide if someone is a refugee and giving asylum seekers less money and making it harder for them to live. The number of asylum seekers has been shown to go down more with the first method than with the second. But policies that try to limit access to the asylum process are very controversial, both legally and morally, because they touch all asylum seekers, whether or not they need protection.

Scholars agree that since the early 1990s, national asylum laws have become stricter. Recent studies, on the other hand, have found some contradictory trends based on comparing migration policy datasets. Beine et al. (2016) find a general trend towards more limited asylum policies, but De Haas, Natter, and Vezzoli (forthcoming) show that liberalisations of asylum policies have slowed down a lot since 1989 and stopped in 2010. Helbling and Kalkum's research (to be published soon) shows that the conditions and criteria for asylum seekers have become more open. At the same time, De Haas, Natter, and Vezzoli (to be published; Helbling and Kalkum, to be published) and Helbling and Kalkum (to be published) have found that national decision-makers are using stricter controls to stop illegal immigrants from entering the country. So, the argument about making asylum rules stricter is still not over, especially in Europe. Comparative migration policy experts seem to agree, though, that it is harder to get into countries where people seek refuge.

Comparative study has also shown that the level of restrictions on asylum is not the most important factor when it comes to figuring out where asylum seekers go. The main things that cause people to seek asylum are wars, humanitarian crises, injustice in their home countries, and natural disasters. They are also driven by the people they already know and the networks of migrants. But most asylum officials don't have much control over these important factors. This high level of outside factors helps explain why tightening measures haven't worked as well as expected.

Simplifying

Not all policy reactions to the growing number of asylum requests have been about making things harder. In fact, today's decision-makers use rules that make the process run more smoothly. The OECD has seen a movement towards reforms that increase efficiency, such as speeding up the process for deciding whether someone is a refugee or not and focusing on structural reforms. In line with OECD policy polls, we think it would be best to call these large-scale efforts "streamlining reforms." So far as we know, scholars haven't paid much attention to these rules. We think streamlining reforms are worth looking into because they change national refugee systems in a big way and follow a different logic than tightening.

Even so, rules that make asylum work better have been around for a long time. In line with the sociological literature on organisations, which sees these kinds of policy changes as constant practises meant to fix organisational flaws, Triandafyllidou (2003) showed that new management principles in Italian immigration offices were meant to make them more efficient, but they actually led to a practise of "fake efficiency." In a similar way, Eule's compelling study of how German immigration offices work found that they have problems with inefficiency all the time and go through a constant cycle of structural failure and change as a result.

Another part of the literature was about the speeding up of processes in Europe. In Europe, exclusionary accelerated processes were set up at the start of the 21st century. They were started by the so-called London Resolution in 1992. The goal of these changes was to speed up the processing of claims that were "obviously false." They were aimed at a certain group of asylum seekers. By 2005, all 15 EU member states and the 10 new countries that joined the EU in 2004 had put in place some kind of fast-tracked processes to keep people out. The UK's Oakington Immigration Reception Centre, which started using a "fast-track" system in 2000, is possibly the most studied case. But because they only focused on a few things, these changes had a small effect. We will show that comprehensive changes that make things easier have only become popular in Europe since the beginning of the 2010s.

There are two main types of laws that aim to make things easier. The first method focuses on making the process of figuring out if someone is a refugee faster, easier, and more efficient. The goal is to prevent or get rid of backlogs of asylum requests. Oakley made a useful distinction between inclusionary and exclusionary practises when it came to this kind of streamlining: "The main goal of an inclusionary accelerated procedure is to quickly grant a person refugee status, while the main goal of an exclusionary accelerated procedure is to quickly deny a person refugee status." The second way is through structural changes that are meant to reorganise the roles and responsibilities of agencies and different levels of the political system in order to make national asylum systems more efficient and flexible. In fact, when the number of asylum requests changes a lot, buildings related to asylum need to be either made bigger or smaller.

"Frontloading" is a term that is often used to describe changes that aim to make things easier and more efficient. According to this idea, standard evaluations of asylum cases (like health problems) and protections for asylum seekers (like legal advice) are put in place right from the start of the process to decide if someone is a refugee or not. The goal of "front-loading" is to speed up the process by reducing the number of appeals that aren't necessary because first instance choices are better. This is supposed to save money in the long run. In fact, faster wait times in the process of figuring out if someone is a refugee make it more likely that they will be able to join the economy.

Most European countries have recently made big changes to their asylum laws that aim to make things easier. The Netherlands possibly made the most ambitious changes in 2011. In addition to tightening policies, the Dutch parliament agreed to create four national asylum centres to centralise the country's process for deciding who is a refugee. The Dutch rule on asylum now gives people more time to get ready before the interview. The goal is to speed up the next steps of the process and cut down on the number of requests.

Many European countries are now changing their asylum processes based on what the Netherlands has done. This will make the move towards making things simpler even stronger in the near future. France (2014) and Switzerland (2015) have already passed laws that are very close to this one. For example, the French bill wanted to cut the average time it took to decide if someone was eligible for refuge from more than two years to nine months. Another example is Ireland, where a single protection determination process was put in place by the government in 2008. All protection claims, including both refugee and subsidiary protection claims, are now looked at during the first step of the process. In 2011, Greece made another big change to make things run more smoothly. Because the country is always under pressure, both because it is a main entrance to Europe and because its national system is always broken, its parliament passed a new law to simplify the asylum process and set up an independent agency with offices all over the country.

Streamlining changes is done for more than one reason. Since tightening policies doesn't do much to reduce the number of asylum seekers, authorities seem to be turning more and more to reducing policies, which lets them have a more direct effect on policy. The main reason given by national governments is that when more and more people apply for protection in a country, the country can quickly reach its capacity limits. In Europe, people who want to get protection usually have to go through a fairly thorough screening process. This includes interviews about asylum, health checks, language analysis to figure out where the person is from, and sometimes even in-depth, on-the-ground investigations of asylum cases. Such methods for figuring out if someone is a refugee run the risk of becoming overloaded quickly. This is because the trained staff can only handle a certain number of applications in a certain amount of time. When things take longer than expected, it costs a lot more for housing, infrastructure, and government benefits. Also, people are more likely to appeal status choices in situations that are always too busy. In line with this idea, the

OECD has found that one of the main reasons for member states to streamline their processes is to cut down on the number of refugee requests that have been waiting for a long time.

When there are a lot of asylum requests, it's possible that European countries will not only have a hard time taking care of them on time, but also reach the limits of their infrastructure for handling asylum requests. Backlogs make this problem even worse. When something like this happens, it's important to have flexible ways to provide more places to stay, like temporary refugee camps, in a short amount of time.

But one could also say that national decision-makers could give refugee systems more money to help them deal with these problems. Given the way things are right now, it's possible that many countries are hesitant to give their asylum systems enough money. Due to the success of the extreme right in getting people to act, the fact that most people don't like asylum seekers, and tightening budgets, there may not be enough political will and courage in Europe today to increase the number of people who can get asylum.

Friction Points

In the age of globalisation, Western Europe's asylum policies have become a major problem, with a public that is upset, interest groups that are ready to act, and disagreements between political parties. In the next section, we will make some guesses about the structure of the conflicts surrounding tightening and streamlining changes. As we will explain in this section, we think that political players always react to these two policies in different ways. We think that disagreements about tightening will be set up along the standard left-right axis. We say that these preferences come from the new culture conflict dimension. As a result, we think that the amount of support for tightening policies goes up as a political player moves further to the right. On the other hand, we say that there is a split across this left-right axis when it comes to streamlining changes. More specifically, we say that ideological extremism makes people less likely to agree with streamlining changes. In other words, people who are more moderate should be more likely to support making policies simpler.

Here's a possible reason for our first hypothesis. Political scientists usually separate economic policy and cultural policy when talking about major political battles in Western Europe today. The first one is about the difference between government actions and market solutions. The second one is about the difference between liberal and cosmopolitan values on the one hand and authoritarian and nationalist values on the other. The societal cleavage has been linked to the area of asylum policies. In the last few decades, this aspect of strife has become very important in Western Europe. In the past, religion conflicts were at the root of the cultural divide. But because of secularisation, changes in class structure, and globalisation, this dimension of conflict has taken on a new meaning. At the moment, it means that universalist and traditionalist-communitarian ideals are at odds with each other. This struggle has become more political in Western Europe because both the new left and the Greens, as well as the radical right, are working to bring attention to it. While the first group pushed for things like ecology, participatory democracy, and libertarianism, the second group mostly fought against European unity and pushed for stricter immigration policies, which made politics much more based on race. In Western Europe, people on the left tend to have cosmopolitan views, people on the extreme right tend to have nationalist views, and people on the mainstream right usually take a middle ground.

Since the main goal of tightening reforms is to make asylum policies stricter, they are closely linked to the authoritarian/nationalist pole of the new dimension of cultural conflict. So, it seems clear that the fight between the left and the right has a direct effect on where people stand on tightening policies. More specifically, we think that politicians are more likely to agree on tightening policies if they are on the right side of the ideological spectrum. According to this theory, the radical right has been pushing for a more restrictive direction for a long time, while the left and its partners in civil society have been trying to keep things the same or improve the rights of asylum seekers. Comparative empirical studies on immigration in general and on asylum in particular have also shown that moderate groups like the Liberals, Christian Democrats, Conservatives, and Agrarians tend to stand between the extreme right and the extreme left.

When it comes to reducing policies, a different set of rules should be used. We claim that the level of support is inversely related to how far to the left or right the political actors are. In other words, these policies are more likely to be supported by moderate groups like the moderate right, the moderate left, religious groups, and public officials. The goals of speeding up and cutting costs, which are key to streamlining reforms, are thought to be in line with the usually pragmatic way that moderate actors in asylum issues solve problems. They may also support streamlining on the grounds that such changes to the way things are done don't hurt the humane principles they usually follow. In particular, these groups may find relief in the fact that the liberal asylum system that has been the norm in Western Europe since the end of the Second World War is not being called into question by changes to the way things are done. These things might be especially important for humanist groups like religious groups and nonprofits.

On the other hand, people on either end of the political range who are more radical are likely to be sceptical about simplifying policies. We think this is because both extreme groups tend to be very critical of how asylum is handled in the United States right now. So, these players might be hesitant to back policies that aim to improve the efficiency of national asylum systems by speeding up procedures and making structural changes. But the reasoning behind this resistance is based on very different things depending on which groups are at stake. Actors on the radical right usually think that only tougher changes, especially when it comes to how asylum seekers can get in, can solve problems in the asylum field. In other words, these people think that trying to simplify rules is mostly pointless. The extreme left, on the other hand, might be sceptical of streamlining because it could hurt the rights of asylum seekers. These groups may worry that the goal of speeding up the asylum process will lead to bad decisions and that cutting back on protections will hurt people who are looking for safety. More generally, the radical left uses to argue for sweeping immigration reforms that would make the difference between refugees who are politically persecuted and economic migrants irrelevant (for an academic critique of this distinction, see Crawley and Skleparis, 2018). When we look at everything together, we expect to see a conflict between moderate and extreme players when it comes to streamlining policies.

Based on these considerations, we are now equipped to formulate the following two hypotheses:

- **H1**: The level of support for tightening policies increases the more to the right a political actor positions itself.
- **H2**: The level of support for streamlining policies decreases with the degree of extremity on the left-right axis.

A Case Study

As an example case study to test our hypotheses, we will use the so-called urgent changes to the federal asylum law that were passed by both chambers of the Swiss parliament in the fall of 2012. There are two main reasons why this choice was made. First, the parts of this bill are all perfectly matched. As we'll talk about in more detail later in this part, it had the same number of policies to tighten and simplify as it did to tighten. This gives us a great place to look at how different political players feel about the two important asylum policies. Second, this case had a lot to do with politics. This is mostly because the bill was called into question through a vote. Since the final decision on this deal was up to the people, political leaders had a strong reason to talk to the public during the campaign leading up to the vote. This high level of public visibility seems to be very important for streamlining changes to be successful. Generalists, like political parties, won't be able to come up with clear opinions until these rather technical problems are discussed in public. If not, these policies will only be dealt with by experts and professionals who work in the field of refuge. Czaika and De Haas say, "There is often a large gap between politicians' tough talk about immigration and their actual migration policies, which are often much more nuanced and complex." Because it has been politicised, the chosen case gives us a chance to look at how a large number of political players are consciously positioned towards both tightening and streamlining. When this happens, political groups are likely to fight with each other, which could lead to clear divisions.

The urgent changes to the refugee law were passed by both houses of Parliament on September 28, 2012. The parties on the right agreed with the bill, but the parties on the left did not. Under the leadership of the Greens and several civil society groups, many organisations chose to force a vote by gathering the 50,000 signatures needed to do so within 100 days. This ad hoc alliance was able to get the urgent changes to the asylum law on the ballot in January 2013. Along with the people on the referendum committee, the Social Democrats, the Catholic Church, and the Protestant Church all said that the plan should be turned down. On the other hand, the federal and cantonal governments, right-leaning parties, and some conservative citizen groups supported the needed changes. On June 9, 2013, 78.2% of Swiss voters said yes to the bill.

When you look at the details of the bill, you can see that four policies are trying to make things tighter, while the other four are trying to make things simpler. In the first case, the rule that you can't ask for refuge at Swiss embassies was one of the most talked-about policies. Switzerland was the only European country that still had this choice, so the Government pushed for it to be taken away. A second strategy meant that deserters couldn't get refugee status. This move was meant to stop young Eritrean men from leaving the country, since many of them did so because they were forced to do military service for an undetermined amount of time. Also, the policy made it possible to set up special centres where so-called troublemakers (asylum seekers who don't want to work with the officials) could live. Finally, Parliament agreed to shorten the time people have to appeal when their asylum request is denied. The time went from 30 working days to 5 working days for applications that the government thought were really good and for possible deportations. The same cut was made for people seeking refuge who came from a list of "safe countries."

In terms of streamlining, the first strategy was to test a planned structural reform that was meant to cut the average time it takes to process an application for the majority of cases from 700 days to around 100. To do this, the Swiss government used the "front-loading" concept and based their reform on what the Dutch did. Also, the central government got more control over the cantons, which are the 26 member states. This gave them more room to move and helped them deal with the problem of changing numbers of asylum seekers. For up to three years, the Confederation could use its own facilities and buildings without getting permission from the cantons. This is a pretty controversial topic in Switzerland, where the opening of new asylum camps often leads to protests, in part because of fears that more crime will happen. In this way, there were worries that this move would take away from what the cantons could do. In exchange for this compromise, Parliament passed two laws that helped the cantons. First, the Confederation could help the affected cantons pay for extra security costs by giving them flat-rate payments. Second, the amendment said that the central state could give money to programmes for getting people jobs that were run by cantons, municipalities, or other groups.

The empirical study is based on information from structured interviews with elite people. We chose political groups that took an active role in the Swiss vote campaign in 2013 about making urgent changes to the federal law on asylum. We found 31 organisations by looking at different things, like the debates in parliament, the effort to get signatures, voting recommendations, the press, and websites in general. Also, this information was checked against the people who were interviewed to finish the list of organisations. With this practical approach, we're sure that we've included the most important groups. In the weeks before the election, we set up an interview with the person in charge of the issue at stake for each group. We chose to get rid of the organisations that had no effect on the direct democracy campaign in question. Based on a measure of reputational power, this turned out to be true for three companies, giving us a total of 28 observations.

When we use the above criteria, we get a group of actors that is very similar to the group Statham and Geddes (2006) looked at when they did a network study of British migration elites. In fact, the organisations we chose can also be put into three main groups: state players (N = 3), political parties (N = 10), and interest groups (N = 15). Table 4.1 gives an overview of the groups that are included.

Our study looks at three state actors: the Federal Department of Justice and Police, the more specialised Federal Office for Migration, and the Cantonal Ministers of Justice and Police at the sub-national level. There are four left-leaning political parties (the Social Democrats, the Greens, and the youth groups for each), and four moderate right-leaning parties (the Christian Democrats, the Conservative Democratic Party, the Liberals, and the Green Liberals). We also included the far-right Swiss People's Party and its youth group, the JSVP, in our list. As far as interest groups go, everyone in them can be thought of as a part of civil society. This shows that groups with economic interests, like business groups and labour unions, try to stay out of the way when it comes to asylum. Civil society groups were against the bill, except for two conservative groups: Pro Libertate, a patriotic group, and Pikom, an organisation that works for stricter immigration policies. These interest groups include four charities (Caritas, the Charity of the Protestant Churches of Switzerland, Swiss Workers Aid, and the Geneva-based Protestant Social Centre), three domain-specific organisations that help asylum seekers and immigrants ('Solidarity without frontiers' and the two French-speaking 'Coordination against exclusion and xenophobia' and 'Living together'), and three religious organisations (the Federation of Swiss Protestant Churches, 'Judaism', and ' Because so many civil society groups are against the voting measure, there are more people against it (N = 17) than for it (N = 11).

Table 4.1 Chosen Political Organisations

Category	Subcategory	Official name	Self-reported positioning on the leftright scale (0-10)
State actors	Federa administration	Federal Department of Justice and Police (EJPD)	5
		Federal Office for Migration (BFM)	5
	Sub-national administration	Cantonal Ministers of Justice and Police (KKJPD)	6
Political parties	Left	Social Democrats (SP)	2
		Young Socialists (JUSO)	1
		Greens (GPS)	2
		Young Greens (JG)	2
	Moderate right	Christian Democrats (CVP)	5
		Conservative Democratic Party (BDP)	6
		Liberals (FDP)	7
		Green Liberals (GLP)	5
	Radical right	Swiss People's Party (SVP)	8
		Young Swiss People's Party (JSVP)	10

Civil society groups	Conservative groups	Pro Libertate (ProLib)	9
		Pikom	8
	Charities	Caritas	5
		Charity of the Protestant Churches of Switzerland (HEKS)	5
		Swiss Workers Aid (SAH)	1
		Protestant Social Centre (CSPGE)	2
	Immigrant organisations	Solidarity without frontiers (sosf)	2
		Coordination against exclusion and xenophobia (stop)	2
		Living together (vivre)	1
	Religious organisations	Federation of Swiss Protestant Churches (SEK)	5
		Justitia et Pax (JusPax)	5
		AGORA	5
	Human rights organisations	Swiss Democratic Lawyers (DJS)	3
		Amnesty International (AI)	5
	Pacifist organisation	Group for a Switzerland without an army (GSoA)	1

Operationalisation

Now, we'll talk about how our key factors work in the real world. We use a series of questions about their position on the 2013 ballot proposition to measure the dependent variables, which are the views of the chosen groups about tightening and simplifying policies. To help them do this, the eight policies at stake were written down and given to the campaign managers. These included: 1) getting rid of the embassy procedure, 2) making a new rule about deserting, 3) setting up special centres for people who cause trouble, 4) shortening the time you have to file an appeal, 5) testing the planned structural reform, 6) giving the federal state more control over cantons when it comes to the use of facilities and buildings, 7) giving flat-rate subsidies for security costs, and 8) the federal state's financial contrition. Respondents were asked to rate their organization's views on a scale from 1 (strongly disagree) to 5 (strongly agree), with 1 being strongly disagree and 5 being strongly agree. To figure out how many dimensions there are, we use principal component analysis with varimax rotation to factor-analyze the eight things. Table 4.2 shows that this method keeps two factors whose eigenvalues are greater than 1. The findings are mostly what we thought they would be based on theory. The tightening dimension is shown by the first, and larger, factor. As assumed, this factor has a lot of weight on the issues of desertion, the process at embassies, special centres, and shortening the time you have to file an appeal. The second thing has a lot to do with the idea of simplifying. Three of the final four items belong to this second dimension, and each has a factor loading of more than 0.7. This is true for the expanded powers of the federal government over facilities and buildings, the job programmes, and the testing of the planned changes to the way asylum is handled. The flat-rate payments are the only exception. This thing is not biassed because it has about the same amount of weight on both factors. We took the scores of each company on the first and second factor loadings to find out how the actors felt about tightening and streamlining.

Now, we'll talk about the two factors that are on their own. We asked respondents to put their group on a scale from 0 (completely left) to 10 (completely right) to show where they thought it fell on the left-right dimension. In the last column of Table 4.1, each organisation that is part of this analysis says what its opinion is. Concerning how far these self-reported places were from the middle, we figured out how far they were from the middle (5). This means that the most extreme players on both sides get 5 points, while those in the middle get 0.

Table 4.2 Factor loadings of the ballot-specific issue (Principal factor analysis with Varimax rotation)

Issue items	**Tightening (factor 1)**	**Streamlining (factor 2)**
No guaranteed refugee status for deserters	0.9892	0.0556
Ban of applying for asylum at embassies	0.9737	0.0872
Special centres for troublemakers	0.9537	0.1331
Reduction of appeal period	0.9411	0.0803
Flat-rate subsidies for security cost	0.5831	0.6165
Testing of new asylum procedure (Dutch model)	0.4323	0.7245
More federal power on facilities and buildings	0.0467	0.8072
Federal contributions to employment programmes	-0.1376	0.8070
Eigenvalue	4.6981	1.8105
Correlation	0.3771	
Number of observations	28	

Results

We did bivariate correlations to get a first idea of the empirical validity of the two theories we were interested in. Both of these links turn out to be pretty strong, which is what we expected from our theories. This is especially true for the first hypothesis, where the left-right stance and support for tightening policies have a 0.77 Pearson correlation coefficient. It seems that the more to the right a politician is, the more support there is for more limiting policies. For the second theory, there is a -0.56 negative relationship between how extreme an ideology is and how much people agree on streamlining. So, groups with more moderate views are more likely to say they are for streamlining policies than those with more extreme views.

Now, let's see if these trends we've seen hold true in a multivariate setting. Since we only have 28 observations to work with, we chose to use simple models by focusing on only a few factors that could explain the data. We control for the impact of policy core beliefs, actor types, and language region in addition to the left-right and extremity aspects of the organisations' core ideology. For the first, we take into account how racist the different characters are. In order to do this, we follow what Sniderman, Hagendoorn, and Prior (2004) say we should do. We asked the people we talked to five questions about the economic, cultural, and safety risks they thought immigrants posed. When we do a factor analysis with varimax rotation on the answers people gave on a five-level Likert scale, we get a single factor that tells us how much xenophobia there is.

When it comes to types of players, we can tell the difference between political parties, groups in civil society, and the government. The reference group is the state players. When it comes to language areas, we use a variable that can only be one of two things. The number "1" is given to the four groups that are based in the French-speaking part of Switzerland. We chose to take language region into account because elite actors in French-speaking parts of the country tend to be more open-minded about immigration issues than those in the rest of the country. Table 4.3 shows how two OLS regression models turned out. Concerning tightening (Model I), it turns out that the more to the right a group is, the more likely it is to support policies that make things harder. This positive relationship, which is significant at the 1% error range, fits with what we would expect from theory. With the second theory, this is also usually the case. Model II shows that there is a negative link between how extreme an ideology is and how much people want to simplify policies. But this statistical link is only sure to be true within a 10% error range. So, there isn't much real-world evidence to show that moderate organisations are more likely to accept policies that streamline things than extreme ones.

Table 4.3 OLS regression models explaining factor loadings for tightening and streamlining

	Model I Tightening	**Model II Streamlining**
Left-right	0.229***	0.029
	(3.71)	(0.30)
Ideological extremity	0.098	-0.203*
	(1.39)	(-1.86)
Xenophobia	0.177	-0.396
	(1.06)	(-1.52)
Parties	0.512**	0.559*
	(2.46)	(1.73)
State actors	1.659***	0.938*
	(5.43)	(1.97)
French-speaking organisations	0.051	0.078
	(0.18)	(0.19)
Constant	-1.565***	-0.039
	(-4.31)	(-0.07)
N	28	28
Adjusted R^2	0.88	0.44

Notes: T-values in parentheses. Civil society groups are the reference category for the actor types.

$^*p < .10$.

$^{**}p < .05$.

$^{***}p < .01$.

The following are the values of the control variables. Asylum-specific views are not always affected by the level of xenophobia. When it comes to types of actors, the most consistent result is about political parties and the government. These two groups seem to be more in favour of both streamlining and tightening than civil society groups, which are used as a comparison group in this study. But it's important to note that the actor-related gap is much bigger (1% error margin) for tightening than for streamlining (10% error margin). Because civil society groups are usually at a loss in the Swiss political system, they are more likely to be critical. Most of the time, these groups don't have direct access to the arena where decisions are made, unlike state players and parties. Because of this, their worries are less likely to be taken into account in bills passed by parliament. This could make people more opposed to the policies that are put in place. We can't find a clear trend when it comes to where languages are spoken. More specifically, organisations from the French-speaking part don't have any different preferences when it comes to asylum than the other elite players.

Conclusion

Faced with a rise in asylum requests, many European countries have passed "streamlining reforms" since the early 2010s. Streamlining reforms are policies that aim to improve the efficiency of national asylum systems by speeding up procedures and making structural changes. In this piece, we made the case that these policies have been ignored by academics so far. We were able to show that the conflict structures over these two big reform trends follow completely different logics by using structured interviews with elites about urgent changes to the Swiss asylum law. Ideological positions on the left-right line have a big effect on how actors feel about tightening policies. The more to the right a political group is, the more likely it is that people will support these policies. On the other hand, the closer a politician is to the middle of this scale, the more likely they are to support reducing policies. This quantitative study showed that the statistical associations are much more important when they are about tightening policies than when they are about making things simpler.

The main results of this empirical contribution show that reform alliances are very different depending on what is at stake. The radical right is clearly in favour of tightening policies, while the left and its civil society partners are against them. The rest of the actors usually take places in the middle. Due to their important part in most political systems in Western Europe, the moderate right may hold the balance of power when it comes to making more restrictive policies. When the moderate right doesn't have a majority in government, these kinds of changes may be made through deals with the radical right. Streamlining reforms, on the other hand, may be the result of coalitions between moderate and pragmatic forces on the left and right. This is because more radical players on either side of the class struggle have been found to be less likely to support such policies.

More generally, the suggested two-dimensional setting may give a more accurate picture of how the actors are set up. By putting together the views for tightening and simplifying policies, we can guess that there are four different kinds of political organisations in Western Europe that deal with asylum issues in different ways. Even though people on the moderate right may be hesitant to make the asylum system stricter, they may generally be in favour of both tightening and streamlining. On the other hand, people on the radical left might be against both methods. The extreme right might agree with tightening and be sceptical of efforts to streamline. It could be the other way around for realistic people on the left. Even though more research needs to be done to figure out how and to what extent streamlining reforms divide the left and the right, it seems clear that a more nuanced way of looking at things has a better chance of reflecting how actors want policy to turn out than a single policy dimension. In a similar way, Bale said that moderate right-wing parties are more than able to think, talk, and act on their own, even if the radical right is pressuring them on immigration problems. A similar way of telling the right from the left might work for the left. At the very least, our empirical study shows that people on the moderate left are much more likely to start reforms that make it easier for people to get asylum than people on the radical left. But when it comes to tightening, it has been shown that these two groups of people have similar ideas.

Even though this empirical study shows some promising results, there are a number of reasons to take them with a grain of salt. First of all, the empirical case used here only looks at one change. Even though the most important thing about the chosen reform case was that it was exactly balanced (it had as many tightening policies as it did streamlining policies), these results should be taken with a grain of salt when it comes to how well they apply to other situations. It remains to be seen if these kinds of patterns can be seen outside of the unique situation that was studied here. Because the urgent changes to the Swiss asylum law were part of a referendum campaign, the political actors' opinions about streamlining policies may have been much clearer in this study than they would have been in a low saliency situation. In other words, we think that our results only hold true when both tightening and streamlining strategies are well-known among political elites. But since there are a record number of asylum requests right now, both asylum in general and streamlining changes in particular are getting more and more attention, we think that this may soon be the case all over Europe. So, we want to ask for studies that look at the different ways and effects of streamlining asylum laws in different countries.

Chapter 5
Problems and Responses to Asylum Seekers in Europe

The goal of this chapter is to look into the issue of asylum seekers in Europe, who are becoming more common as people move there. There are different ways that people can move. People can move to another country to find work, get an education or start a company, reunite with family, get some kind of protection, seek asylum, or for other or a mix of reasons. For example, climate change and global warming are likely to cause a lot of people to move around in the future.

Asylum seekers, also called "asylees," are carefully defined as humanitarian migrants or people who need protection, like refugees who are protected by the Geneva Convention of 1951 and its 1967 Protocol. The word "migrant" is used for anyone who moves to another country with the intention of staying for a certain amount of time. The Organisation for Economic Co-operation and Development (OECD) says that the term "humanitarian migrant" refers to people who have successfully applied for asylum and have been given some kind of protection, "be it refugee status, subsidiary or temporary protection" Instead, asylum seekers are people who have officially asked for refuge but are still waiting for their case to be heard. When migrants get to a country's land and ask for protection, the assessment process starts. Asylum cases are usually handled in three steps: interview, assessment, and appeal if the decision isn't what the person wants. Also, it's important to keep in mind that there are rejected asylum seekers and illegal immigrants who are part of Europe's immigrant population even though they don't show up in official figures. Undocumented migrants, who are also called illegal or irregular migrants, are people who stay in a country after being turned down for humanitarian migrant status or who do not apply for refuge.

The European Union (EU) is facing new problems because more people from the Middle East and Africa want to come to Europe. Civil wars, genocide, and policide are some of the threats that lead to more asylum seekers and migrants. Human rights violations, poverty, and a lack of economic chances in origin countries are also factors. In 2014, the number of refugee requests in the OECD area reached its highest level in 20 years. This was partly because the security situation in Syria and Libya was getting worse. In 2015 and 2016, the number of people looking for refuge went up sharply. Because of the number and variety of new refugees, it's hard to predict how many asylum seekers will come from outside of Europe, even though it's likely that more big groups will come in the future, so asylum movement should be thought of as a steady thing.

This research has three goals: first, to show that the recent "asylum crisis" is really a "policy asylum crisis" that puts pressure on a small number of Member States, namely those at the EU's borders; second, to show where the EU's asylum policy falls short; and third, to introduce and discuss a new proposal to fix some of the system's flaws. A contextualised study of the literature is used to answer the first two research questions. After figuring out the main things that cause and explain why asylum seekers move to certain countries, an overview of policy responses to recent unusual migration is given. The main problems that still keep fair and effective answers to humanitarian questions from being found are explained. To help with the third goal, this study talks about an Italian solution that could help with security and integration problems that are widespread. Interviews were done with the people who came up with the answer and with some local and national policymakers to find out what the project's strengths and weaknesses were.

Most of the research on where different ethnic groups choose to live is about foreign migration, not asylum. There are different ideas about why people move from one country to another. Some studies say that immigrants are drawn to states with rich welfare programmes, while other studies say that welfare programmes have little or no effect on where immigrants choose to live. There is also some evidence that migration rates rise with linguistic proximity. However, linguistic proximity seems to be less important for migrants coming from countries with low secondary school enrollment, especially to English-speaking countries. Also, there is proof that network effects, measured by the number of immigrants from the same country who already live in a country, have a big positive effect on new immigration flows.

Even though the theory literature on international migration can't be directly applied to asylum migration, it can help researchers figure out where asylum flows are coming from and how they are spread across host countries. There are five types of pull factors that cause people to move: economic, historical, political, geographical, and policy-related. Specifically, migration decisions can be influenced by the following: the economic performance and the expectation of employment in the destination country; the establishment of earlier migration flows in certain destination countries, where language ties, communication links, and cultural networks can greatly reduce the costs and risks of migration; the liberal reputation of a country in terms of its openness, integration of migrants, and adherence to international norms; and the liberal reputation of a country in terms of its openness, integration of migrants, and adherence to international norms.

Some econometric studies have looked at asylum applications from the sending countries' point of view to find the main push factors. Other studies have focused on the role of conditions in the destination countries as pull factors in refugee migration. Also, some researchers have looked at both factors that push and pull people to seek protection.

Schmeidl (1997) used regression analysis to find that political indicators, like genocides and civil wars with foreign military involvement, were the best predictors of changes in the number of refugees in over 100 countries from 1971 to 1990. Davenport et al. (2003) and Moore and Shellman (2004) also suggested that civil wars, genocide, and "politicicide" efforts played a role in explaining things. But Moore and Shellman (2004), who looked at about 175 countries to find out why internally displaced people and refugees were forced to leave their homes from 1952 to 1995, found that high levels of dissident violence have a bigger effect than civil wars, genocides, and politicides. Their study shows that governments and rebels who act violently are the main causes of forced migration flows. In the same way, Davenport et al. (2003) showed that political dangers from the government and from dissidents were the main reason why people from 129 countries left their homes from 1964 to 1989. Hatton (2011) found that high levels of terror and bad living standards were the main reasons why 56 of the most violent countries in the developed world had so many asylum requests from 1982 to 2006.

In a recent study, Hatton (2017) looked at the trends in asylum applications from 48 origin countries to 19 destination countries from 1997 to 2014. He found that bad economic conditions at home lead to asylum migration, and asylum seekers are drawn to countries with less strict asylum policies and networks of migrants already there. In particular, "asylum seekers who are already there might be able to help newcomers find their way in the country of destination and look for work." In fact, migrant communities help people who want to leave their home country by giving them knowledge and cultural support. Movement leads to more movement because "migration in the past lowers the cost of migration in the future," which is why it's important to build networks. Interviews with key informants in the Netherlands, Belgium, and the UK also showed how important pre-existing migration networks are. "For almost all interviewees, the presence of friends, relatives, or compatriots in the country was reported to be the most important factor in deciding where to seek asylum," the report said. Robinson and Segrott's (2002) talks with asylum seekers to learn more about how they make decisions showed that family and friends are the most important people in their lives.

Thielemann (2006) looked at the issue of "pull factors" in a more thorough way. He used data from 20 OECD countries from 1985 to 1999 and came to the conclusion that the most important reasons for an asylum seeker's choice of destination country are not how generous the welfare benefits are, but rather historical migrant networks, relative employment opportunities, and a country's liberal reputation. Angeloni (2016) found that the number of people seeking protection for the first time in 30 European countries between 2014 and 2015 was related to the level of GDP (as measured by purchasing power standards) and the number of refugees per 1000 people in host countries. Neumayer (2004) looked at the number of people who asked for refuge in 17 OECD countries from 1982 to 1999. Some of these results are similar to what he found. His research showed that a country's general level of economic growth (measured by GDP per capita), the number of left-wing governments in that country, colonial and language ties, and its location all affect where asylum seekers choose to go. Also, Jacobsen (2006) says that asylum seekers are usually drawn to urban centres because they are more likely to build some kinds of social capital where there are a lot of economic resources and chances, such as schools for their children. Lastly, there are things like public opinion and how people feel about immigration that can have a good effect on how many refugees and asylum seekers come to a country.

The Challenge of Equitable Responsibility Distribution

Article 78(1) of the Treaty on the Functioning of the European Union (TFEU) says that the Union creates a common policy on asylum, subsidiary protection, and temporary protection. Also, Article 80 of the TFEU says that the Union's policies on border checks, asylum, and immigration, as well as how they are carried out, must be based on the principle of solidarity and fair sharing of responsibility, which includes the costs, among the Member States. In the last few years, more and more people from Africa, Latin America, and Eastern Europe have moved to the European Union, especially in Southern Europe.

In 2016, about 1,204,300 people seeking refuge for the first time did so in EU Member States. This is about the same number as in 2015, when 1,257,000 people seeking asylum for the first time were registered. Both numbers are almost twice what they were in 2014. In 2014, about 562,700 people asked for protection for the first time. Germany had the most first-time applicants (60 percent of all first-time applicants in EU Member States). This was followed by Italy (10 percent), France (6 percent), and Greece (4 percent). These numbers show that, despite some recent changes to the law, the burden-sharing system for examining asylum requests was not working as well as it should have, since some EU Member States are hit much harder by migrant flows than others.

Even though the European Commission presented key actions and a comprehensive strategy in its European Agenda on Migration in 2015, the asylum distribution shows that new asylum seekers choose where to go based on how different countries in the EU handle asylum. In fact, a country's asylum policies do affect the choices of asylum seekers, who may choose where to apply "not to maximise their income in the strict sense, but to try to increase their chances of being accepted as refugees." The number of refugees relies on where asylum seekers want to go, how many people want asylum overall, and how each country handles refugees. Asylum policy is made up of two separate but closely related parts: managing asylum seekers and resettling refugees from other countries in a safe way.

Resettlement is the process of moving non-EU citizens or stateless people who need international protection and don't have a country of their own to an EU state, where they are accepted on humanitarian grounds or as refugees. Relocation, on the other hand, is the process of moving an applicant from the territory of the Member State that is looking into his or her request for foreign protection to the territory of another Member State. The Dublin III Regulation (which was passed in 2013 and replaced the Dublin II Regulation, which had replaced the Dublin Convention of 1997) says which Member State is in charge of looking into a foreign protection application. To stop people from applying for asylum in more than one country, the Dublin system says that an asylum claim can only be looked at by the country where the person first entered. Member states that get people moved should get €6,000 per person, while member states that send people should get €500 per person. For each person who is moved, the EU budget should give the Commission 10,000 euros from the EU budget to help the Member States with their resettlement efforts.

These money transfers are important because countries where asylum seekers and refugees travel and arrive generally have to pay some short-term and long-term costs. Short-term costs are related to the first reception phase and, in general, include the costs of administrative procedures (mechanism of identification, registration and fingerprinting, health check-up, and other legal issues) and giving applicants material support, such as housing, clothing, food, and cash. Measures of social integration (such as cultural orientation, language lessons, vocational or other education, and schooling for children), housing, social benefits, and medical and mental health care all have long-term costs. Also, governments may have to pay for the cost of sending away people who broke the law to get into their country. Getting rid of rejected asylum seekers is often hard and expensive because "finding people who may have gone underground takes time and uses up scarce public resources."

Lahav and Guiraudon say that "the official goal of policy cooperation has often been reported to be the sharing of the cost of hosting asylum seekers among EU states as well as the harmonisation of rules" to stop people from "shopping for asylum." Even though refugee policy is becoming more "communitarian" or "Europeanized," there are still differences in how each country handles asylum. This is because each country has different social, political, and geographical conditions, as well as different experiences and customs. Different asylum recognition rates are caused by differences in laws and legal practises, which "leads to a rather unequal sharing of the burden for asylum applications and accepted refugees." To get a fair distribution of tasks among EU Member States, the question of how to share the load has been and still is a major source of disagreement. Even in the past, people who were looking for safety did not have much luck. Neumayer has focused on how, from 1980 to 1999, the rates of acceptance of asylum cases in Western European countries were very different. So, there isn't much proof that the norms of solidarity and fairness have made a big difference in how the Member States handle forced migration, even though these norms are often mentioned in official EU documents and communications.

To make sure that those who need security get it, refugees and people looking for asylum should be spread out among countries based on a mandatory burden-sharing plan. On the other hand, a voluntary method is likely to lead to people who don't pay their fair share. Without binding governance mechanisms, most countries are tempted to outsource migration control by accepting as few asylum seekers as possible in the hopes that others will take on the burdens of the relocation plan. So, in September 2015, the Council made two decisions that are legally binding. These are Council Decision (EU) 2015/1601 and Council Decision (EU) 2015/1523. They set up temporary and exceptional relocation measures to help Italy and Greece, two Member States that are under a lot of pressure to take in asylum seekers. But because some EU Member States want to keep the voluntary nature of EU solidarity measures in asylum policy, the programme to move people that was needed by the two Council Decisions didn't work well and took a long time to put into place.

The Member States have taken different steps to deal with the huge number of refugees who have arrived in recent years. At first, some countries changed their laws about migration, reorganised their government offices, and spent more money on public services to process protection requests and welcome refugees. But in recent years, some countries are putting limits on the number of foreigners who can enter in order to deal with the growing stresses that come with more globalised asylum flows. There are different ways that individual countries can stop people from asking for asylum. For example, they can make it harder for potential asylum seekers to enter their country for political or electoral reasons, or they can change the way they handle applications. Other countries can stop people from asking for refuge by not letting them work while their cases are being processed.

Fig. 5.1 - Arrival of refugees and migrants by sea and main hosting countries in 2016. Source: UNHCR

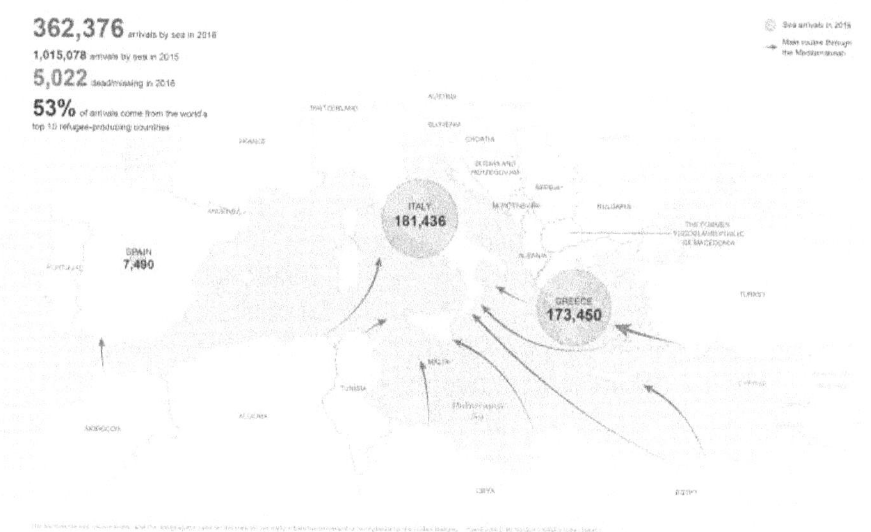

So, some EU Member States, which at first welcomed foreigners who were leaving war-torn countries, have started to change their laws to limit the rights of people who want to seek asylum. For example, the Integration Act, which was passed in Germany in July 2016, took away some of the special rights that refugees and asylum seekers used to have. It did this by trying to "find a middle ground between integration efforts and hard-line calls to stop more asylum seekers." In a similar way, other countries have made or planned to make big, restrictive changes to their asylum laws and border policies in order to make their countries less appealing to people looking for asylum. Legal walls were sometimes used in conjunction with actual walls. Some countries, like Bulgaria, Croatia, and Hungary, have put up fences along their borders. Others, like Austria, Denmark, Germany, Norway, and Sweden, have briefly brought back border controls to stop the flow of undocumented immigrants. But strict asylum rules aren't enough to stop people from using smugglers to try to get into Europe if they want asylum. In fact, stopping immigration by militarising the border has a number of problems: it raises the cost of smuggling, makes it harder for people who keep crossing the border illegally, and causes more deaths at the border. As a result of the growing number of preventative measures and restrictions on entry, asylum seekers are driven to enter the EU illegally. This makes Europe "one of the top destinations for human trafficking" and the Mediterranean one of the seas where the number of deaths is rising.

In 2016, just like in years past, a lot of refugees and migrants tried to get to Europe by crossing the Mediterranean. They risked their lives on boats and dinghies that weren't made for crossing the sea. Figure 5.1, from the United Nations High Commissioner for Refugees (UNHCR), shows that 5022 people died or went missing on these dangerous trips in 2016, which is 33% more than in 2015. At the same time, it should be noted that many people have been saved by sea rescue operations since the beginning of 2016. This is partly because Italy has been very involved in these operations. Italy is a leader in controlling the borders of the European Union and meeting humanitarian obligations. Italian missions have recently benefited from the 2016 change of Frontex, the European Agency for the Management of Operational Cooperation at the External Borders of the Member States of the European Union, into the "EU Border and Coast Guard Agency," which is more independent and has much more power to directly implement border protection policy.

Table 4.1 shows some facts and figures about migration in Italy for the five-year period 2013–2017. The numbers came from the Economic and Financial Document 2017, which was sent to the EU in April 2017 by the Italian Minister of Economy and Finance. In the second column of Table 4.1, you can see that the number of visitors to Italy has grown at an exponential rate, from 22,000 units in 2013 to 104,000 units in 2015 and 176,00 units in both 2016 and 2017. Assuming a constant scenario, which means that migration flows don't get any worse, the third column shows the total costs of the migrant crisis, which include costs for housing, sea rescue, health care, and schooling. The EU's part of the External Borders Fund, the Return Fund, the Refugee Fund, and the Integration Fund for non-EU country nationals are listed in the fourth column. Assuming that everything stays the same, the last column shows the net spending, which is the difference between the total spending and the EU funding.

Table 5.1 Data and estimates concerning migration in Italy (years 2013-2017)

Year	Number of migrants in reception facilities	Gross expenditure incurred for migrant crisis (in € million)	EU subsidies for migrant crisis (in € million)	Net expenditure incurred for migrant crisis (in € million)
2013	22,118	1324.9	78.8	1246.1
2014	66,066	2030.4	70.3	1960.1
2015	103,792	2665.6	106.6	2559.0
2016	176,554	3719.3	120.8	3598.5
2017	176,523	4304.0	91.0	4213.0

Source: Minister of Economy and Finance (April 2017) ® Springer

So, the total effect on Italy's budget is likely to go up from 2.5 billion euros in 2015 to 3.6 billion euros in 2016 and 4.2 billion euros in 2017. Figure 5.1 shows that Italy's response to migration cannot be supported by EU financial incentives alone. The sharp rise in Italy's spending is mostly due to the country's location, as asylum seekers see it as a place to pass through. It is also due to the failure of the emergency relocation scheme, which was supposed to move asylum seekers from Greece and Italy, where they first arrived, to other Member States.

The failure of the emergency relocation plan to work rests on how well the Member States are able to coordinate their policies. For a truly European policy on asylum, processes and standards in different countries need to be more closely aligned. Unfortunately, there are still differences between countries when it comes to refugee seekers' access to welfare and jobs. The time it takes to process asylum claims is not the same in every country. According to the OECD (2016), the average time it takes to process an asylum claim runs from 2.5 months in Belgium to 10.5 months in Luxembourg. Also, EU states have different rules about whether asylum seekers can work while their claim is being processed. For example, asylum seekers who are still waiting for a decision can work right away in Greece and Sweden, or they can apply to work after 2 months in Italy, 3 months in Austria, 6 months in Spain, or 9 months in Hungary. However, Austria, Germany, and Hungary have even more restrictions on the labour market. Also, there are a lot of differences in how refugee seekers are taken care of in different EU countries, from open reception centres to detention centres. Many of these places to stay are not good places for asylum seekers to live because of how they are set up.

To deal with long-term migration flows successfully, we need a stronger monitoring system for putting into place mandatory and permanent plans for sharing the load. In particular, harsh economic sanctions and punishments should be set up and put into place quickly if Member States don't follow EU laws. To make sure that asylum seekers don't have to wait a long time in limbo and in places that aren't up to par, there should be stricter dates for different parts of the process and clearer standards for where they can stay. But punishments and suggestions aren't always enough to get everyone to follow the concept of fair sharing of responsibility and solidarity. Some people may have negative feelings or strong reactions, which could make it harder to reach the goals of policy coordination. This is especially true when political leaders haven't done much to prepare their people for changes in migration by explaining the possible social and economic benefits for hosting countries. This is the most important part because integration can't happen without good attitudes in the host towns. Asylum seekers are treated less and less like welcome guests and more and more like a threat to security by the governments of the countries where they first arrive or pass through. In general, "many different national historical, cultural, and political factors affect how a country feels about immigration." By looking at how people in a community feel about foreign groups, like immigrants, some scholars have found a link between negative attitudes and socio-economic factors like schooling and political orientation.

Meuleman et al. (2009) and Scheepers et al. (2002) found a link between negative attitudes and high unemployment rates. This is likely because people who are struggling financially tend to be against immigrants. In the same way, another study found that the chances of getting asylum are lower for people from poorer countries and when certain things are true in the country where they want to go, such as "when unemployment rates are high and the idea that asylum seekers are too many is common." Even though people seek refuge more because they need to stay alive than because they need a job, the state of the labour market is very important because immigration has no effect on crime in areas with low unemployment but has a big effect in areas with high unemployment. Asylum seekers are often portrayed as illegal workers instead of real refugees or people running away from dangerous situations. Johnson (2011) said that resettlement and integration have become less popular over time because states started to see refugees as economic and environmental burdens as well as possible security threats. In 2015, refugee seekers made up only about 0.1% of the total OECD population, and even in Europe, they made up less than 0.3% of the total EU population. This is a lot to worry about.

In March 2016, the European Union and Turkey came to an understanding to stop the growing number of people coming from countries outside of the EU and to ease the pressure on Greece. The goal of this deal should be to stop people from coming into the EU illegally and in a chaotic way through the Greek islands. In light of the EU-Turkey Statement from March 18, 2016, all new irregular migrants and asylum seekers who come from Turkey to the Greek islands and whose refugee claims have been rejected should be sent back to Turkey. Also, under the "one-for-one" relocation plan, for every Syrian that Turkey takes back from the Greek islands, another Syrian from Turkey should be moved to an EU member state. Under this deal, the EU should pay up to 6 billion euros to Turkey. Carrera and Guild (2016), on the other hand, say that the plan brings up some procedural and legal questions about the EU Member States' human rights responsibilities.

Also worrying is the fact that the British people chose to leave the EU on June 23, 2016, when they used Article 50 of the Lisbon Treaty to do so. It's scary that the Leave vote won the referendum on the UK's membership in the EU because people were afraid of immigrants and losing control of their country . This never-before-seen move to stop the EU from getting involved in UK politics could throw the EU's system into chaos. In order to handle their own migration problems on their own, many European countries try to get as many non-EU countries as possible to sign bilateral deals that outline how asylum seekers can be sent back to their home countries.

Traditional and Modern Approaches

As was already said, some countries have changed their laws to make it harder for people to ask for refuge. Millbank (2001) says that developed countries can stop the flow of asylum seekers if they pay more attention to improving conditions in source areas instead of making it harder to get into the country and making the asylum process harder. In the literature, different estimation models have been used to explain how help is given by testing how different donor countries act. "A $1,000 increase in the GDP per capita of source countries would cut asylum requests by about 20%," according to some estimates. So, more money should be spent on helping refugees close to home, in part to stop people from moving on without their permission. This idea, which was first put forward by the UNHCR under the name "regional prong," seems to be the best of all the possible answers, even though improving conditions in source countries is still a difficult, expensive, and uncertain goal. In fact, "some empirical findings generally suggest that a general support of democracy, economic development, and trade will not reduce migration, at least in the medium run." Also, the amount of help given to a country can make it less likely that democracy will be practised there. Neumayer said that how well a country respects civil and political rights and personal moral rights should be a big factor in how much aid it gets. This means that countries with good records in these areas should get more aid.

In the past, some complicated migration flows were handled by putting asylum seekers in centres outside of their home country. This plan, which is called the "Pacific solution," was mostly set up by Australia and the United States. They did this by signing bilateral deals with each country. Several islands were taken out of Australia's territory so that asylum claims could be made on them. Nauru and Papua New Guinea were chosen as places to set up offshore processing centres, which are run by the International Organisation for Migration. This was done to discourage and reduce the number of unwelcome immigrants. This approach, which Australia used from 2001 to 2008 and then again in 2012, was also used by the USA, which gave money to Mexico "to do deportations and to strengthen its southern borders." Italy also helped pay for a number of detention camps in Libya, and more agreements were made in 2017. But the Pacific model should be looked at carefully because it could lead to violence and human rights violations in holding centres.

So far, several solutions have been suggested: (i) making a humanitarian corridor, safe zone, buffer zone, no-fly zone, and even a no-drive zone, all inside Syria, where people who are fleeing the bombs can be taken care of; (ii) allowing the navy to stop ships carrying migrants and, if possible, forcing the ships back to the territorial waters of the countries where they came from; and (iii) taking care of the identification, registration, and paperwork for the migrants

Previous studies have shown that the Dublin III Regulation, which says that migrants' asylum claims must be looked at by the first EU country they enter, doesn't work well. Even though this rule is often argued about, it has many real benefits. First, it wants to make sure that asylum seekers don't move around Europe again after they've reached the closest European country to find out, for the first time, if their request for international protection under the Refugee Convention will be accepted. For an asylum seeker, it doesn't make sense to travel to a faraway country as a preferred destination if the government of that preferred country won't accept the asylum application. The asylum seeker will just lose more time and money by doing this. Aside from that, the Dublin III Regulation is meant to stop people from "shopping" for asylum. It does this by making it illegal for asylum seekers to ask for asylum in more than one Member State or choose Member States with better acceptance rates, reception facilities, or social aid programmes. The Dublin III Regulation is also meant to protect the safety of EU citizens, who can't stand it when unnamed asylum seekers move from one EU state to another (Constant and Zimmermann). Lastly, one good thing about the Dublin mechanism is that it makes it easy to find out which Member State is responsible for evaluating an asylum claim, so that there are no conflicts of jurisdiction.

Still, it is clear that something has not gone in the right direction, as shown by the fact that the same European Commission keeps making suggestions to change the Dublin III Regulation, which is used in different ways by each Member State. On the other hand, if a country doesn't want to be flooded with asylum seekers, it can avoid registration and cut off the fingers of asylum seekers. On the other hand, asylum seekers have a reason to lie about who they are and have to pay smugglers to get to where they want to go in an illegal way. Member states don't think twice about putting the military on their own borders in order to stop illegal movement. Militarising and tightening border controls are dangerous and ineffective solutions. They cost a lot, hurt a country's economy, make humanitarian crises worse, and increase the demand for and price of smugglers' services, as well as the number of people who risk their lives and travel on dangerous routes. Strengthening border controls can have unintended results, like "reorienting flows and changing some routes." This could put refugees at greater risk and make them more vulnerable.

But besides the Dublin system, the biggest problem with getting Member States to work together is that they don't all follow the Asylum Procedures Directive the same way. Several studies show the many reasons why the EU hasn't been able to come up with an effective and fair refugee policy. EU countries sometimes use low standards to discourage refugee seekers from coming to their country. Member states are put in competition with each other, which leads to a "race to the bottom" because they are perversely encouraged to "free ride." Member states still have very different rates of accepting asylum, administrative standards, judicial processes, protection systems, and conditions for receiving people. These differences make it easier for people to move around and break the rules. This situation has a lot of bad things about it, like people dying, asylees getting angry, smugglers making money illegally, Europeans feeling bad about migration, diplomatic tensions between Member States, and wasting public money on trying to protect national borders. The lack of a common asylum process, federal asylum courts, and executive powers is a big reason why the European refugee system hasn't worked. This is because EU governance isn't unified. The problem has gotten worse because of how the EU governs refugee policy and border control. This puts national sovereignty against Union values.

Some changes to the law are proposed to solve this problem. For example, "the current Asylum Procedures Directive should be changed into a new Regulation establishing a single common asylum procedure in the EU." But "it is very unlikely that all 28 EU Member States will fully harmonise and agree on how to make decisions about asylum applications." One interesting piece of recent research says that decisions about asylum should be made at the federal level to help even out the differences between Member States. In particular, the studies call for "the creation of a centralised EU agency with decision-making powers to evaluate asylum claims" or for the EASO to be given these powers. The switch from a national to a common international refugee status determination system could lower processing costs and free up money to help frontline receiving countries. This is because "economists suggest that reallocating the funds now spent on the many, often very complicated, domestic asylum systems would be more than enough to fund this system." For methods to reduce costs, registration, selection, and distribution systems need to be set up in the same way.

Den Heijer et al. (2016) agree with the analysis behind these suggestions, but they are hesitant to support federalization as a solution to the problems with asylum. This is because federalization could add another level of fragmentation and make it harder to manage asylum if there isn't also a transfer of power in the areas of border control, the return programme, and detention. Also, a full centralization of power could "undermine the constitutional principle that the Member States are ultimately responsible for their own internal security" Some EU Member States don't want to give up their right to make decisions on their own, which makes it hard for the EU to become more centralised. This could increase the risk of paralysis because all EU Member States need to agree on the same thing. Den Heijer et al. (2016), on the other hand, say that it is easier to come to an agreement with the government of a specific Member State that would be willing to take the lead in making a fair and sustainable system work, giving EASO and Frontex the power to observe or take part in the process of receiving and identifying people. So, this approach seems more likely to work in Europe than putting asylum decisions under the control of the federal government. It is also more likely to work than setting up extraterritorial processing zones, which is what the American and Australian models are based on.

In the context of European policy, this could be done by giving Italy, a country that is geographically hurt by the growing border security measures put in place by other European countries, a new and important role. Figure 5.1 already shows that this is likely true, since Italy and Greece had the most people arrive by sea in 2016. Italy has 7500 km of shore, but because of its size and location, it is not able to keep an eye on all of its borders. In light of this, the question is whether it is possible to turn a threat into a chance by making things better for asylum seekers, Italy, and other EU Member States. This seems possible if Italy, after reorganising its real estate and human capital in the right way, agrees to play a central role in helping the EU's migration strategy by temporarily managing and housing asylum seekers. In a recent study that took about a year to do, this approach was proposed as a possible answer. Di

Pasquale et al. (2016) did the work under the direction of Milena Gabanelli, the founder of Report. The study's authors have found a number of Italian buildings, such as confiscated mafia assets, empty barracks, old schools, old hospitals, old hotels, and old offices, where asylum seekers could live and get help with things like education, health care, language support, cultural orientation, and job training. In particular, a first facility census found that some Italian regions have a number of public buildings that are not being used. Some of these buildings only need simple repairs before they can be used again. Based on the assumption that about 200,000 people will visit each year, the study says that 400 places should be made usable, which would cost about 2 billion euros. The same study suggests that about 25,000 full-time workers, like teachers, trainers, and psychologists, would be needed. This would cost about 750 million euros per year. Also, if there was one doctor for every place, about 400 doctors would need to be hired, which would cost about 15 million euros per year. Lastly, the projected 1.4 billion euro cost of food and public utilities (such as electricity, water, gas, and heat) should be added. So, this study suggests that the total yearly cost could be around 2.165 billion euros.

In short, Italy could be a major hotspot network for the first phase of arrival and reception of asylum seekers, as long as the European Union pays for it and each Member State agrees to take its share of people in need of protection who have already been identified and trained in Italy. This first phase would last about six months. So, EU Member States could get rid of expensive, time-consuming administrative chores and policy measures, which would be good for public safety, social order, and the peace of the community as a whole. Also, the Italian answer could be made better by letting asylum seekers say and explain why they want to live in a certain Member State. Except for when a child is alone and when a family is reunited, the Dublin system doesn't care if an asylum seeker wants to apply in a certain Member State. But there are other important reasons why asylum seekers like some host countries more than others. These include "family and social ties, language skills, preexisting ties with a country, matching skills to job opportunities, etc." The desires of asylum seekers should not be undervalued as important factors for a quick and successful integration, as this encourages them to follow clear, right, fair, and democratic rules on their own. On the other hand, ignoring a priori asylees' preferences about their chances of integration increases their sense of being left out of society and makes them more likely to join secondary groups.

Without a question, the above proposal could make it harder for people to sneak things across borders and stop more tragedies from happening. Also, the Italian programme would try to reach the goals of a harmonised approach by making sure there is more rationalisation, interaction, and economies of scale.

This would be done, in part, by avoiding the spread of unnecessary national rules and administrative procedures that slow down and make it harder to help people who need protection in the EU. In fact, "policies that aren't coordinated lead to a prisoner's dilemma in which each member spends a lot of money inefficiently on border controls, sub-optimal asylum and humanitarian policies, and inefficiently restrictive policies on illegal immigration."

As with any other European initiative, the Italian model is more likely to work well when the Member States, the EU, and asylum seekers all want to work together. On the other hand, an unfriendly and non-collaborative environment, coercion, prohibition, conflicts, tensions, a sanctions regime, or even unrealistic expectations can take the focus away from the main goal of building and sharing an effective and efficient asylum system. In this case, it's important to note that when asked what they thought about the Italian plan, a number of European deputies said they thought it was interesting and doable. Most importantly, the EU Commissioner for Migration, Home Affairs, and Citizenship said that such an idea could be accepted and financially backed if it was part of a national plan that the Italian government officially sent to the European authorities.

People like the idea because they think it has the ability to make the asylum system more functional, logical, and cost-effective. In particular, the fresh and new approach suggested here has a number of good points.

First, it makes it easier for Member States to work together. They wouldn't have to pay as much for the administrative and operational tasks of the first phase (like identification, registration, fingerprinting, reception, deciding if someone needs asylum, protection, or to be sent back), and they wouldn't have to spend as much on defensive measures (like high security fences, stricter border controls, etc.).

Also, this option should discourage asylum seekers from using illegal means or smuggling networks to get to their preferred country. This is because Italy should be the only European country that can deal with their claim in a unified way, by managing their return (if their application is denied) or their six-month stay before they are resettled in another preferred Member State (if their claim is accepted and the preferred Member State is not Italy).

Also, the Italian proposal should lead to a lot of cooperation from the other Member States, who all have an interest in defining in advance the skills needed of the asylum seeker. After an appropriate 6-month programme (which the other Member States should agree with Italy on based on their own labour markets), the asylum seeker could arrive in their countries as a person who is easier to hire and doesn't need help from the government or money.

Also, the plan proposed here saves time and money because most of the money and people (including EASO and Frontex staff) should be gathered in one country, taking advantage of economies of scale and experience in running and monitoring activities. In fact, there is no doubt that this solution stops the Member States from wasting public money on ineffective and inefficient administrative procedures and repressive actions, while the concentration of European expertise and support in Italy could lead to a fast, uniform, and efficient system that solves problems caused by a lack of EU staff or their dispersion.

Also, this plan doesn't involve rethinking the Dublin system as a whole, since the system could be made more efficient without raising sovereignty concerns or needing more resources. By getting rid of defensive measures and administrative procedures in other Member States, money could be saved that could mostly be used to fund Italy. Italy should then be in charge of processing asylum claims under a single procedure that is fully based on international standards and European humanitarian standards.

After explaining why the above plan should be seen as a good way to balance different interests, it is important to explain why only Italy, and not the other Member States, should play a key role in the European asylum system. At least five good reasons exist.

First of all, as a transit country, Italy is physically punished more than other Member States by the Dublin mechanism rule, and the other Member States don't want to change the rule that says the first country of entry is responsible for all the administrative work. In light of recent failures and resistance to changing the "country of first arrival" rule, Italy is forced to be an overburdened frontline state and doesn't have many other options to deal with the (undeclared) desire of some Member States to get out of their duty to share the burden. On the contrary, Italy has every reason to come up with and propose changes that the other Member States can easily agree to and use. Also, Italy could use this situation to boost investment and job growth by repurposing its assets and creating jobs and other economic chances in many different areas, thanks to the EU aid.

Second, because Italy is in the middle of two continents, it has been working with northern African countries for a long time on both official and informal diplomatic efforts to stop illegal migration across the Mediterranean. Because of its location in the world and its history, Italy has been one of the most active European countries when it comes to supporting and negotiating programmes and bilateral agreements with countries of origin and transit to make it easier for people to go back home and stop illegal migration. This good network of relationships can grow and be used more easily if other third countries are asked to deal with one country that also works for the interests of all of Europe.

Third, because of recent events in history, Italy has already learned how to handle asylum requests in an emergency. This is a strength that makes Italy the best country to deal with asylum problems in a professional and organised way. "Italy plays a key role in making sure that this kind of management happens, and it is making a huge financial effort to help the European Union meet its humanitarian obligations."

Fourth, Italy has a large and strong network of organisations that help people in need, especially when it comes to rescue operations and emergency medical services. "In Italy, local government, network assistance, NGOs, volunteer groups, and other local actors who deal with immigration all play a major role in putting the country's immigration policy into action," even though multiculturalism the Italian way isn't perfect.

Fifth, there is nothing that would stop Italy, which has about 60 million people living there, from extending and stabilising the stay of refugee seekers in the long run. In fact, a country like Italy, which has a very high life expectancy and a low birth rate, may be able to ease some of the problems caused by an ageing population by integrating immigrants, who tend to be younger than locals. Eurostat says that Italy needs more immigrants because, without immigration, its population could drop below 51 million people by 2050. Also, the flow of asylum seekers could be a way to bring back at least some of the people who used to live in some old Italian villages that are in danger of disappearing because their original people don't want to work in farming or making things.

Obviously, some questions need to be answered better before the Italian solution offered here can be used. In particular, it needs to be looked into whether there is political agreement at the central government level to back this plan. Also, it should be looked into how many mayors are willing to use public buildings for immigration causes, even if it goes against what the people want. In democratic countries, the support of the people is key to the success of any project. Also, there needs to be more information about the legal and technical timelines for converting buildings, since some of them might need more major changes to meet safety standards. Also, the kind of help that should be given to non-profit organisations, which have played an important and unique role in helping with migration emergencies so far, should be looked at in more detail. These things, along with finding a way to make sure that tasks are shared effectively and fairly in the EU, could be the next steps for research.

Conclusion

Many European countries' asylum processes are under a lot of stress because of the unusually high number of people trying to get in. Asylum is becoming an important social and political test of how well European countries can work together. The study has shown that there is still a lack of long-term cooperation on how to deal with asylum issues, even though many countries are trying to reduce their own burdens in the short term through the Dublin system. But the most important thing is that the flow of asylum seekers is not a temporary problem. Instead, it should be seen as something that will continue for the next few years or decades.

After pointing out the physical or legal barriers that European countries are putting up to stop asylum seekers from moving there, the study has come up with a good way to connect different points of view. With this new answer, Italy could take the lead in putting in place a fair and long-lasting system that meets all EU and international standards. Because it is hard or impossible for Member States to agree on asylum policies or to give more power to the EU, the Italian plan may be seen as a good middle ground between the EU's centralised process and keeping the controversial state of the art.

There are many reasons to support and adopt this solution. There are ethical and social implications, such as better protection for people outside of the EU and a greater sense of security among EU citizens. Specifically, (i) Italy can count on financial and human support of the EU to manage the flow of asylum seekers in the best economic and humanitarian way; (ii) the deployment in the Italian country of European supporters and police force, including Europol and Eurojust, should minimize sentiments of insecurity and safety risks among the citizens, who could see the Italian mission as an opportunity to requalify unused building, improve employment rate, and face demographic decline; (iii) the other Member States can see disappear the needs for repressive actions and costly administrative procedures, being only bound themselves to receive a certain number of people, already trained according to their instructions and according to a planned schedule shared with Italy; (iv) asylum seekers would have no reason to search for possible better claim assessment by entering irregularly in Member States different from Italy, which would be essentially the only country that can deal with their applications by using the same procedure for all applicants, under the EU control, and by taking into account the asylees' preferences; (v) the criminal human traffic of smugglers would be winded up, thanks to the rule that the other Member States cannot in general process asylum claims; (vi) the further strengthening of Italy's partnership with third countries should ensure legal pathways to Europe.

In short, such a plan could combine the national goals with the EU's interests in a way that works. Both groups want to save lives, protect national security or public order, stop illegal migration, break the business model of smugglers, improve the quality of international protection and humanitarian programmes, improve cooperation, and make sure that resources are used effectively and efficiently. Of course, the Italian solution should be put forward and made official by qualified institutions. After this process, it's not impossible that the EU could recognise and back a big, helpful project, both legally and financially.

Chapter 6
Border Security Management in Europe

The European Union (EU) and a few other countries have the most extensive border control system in the world. Border management is generally only thought of in terms of physical control of borders and the flow of goods and people through ports of entry. However, it also has to do with managing immigration and reducing cross-border threats like crime and terrorism. Since the start of the European migrant crisis from the Middle East and North Africa in 2011, when the Syrian civil war and the fall of Libya both happened, some EU member states have made big changes to how they control their borders. This has made people wonder if it's possible to turn back the clock, since migration rates have gone down since 2015, when the crisis was at its worst, or if the changes made by some member states and being thought about by others will really change the way borders are managed in Europe.

We will look at the current European policies and structures as well as recent policy changes in certain areas of each of the three aspects of border management mentioned above. This will help us understand some of the most important parts of Europe's changing approach to managing and protecting its internal and external borders. More specifically, we will look at problems related to the status of the Schengen area and the control of external borders with non-EU/Schengen countries, the management of immigration within the European Union and its member states, and the role of the EU in fighting cross-border threats.

From the point of view of American officials, one reason to look at homeland security issues (like border security) in other countries is to find out how other countries solve problems that are similar to ours. This could help U.S. policymakers avoid making the same mistakes that were made abroad and keep them from having to "reinvent the wheel" when ideas for policy that worked well overseas are brought to the U.S. Hopefully, this study will also make people think about possible policy directions and/or areas to look into as the U.S. keeps trying to improve its immigration and border security policies.

The scholarly literature on border and migration studies has written a lot about border management and immigration in Europe. However, much of the more recent literature has focused less on policy and more on the geospatial, political, or cultural aspects of European borders and border regimes. For example, Bellanova and Duez look at the European Border Surveillance (EUROSUR) project in the setting of the Mediterranean. They look at how the idea of a border has changed and what makes up a "area of control." Other scholars, like Longo, say that borders shouldn't just be seen as places, but as "... thick, multifaceted, and binational institutions."

From a political point of view, Jeandesboz focuses on the way EU border control activities are communicated to the public, especially how EU actions are explained to the public. On the other hand, Vaughan-Williams looks at how the opposing discourses of "humanitarization" and "securitization" affect political action. Beznec says that the EU has caused a "crisis of territoriality" in its member states, which means that a new political and conceptual framework of the border has to be made.

Among the studies of border culture in Europe, Zaittoi says that there is a culture of border control in Europe that affects how problems are seen, who should be involved, and what practises should be used. Kramsch, Aparna, and Degu look at the geographic boundaries of national cultures from a linguistic point of view. They say that the introduction of migrant languages into Europe weakens the connection between language and territory, as well as what they see as the inward-looking and secure idea of European territories.

As the above summary of some of the most recent literature shows, scholars have looked at European border management problems from a variety of angles. However, as was mentioned, scholars tend to focus more on the conceptual and theoretical aspects of the problem.

History

Europe's border management is a strange mix of international deals, controls over multiple states, and different national policies. This shows the tension in Europe between centrifugal and centripetal forces that, on the one hand, pull EU member states closer together towards a common federative state and, on the other hand, assert the individual identity, sovereignty, and political autonomy of each of the nation-states that make up the EU. The European Union started with the creation of the European Coal and Steel Community in 1950 and the European Economic Community in 1957. It is based on efforts to not only pool Europe's economic resources and promote trade within Europe, but also to work towards a federation of European states under a supra-national authority (a kind of "United States of Europe") as a way to stop the kind of destructive European fighting that led to two world wars.

Even though the EU is still a long way from being a real federation and probably won't ever be one, EU institutions are now in charge of areas of public policy that were once the responsibility of national governments. For example, since the EU member states form a single economy, the EU has the power to regulate economic issues like agricultural policy, banking, product standards, environmental protection, food and water safety, energy policy, trade agreements with non-EU countries, antitrust efforts, and a wide range of other things. Also, the EU has power over monetary policy for the 19 countries that are part of the Eurozone. This is because these 19 countries all use the same currency, which is managed by the European Central Bank (ECB).

The European Union is run by seven institutions: the European Commision, the European Parliament, the European Council, the Council of the European Union, the Court of Justice of the European Union, the European Court of Auditors, and the European Central Bank. The European Commision, which is based in Brussels, is the EU's executive and bureaucratic arm. Its job is to oversee and manage the different areas of EU duty, to suggest laws to the European Parliament (EP), and to make sure that EP laws are followed. The European Parliament (EP), which is based in Strasbourg, is in charge of budgets and passes laws based on recommendations from the European Commision. Members of the EP (MEPs) are chosen by popular vote in districts that are roughly the same size as their populations across the EU. This means that bigger countries get more places. For example, Germany has 96 MEPs (out of a total of 751), but Malta, which has less than half a million people, only has six MEPs.

The European Council, which is based in Brussels, is a kind of policy coordination shop made up of the heads of government in Europe. It usually meets four times a year to talk about and plan strategic policy. The Council of the European Union, which is based in Brussels, is the way that the governments of EU member states can change EU laws and policies. Members of the Council will change based on what policies are being talked about. For example, EU energy policy will be talked about and made by the energy ministers of member states, while agricultural policy will be talked about and made by agriculture ministers, etc. The Council of the EU will vote on issues based on a simple majority (15 member states voting in favour), a qualified majority (55 percent of the member states representing at least 65 percent of the EU's total population), or unanimously, depending on the issue. The Council's voting method is meant to strike a balance between what the majority of people in the EU (i.e., the large member states) want and what the small member states want. Adding new countries to the EU is one important problem that needs a unanimous vote. This means that even the smallest member states have a say in this process.

Since it is directly elected by the people of the member states, the European Parliament speaks for them, while the Council of the European Union speaks for their governments. This is similar to how the lower house of the German parliament speaks for the people, while the upper house speaks for the state governments.

The EU's major decision-making bodies are the European Parliament and the Council of the European Union. The Court of Justice of the European Union, which is based in Luxembourg, is the EU's judicial branch. It is in charge of interpreting EU law and resolving legal issues between member states. Lastly, the European Court of Auditors makes sure that EU funds are handled well, and as was mentioned earlier, the European Central Bank is in charge of monetary policy.

During the first decades of these European supranational structures, the borders between member states were policed and ports of entry were controlled, but many goods could cross the borders without paying customs duties. This meant that border management issues were firmly in the hands of each member state, similar to how border management was handled in the North American Free Trade Agreement. In 1986, when the Single European Act was passed by the parliament of what was then called the European Community (EC), another name for what is now the European Union, things began to change in how borders were managed in Europe. Article 13 of the Single European Act called for "free movement of goods, persons, services, and capital" across the borders between member states. This was an important rule because it paved the way for the removal of border controls between at least some EU countries, even though at the time it was more of a statement of intent than a real policy change.

Along with the strategic goal of a borderless Europe, a number of international agreements (bilateral, trilateral, and multilateral) were signed between different European countries in what was then called the European Community (EC) for the exchange of information between their police and intelligence agencies on trans-border threats. This made it easier for police and intelligence agencies from different countries to work together and coordinate across national borders. As part of this trilateral customs union, Belgium, the Netherlands, and Luxembourg got rid of border controls between them in 1970. This was the first time this had been done between three countries. The success of the Benelux agreement led to a larger multilateral deal to get rid of border controls between the Benelux countries and France and Germany. This multilateral agreement was signed in the town of Schengen in Luxembourg in 1985. When it went into effect in its current form in 1995, it led to what is known as the Schengen System, which is a framework with open internal borders between member states of the system (most of which are EU members, but not all EU members are members of the Schengen system). By the mid-1990s, the Single European Act called for open borders, which were being done in practise through the multilateral (between different national governments) Schengen framework. Because of this, it was necessary to link Schengen to the legal and institutional framework of the European Union. This was done through the Treaty of Amsterdam in May 1999. Some Schengen countries, like Norway, Switzerland, Iceland, and Lichtenstein, are not part of the EU, and some EU countries are not part of most or all of Schengen, like the United Kingdom, which is about to leave the EU, the Republic of Ireland, Romania, and Bulgaria (because of concerns about the rule of law in these countries). In a nutshell, the different agreements that have been signed over time and make up the current Schengen system not only got rid of border controls between Schengen Area countries, but they also set up common border controls, procedures, and information-sharing at "external borders," which are land borders, maritime borders, and all ports of entry from non-Schengen Area countries (air, sea, and land). The Schengen system does not completely get rid of border controls between its members, though, because the agreements include ways to briefly bring back national border controls in times of crisis or during big national events like sports games, anniversaries, etc.

In terms of immigration, the countries in the Schengen Area also decided to make a short-term visa for visitors from outside the Area. Aside from these short-term visitors, non-EU and Schengen country citizens have always been subject to the immigration laws and policies of each member state. However, they have decided on common standards for how asylum-seekers are received and processed. In order to stop smuggling, human trafficking, and terrorism that crosses borders, the EU and Schengen frameworks set up common databases (the Schengen Information System, version II, and the Visa Information System) to keep track of everyone entering and leaving the Schengen Area and to stop people from entering one country's border who have already been turned away at another country's border (or to catch people for whom a European Arrest Warrant has been issued).

Lastly, when it comes to coordination and cooperation, EU countries with land and/or sea borders can ask other EU countries for help with border security through the European Border and Coast Guard Agency. This agency used to be called Frontex, which stood for the European Agency for the Management of Operational Cooperation at the External Borders of the Member States of the European Union. It was set up in 2004. The new European Border and Coast Guard Agency is still called Frontex. It helps make uniform training standards and does assessments and risk analyses. The agency can also send Raid Border

Intervention Teams (RABITs), which are made up of border guards from other EU countries and sent to an external Schengen border to help a member state that is having trouble keeping its border safe. Also, the Dublin Convention of 1990 and the Dublin II Regulation of 2003 allow for cross-border surveillance, hot chase across borders, and faster extradition between EU member states.

The conversation above shows how the rules and policies of Schengen and the EU have changed over many years. After 2015, which was the start of Europe's worst migration crisis since World War II, a number of Schengen/EU countries started to question the value of free movement of people within the Schengen Area. At least for now, political trends suggest that we are likely to see a return to more restrictive European border management policies and a weakening of the Schengen system.

Migration Stress on the Schengen Region

On April 15, 2011, a fight between France and Italy over refugees was one of the first signs that things might not be going well in the Schengen Area. At that time, about 25,000 Tunisians came by boat to the Italian island of Lampedusa, which is close to the coast of Tunisia, to ask for refuge. Asylum seekers must stay in the first EU country they enter and ask for asylum there, according to the Dublin Regulation. The host country is expected to feed, clothe, and house the migrants, as well as process their asylum requests. This will help the country figure out who is suitable for asylum and should be given refugee status, and who is an economic migrant who should be sent home.

From an EU-wide point of view, the problem with these rules is that most EU countries don't border areas where a lot of asylum-seekers cross. Because of this, countries like Spain, Italy, and Greece have to deal with a lot of migrants and have to pay a lot of the costs of taking care of them and processing their applications. In April 2011, the Italian government refused to house and feed about 25,000 people. Instead, it helped them move to other parts of the EU, where they could probably ask for asylum. So, the Italian government gave the refugees a temporary "humanitarian passport" and let them go so they could go to other countries in the Schengen Area. Not surprisingly, France, Belgium, and Germany all protested the Italian move and said that it broke EU rules about how to deal with refugee seekers. Two months later, France briefly put back border controls at its border with Italy and stopped Italian trains from entering France for six hours. Even though the situation was solved pretty quickly in the end, it was a sign of things to come because EU countries without external Schengen borders did not have to deal with large numbers of migrants at the time. Technically, the French were within their rights when they decided to close the border for a short time. At the time, the Schengen Borders Code said that any country could put up temporary border controls for up to six months if there was a threat to "public policy or internal security."

France's decision to temporarily close its border in 2011 may have been what led to Chapter II, Article 26 of the 2016 version of the Schengen Borders Code, which says that "migration and the crossing of a country's borders by large numbers of third-country nationals should not, per se, be considered to be a threat to public policy or internal security." But since the new version of the Schengen Borders Code still lets countries briefly close their borders for security reasons, migrant traffic has just been reclassified as a security threat in some cases. Eventually, the EU member states realised that the Dublin Regulation was unfair and put an unfair amount of stress on a few southern European countries that took in the vast majority of refugees. In 2016, the European Commision, which is the EU's governing body, suggested a way for some asylum-seekers to move to a less-crowded EU country and apply for asylum there. This would happen if a country was overwhelmed by a large number of migrants. This plan did not go over well with everyone. Those who opposed it said that forcing them to accept migrants was a huge violation of national authority and that it was up to each member state to decide if they wanted to let migrants in or not. In the end, this problem has yet to be decided, but it has made people in several eastern European countries, such as Poland, the Czech Republic, Slovakia, and Hungary, less happy with the EU.

In 2015, a huge number of people from the Middle East and North Africa tried to move to Europe and ask for refuge. This put the Schengen system to the test again. In that year, there were more than 1.2 million new refugee claims. In 2018, there were just over 635 thousand new asylum claims across the EU. Just over a million of these migrants entered the EU by sea through Greece, Italy, or Spain. In answer to the large number of migrants coming through Greece and the Balkans into central Europe, most EU/Schengen countries decided to put back border controls on their internal Schengen borders. In September 2015, Germany put back border controls at its border with Austria. Soon after, Austria put back controls at its borders with Italy, Hungary, Slovenia, and Slovakia. In answer, Slovenia and Hungary put up border checks on the southern parts of their countries. By the middle of 2016, Sweden, Norway, Denmark, Belgium, and France had all joined the list of countries putting back temporary border controls on their internal Schengen borders. Since then, all of these countries have put up "temporary" border controls and then taken them down, apparently to slow the flow of migrants. Since Article 26 of the Code no longer lets stopping cross-border migrant flows be used as a reason for re-imposing border controls, these changes are seen as a way to stop security threats from "significant secondary movements," which is when migrants move from the country where they are seeking asylum to another country.

At the moment, it is hard to say what the future holds for a Europe without more or less permanent interior border checks. An analysis by Tobia Etzold and Raphael Bossong of the German Institute for International and Security Affairs suggests that border controls within Europe are likely to become permanent. The nature of these controls and how much they are felt vary from country to country, as some countries do random checks, others only check at a limited number of crossing points, and others use licence plate readers and other technology that makes border checks less obvious. Some work is being done to stop Schengen countries from repeatedly extending "temporary" border controls for six months and to limit such measures to one year. However, this is unlikely to be acceptable to some of the major Schengen signatories, and they could take back border security functions on the grounds that national security issues are the responsibility of EU/Schengen member states and not the EU as a whole.

The coalition agreement that was signed in early 2018 reaffirms Germany's "right" to set up border controls until the EU comes up with a stricter policy for the Schengen external borders and the distribution of asylum-seekers across the EU. This could be a sign of where the political winds are blowing when it comes to keeping border controls. Germany is arguably the most important EU member state. As we've already said, Germany is not the only EU country to re-establish border controls. A number of other EU countries have done the same thing in order to stop illegal immigration and terrorism threats, and these steps seem to be politically popular with at least a large minority.

According to a study released by the European Commision in December 2018, only 55 percent of respondents thought the Schengen Area made security better. Thirty percent of respondents thought it made security worse, and 15 percent didn't know if it was good or bad for security. European politicians will probably have to take into account this rather large minority of European citizens who think Schengen arrangements hurt security or could hurt security. This is likely to mean that they will want to limit the traditional freedom of movement across internal Schengen borders more permanently. At the same time, three-quarters of the people surveyed by the European Commision agree that the Schengen Area has helped Europe's economy in a big way. A big part of each country's people will want more security and less immigration, but the majority will want to keep the economic benefits of Schengen. European politicians will have to find a way to satisfy both groups. This is likely to require some kind of compromise to avoid the permanent re-establishment of border controls on internal Schengen borders with cameras that can read licence plates at border crossings, police checkpoints inside member states, and the random re-establishment of full border controls at different border crossings and at different times. European officials will probably be interested in how the new border crossings between Northern Ireland and the Republic of Ireland work. They want to see if this can be a test case for using technology and other measures to make border crossing easier (or not), depending on what happens.

There is no sign that terrorism and migration, the two main reasons why Schengen countries want to bring back border controls, are going to go away. Terrorism tends to go up and down, but there is no proof that Jihadist and other groups from outside the EU have stopped targeting Europe. As far as migration demands go, the number of migrants coming from the Middle East is not as high as it was during the 2015 crisis. However, the ongoing economic and social problems in Afghanistan, Iran, and Iraq are likely to keep people from those countries wanting to leave. Also, it is unlikely that the millions of Syrian refugees in Turkey, Jordan, and Lebanon, as well as the internal refugees in Syria, will be sent back home in the near future. This will keep pressure on people to move to Europe. As Turkey is often the entry point for these migrants into the Schengen Area, the March 2016 deal between Turkey and the EU on readmitting migrants who arrive on Greek islands in the Aegean Sea could explain a lot of the drop in refugee flows from the Middle East after 2016. In July 2019, Turkey said it would no longer follow the rules of the agreement. It has since returned to the agreement, but EU member states can't be sure it will stay in place forever.

Also, the closing of the Aegean path has led some Middle Eastern migrants to try to get to the Schengen Area by crossing the dangerous Mediterranean from North Africa to Spain and Italy. Also, population growth and rising numbers of young people in sub-Saharan Africa, as well as the chaos in Libya, have led to more and more African refugees. Between 2010 and 2017, the number of Africans trying to get to Europe more than doubled. In short, the main reasons why lasting internal border controls might be put back in place in some form are not likely to go away.

Handling Migration

The member states of the European Union are mostly responsible for immigration issues, but not all of them. This is different from many other areas of economic action and regulation. This shouldn't be a surprise, since the ability to decide who is a citizen is a key part of the idea of national sovereignty, and member states are sensibly reluctant to give up this power. Still, over time, EU member states have given in to EU institutions on some parts of immigration law and policy. For example, as we've already talked about, temporary access (for tourists and other short-term visitors) is granted across the Schengen Area by the country that serves as the first point of entry for non-Schengen Area citizens. This common visa is often called a "Schengen Visa." Also, Title III of the Treaty of Rome from 1957 says that every EU country must let people from every other EU country live and work in the country. In fact, the United Kingdom, which is not part of the Schengen area and doesn't accept Schengen Visas, has been unhappy with the free movement of workers rules of the European Union for a long time. The fact that people from other EU countries have been able to live and work freely in the UK was one of the reasons why the UK decided to leave the EU.

Members of the EU are bound by the 1951 United Nations Convention and Protocol Relating to the Status of Refugees (Refugee Convention), which says that countries can't send back people who have been given refugee status because they have a "well-founded fear of being persecuted because of their race, religion, nationality, membership in a particular social group, or political opinion." Since 2013, EU member states have had to follow the current version of the Asylum Procedures Directive (APD) when it comes to receiving and evaluating asylum requests (except for the UK, Ireland, and Denmark, which chose to opt out of all or some of the current APD's measures; at the time this article was written, the UK was still a member of the EU). Part of the reason for making a common process for applying for asylum was to stop "secondary movements" of asylum seekers from one EU member state to another in search of better conditions for applying for refuge. The APD decides which member state will look at an asylum application (as we've already said, this is usually the first member state the candidate steps foot in), how individual asylum applications are handled, and how appeals are handled.

Standardising how asylum applications are evaluated and sticking to the non-refoulement principle do not necessarily mean that the European Union and its member states know what they can and cannot do with applicants who may have been foreign fighters, involved in terrorism, or committed serious crimes. Article 33 of the UN Refugee Convention says that the concept of nonrefoulement does not apply to people who threaten national security or who have been convicted of a serious crime and are seen as a threat to the public. At the same time, the EU Charter says that people have an inherent right to not be sent back, no matter where they come from or how dangerous they are. Even though it is illegal to send a migrant back to his or her home country if his or her asylum application was denied on the grounds that he or she poses a threat to public safety or for any other reason, this does not mean that he or she will be allowed to stay in an EU member state. Most people don't think it goes against the principle of non-refoulement to send a migrant whose request for refuge has been denied to a third country where he or she is not likely to be persecuted. So, in 2016, the European Union made a partnership agreement with third countries in Africa and the Middle East as well as a number of bilateral treaties to allow for the resettlement of migrants who were not given refugee status in those countries and to stop the flow of migrants into Europe.

EU member states are free to decide their own immigration and naturalisation policies, as long as they follow the UN Refugee Convention and common asylum processes and standards. Most EU member states require immigrants who want to become citizens to know the language, understand the legal and political system, act in a responsible way (like not having a criminal record or being unemployed for a long time), and show a willingness to become part of the larger society and accept its values. Different European countries have different rules about how long a regular resident must wait before they can become a citizen. In Austria, Italy, and Spain, the waiting period is ten years. In Germany, applicants for citizenship must have lived in the country as permanent residents for at least eight years. In France, the Netherlands, Sweden, and the Czech Republic, the waiting period is only five years. No EU country automatically gives citizenship to children born in the country to foreign citizens. However, some EU member states let children get citizenship when they are born if their parents have lived officially in the country for three to ten years.

Citizenship can also be taken away by a European country if someone gives up their citizenship on their own, if they commit fraud during the naturalisation process, if they live abroad for a long time, or if they serve in a foreign army. Several EU countries also let people lose their citizenship for crime or not being loyal to their country. This can include serious crimes (Netherlands, Belgium, Denmark, Bulgaria), going against the constitution (Estonia, Latvia, Lithuania, France, Denmark), showing lack of loyalty (Ireland, Cyprus, Malta), hurting national interests (France, Greece, Romania, Slovenia, and the UK), and/or being involved in terrorism (France, the UK, and the Netherlands). Overall, then, European countries are mostly in charge of immigration issues, even though they can't act on their own as much when it comes to international agreements and EU rules about migrants asking for asylum. But immigration policy has become a big issue in Europe, which has led to the rise of governments that are mostly against immigration in Hungary, Poland, Austria, Italy, Denmark, the Netherlands, and other EU countries. This makes it very unlikely that EU member states will create common immigration rules and policies that go beyond what is already in place for asylum-seekers. But the reality of immigration is that most people try to get official refugee status by applying for asylum. This makes it hard for member states to make and implement their own immigration policies at a time when the public is increasingly supporting national politicians who want to stop the flow of migrants. Even though this hasn't led to real calls to leave the shared asylum policy yet, it has led member state governments to try to change the policy. As long as the EU changes its refugee policies to meet the needs of its national governments, the system is likely to stay in place. If it doesn't do this, however, member states could pull out of the ADP or refuse to accept its rules, as Ireland, the UK, and Denmark have already done. In fact, as we've already said, the UK's decision to leave the European Union was influenced by its dislike of the EU's rules and policies on the free movement of people across borders. Populist politicians in other parts of Europe, like Marine Le Pen in France, have also called for their countries to leave the EU for similar reasons.

Like when we talked about re-establishing border controls at internal Schengen borders, the main reasons for limited the freedom to move across borders—fear of terrorism and fear of waves of migrants—are likely to have an effect on immigration policy in each member state. Already, the rules for immigration for people who are not looking for refuge have become stricter, and EU institutions have been put under a lot of pressure to change the common asylum system. At the moment, the European Council is looking at seven legislative proposals made by the European Commision to change the way the asylum system works. This could help ease the main worries of member states that the current system doesn't do enough to process asylum seekers and send back those who don't qualify. The proposals include changing the Dublin system so that asylum seekers aren't forced to claim asylum in the first EU country they arrive in. Instead, they would be spread out more evenly among member states. The proposals also include creating an EU asylum agency to be in charge of common ways to evaluate asylum applications, starting common asylum processes and procedures (including stricter rules to stop abuse), and setting up common rules for resettling refugees in t. Even though it's too soon to tell if all of the member states will agree with these latest proposals, it seems likely that if the EU doesn't fix its common asylum policies, the member states will take back this part of their national sovereignty, just like some of them are doing with border controls. After all, if the goal is to have better control over who is in a member state, border controls will be less effective if EU asylum policies allow people who are seen as either a danger or an economic migrant to live and travel in the member state.

European Union's Efforts in Addressing Cross-Border Risks

As with immigration, attempts to stop illegal activities and threats that cross borders in Europe are based on a mix of EU-wide systems, national measures, and agreements between EU member states. Controlling borders is a big part of a country's territorial sovereignty and making sure its citizens are safe, so national governments in the EU have tried to keep their monopolies on this problem. At the same time, Schengen means that internal EU borders can't be treated like external borders (and some EU countries, like Germany, don't have external land borders with Schengen right now). On the other hand, the agencies that deal with cross-border threats like smuggling, human trafficking, and international terrorism are national agencies. This is because they gather information or enforce laws, which are mainly the responsibility of the member states and not the EU.

The European Union's main job in fighting smuggling, human trafficking, and cross-border terrorism is to help member states share information and coordinate their actions. The Schengen Information System, version II (SIS II), which was already stated, is the most important way that information is shared right now. SIS II is a shared IT system that lets law enforcement, border control, customs, citizenship, car registration, and the courts share information about criminals and illegal goods. Member states share information about criminal suspects who are accused of serious crimes, people who have been denied access to the Schengen Area (or deported from it), missing people, known cases of identity fraud, and people who have been subpoenaed or otherwise ordered to appear in court, as well as stolen vehicles, guns, equipment, documents, credit cards, and other items. SIS II works by sending "hits" (alerts) about these people or things to the national authorities listed above who work inside their own countries and at the external borders and ports of entry into the Schengen Area, such as airports and seaports. Each member state is in charge of running its own national database and a national SIRENE (Supplementary Information Request at the National Entries) bureau. The SIRENE bureau is in charge of coordinating information on alerts around the clock, including providing additional information, confirming the identity of people who are wanted, letting member states know when an arrest or other action has been taken on a hit, and other similar tasks.

The European Border and Coast Guard Agency (Frontex), which was already stated, is in charge of a second way for information to be shared within the European Union. Frontex gives member states information about smuggling, human trafficking, terrorism, and other threats to border security based on what law enforcement, intelligence, and other agencies in member states report to it through the Frontex Risk Analysis Network (FRAN). FRAN indicators include data on illegal border crossings, refusals of entry, the discovery of fake papers, people who overstay their visas, deportations, asylum requests, and other information.

Europol, which is the European Agency for Law Enforcement Cooperation, is a third way that the EU shares information. Law enforcement is a national job in the EU, but Europol acts as a kind of clearinghouse/fusion centre for sharing intelligence and other information between EU member states and, through bilateral cooperation agreements, with sixteen non-EU countries and international organisations like Interpol. Europol helps a wide range of national law enforcement agencies, including those that deal with immigration, border security, financial crimes, terrorism, organised crime, and other things. Europol does more than just make it easier for people to share information. It also offers analysis and support for operations, technical expertise, and strategic threat assessments. The European Cybercrime Centre, the European Counter Terrorism Centre, and the European Migrant Smuggling Centre are some of the analysis centres that Europol runs on its own.

The European Union Judicial Cooperation Unit, or Eurojust, is another way to work together. Eurojust was created in 2001 to help EU member states work together and help with investigations and trials. The agency can ask a member state to investigate or prosecute a crime, make it easier for member states to work together to form joint investigation teams, figure out where it might be best to prosecute crimes that happen in more than one member state, and help Europol with its information-sharing and support duties.

The "Solidarity Clause" of the Treaty on the Functioning of the European Union (TFEU) says that member states can ask for help from the EU right away in times of crisis. Teams of police officers from other member states can be sent by the EU. As we've already said, Frontex can get RABIT teams from other member states to help with border security. The same method can be used to put together Joint Investigative Teams (JITs), do Joint Customs Operations (JCOs), and use joint Financial Intelligence Units (FIUs) to look into common financial crimes.

In short, the European Union has put in place a number of ways to help fight risks that come from other countries. There are, of course, differences between some EU member states and the EU here as well. One of the many reasons why Britain left the EU was because its government wouldn't follow the strict rules that EU agencies use to protect personal information. Still, there is no sign that cooperation between member states through these EU platforms, institutions, or frameworks is a problem in the same way that common ways of dealing with migrants or open internal borders are. The UK's planned exit from the EU is expected to make it harder for the EU and the UK to share information and work together, but it is unlikely to change the EU's existence or future.

Conclusion

The European Union is very important for managing borders in Europe, and if you look at the Schengen Area as a whole, it might be the world's largest and most complicated system for managing borders. As the European Union has grown stronger at the cost of individual national governments, EU institutions have taken over more and more areas of public policy. Border management is one of those areas. Not surprisingly, as the EU's power and authority have grown, there have been more calls for limiting or even getting rid of the supranational body's power and giving the member states back their national autonomy. In the last 20 years, the EU has had to work hard to keep the Euro stable, deal with the global financial crisis of 2007-2008, stop economic nationalism (movements towards more economic independence) in some of its larger member states, keep trade ties stable with the U.S., China, and Russia, and, of course, deal with a wave of migration. These problems have hurt the EU, and the United Kingdom's choice to leave the EU is the most dramatic example of how badly they have hurt the EU. The EU is about to lose a member state with a lot of influence around the world and the second or third largest economy in the EU, depending on how the size of the economy is measured. This is likely the biggest problem the EU has faced since it was founded.

As we've already said, these shifting forces can also affect other countries, but there are no signs right now that any other EU member state is seriously considering leaving. To stop the EU from falling apart in the future, however, paradigms may need to be changed in a number of law and policy areas, and border management seems to be one of them. Even though there are no signs that EU institutions, platforms, and mechanisms for managing borders, especially when it comes to cross-border threats like smuggling, human trafficking, and cross-border terrorism, will change in a big way, the paradigm is changing when it comes to the Schengen internal borders, the free flow of people and goods, and how migration and asylum are handled. It's hard to say what the future will look like in these areas, but current trends seem to point towards some kind of permanent border controls on internal Schengen borders, possibly using technology to make crossing a border feel less like crossing a border. In this context, it will be interesting to see how the British and Irish governments (with the EU's blessing in the case of the Irish government) try to avoid making a "hard" border again. Also, fears of migrants (both in terms of how many there are and how they might become radicalised) are causing people to try to change the way EU refugee processes work so that national governments can have more control over who is allowed to live in their countries. So, the paradigm is changing in this area, too, towards more control by member states. This may also happen in the area of asylum if the EU can't come up with reforms that are acceptable to its member states. All of this doesn't mean that the European Union is going to end soon. Even when it comes to problems with managing borders, the EU has a lot to offer its members that makes up for its flaws. The people of Europe and most leaders (with the UK being a notable exception) still want the EU to stay together. So, even though parts of the way borders are managed are changing, sometimes in pretty big ways, the EU, with its laws, institutions, policies, and the shared European identity it helps to build, is not likely to go away.

When it comes to controlling borders and managing migration, the changes happening in Europe are a sign of a larger trend in the developed world. Other wealthy countries outside of the EU are also having trouble with both of these problems. They are making plans to better control their land, air, and sea borders and to limit migration. The United States, for example, has seen a huge rise in people being caught along its south-west border (nearly a million in 2019, which is more than double the number of people caught in 2018 and three times the number of people caught in 2017) and has also made it harder for people to get protection. refuge-seekers from Central America who come to the US through Mexico can no longer ask for refuge in the US. Instead, they must ask for asylum in Mexico or somewhere else. This rule could change, though, because of ongoing court cases. Australia has used a plan called the "Pacific Solution" to send asylum-seekers to other countries and has always said no to anyone who comes to the country illegally by sea. Japan, South Korea, and Israel are three other developed countries with strict rules about immigration and refuge. In short, the changes we are seeing in Europe are part of a larger global trend that is driven not only by security concerns and fear of terrorism, but also, and perhaps mostly, by population growth in poor countries that is causing waves of migrants and fears that unrestricted migration will lead to unwanted social and economic changes (though this fear is by no means new). Demographic projections show that most of the world's population growth will happen in the developing world, especially in sub-Saharan Africa, well into the middle of the century. Since it's likely that these countries won't be able to support their growing populations (in part because climate change is making food and water more scarce), this suggests that migration pressures from poor countries to rich countries will grow and cause more resistance. We are already in a time of pulling back, when people won't be able to move around as freely as they did from the middle of the 20th century to the beginning of the 21st century.

Some of the policy problems that the EU is facing, which we talked about above, could teach the US something. The United States is, of course, one country, and the lines between states are not foreign borders. The federal government is officially in charge of border security and immigration policy. But the federal government often depends on state and local governments to help with law enforcement and services along the border and with migrant groups inside the country. Some parts of the European Union's frameworks for better cooperation between member states and between member states and EU institutions could be changed and used to improve cooperation between states (especially when a state's authorities might be overwhelmed by a large number of migrants), between state and local authorities in the same state, and between federal authorities and state and local authorities. With some changes, the U.S. border security and immigration system might work better if it used the same kinds of information sharing, task groups, and agreements to help each other that are used in Europe. In the same way, some of the ways the EU handles asylum and immigration could, with some changes, help shape US policy, especially if the federal government gave states more power over where refugees are resettled and where they look for new immigrants with certain skills. Obviously, as the Europeans have shown, border security and immigration policies that work well are a pipe dream. However, real lessons have been learned, and many of them could help U.S. officials. In short, when it comes to this and other parts of homeland security, there is a lot of knowledge and experience outside of the United States, and some of it may be useful to American policymakers and help them make better decisions if it is changed in the right way.

Chapter 7
Mediterranean Migration Dynamics

In 2015 and 2016, more people came to Europe than at any time since World War II. In each of these years, more than 1.2 million people asked for refuge in the EU, while only 625,000 did so in 2014. These more applications did not cause the crisis that followed; they just showed that the Common European Asylum System (CEAS) was still not working well and had problems. So, the so-called "refugee crisis" in Europe may be better called a crisis of the CEAS. On paper, this system with clear distribution rules and shared protection standards was put in place in 2012 through several EU directives and the Dublin regulation. However, since the end of summer 2015, it has become very clear that it has not been put into place. At that time, the Dublin system had already broken down. Under this system, border countries are responsible for any asylum seeker who enters the Schengen area through their land. However, border countries were letting asylum seekers go to traditional host countries in Western and Northern Europe. States that didn't get many asylum requests were hesitant to adopt methods for sharing responsibility, and some Member States were openly against the idea. Some countries, like Germany, Austria, and Sweden, which had been welcoming to refugees at first, closed their borders and briefly stopped using the Schengen system. Even though this action was in line with EU law, it called into question freedom of movement, which is one of the most important parts of European integration. This made the crisis worse.

Also, the deaths of thousands of migrants at the Union's borders and some of the steps taken to stop refugees from coming to Europe have made people question the EU's role as a supporter of human rights around the world. At the same time, the problem has gotten a lot of attention from the media and has become very political. This, along with the rise of populist parties, has put a lot of pressure on EU institutions and member governments to find solutions. Along with the trauma of the Eurozone, this crisis and its aftermath have the ability to do a lot of damage to the EU integration project as a whole. Even though the EU has worked together on refugee policies for almost 20 years, there isn't a coordinated approach during times of crisis. This is strange, and it makes us think about and question the state of integration in this policy field.

So, this chapter gives a short summary of how and why the crisis started and how it grew. It also looks at what the EU and its Member States did to deal with the crisis so that we can judge how well the Union did and what that means for future cooperation.

European Refugee Crisis

Civil war, long-lasting conflicts, terrorism, worsening internal security, and rising poverty in many countries, especially in the Middle East, Africa, and Southern Asia, have caused large numbers of civilians to leave their homes in recent years. This has led to a situation called "mixed-motive migration," which means that people are both running away from persecution and trying to improve their social and economic lives. Yet, most of the people who moved to the EU came from war-torn places like Syria, Afghanistan, and Iraq. The war in Syria, which forced more than 5 million people to leave their homes by 2017 at the latest, has been by far the biggest reason for the sharp rise in migration, both in Syria's neighbours and in the EU. So, it should be noted that neighbouring countries like Lebanon, Jordan, and Turkey, where a lot of refugees went, had a hard time taking care of and integrating them because the camps lacked basic resources and money, their own security was getting worse, and tensions were rising within their own populations. Since the rest of the world didn't do enough to improve the conditions of the camps and because there were no plans for people to be moved to another country or other legal ways to enter, many people who were temporarily housed in their home area kept moving towards Europe.

In the years before 2015, there were already signs of a coming crisis in Europe. Along with the steady rise in the number of refugees coming to Europe, there has been a sharp rise in the number of shipwrecks and deaths in the Mediterranean. In response, the Italian government launched "Mare Nostrum" in 2013 to improve earlier search and rescue efforts in the area. However, "Mare Nostrum" was replaced by the much smaller EU operation "Triton" the following year. From spring 2015 on, the number of migrants entering Italy and Greece was especially high. This made it more likely for these countries to not properly register migrants, which made it easier for them to get to the North. In the end, "the Dublin system fell under its own weight" because it was inherently useless and made things take longer by adding more paperwork. With the routes moving more and more to the Eastern Mediterranean and Western Balkans, and with more and more evidence that asylum seekers were routinely detained and treated inhumanely in Hungary, which at the time was the EU country that took in the most asylum seekers, the German government unilaterally suspended the Dublin regulation for Syrians in August 2015. This meant that they could apply for asylum in Germany, regardless of where they first came from.

But about three weeks later, when a huge increase in people coming to Bavaria put pressure on the German government, it changed its mind to some extent and put back border controls at the internal Schengen border with Austria. This started a chain reaction that led other countries along the Balkan route to set up border controls so they wouldn't become a "dead end" where unwanted people could get "stranded." Sweden, Norway, Denmark, and Belgium later did the same. In October 2015, Hungary decided to build a fence along its borders with Croatia and Serbia because there were more people asking for asylum and the EU wasn't doing enough to manage border control on the outside. By taking this step, Hungary was able to move migrant flows to nearby countries, especially Slovenia. So, because of these choices, the "Western Balkans route" was shut down. This left tens of thousands of people stuck in Greece, where they often had to live in terrible conditions.

The EU's Handling of the Crisis

In May 2015, as the situation was getting close to its worst point, the European Commision put out its "European Agenda on Migration" between two emergency summits of the European Council. In it, the Commision laid out both immediate steps that need to be taken to deal with the problem in the Mediterranean and steps that will be taken over the next few years to improve how the EU manages its migration policy. After the first "implementation package" was passed on May 27, 2015, the European Commision put forwards a set of comprehensive priority measures in September of the same year. After working on the agenda for two and a half years, the Commision added a roadmap to its original plan in preparation for the European Council's summit on migration on December 14, 2017. The roadmap laid out specific goals and a time limit for creating a complete asylum policy. This section describes the measures that have been suggested since May 2015 and, to a lesser extent, looks at how they are going and whether or not they are right.

Given that the European Commision believes that "only a comprehensive approach works," which means "combining a variety of international and external policy tools," the following analysis groups measures by the factor they affect. Even though the measures are listed under different parts, they often go together and should be looked at as a whole. The following analysis focuses on the following measures: (1) hotspots and emergency support for affected Member States, (2) relocation, (3) resettlement and other legal ways of entry, (4) the CEAS reform, (5) addressing irregular migration through border controls and fighting smuggling and trafficking, (6) return and readmission, (7) the EU-Turkey Statement, (8) additional cooperation with third countries as well as (trust) funds to help regions of origin.

In June 2015, the European Council agreed to help Greece and Italy, which had the most refugees at their borders, by using a method called the "hotspot approach." This was done to deal with one of the most important problems caused by the crisis. It tries to help them by sending out Migration Management Support Teams. These teams work in five key areas: making functional hotspots, putting relocation decisions into action (see below), making sure migrants who don't qualify for international protection are sent back, improving border management, and making sure there are enough places to stay (European Commision 2015a; Statewatch 2015). In order to do these things, EU organisations like Frontex, the European Asylum Support Office (EASO), Europol, and Eurojust work with local governments to help with operations on the ground. While this is going on, other Member States must provide enough experts and tools to help these Migration Management Support Teams.

The agencies' jobs are meant to support each other, and they are supposed to help the Member States with registering, identifying, fingerprinting, debriefing, and sending back asylum seekers. When Hotspot facilities were built and temporary relocation decisions were made in 2015, it gave Greece and Italy a reason to register migrants the right way, as required by the Eurodac regulation, if they wanted to take advantage of the relocation plan.

Even though building and implementation of the hotspots took a long time, it seems that they have brought more order and greatly increased the number of people who sign up and get their fingerprints taken. But there has been a lot of criticism about: 1) the lack of a specific legal act or framework governing the hotspot approach, which challenges the fundamental rights of refugees (Menendez 2016, 408); 2) the approach's failure to relieve the pressure from Greece and Italy as planned, which may be because Member States didn't hire enough experts for the Support Teams; and 3) the chaotic conditions: medical services, catering, security, and housing. As a result of this, a number of NGOs left camps, which is said to have made things worse in the hotspots. Four years after the method was put into place, the situation has become much worse, especially on the Greek islands, where there are too many people and not enough basic care. The most obvious effects are suicidal thoughts and prostitution. Michael O'Flaherty, head of the EU's Fundamental Rights Agency, called the situation "the most worrying fundamental rights issue we are facing anywhere in the European Union."

Aside from Italy and Greece, the EU has helped the Western Balkans outside of the hotspot framework to "improve reception conditions and capacity for migrants and refugees and build capacities to strengthen migration management systems." In addition to the hotspot approach, there are two other ways to help financially and physically hard-hit states like Greece and Italy. Since 2015, other Member States have sent more than a million blankets, mattresses, beds, tents, teams, and equipment, as well as shelter and medical supplies, through the EU Civil Protection Mechanism. The "Asylum, Migration, and Integration Fund" (AMIF) and the "Internal Security Fund" (ISF) both helped pay for "migration management" in a financial sense. Emergency Support Instrument (ESI) money is added to these two funds to help refugees in Greece who need help right away. This is done in cooperation with UN agencies, NGOs, and foreign organisations (ibid.). So, as of January 2020, Greece, for example, had gotten around 2.23 billion Euro in emergency aid since 2015 through AMIF (1.18 billion Euro), ISF (415.4 million Euro), and ESI (643.6 million Euro) (European Commision 2020).

Overall, the Commission's budget proposal for the period 2021-2027 calls for almost a tripling of funding for migration and border management compared to the previous long-term period. This is a 75% increase in the funding that was originally planned for migration until 2020. The institution also called for the creation of an Asylum and Migration Fund to strengthen the CEAS, legal migration, and integration, as well as to fight irregular migration and make the system work better.

Relocation

A "temporary emergency relocation scheme," which is the process of moving people who need international protection from one EU Member State to another, is another way to deal with the problem of sharing responsibility. The relocation programme was made because the Dublin system hasn't been able to handle the problems caused by a large number of asylum seekers coming into the Union. This puts a lot of duty on countries with EU borders, especially Greece and Italy. After the Council made a first decision on September 14 to move 40,000 asylum seekers from Italy and Greece to other Member States, they made a second decision on September 22 to move 120,000 protection seekers (50,400 from Greece, 15,600 from Italy, and another 54,000 to be decided) within two years. This decision was based on a binding distributing key that took into account population size (40%), total GDP (40%), unemployment rate (10%), and the affluence of the country. The choices made in the Council were especially controversial, and many Central and Eastern European Member States, especially the Czech Republic, Hungary, Romania, and Slovakia, voted against a plan to move people temporarily against their will. Slovakia and Hungary even sued the European Court of Justice (ECJ) in November 2015 over the EU's required asylum quotas. The ECJ, however, threw out the case.

The agreed-upon plan didn't work as well as it could have because some member states didn't want to take part and because of practical and logistical problems. By the time it ended in September 2017, about 27,700 people had been moved because of it. But because thousands of people who were qualified were still waiting for their transfer, the Commision urged the Member States to keep working on their own, with financial help from the Union. So, by October 2019, 34,690 asylum seekers, or 96% of the people who were qualified, had been moved. But this number is only 35.3% of the 98,255 places that Italy and Greece are officially allowed to have. The difference is caused, in part, by the narrow meaning of who is eligible. Only asylum seekers from countries with an EU-wide recognition rate of 75% or higher were eligible for the programme, which meant that a lot of people, especially in Italy, couldn't use it. EU auditors say that at least 445,000 Eritreans, Iraqis, and Syrians may have been eligible in Greece alone. However, because the Greek and Italian governments didn't have enough resources, the EU-Turkey date was made up. Statements and lack of trust on the part of many refugees kept them from signing up for the programme. Because of this, these two countries kept getting pressured.

Also, Member States were different in how determined they were to meet their legal responsibilities and how hard they worked to do so. In June 2017, the Commision started an infringement process against Poland, the Czech Republic, and Hungary because they had either not moved a single asylum seeker or had stopped promising to do so for almost a year. Critics also say that the scheme didn't take into account asylum seekers' preferences, their ability to pay, and their personal and family situations when choosing where to move them. Like the Dublin system, this distribution system was based on the idea that asylum systems across the EU should give similar levels of protection and access to welfare. But case law from both the European Court of Justice and the European Court of Human Rights has shown that some Member States, especially in Southern Europe, failed to meet even the most basic standards.

The temporary emergency relocation plan went against the current Dublin regulation's "first-country-of-entry" rule. It could be seen as the EU's first step towards dividing the duty for refugees among its members. But because it was only there for a short time, it didn't create a long-term option to Dublin. So, in December 2015, the Council started talking about a permanent plan to move people. But at the beginning of 2016, the talks stopped because of resistance.

As an alternative, the Commision came up with a plan for a "Dublin plus" regulation. This regulation would keep the rules that are already in place, but it would also include a "corrective fairness mechanism" that would allow refugees to be moved around in times of crisis to relieve the pressure on countries on the outside of the EU's borders. The European Council suggested that people who are saved should only be sent to controlled centres set up in Member States if they want to. This is what international law says should happen. The focus on voluntary actions makes this vision unlikely and makes us wonder which country is ready to build these centres and take in refugees whose asylum claims have been found to be valid.

A possible solution seemed to take shape after tough negotiations, which were complicated by the fact that the temporary relocation plan wasn't perfect and that people had different ideas about what it means to be "solidarity" and what it means to be "voluntary" when it comes to helping asylum seekers. A plan from the Bulgarian Presidency called for a dynamic model that would separate "three phases of the crisis mechanism: normal circumstances, challenging circumstances, and severe crises." These phases would be linked to different actions taken by different EU institutions and monitored by different EU institutions. To help EU countries with their borders through solidarity, financial, expert, technical, and operational support would be given automatically when things get harder. The external dimension would be dealt with by working with third countries of origin, transit, or first asylum. Notably, the plan wants to replace these measures with "targeted allocation based on strong incentives and, as a last resort, on the basis of a Council Implementing Decision as an effective guarantee of triggering allocation." In other words, the Commision gave up on its more ambitious plan to create an automatic system for relocating people in favour of giving Member States more freedom and willingness, leaving room for national resistance. Insisting on the first-country-of-entry approach would mean that external border states would continue to be in charge of asylum seekers, which would put more pressure on their authority and ability to get things done. Greece and Italy would no longer be able to let migrants go to other countries because of the strict registration rules in the new Eurodac law and the increased focus on stopping "secondary movements." As a result, there would probably be another crisis, which would start with people moving on their own and end with a forced Council decision. Even though things have changed under the Finnish and Croatian Presidency, and there hasn't been a compromise based on the Bulgarian model, it's clear that by early 2020, no progress has been made towards a fair division of responsibilities between states, which would protect asylum seekers and guarantee their rights under EU law.

Resettlement

Resettlement is the process of letting displaced people who need protection from outside the EU into the Member States. This is done so that refugees don't have to take dangerous routes across the sea or risk their lives by going to people smugglers. Before the EU Turkey Statement, which led to the transfer of about 21,000 Syrians by March 2019, the heads of state and government agreed on a plan to move 20,000 people in Europe over the course of two years. Through this plan, more than 24,000 refugees will have found safety in Europe by March 2019. However, nine Member States had not given by September 2017. In fact, each Member State and some associated states had agreed to resettle a certain number of people in need through national and international programmes. Because of this process, there are big differences between the Member States in terms of how they choose people, how long the process takes, and how many places they have. So, in July 2016, the European Commision suggested a permanent framework for resettling people across the EU with a single set of rules.

Since the first ad hoc programme was only set up for two years and resettlement from Turkey was limited, the Commision asked Member States in its December 2017 roadmap to bridge the transition to the Union Resettlement Framework by pledging 50,000 places by February 2018 and putting them into action by May 2019, with a 50% target in October 2018. As of December 2019, 41,300 people had been resettled through the programme. In response to the Commission's call, Member States have agreed to accept another 30,000 refugees in 2020. The EU-Turkey Statement said that these resettlements were meant to focus on people moving from Turkey, Lebanon, Jordan, Libya, Niger, Chad, Egypt, Ethiopia, and Sudan. This was done "to help stabilise the situation in the central Mediterranean." In particular, the EU started working with the United Nations High Commissioner for Refugees (UNHCR) through the EU Trust Fund for Africa to move refugees from Libya to Niger and Rwanda through the "Emergency Transit Mechanism" (ETM) so that they could be resettled in European countries.

So far, family reunion has been the only legal way for refugees to get into Europe besides being resettled. Still, the Commision also started a "study on the feasibility and added value of sponsorship schemes as a possible way to safe channels of admission to the EU." Also, the Commision asked Member States to start pilot projects with African partner countries on legal economic movement as part of the Mobility Partnership Facility. This tool, on the other hand, seems to be mostly designed to meet labour needs. In the same way, the EU gives a number of (other) legal (temporary) entry options for highly skilled and seasonal workers, students, and researchers. However, these options don't really help people who are trying to get away from danger.

CEAS Reform

The first set of EU laws on asylum only set basic standards that everyone had to follow. The second set of EU laws in this area didn't do much to change the status quo ante. In the wake of the crisis, it became clear that the lack of harmonisation of asylum laws had (significantly) added to it, including by causing different migration pressures in different parts of the EU. So, on May 4 and July 13, 2016, the Commision suggested seven changes to the law that are closely related to each other. At the centre of these proposals was the new Dublin IV regulation. The other goals were to (1) set up a European Union Agency for Asylum, (3) make the Asylum Procedures and Qualification Directives into laws, (5) change the Reception Conditions Directive, (6) decide on a stronger Eurodac regulation, and (7) set up a Union Resettlement Framework. The goal of these reform proposals was to "limit secondary movements and make asylum procedures more efficient" by finding a balance between responsibility and solidarity and by harmonising rules about procedure, reception, and qualification so that people wouldn't be encouraged to go to a certain Member State with better conditions. On September 12, 2018, two more ideas were added to these proposals: (8) Along with a stronger EBCG, the Commision also put forwards a proposal for a revised Return Directive, on which the Council agreed in part in June 2019 on a common negotiating stance. The latter aims, among other things, to make processes faster and clearer, to get migrants to work together, to make detention easier for security reasons, and to allow, if necessary, returns to "safe third countries."

Even though the Dublin reform and the planned Asylum Procedures Directive haven't moved forwards much because of disagreements in the Council, most of the other laws have made progress by early 2020: The main thing that the co-legislators agree on when it comes to the Eurodac Regulation is that it will make it easier for law enforcement agencies to gather more data and use it. The adoption of a new EU Asylum Agency, which would make sure that all asylum applications are evaluated the same way and give technical and operational help to Member States, depends on how far the remaining CEAS reform plans get. Both the Qualifications Regulation and the Reception Conditions Directive have hit the point where Council and Parliament are negotiating them. They want to change the common criteria for judging asylum applications and set common standards for reception, such as the right to work no later than nine months after applying for protection and making sure that minors get an education and care, while preventing secondary movements by putting limits on where people can move. Trilogue talks have led to temporary agreement texts, but the Council didn't agree with them, and the

European Parliament didn't like the changes that the Council made. Because of this, trilogue talks have been put on hold since. Lastly, the EU Resettlement Framework will decide how many refugees can be taken in, how they will be split between Member States, and which areas will be given preference. Like the Reception Conditions Directive and the Qualification Regulation, talks for the trialogue have stopped moving forwards.

Concerning the Asylum Procedures Directive, one of the points of contention is a list of safe third countries and safe countries of birth that is the same for both. Member States use the second tool to list countries that are thought to be safe to live in because they have a stable democratic system and follow international human rights laws. The "safe country of origin" idea allows for a faster review process, but using "safe third countries" and "first countries of asylum" could lead to an application being ruled inadmissible. Critics said that the new regulation would make it harder for asylum seekers to appeal a decision that was made against them and to legally stay in the country where an application was made while an appeal was pending. Because of this, a standardised EU list could lead to protection rules that are based on the lowest common denominator.

Trafficking and Smuggling

Since one of the objectives of the Commission's Agenda on Migration is to fight against the business of smuggling and trafficking in people as well as illegal migration, the EU has started a number of things. From its meeting on October 18, 2018, the European Council came to the following conclusion:

> The fight against people-smuggling networks needs to be stepped up: work with third countries on investigating, apprehending and prosecuting smugglers and traffickers should be intensified, with a view to preventing people from embarking on perilous journeys.

In February 2019, Europol set up a European Migrant Smuggling Centre to help EU member states work together better. In terms of the sea, the EU runs three main military missions: Poseidon, Themis (formerly Triton), and Sophia. This is in addition to helping operations like Hera, Indalo, and Minerva. Since June 2015, the EU has tripled its spending for the missions Triton (which has been going on since 2014) and Poseidon (which has been going on since 2006), making up for the cuts caused by the end of Mare Nostrum. Both Poseidon and Themis (which replaced operation Triton in February 2018) focus on border control and monitoring. Themis works in the Central Mediterranean, while Poseidon works along the Greek sea borders with Turkey . Since one goal of the operations is to help people in situations, many refugees in trouble at sea could have their lives saved. Between January 2016 and June 2018, Triton/Themis saved 250,000 lives and Poseidon saved another 82,000. Notably, migrants helped by Operation Themis must now get off the boat at the nearest port, not just on Italian soil. But, even though both areas of operation have grown a lot since June 2015, Themis and Poseidon only step in when something goes wrong near the EU's borders.

The EUNAVFOR MED operation Sophia, which started in June 2015, is the third navy mission. Its major goals at first were to stop trafficking and smuggling and to stop more people from dying on the high seas of the Mediterranean. To reach these goals, it wants to find, seize, and get rid of boats used by people who smuggle or trade migrants. By the end of June 2018, the mission had saved almost 45,000 lives, caught about 150 people who were trying to bring drugs into the country, and destroyed about 550 boats.

In August 2016, the mission's goals were changed to include training the Libyan coast guard and navy. According to the International Organisation for Migration (IOM), Libyan authorities probably saved almost 5,000 migrants in the first three months of 2018. However, reports of refugees being abused and mistreated by the Libyan coast guard, which is accused of being involved in smuggling, as well as cases of interference with civil rescue operators like Seawatch in which several people drowned, led the EU to set up a monitoring system for the Libyan coast guard. Yet, from the first monitoring report in March 2018, the Commision came to the conclusion that "capacity and professionalism are getting better," but that "effective monitoring could be improved by a continued presence of EUNAVFORMED personnel in the operation centres of the Libyan Coast Guard." Regarding its support for Libyan authorities, the EU is accused of using the Libyan coast guard to "operate refoulement by proxy" on its own behalf, "with full knowledge of the Libyan Coast Guard's violent behaviour and the detention and inhumane treatment migrants would face if they were returned to Syria." Campbell says that the current cooperation is similar to operations under the EU-Turkey Statement and the former Hera joint operation with the Senegalese and Mauritanian coast guards in that it "uses the coast guards of bordering countries to do what European coast guards can't do, which is physically stop people from getting to Europe." Even with these worries, Sophia's job was extended until March 31, 2020, in September 2019. Since then, naval assets have been put on hold briefly.

Over time, people have had different ideas about what to do with illegal immigrants who are saved at sea. In addition to European processing centres, plans were made for sites outside of Europe where people could get off the ships. The Commision says that a "regional arrangement could work by identifying partner countries and working with the UNHCR and IOM to make sure that those who get off the boats can be sent to existing EU resettlement schemes if they need protection or to IOM-run return and reintegration programmes if they don't." In fact, the Commision was clear that, in order to avoid creating a pull factor, "resettlement options will not be available to all disembarked persons in need of international protection, and points of reception should be set up as far away as possible from points of irregular departure." This method could hurt the Union's reputation as a defender of human rights and international law in a big way. Stefanov (2018) questions the whole idea of setting up refugee centres in third countries. He does this by pointing out the legal and jurisdictional confusion as well as how hard it is to keep the centres safe and in control from the outside. Also, this approach really relies on the agreement of third countries, which they are unlikely to give unless they get a lot in return.

During the same time, Italy's populist alliance government closed its doors to refugees saved at sea by NGOs, putting them in a very dangerous situation. France, Germany, Italy, and Malta tried to set up a fast-track plan for disembarking and relocating these migrants, but they didn't get enough backing from other Member States. This stopped a de facto change to how the Dublin Regulation divides up who is responsible for what.

Due to Frontex's restricted abilities and powers to "protect" the EU's external borders, the Commision proposed a European Border and Coast Guard Agency (EBCG) in December 2015. It was quickly negotiated and went into effect in October 2016. The EBCG is a big step up from the old Frontex because it has more resources, a bigger job description, and more freedom from Member States. For example, it has to do mandatory vulnerability assessments of how Member States handle their borders on a regular basis. If Member States find problems and don't fix them, the EBCG's "right to intervene" can be used by a qualified majority in the Council to send border guards to a Member State, even if that country doesn't want them there. Even though some moves towards integration have been taken, critics have said that the EBCG fails to create a common European border management. This is because the Member States are still responsible for a lot of things, like putting in place border controls.

The body has had trouble doing its job for a long time because the Member States haven't given it enough people or resources. In November 2019, the Council passed a revised regulation to better equip the EBCG, such as by giving it a standing corps of up to 10,000 operational staff, and to strengthen its role in return and border control. The agency now has the power to deploy its forces outside of EU territory and in neighbouring countries, as well as to collect information and travel documents and pay for return operations.

Aside from working at sea, the EU has been putting more and more emphasis on border control (or "border protection," as it is often called). They say this is important to make sure the common Area of Freedom, Security, and Justice works. Frontex helps countries like Hungary and Croatia, for example, by sending officers and tools to watch the borders. When these controls are combined with the fact that there are no legal ways to get in, they have serious effects. Since the supposed closing of the Western Balkans route hasn't stopped forced migration and refugees and other migrants are still trying to get into EU territory, these border controls actively stop people from using the EU's protection system. Because of this, the Bosnian camp of Vucjak has become a well-known example of the horrible conditions refugees face when they are stuck in countries that can't help them. Even though this is a big problem on its own, it's made much worse by accusations that the Croatian border police do things like push people back illegally all the time .

Return and Re-Admission

European leaders think that returns are an important part of how the CEAS works, but the return rate has gone down from 46% in 2016 to 37% in 2017. This means that return decisions are often not carried out, which is partly because the countries of origin don't work together. Legally, returns are based on the EU Return Directive and depend on readmission deals. This means that third countries agree to take back both their own citizens and citizens of other countries who are living in the EU illegally. By the summer of 2019, the EU had signed 23 deals to do this.

European leaders decided that Frontex's supporting role, including in working with third countries, should be strengthened by giving it more money and a bigger job. This was about controlling the borders and sending back illegal immigrants. The agency has at least three pools of return experts, escorts, and monitors who can be sent out when asked to by a Member State. Setting up an independent return department, making national operational plans, and moving forwards with "pilot projects to develop and test innovative solutions for joint management of returns" were all ways to make European and national return policy even more effective. While this was going on, the EBCG's part in operating returns was criticised by many people because of reports that there wasn't enough internal monitoring of wrongdoing.

In September 2018, the Commision proposed a new Return Directive to "reduce the length of return procedures, ensure a better link between asylum and return procedures, and ensure a more effective use of measures to prevent absconding." This was in response to repeated requests from the European

Council and Council to make return more efficient. In June 2019, the Justice and Home Affairs Council agreed on a number of changes to the proposal. These changes included extending the maximum length of entry bans from five to ten years and making it possible for Member States to decide that returnees pay for their own removal and detention costs. By the end of 2019, the European Parliament had not come to a decision.

Over the years, the EU has become much more determined to control migration by relying more on return in a world where third parties are being asked to do more. During his meetings in October 2019, the responsible Commissioner, Margaritis Schinas, said that he wants to sign more readmission agreements in addition to harmonising the rules for returns to make them more efficient. In May 2019, the EU made a change to the Visa Code Regulation that made it easier to use visa policies as a tool to get third countries to work with them more on return.

When the EU's efforts to solve the refugee problem from the inside didn't seem to be working, it tried to find more solutions from the outside. The "EU-Turkey Statement" from March 18, 2016, is the most important part of this plan. It builds on the "EU-Turkey Joint Action Plan," which was put into action on November 29, 2015. It has the following as its main parts: (1) As of March 20, 2016, people who crossed into Greece illegally through Turkey were sent back to Turkey. This is true for all migrants who haven't asked for protection or whose requests have been turned down as "inadmissible" or "unfounded." (2) A transfer plan in which one Syrian is sent back to Turkey for every Syrian already living there who is sent to the EU. This system could send up to 72,000 refugees back to their home countries. (3) Turkey said it would do what it took to stop new land or sea routes to the EU. (4) In exchange, the EU would give Turkey: (i) visa-free travel, as long as Turkey took the steps needed to meet the rest of the requirements; (ii) 3 billion euros from the "Facility for Refugees in Turkey" fund and another 3 billion euros to be spent on specific projects to help Syrian refugees in Turkey; (iii) more talks and work on improving the Customs Union; and (iv) the return of flights between Turkey and the EU.

Observers say that the EU-Turkey Statement is a big reason why fewer people are entering Greece through Turkey. In fact, the number of people who came to Greece dropped by 98% between 2015 and 2016, and the number of people who died or went missing in the Aegean Sea dropped by 94%. This trend continued in the years that followed. Yet, the EU-Turkey Statement has been called into question because it agreed with closing the Western Balkans route, said that conditions in Greece were not good for refugees, and said that several EU countries would start checking people at their own borders. Also, the number of people who came to Greece each month was going down before the EU-Turkey Statement. This could have been because winter was coming and the weather was getting worse. Also, the fact that there haven't been many returns under the EU-Turkey Statement up until March 2019 shows that it didn't have a large-scale effect. Still, the projects funded by the facility have helped improve the lives of Syrian refugees in Turkey. For example, they have given Syrian refugees (partial) access to education, health care, vaccinations, and monthly cash transfers, even though EU Member States didn't agree on how to pay for the second tranche until June 2018.

Still, there are many things wrong with the EU-Turkey Agreement. (1) There have been questions about whether Turkey's asylum security meets international standards. Claims that the Turkish government and courts don't have enough skills and experience are at odds with the UNHCR's assessment that Turkey now "provides protection and assistance to asylum seekers and refugees, no matter where they came from." This is based on the Law on Foreigners and International Protection. Human Rights Watch also said that Turkish border guards shot at refugees who were trying to cross the border, and Amnesty International said that a lot of Syrians have been sent back to Syria. (2) Declaring Turkey a safe third country helped solve some of the legal problems with sending refugees back to Turkey. This is a practise that can be seen as problematic and may now be seriously contested because of the steps taken after the failed coup in July 2016. (3) By making the deal with Turkey such a big part of the EU's response to the crisis, the Union has put itself at risk of becoming very dependent on Turkey and easy to blackmail by a leader with clear authoritarian tendencies. This fear has come true, as President Erdogan has used migrants as a bargaining chip many times since his military offensive on northeastern Syria began in October 2019.(4) The situation in Greece isn't covered in a logical way. The deal doesn't include refugees who came to Greece before March 20, 2016, which was estimated to be more than 46,000 people at the time. In fact, the agreement to send people back did not help Greece much, because many refugees now apply for asylum in Greece instead of their prefered country of choice to avoid being sent back. So, the share of returns in 2016 was only a small part of the total number of entries. (5) People have been moving in slowly. From April 2016 to March 2017, 3,656 Syrians moved from Turkey to the European Union (EU). At this rate, it would have taken the EU about 13 years to fulfil its plan to resettle all Syrians. (6) The agreement doesn't do what it was supposed to do, which was to create safe, legal ways to get to Europe. This is because places were taken from promises already made under resettlement and removal programmes. (7) The "EU-Turkey statement" doesn't have any legal force and hasn't been made a part of the EU's structure. So, EU institutions can't be held responsible for it.

This gets around the normal checks and balances in the EU, like the ECJ's review. The message was used as a model for other deals. The closing of one route is not going to stop people from coming to Europe. Instead, it will make people take even more dangerous routes to get there. So, the cooperation between the EU and Turkey turns out to be a band-aid solution that moves the problem and doesn't give all people in need the protection and integration they need. This is especially true in a country like Turkey, which is already home to millions of refugees while making it harder for people to seek asylum in Europe.

Cooperation with Third Countries

From the EU's point of view, migration and refugee issues can't just be dealt with when migrants reach Europe. They must also be dealt with in the countries where migrants come from and pass through. On October 18, 2018, the European Council again stressed "the importance of further preventing illegal migration and strengthening cooperation with countries of origin and transit, especially in North Africa, as part of a wider partnership." This relationship includes Egypt and the Arab League. As the route across the Central Mediterranean to Italy became the most popular in the second half of 2016, the European Council met in Malta in February 2017 and agreed to work with Libya to cut down on illegal migration and stop people from taking that route. In November 2017, the EU, the African Union, and the UNHCR also set up a joint migration task group to improve how they work together on migration in Africa, especially in Libya. Yet, especially about the last one, the Commision admitted in March 2019 that "continued efforts are needed to end the untenable situation on the ground." It planned to reach this goal by continuing to get people out of detention centres, helping them get off the boats, coordinating resettlement, and making it easier for people to return on their own. In 2018, the most common way to get from Morocco to Spain was through the Western Mediterranean. Because of this, the EU decided to step up its cooperation with Morocco. This includes a 140 million euro programme to improve border control, the finalisation of a readmission agreement, and more development aid through the North African Window of the EU Emergency Trust Fund for Africa.

In June 2016, the European Commision announced a New Partnership Framework (Migration Compacts) "with key third countries of origin and transit using a mix of incentives tailored to produce concrete results in stopping the flow of irregular migrants and helping third countries develop in order to address the root causes of irregular migration." In addition to "getting to the root of the problem," these agreements focus on return and readmission, legal ways to move, stopping trafficking and smuggling, and saving lives at sea.

The EU Trust Fund for Africa and the External Investment Plan are used to help pay for the framework. Mali, Niger, Ethiopia, Lebanon, Senegal, Nigeria, and Jordan were named as countries that should be a focus. Partnerships add to the Global Approach on Migration and Mobility, the established Rabat, Khartoum, and Budapest Processes, and the Regional Development and Protection Programmes. They build on the European Neighbourhood Policy review of 2015, the Western Balkans Leaders' meeting in October 2015, the Valletta Summit on migration a month later, the EU-Turkey Statement, and naval operations Sophia, Triton/Themis, and Poseidon.

One and a half years after it started, Mali, Nigeria, Niger, Senegal, and Ethiopia started putting it into action, and work continued with other countries in North-West Africa and Asia (European Commision 2017i, 1). As a result, (1) political dialogue has been strengthened through regular meetings, the deployment of twelve migration liaison officers, and cooperation with EBCG and Europol. (2) A Joint Investigation Team was set up with Niger to fight against smuggling and trafficking. This team could serve as an example for other countries. Also, local income support has given people in the north of Niger an alternative way to make money besides piracy, and the EU has kept giving 147 million Euro to the G5 Sahel Joint Force. In Niger, five transit centres that offer help, medical care, and emotional support were set up with the help of IOM. Migrants in Libya were also given protection, and the Commision pays for their voluntary return. (4) "Migration management systems" were made better with the help of IT and by keeping track of movement and population. (5) The EU wanted to make a total of 188,000 new jobs in Ethiopia, Kenya, Somalia, South Sudan, West Africa, and the Sahel. Aside from that, more than 1.6 million people began to get basic social services.

From the EU's point of view, more progress was made until May 2018: (1) The Commision urges the Libyan authorities, among other things, to keep their promises to help with humanitarian evacuations through exit visas, give access to detained refugees, improve the conditions in detention centres, and register all migrants who get off boats. (2) Talking and working together with African partners like Ethiopia, Guinea, The Gambia, Cote d'Ivoire, Egypt, and Nigeria has become even more important. This includes managing borders, smuggling, and return. (3) In the Horn of Africa, the Regional Operational Centre for the Khartoum Process, which aims to improve joint investigations into smuggling, has made progress. Under the "Better Migration Management Programme," government officials have been trained in border management and migrant rights. (4) Morocco kept working with Spain to keep an eye on the border.

In general, these agreements should be seen as part of the EU's partnership with Africa, which was reaffirmed at the fifth summit with the African Union on November 29 and 30, 2017. In terms of migration and mobility, the Unions and UNHCR reaffirmed their shared resolve to protecting migrants in Libya and on routes that lead there. Also, by the end of 2017, the EU had taken part in 14 Peace Support Operations in Africa, helping to build peace, stop conflicts, and train military, police, and legal staff. With help from the EU Trust Fund for Africa and missions in Niger and Mali, the Nigerien government and IOM were able to save more than 1,100 refugees in 2017.

Aside from Africa, the EU has signed readmission deals with countries in Asia and the Western Balkans. These countries are also places where they work together. At their summit on June 28, 2018, European heads of state and government came to the conclusion that "cooperation with and support for partners in the Western Balkans region remain key" to share information about migration flows, stop illegal migration, improve border protection, and make it easier to return and readmit people. Since the Western Balkans meeting on October 25, 2015, agencies from the EU, UNHCR, and IOM have kept in touch through weekly and monthly video conferences.

Setting up of Trust Funds in Neighboring Countries

To stop more people from coming to Europe, the EU has set up a number of trust funds that pool a lot of money from different sources to help people who are already there. In response to the refugee situation, there are four main funds in place right now, besides the Facility for Refugees in Turkey that we talked about above:

The EU Regional Trust Fund in Response to the Syrian Crisis, also called the "Madad" Fund, was set up in December 2014 to deal with the regional problems caused by the Syrian crisis. It helps Syrian refugees in Syria and in neighbouring countries like Iraq, Jordan, Lebanon, Egypt, Turkey, and the Western Balkans. More specifically, the Madad Fund wants to help 1.5 million Syrian refugees and other displaced people in Iraq by giving them health care, education, child protection, water infrastructure, and better economic and social chances. It wants to give young people hope for the future and make things easier for the countries that take in refugees. By June 2018, 1.5 billion euros had been given by 22 EU Member States, Turkey, and the EU budget, and 920 million euros had been spent on almost 50 projects.

The Bekou Trust Fund for the Central African Republic was set up in July 2014 to pay for actions related to peace and transition, such as health care, job training, and helping refugees. By the end of 2017, the amount of money pledged had grown to 236 million, and 149.3 million Euro had been given to

15 projects. These projects focus on rural development, infrastructure, water supply, sanitation, and helping people who have been moved.

(3) The Emergency Trust Fund for Africa was set up at the Valletta Summit in November 2015. Its goal is to address the root causes of instability, forced displacement, and irregular migration, as well as improve access to basic social services and boost the economy and job market. It is broken up into three windows for people from the Sahel/Lake Chad area, the Horn of Africa, and the North of Africa. Programmes put economic and equal opportunities, resilience, security, and growth at the top of their list. By March 2019, a total of 188 programmes and €3.6 billion had been used to make life better for people who want to move to Europe from Africa.

The EU works with the International Organisation for Migration (IOM) and the United Nations High Commissioner for Refugees (UNHCR) to help refugees and people who have moved within their own country. They do this at disembarkation points, inside and outside of detention centres, and in host towns. There have been many reports of migrants in Libya being abused and exploited on a large scale. In April 2017, a new 48 million Euro package was passed to improve the living conditions of migrants, including in detention centres. In March 2018, a 50 million Euro programme was passed to help migrants and the communities where they live. Notably, by July 2018, these programmes had helped 52,200 refugees and vulnerable migrants directly with non-food items and hygiene kits, 26,000 people with medical care, 3,500 Libyan families with basic needs, and four Primary Health Care Centres with medical equipment. The EU and UNICEF also work together to help get children out of holding centres and meet their basic needs. Still, Libyan municipalities are stabilised by fixing up schools, hospitals, nurseries, police stations, and strengthening water, sanitation, and social infrastructure. Other programmes focus on training Libyan officials on human rights and "integrated border management." For example, the Libyan coast guard gets training and important equipment through this fund, and pilot activities are done "to increase capacity for border management."

(4) After a suggestion from the Commision in September 2016, co-legislators quickly agreed to set up an External Investment Plan (EIP) within less than a year. The goal of the EIP is to "use EU funds to leverage private investment in the development of Africa and other parts of the EU's neighbourhood." According to the Commision, most of these investments will go towards improving social and economic infrastructure, such as municipal infrastructure and services in close proximity, helping small and medium-sized businesses, and working on microfinance and job creation projects, especially for young people. In September 2017, a new law set up the European Fund for Sustainable Development (EFSD) as the main way to make the EIP work. By March 2019,

EIP projects had been given €3.7 billion, which helped create jobs and boost growth in the European Neighbourhood and Africa.

Den Hertog makes it seem possible that the real plans and goals for these funds might be more focused on the EU's short-term security needs. In the same way, a CONCORD study on the effects of the EU Trust Fund for Africa (EUTF) and Migration Compacts raises "concern that the EUTF is being used as a political tool focusing on quick-fix projects" and "contributing unintentionally to inhumane treatment of migrants and refugees, as in the case of Libya."

Conclusion

Given the wide range of internal and external policy measures, it's possible that the EU's overall reaction to the crisis has been stronger and more thorough than most people think. But because the issue as a whole has caused deep divisions in the European Union and its societies, the EU has not been able to come up with good internal answers, especially a way for Member States to share responsibility that will last. The rising securityization and externalisation of responsibilities under international law may slow migration in the short term, but it also keeps many people who are fleeing persecution or violent conflict from getting protection. In this way, the EU not only backs away from its share of global duty, but also accepts and, in fact, encourages the suffering, mistreatment, and exploitation of refugees. Fighting "irregular migration" to keep control and keep refugees from being taken advantage of by smugglers and human traffickers doesn't make sense when there isn't enough legal access for asylum seekers and only a small number of people in need are resettled. Cooperation with countries of origin to create new opportunities and safety at home is a good start, but putting more conditions on third countries to get them to help with return and "border management" is just a way to get out of doing what needs to be done. Overall, security-focused measures have come to take precedence over humane ones. The Commision is likely to take the same approach with its new Pact for Asylum and Migration, which will be introduced in the spring of 2020, just like Finland and Croatia did in the past.

So, the EU still doesn't seem ready for a new wave of refugees and other migrants as long as there isn't a fair compromise based on international duty and solidarity. A Common European Asylum System that aims for substantial harmonisation between Member States, for example on the qualification, reception, and redistribution of asylum seekers, as well as on asylum procedures, would do a lot to give refugees and asylum seekers across the EU legal certainty and clear rights and duties. However, it is unlikely that this kind of harmonisation will happen in any substantial way, despite the legislative acts that are already in the works.

Chapter 8
Legal Immigration in the Years Ahead Between EU and Africa

Will economic growth in poor countries make people move there less or more? It's hard to answer this question. Certainly, the way many politicians in Europe talk shows that they think giving aid or addressing the "root causes" of migration will stop people from leaving. The idea is that people move because there aren't enough jobs, there are wars, or the climate is changing, and that the effects of all of these things can be lessened by putting money into targeted help. This part will try to show that this way of thinking is too simple. Yes, European leaders should use aid money to create jobs and help the economy grow, and they should also make sure the borders are strictly enforced. But if they don't help create new legal ways for workers to move, they won't be able to handle this movement in the long run or take advantage of the good things it might do for European labor markets.

Migration and development have a complicated relationship, but there is a lot of evidence that growth can lead to more migration (see Figure 8.1). There is clear proof of an upside-down U-shaped relationship between migration and economic growth. In spite of what officials say, economic growth and migration, up to a certain point, go hand in hand. We call this the "mobility transition," and the "hump" happens between US$7,000 and US$8,000 PPP, which is an upper-middle income country. Even with more help and economic investment, it will take a long time for many poor countries to "get over the hump" at their current growth rates.

When we apply this US$7,000-$8,000 PPP barrier to sub-Saharan Africa, we see that most countries fall on the left side of the inverted U (see Figure 8.2). The countries that are above the US$7,000 PPP threshold are shown in yellow. However, most countries are below that amount. Because of this, it's possible that more people will leave these countries in the years to come.

Fig. 8.1 - To a point, development and emigration go hand in hand

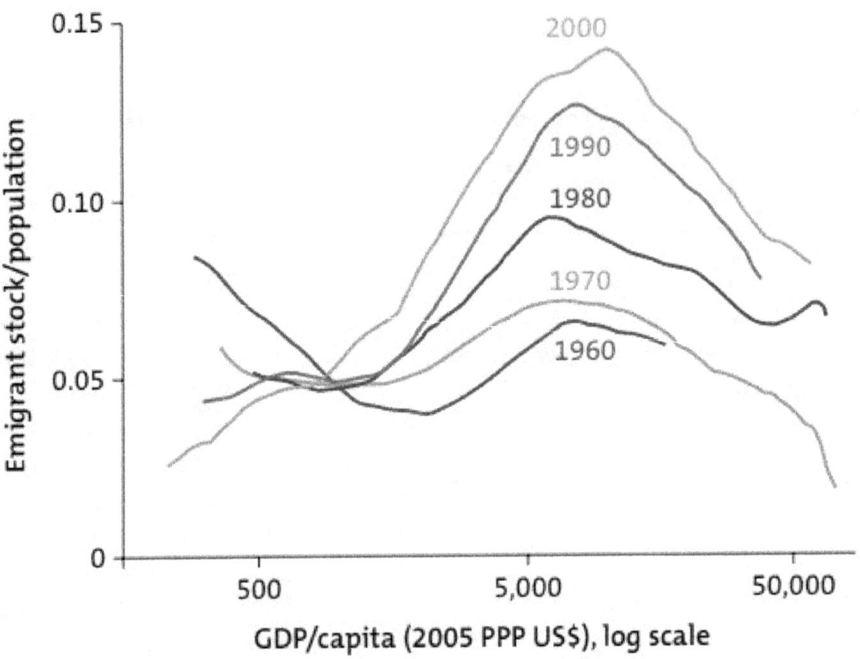

Source: World Bank data quoted in M. Clemens, Does Development Reduce Migration?, CGD Working Paper 359, 2014

Fig. 8.2 - Most sub-Saharan African countries will experience More migration in the decades to come

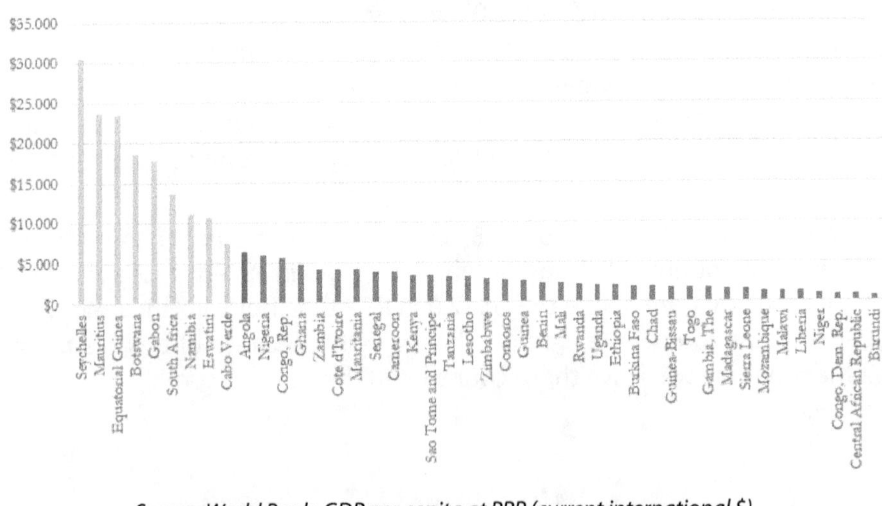

Source: World Bank, GDP per capita at PPP (current international $)

This link between economic growth and people leaving is not a perfect science. There are a lot of reasons why a country wouldn't follow this trend, but the biggest ones are war and climate change. But there are six major reasons why countries tend to follow this pattern. These reasons seem to be the same for all of the countries in Figure 8.2.

1. Demographics. At early stages of development, rising incomes cause child mortality to fall quicker than fertility. That means a rise in the youth population. Not only does this mean there are normally too many people for the number of jobs, but young people are also more likely to move.
2. Credit constraints. Migration is expensive - paying for recruitment fees, insurance, transportation, education, visa fees and passports. Eventually, migrants will earn more money by moving, but these benefits accrue in the future. As a country develops, people gain more and more money, they gain access to loans and other financial markets, and they are more likely to know other people who have moved, who send money home in the form of remittances. This money allows new people to afford the journey.
3. Information. Once a few people have moved, they provide information to those people back home - about job searching, earning potential, cost of living, marriage partners, legal formalities, and ways to move. This reduces the risk of moving 'blind'.
4. Structural change. As a country develops, some sectors increase, and others decline. This is why we see so much rural-to-urban migration. But some of those people may want to move abroad rather than adapting to this new reality.
5. Inequality. As we all know, economic development doesn't benefit all people equally. Some people may feel like they're not benefiting from the growth of their country, and feel that they could do better in a different one.
6. Immigration barriers abroad. Up to this point, we've just talked about changes in the demand for migration, but the supply of opportunities matters too. As a country gets richer, they're more likely to produce higher-educated and skilled people, who are more in demand abroad.

And movement can help the economy grow. By moving, migrants can earn more money and learn more, which lets them spend more on meeting their basic wants and making investments for the future. Migration can lead to higher wages and more economic growth in the country of birth through higher incomes, more money sent home, more spending, the transfer of knowledge and technology, and investments by migrant households. In the countries where they end up, refugees can fill jobs that aren't being filled and help with services, taxes, and social security. In this way, migration and development are inextricably tied. More people leaving a country can be a sign of and a cause of more development. And, over time, in a stable environment, development will bring about enough economic growth to push the community past the curve to the point where migration forces start to go down.

How does this affect sub-Saharan Africa? What do we know? In sub-Saharan Africa, the number of people of working age is growing quickly. This is because the death rate for children under five has gone down, which is a big step forward in terms of growth. But it also makes things hard. Last year, the International Monetary Fund found that sub-Saharan Africa will need to create 20 million new jobs every year to keep up with its growing population. And these jobs need to be in high-skilled fields that add more value. At the rate of growth that is happening now, it will be hard for local labor markets to meet this demand. Given these demographic trends and the other five factors in the region, migration from sub-Saharan Africa is expected to increase in the coming decades. Most people will choose to move within the same country, and the number of people moving within the same country is growing faster than the number of people moving abroad. But others will look for work in other places, like Europe, to make a better living and send money back home.

This is a big chance for Europe to do something good. Europe is going through big changes in its population. By 2100, its working-age population is expected to be almost 30% smaller than it was in 2015 (see Figure 8.3). This is because birth rates are low and people are living longer. This change is already having an effect, as the private sector in many countries is asking for a rise in the number of workers and in the skills they have. If Europe wants to keep growing and keep its social programs going, it will need a big increase in the number and types of people who could work there.

So, if Europe wants to use migration to help improve both its own countries and sub-Saharan Africa, it has to do three things:

- Enact robust border enforcement which includes a humane and effective security system, and managed returns and reintegration efforts with countries of origin;
- Target aid and development efforts in countries of origin, particularly those aimed at employment creation and general economic growth; and
- Promote new kinds of legal labour migration pathways to manage migration in a mutually beneficial way.

Only by pursuing all three of these routes in tandem can Europe manage this demographic pressure in the years to come.

Fig. 8.3 - Population Division World Population Prospects

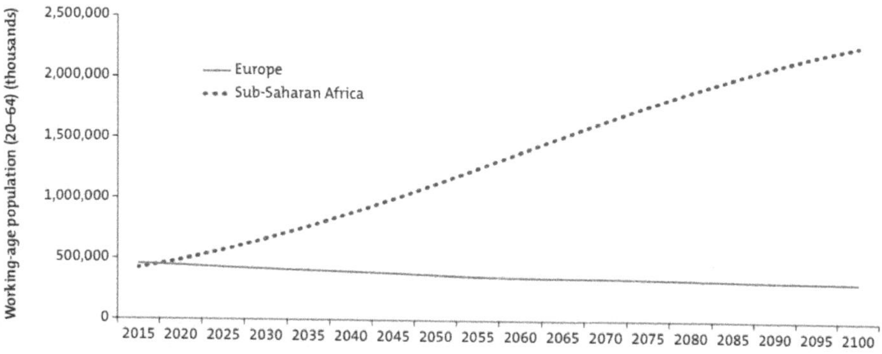

Source: UN DESA, "Population Division World Population Prospects", 2017.

Note: This projection uses the "medium-variant", which assumes a continuationof recent levels of net migration (the difference between the number of immi-grants and the number ofemigrants for a given country or group of countries).For more information, see United Nations Department of Economic and SocialAffairs (UN DESA), "World Population Prospects: The 2017 Revision, KeyFindings and Advance Tables", 2017; and UN DESA, "Population Facts", 2017.

EU and Its Current Progress

In May 2015, the European Commission put out the European Agenda on Migration, which is a very detailed plan. It was made to deal with the "crisis" of refugees in 2015 right away. It was built on four bases that would help better manage migration in the medium- and long-term. Under these pillars, the Commission has done a lot, like increasing the number of refugees who are resettled, helping Member States manage their borders, funding integration projects, fighting smuggling networks and trafficking, and working on development and security in the countries where refugees come from through the European Union Trust Funds. By doing this, the Commission has had a lot of success, such as reducing the number of people who come to the country without permission (see Figure 8.4).

Fig 8.4 - The number of irregular border crossings into Europe has fallen since 2015

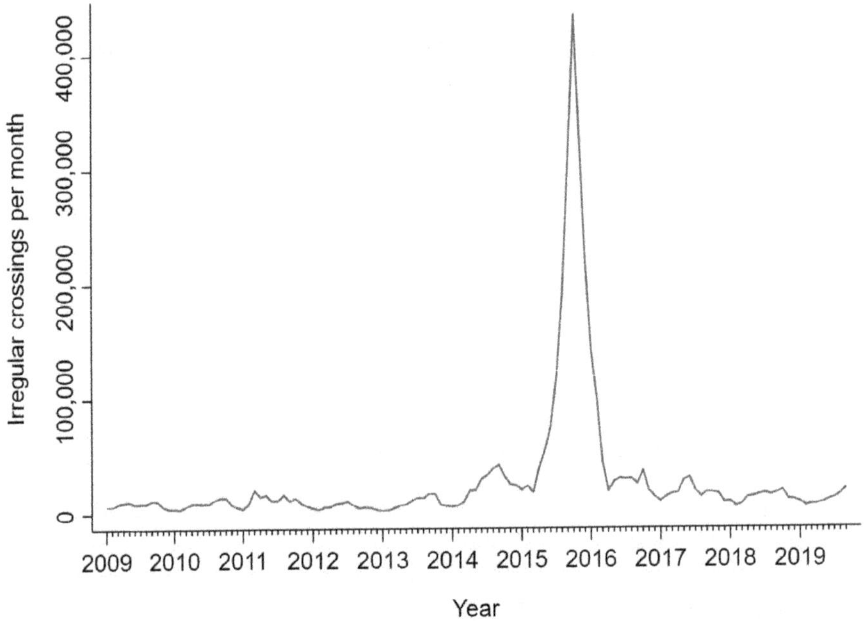

Source: FRONTEX (European Border and Coast Guard Agency), updatedSeptember 2019 at https:// frontex.europa.eu/along-eu-borders/migratory-map/

But given the above demographic predictions and other things that are out of the Commission's control, like foreign wars, migration, and climate change, the future is not a sure thing. Also, most of the Commission's wins so far have come from the help of other countries, which may not be a given in the future. And because there isn't a wide agreement in Europe on how to best handle migration, European states often have to come up with answers on the spot.

Even though both growth and border controls are important, the Commission has agreed that they are not enough to stop illegal migration. Europe needs new kinds of legal paths for migrants in order to lower the incentives for illegal migration, bring in the right kind of talent and skills, and make it possible to tailor admissions to the needs of the labor market. Without these paths, the EU's economy will not grow as fast as it could. So, the fourth pillar of the European Agenda on Migration is supporting new legal paths. These paths come in three different forms: bringing in new talent, the Blue Card Directive, and pilot projects that are planned across Europe. These measures show how little room the Commission has to move, since Member States still have the power to decide how many people from other countries can come to work there.

In 2017, the Commission came up with the idea of legal migration pilot projects to "replace irregular migratory flows with safe, orderly, and well-managed legal migration pathways; and to encourage cooperation on issues like preventing irregular migration, readmitting irregular migrants, and sending them back." The Commission put out a "Concept Note on the Pilot Projects on Legal Migration" the following year. It named the target countries, explained how to apply, and named the sources of funds. The Directorate-General for Migration and Home Affairs paid for the Mobility Partnerships Facility (MPF), which was a system that could be changed quickly and was flexible.

The Belgian Development Agency, Enabel, was one of the four Member States that asked the MPF for money. Its "Pilot Project Addressing Labour Shortages Through Innovative Labour Migration Models" is directly using the Global Skill Partnership model to train information and communications technology (ICT) workers for jobs in Morocco and Flanders. Even though it's too early to judge how well the test worked, everyone involved has said that a project like this is needed to meet the needs of both sides. All pilot projects that are paid for by the MPF invest in skills and people capacity. For example, training or internship programs are run in European Member States as part of these investments.

Global Skill Partnership

Member States are the only ones who can decide how many and what kinds of workers can cross their lines to work. The Commission can't suggest a "common migration policy" like the Common European Asylum System. But it does have an important part to play in promoting, making it easier for, and helping to create new legal ways for people to move to Europe to work.

One way to do this is through a Global Skill Partnership. It is a deal between two parties with equal power. The country of destination agrees to give the country of origin the technology and money it needs to teach potential migrants with the skills it needs in the country of origin before they move. This way, when migrants arrive in the country of destination, they already have the skills they need to integrate and contribute best. The country of origin agrees to provide that training and gets help for teaching people who are not migrants. This adds to human capital instead of taking it away.

For example, both Morocco and the Flanders area of Belgium have said they need more people with training in ICT. Belgium has decided to pay for and help train ICT workers in Morocco. Some of these people will stay and work in Morocco. Others will move to Flanders to work for companies based there. When they get there, this last group will also get language and integration training and be linked up with local migrant networks.

Global Skill Partnerships is different from other programs in this area in six ways. Partnerships for Global Skills:

- Manage future migration pressure, addressing many legitimate concerns about migration in countries of destination (such as integration and fiscal impact) and in countries of origin (such as skills drain).
- Directly involve employers in the country of destination to identify and train for specific skills they need that can be learned relatively quickly.
- Form a public-private partnership for semi-skilled work - jobs that take between several months and three years to learn and do not require a university degree.
- Create skills before migration, with cost savings to the country of destination and spillover benefits from training centres in the country of origin.
- Promote development by bundling training for migrants with training for non-migrants in the country of origin, according to the differing needs of each. Such training occurs in two tracks: a "home" track for non-migrants, and an "away" track for migrants. Trainees can pick which track to go down - those who choose to migrate could also receive additional training in soft skills, for example in different languages or other facets of integration.
- Are highly flexible. Any agreement can, and must, be adapted to the specific country needs in both destination and origin.

Who does this kind of plan help? In a sense, everyone was involved. Europe, which has many countries of destination, gets migrants who are skilled enough to make the most of their time there and fit in quickly, without being a total drain on money or people. They can control how and why people move there, picking those who have the right skills, can contribute quickly, and fit in quickly. Because of this, countries of destination gain in four ways: 1) dealing with their own population changes, 2) reaching their development goals, 3) making it easier for migrants to fit in, and 4) helping to stop illegal flows.

The country of birth gets new technology and training facilities, an increase in human capital from those who stay, the possibility of remittances from those who leave, and less pressure to take in new workers.

Those who are taught can move regularly and safely, or they can stay where they are and get better skills to enter the local job market. All of them can make more money, which has other perks.

And everyone else gains from skills gaps being filled, including those with secondary jobs that depend on those roles being filled and those who will fill new jobs created by those who move and stay.

In the current political climate, it is tough to make new legal ways for people to move for work. More and more lawmakers want to close national borders and cut the number of immigrants. But we think that even the most conservative Member States are likely to adopt the Global Skill Partnership approach because of the following:

- The number of migrants admitted is small and therefore unlikely to attract much political attention;
- Migrants have been selected and brought to the country of destination to meet specific skills needs that locals are unable to meet, and have already been provided with language and integration training;
- The potential migrants will be screened and vetted before they enter the country of destination and easily tracked after they arrive, thereby satisfying security concerns;
- The model meets the desire among countries of destination to participate in the "development" of countries of origin; and
- It provides countries of destination with a practical and pragmatic way to control some migration flows and shift irregular flows into regular pathways, thereby satisfying voter demand for a "managed" immigration policy.

Recommendations for EU

Due to the size of the above-mentioned demographic changes, Europe cannot wait until migrant flows become more obvious to start a Global Skill Partnership. This tool should be tried out now, while migration is still manageable, before the size and speed of movement make it hard to try new things. So, we think this is a great time for the new Commission to expand the size and scope of these legal labor migration projects and try out new ways to make sure that migration is good for everyone.

Ursula von der Leyen, the new President of the European Union Commission, and her team recognize the need for a more comprehensive approach to migration. This means working together with both countries of origin and countries of transit to create legal ways to bring in the skills Europe needs so badly. In September 2019, President-elect von der Leyen sent mission letters to all Commissioner-Designates. These letters explained each person's portfolio, objectives, and institutional responsibilities for the years 2019–2024. She also explained how these different roles work together to meet the political goals of the new Commission. Josep Borrell, the "chief diplomat" of the European Union, will work with Ylva Johansson (Home Affairs), Margaritis Schinas (Protecting our European Way of Life), and Jutta Urpilainen (International Partnerships) to manage migration within and to the European Union.

Commissioner Johansson will be in charge of most of the migration area. She will be in charge of the Directorate General for Migration and Home Affairs (DG HOME). Von der Leyen gave her the job of coming up with a "New Pact on Migration and Asylum." She will also have to fix the refugee system, work for long-lasting search and rescue efforts, fight trafficking and smuggling, expand Frontex's work, and put the rules about free movement in the Schengen Area into place. Also, her letter about her goal has two interesting side points:

> You should focus on ensuring there are genuine legal pathways to the European Union, both through the resettlement of those in need of international protection and through employment opportunities for skilled workers. I want you to work closely with the High Representative/ Vice-President and other Commissioners to develop stronger cooperation with countries of origin and transit. You should work closely with Member States to step up efforts to develop a more robust system of readmission and return. [their emphasis]

Clearly, the incoming president of the European Commission knows that legal ways to move to Europe need to be strengthened and that a good policy framework for migration requires close cooperation with partner countries.

The new Vice-President in charge of "Protecting our European Way of Life" will be in charge of Commissioner Johansson's responsibility. The media has criticized this title for using the same language that the far right uses to talk about immigration and for making it sound like there is a European way of life. In answer, Commissioner Schinas made it clear during his hearing that he sees the "European way" as a commitment to inclusion, solidarity, and diversity. His job will be to help put the "New Pact on Migration and Asylum" into action, and he will be focusing on:

> creating pathways to legal migration to help us bring in people with the skills and talents our economy and labour market need.

Lastly, Commissioner Urpilainen, who is in charge of "institutional partnerships" and the Directorate-General for International Cooperation and Development (DG DEVCO), will help the EC's efforts on migration by:

> to reach comprehensive partnerships with countries of migration origin and transit, bringing together all instruments, tools and leverage. You should therefore be ready to adapt bilateral funding to achieve our objectives on migration management. [their emphasis]

Even though all three portfolios still put a lot of stress on border enforcement and security, these statements are a welcome shift toward a more practical way of managing migration that could be good for the countries where people come from, pass through, and go to. It is interesting that the "carrot" of more legal ways to get to the U.S. is presented as a "stick" in the form of higher returns and re-admission agreements.

But there are also worrying signs of conditionality, which could involve using "all instruments, tools, and leverage" to get such deals while giving little in return. It says a lot that Commissioner Urpilainen's job description doesn't mention how important legal routes are for economic growth in countries of origin, transit, and destination, and how important it will be to promote these for decades to come. If the new Commissioners want to do a good job with their jobs, they will need to put money and time into both regulation and new legal ways for people to move to work.

Even though both more work on development and tighter border controls are needed, they are not enough to stop illegal movement. The outgoing Commission has admitted this. Europe needs new kinds of legal paths for migrants so that there are less reasons to move there illegally, the right kind of ability and skills come there, and admissions can be based on what the labor market needs. So, the fourth pillar of the European Agenda on Migration is supporting new legal paths.

So far, the focus on police and border security has gotten a lot more money and attention than this fourth pillar. But, as shown above, the incoming Commissioner's mission papers talk a lot about legal ways to do things. How can President von der Leyen and her team do that? Our "Roadmap for the New European Leadership" gives the European Commission four ways to make new partnerships to handle migration in a way that is good for everyone.

Make and support new legal ways for workers to move from one country to another that have more tangible benefits for both countries. Such efforts can add to the development and security work already being done in sub-Saharan and North Africa, lessening the need for illegal routes and giving Member States more power. The building blocks for these kinds of attempts have already been set up by the Commission. The fourth pillar of the European Agenda on Migration gives a framework for making and promoting new kinds of legal pathways, and the trade ties that are already in place with sub-Saharan Africa can be used as a starting point for talks. The Commission can help Member States by giving them the tools, ways to work together, and advice they need to put in place new kinds of legal paths. We agree with the results of the recent "Legal Migration Fitness Check," which asks the Commission to harmonize conditions, processes, and rights to make the system less fragmented.

Pilot and grow projects between Europe and sub-Saharan Africa that are part of the Global Skill Partnership. A Global Skill Partnership is a way to control migration, stop irregular migration flows, shape the conditions under which migration happens, and make sure that migrants come to Europe with the skills they need. It is also a tool for development in the place where it started, helping to build long-lasting institutions that create human capital and build capacity. As we've already talked about, the Commission is already helping similar projects, and it should keep doing so by increasing and diversifying the funding and support available to the MPF and letting Member States know about the chance based on their needs and goals now and in the future. The Commission should also look at similar projects, like the one between Germany and Kosovo in the building business, to see what they did right and what they did wrong.

Try out projects from the Global Skill Partnership in Africa. Many people from sub-Saharan Africa will not want to go to Europe. Instead, they will want to find work in their own area. The Commission can pay for agreements between a country of origin, like a developing country in sub-Saharan Africa like Niger, and a country of destination, like a more developed country in North Africa like Tunisia. With this kind of partnership, both local and foreign workers in the country of destination could learn skills that complement each other. For example, people from Niger could learn basic construction skills while people from Tunisia could learn middle-management skills. This makes a workforce that works well together and relieves pressure on both governments.

Be a voice for migration in Europe that is good. These kinds of activities will need more money, more coordination, more partnerships, and, most importantly, more leadership. Here, we talk about the many benefits that can come from moving if it is done right and suggest a way to get these benefits. But for this to work, it will take political will and commitment from Member States, as well as a positive message from the people across Europe. It is very important for the Commission to continue to speak out in favor of labor migration (which is necessary because of the changes in the population that are already happening) and to show off the good results from the test projects. We have a real chance to make new kinds of movement easier, but this will only happen if the Commission takes the lead.

What the Future Holds: Migration from Africa to the EU

In Europe, the words "migration" and "crisis" have often gone together in the last few years, as the number of undocumented people entering the European Union hit levels that had never been seen before between 2014 and 2018. The focus of public opinion and policymakers has been on problems that already exist and quick solutions. This is shown by the EU-Turkey statement from March 2016 and the deals with transit countries in Africa (Niger, Ethiopia, and Libya). In fact, efforts to "externalize" border control have been successful in reducing the number of illegal arrivals to Europe. In 2016, the number of illegal arrivals to Greece dropped by 98%, and since the middle of 2017, the same thing has been happening in Italy (-93%). Evidence shows, though, that even if restrictive migration policies work, they can't stop movement completely. Even though the "migration crisis" in Europe is over, this means that people will still come to the EU illegally after the crisis is over. So, long-term solutions are desperately needed.

At the same time, the idea that migration to the EU will increase in a way that can't be stopped seems to be growing. The population of Africa is expected to double between 2010 and 2040, from 1 billion to 2 billion people. This is four times as many people as live in the EU28. People are worried that population growth could have a "multiplier effect" on migration from Africa to Europe, which could lead to more people moving from Africa to Europe. In this part, we're going to try to find out if these fears are real. We try to figure out what might happen in the future by looking at data from the past 50 years of movement from Africa to Europe. We do this because we think that a projection of expected migration trends based on facts should be used to plan for the future and help the EU and its Member States make better plans and policies.

Like making any kind of prediction, this is not an easy job. Forecasting future changes in migration stocks is hard because different countries have different ideas about what migration is and because data are often sparse and have problems. Also, it is hard to get a complete picture of all the reasons why people move. Most attempts to guess the future of a population's demographics, then, treat migration as something that can't be predicted and instead rely on scenarios that assume migration stays at a constant level compared to past trends. Of course, forced migration and migration because of a fight are the hardest to predict and may need this kind of treatment. But structural factors could help us figure out how strong, where, and when other migration waves will happen.

In this chapter, we look more closely at one type of migration flow—the net outflow of people from African countries to the EU. By looking at how things have been in the past, we can see that many of the things that seem to cause bilateral migration on a world scale don't seem to be true in this case. Instead of showing a problem, we flip it on its head and try to directly predict future flows. In order to be as exact as possible, we give country-specific predictions of net emigration to the EU from 56 African countries and other territories identified by the United Nations Department of Economic and Social Affairs (UN DESA) between 2020 and 2040.

Even though the number of people living in Africa is likely to double in the next 50 years, we think that migration from Africa to Europe will not reach levels that have never been seen before. Even more, it is not expected that the number of Africans moving to the EU will rise in a straight line with the growth of the African population. Instead, the number of Africans moving to the EU is expected to stay pretty stable.

Our predictions show that migration from Africa to Europe will continue to be a problem for EU policymakers, but it won't be a problem like this has never been before. As a result, it will be important to get ready for what could be large migration flows from Africa, but the EU as a whole can handle this task.

Historical Patterns in African Migration to Europe

Before we can predict how people will move from Africa in the future, we need to know how they move now and how they have changed in the past few years. To do this, we mix data from the World Bank on migrant stocks over 10 years between 1996 and 2000 with data from the UN on migrant stocks over 5 years between 1990 and 2019. For the time period when the two datasets meet, they do not show the same number of migrant stocks. We combine them by figuring out a country-specific factor that we then use to fit World Bank (WB) data to UN data. For each African country, we divide the number of migrants reported by the UN in 1990 by the number of migrants reported by the WB in the same year to get this factor. Lastly, since WB data is given every 10 years and UN data is given every 5 years, we interpolated stock and population data for 1965, 1975, and 1985.

Today, about 3.1% of Africans live abroad, which is less than the average of 3.5% per person in the rest of the world. Compared to Europe, where 8.2% of the population lives outside the country where they were born, and Latin America, where 6.2% of the population has crossed an international border and now lives abroad, this share is even smaller.

Figure 8.5 shows how the number of Africans who live abroad as a percentage of the continent's total population changes over time (dotted line). If we separate migrants from sub-Saharan Africa (SSA) from migrants from

Northern Africa (NA), we can see that until very recently, the number of people living outside of their country of birth went in two different directions. Before 1970–1980, there were more people from sub-Saharan Africa living abroad than from North Africa. But as time went on, more and more people from Northern Africa moved away, while the number of people from Southern and Eastern Africa (SSA) stopped going anywhere. Since 2010, this trend has changed, but there is still a big gap between the number of Northern Africans and Sub-Saharan Africans who move abroad. Today, the number of Northern Africans living abroad is almost twice as high as the number of Sub-Saharan Africans.

Fig. 8.5 - Stock of African emigrants / Total population of origin

Source: authors' elaborations on UN DESA and WB data

We will now talk about Africans moving to the EU. To put this into perspective, we look at the 3.1% of Africans who have left their home country. About half of these people have left the continent. Even fewer people who have left the area have made it to the European Union. Only 26% of all African refugees are in the EU as of today. Still, as Figure 8.6 shows, there are almost ten times as many African refugees living in the EU in 2019 as there were in 1960. If we look back at the last thirty years, from 1990 to 2019, the number of African refugees in the EU has more than doubled, from 4.6 million to 10.3 million. This rise affects both people from SSA and North American countries. But because NA is close to EU countries, the number of NA migrants staying in the EU has always been higher than the number of SSA migrants. But in 1960, only 22% of all Africans living in the EU were SSA migrants. This share has slowly grown over the years, hitting 36% in 1990 and 46% in 2019.

Even though there was a "migration crisis" from 2013 to 2017, Africans still only make up 2.0% of the EU's total population. From 1% in 1990, this share has doubled, but most of that happened in the late 1990s and early 2000s, not now. It's also interesting to note that, even though several EU countries have made it harder for African migrants to use legal routes, movement from the continent hasn't stopped. Instead, most people are now using illegal routes. This shows that structural reasons that cause migration tend to be stronger than policies that try to stop it, making it hard to stop flows.

Fig. 8.6 - African migrants in the EU28

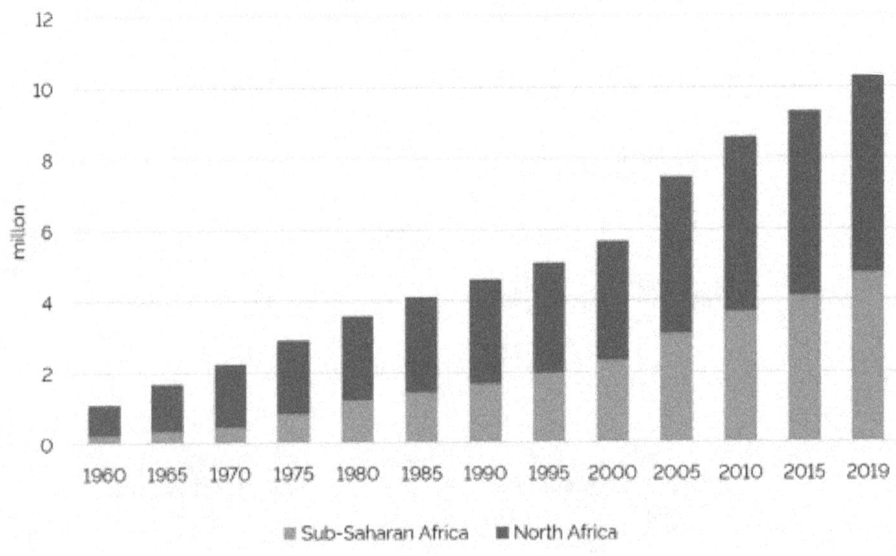

Source: authors' elaborations on UN DESA and WB data

What Shapes African Migration to Europe

Migration is hard to "stop" because African migration to the EU has mostly gone up regardless of policies on the European continent. This raises the question of what are the structural causes that actually shape migration from Africa to the EU. Below, we'll talk about net emigration, which includes people who move back to Africa from the EU. So far, there isn't much evidence of people moving back from the EU to African countries, except for a few cases that happened recently, like the return of Angolans.

Focusing on the amount of people from Africa who move to the EU has two big advantages. First, it lets us ignore movements inside of Africa as long as they don't cause big movements outside of Africa. Migration within Africa is much harder to plan for because almost all forced migration on the continent is part of it. As everyone knows, most forced migrants stay closer to where they came from than foreign migrants. For example, in 2018, two-thirds of forced migrants in the world had left their homes but not their country. These people are called internally displaced persons, or IDPs. Of those who did cross an international border, 85% went to neighboring countries or other countries in the same area. Forced migration is the hardest to predict, both in terms of time and intensity. This is because it is affected by sudden changes in political and social conditions in the countries of origin. Also, the number of forced migrants who decide to cross an international border can depend on a lot of hard-to-measure factors in the country of origin, such as where the conflict is happening, who is being targeted, and how likely they are to leave. By focusing on the number of Africans who move to Europe without being forced to, most of the forced migrant flows can be ignored. This makes it much easier to make predictions.

Second, focusing on net emigration to the EU as a whole instead of to each Member State lets us study the factors that cause migration to a macro-region. This gets rid of country-level differences that might hide deeper trends and gives us more accurate predictions (since we don't have to guess where African migrants will end up in Europe). Because we focus on the whole EU, there are a lot of non-EU citizens who move around in the EU, both legally and illegally.

Our predictions of migration flows over five years are based on a simple subtraction between stocks over five years. This is called "stock differencing." We know that there are other, more detailed ways to predict migration flows. However, we use this raw measure as a first approximation that other researchers may want to build on in the future. There are a number of reasons why stock differencing might both overestimate and underestimate net movement rates. It tends to overestimate how many people leave: Because children born to foreigners in EU countries are counted as migrants from the origin country as long as they don't become citizens of the host country (which can take a long time since no EU country has a pure ius soli law) and because it doesn't take into account return migration, which is low now but is likely to rise in the future. It could also lower the number of Africans who move to the EU net: 1) When Africans living in the EU get the citizenship of the host country or change citizenship within a five-year time, and 2) When Africans living in the EU die. Even with these caveats, we think stock differencing gives a good estimate of net migration, and we'll leave it to future study to try to improve our estimates.

We start with the results of gravitational models to look at variables of African migration to the EU. We want to find out, in particular, if the level of income, the number of young people, the presence of diasporas in the destination area, or the end of the Cold War has made Africans more or less likely to move to the EU. To do this, we first figure out the net emigration rates (the number of people who left the country of origin per 1,000 people who lived there at the beginning of the 5-year period), set all negative emigration rates to (very close to) zero, and take the natural logarithm of the variable that is left over. Then, we use UN data to figure out the total number of people and how old they are, and we use WB data to figure out the average GDP per person (in constant dollars). We figure out our regressions based on 5-year data for 53 African countries from 1965 to 2019. This spans more than 50 years. In Table 8.1, our results are shown according to three different models.

Table 8.1 Drivers of net emigration rates: Results of a multivariate panel regression

DV: Net emigration rates (logged)	**Model 1**	**Model 2**	**Model 3**
Net emigration ratestj (logged)	0.65 (0.04) ***	0.28 (0.04) ***	0.28 (0.04) ***
Migrant stock / pop	5.5 (4.3) ***	-20.4 (4.3) ***	-20.0 (4.4) ***
GDP pc (logged)	0.55 (0.33) .	-0.1 (0.7)	0.2 (0.5)
GDP pc (logged, squared)	-0.33 (0.22)		-0.02 (0.04)
Age group 15-35 (% of total population)	-0.6 (1.4)	-1.5 (1.4)	-1.6 (1.4)
Post-Cold War	0.19(0.14)	0.27(0.12) *	0.18 (0.12)
Constant	-2.7 (1.2) *	0.24(0.57)	-0.8 (2.0)
Year effects	YES	YES	YES
Fixed effects	NO	YES	YES
N	491	491	491

Standard errors in parentheses.

*Significance levels: . = .10 * = .05 ** = .01 *** = .001*

Model 1 shows the results of a traditional multivariate linear regression. It gives diasporas ("migrant stock/population") and past net emigration rates (the number of people who moved away from a country) new meaning. It also has a small effect on economic growth, but only in a linear way. The quadratic term has no effect. But a correct estimation in a panel setting should always include fixed effects: by only looking at variation within a country, fixed effects models avoid misinterpreting effects found at the "systemic" level that disappear when looking at the country level. In other words, they prevent some ecological fallacies. Fixed effects also have the important advantage of being able to account for things that are known to cause migration but don't change over time, like distance, ties to past colonies, or a common language.

Models 2 and 3 show the results after set effects are added. As can be seen, net migration from African countries to the EU seems to be driven by very few variables. First, it is shocking that the role of diasporas in bringing more people from Africa to the EU has been turned around. Even more surprising is the fact that family reunion is one of the main ways Africans move to many EU countries. Second, study from the past has shown that people between the ages of 15 and 34 are more likely to move. However, changes in the size of this age group in each African country's total population between 1960 and today don't seem to have had a big impact on migration from Africa to the EU.

Third, even economic growth seems to play a small part. Past research has shown that net emigration tends to follow a "hump-shaped" curve as a country develops: as a country moves up from low income levels, net emigration rates tend to rise as well, until the country's GDP per capita at purchasing power parity (PPP) reaches about 5,000 international dollars. After that point, as average wages go up, the (net) number of people leaving starts to go down, because people are both more able to leave and less likely to do so. Since the average GDP per person in sub-Saharan African countries is less than 4,000 international dollars at PPP, which is well below the peak of the so-called "migration hump," we should expect net emigration to rise as countries get better.

But Model 3 shows that this doesn't seem to be true for African migration into the EU over the past 50 years. Changes in economic development don't seem to have a big effect on migration flows, and the fact that the quadratic term isn't significant suggests that there isn't a "humped" relationship. To learn more about these results, we used our information to repeat the results of previous studies. We can find the "migration hump" when we look at all net departure rates from all countries in the world. However, when we only look at sub-Saharan African countries, we find that the trend is very different. Figure 8.7 doesn't show a "hump," but it does show what could be called a "migration plateau": net emigration rates from every African country to every other country in the world don't follow the typical inverted-U shape, but instead stay about the same at most levels of economic growth. Even if we only look at the flows from Africa to the EU28, the graph still looks more like a plateau than a hump.

Going back to our models, we also don't find strong evidence that net emigration rates from Africa to the EU28 are going up over time. When looking for a post-Cold War effect (on flows from 1990 to 1995 and later), only Model 2 finds a significant effect. On the other hand, yearly controls show a large increase from 2000 to 2005, which slows down from 2005 to 2015, but then picks up again in the last part of our series (2015 to 2019).

Fig. 8.7 - Relationship between GDP per capita and Net Emigration Rates

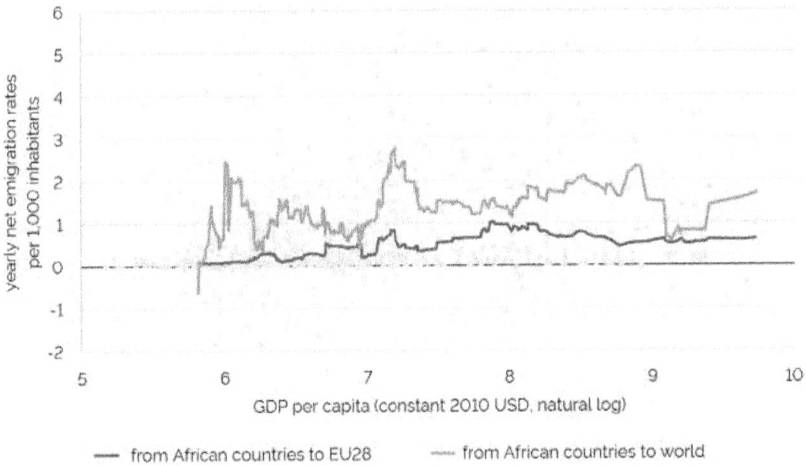

Source: authors' elaborations on UN DESA and WB data.

Solid lines represent moving averages (period 30).

The most important thing is that our models seem to show that past net emigration is a very strong forecast of future net emigration of Africans to the EU28. Then, it should be possible to predict how many Africans will move to the EU in the future without having to think about how many traditional variables will change in the future. Instead, you could just look at how many Africans left the EU in the past. But because the role of diasporas seems to have an unexpected effect on future flows, predictions based only on past migrant flows could overestimate future flows as the diasporas in Europe grow.

There might be something even better. Our models show that there is a strong link between emigration flows over time. This makes it important to look at stocks directly, or better yet, the percentage of a country's population that is made up of migrants. Clearly, if the number of Africans who moved to the EU in the past is a good predictor of the number of Africans who move there now, then the trends in the number of migrants should be even more similar and, therefore, easier to predict. This seems to be the case: when we look at how the number of African migrants living in the EU has changed over time, we find that they are very stable, with a 0.97 link between the number of migrants and their 5-year lags.

A possible worry could be that, since Africa's population is expected to double from 1 billion to 2 billion people between 2010 and 2040, even a strong trend in the recent past can't help us predict what will happen in the future.

But based on what has happened in the past, these fears should be put to rest. Between 1950 and 1985, Africa's population went from less than 250 million to more than 500 million, and then it doubled again to reach 1 billion by 2010. But the number of migrants relative to the population has been going in a much more steady and, therefore, more expected direction. For example, Nigeria's population has doubled twice, from 45 million in 1960 to over 100 million in 1995 and then to 200 million in 2019. This is in line with the general trend in Africa. Figure 8.8 shows, however, that the ratio of migrants to natives has followed a very clear trend.

Fig. 8.8 - Nigeria: total population and migrant stock ratio to the EU28

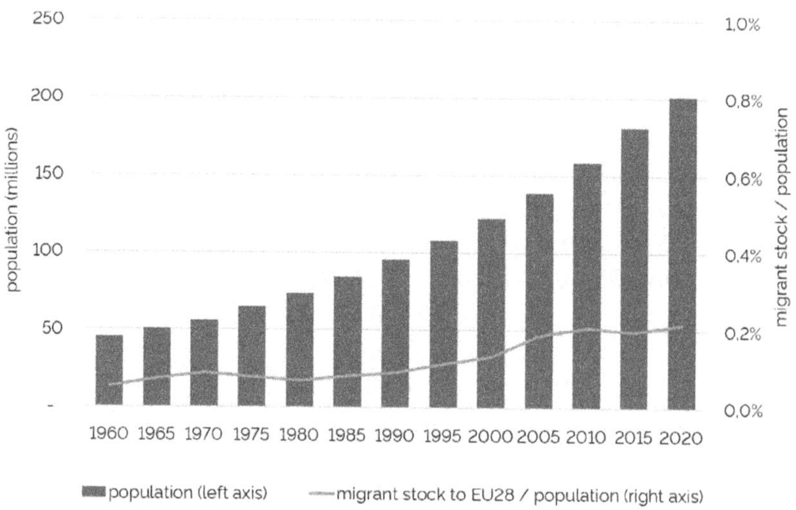

Source: authors' elaborations on UN DESA and WB data

Predictions for the Future

In the last part, we showed that net emigration rates from African countries are not strongly linked to most of the things that are usually thought to cause them. To predict how many Africans will move to the EU in the future, we look at how the ratio of Africans living in EU countries to the total population of each African country at the beginning of each 5-year period from 1960 to 2019 changes.

Our sample is made up of 56 of the 58 African countries and other areas listed by UN DESA. South Sudan and Mayotte are left out because they don't have any data on migrant stocks. We make predictions about how many people will move to the EU28 and to the EU27 (all Member States except the UK). Then, we use the low, medium, and high versions of UN DESA's (2019) population estimates to figure out how many African people will live in the EU between 2025 and 2040. Lastly, we use stock differencing to figure out how many people will leave the country in the future.

We use single, country-specific ARIMA (autoregressive integrated moving average) models to make predictions about how many Africans will move to EU countries in the future. We use the methods that Hyndman and Athanasopoulos (2018)25 have come up with to choose between different ARIMA model specs. Then, we look at the forecasts by hand and make changes for a few big countries where the chosen predicting method gives results that are clearly wrong. We are right about Djibouti, Eritrea, Morocco, and Tunisia, which are four of the 56 African countries in the EU27 forecast, and about six countries in the EU28 forecast, which are the same four plus Somalia and Zimbabwe. The results of our predictions are shown in Figure 8.9. As you can see, migration from Africa to the EU28 is likely to stay strong but not reach levels that have never been seen before. Even though Africa's population is expected to double between 2010 and 2040, migration rates from Africa to the EU are expected to level off and stay within the same range as in the past. In particular, our predictions say that between 220,000 and 300,000 Africans will move to the EU28 every year between 2020 and 2040, with 260,000 being the most likely number. About 200,000 of these will go to EU27 countries each year, while the rest will go to the UK.

This means that the number of African citizens living in the EU28 who do not have EU citizenship is expected to rise from 10.3 million in 2019 to between 14.9 and 16.6 million by 2040. Compared to the overall population of the EU28, which the UN says will be 513 million in 2019 and drop very slowly to 507 million in 2040, this is the same as a rise from 2% today to between 2.9% and 3.3% by 2040, with 3.1% being the most likely number.

Even though there is evidence that the changing age distribution of Africans did not have a big effect on net migration from the continent to the EU in the past, it could be interesting to see if our univariate models pick up any change in the near future. So, we recalculated our predictions by dividing the number of emigrants by the percentage of each African country's population between 15 and 34 years old. According to study, this age group is the most likely to move. Figure 8.10 shows the migration flows to the EU27 over the next five years. It shows our central forecasts and the sum of the country-specific estimates for people aged 15–34. Estimations of migration will be more different in the first ten years after 2020, but by 2040, they will all be about 200,000 per year. Overall, around 190,000 people are expected to move each year, which is less than the 210,000 people who move each year when the total population is used.

Fig. 8.9 - Past realisations and forecasts of net yearly Emigration from Africa

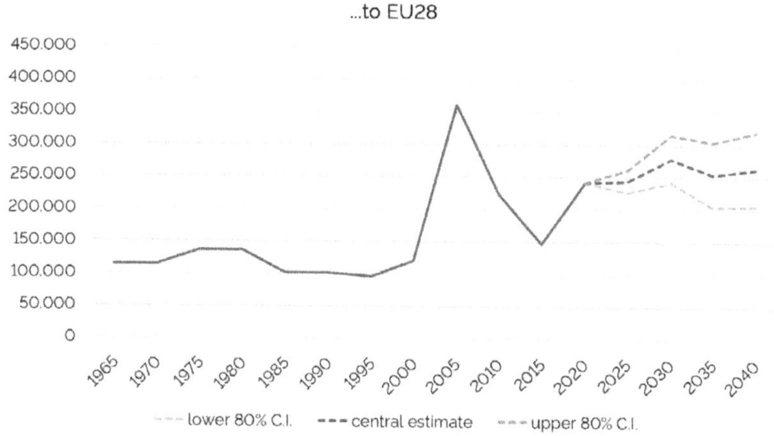

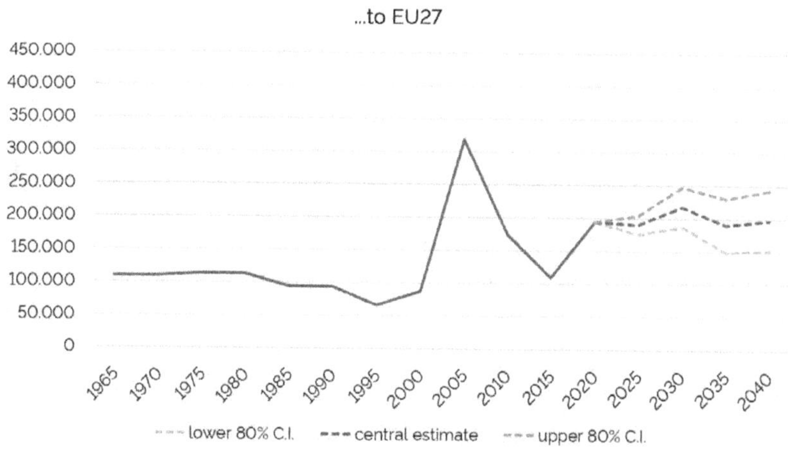

Source: authors' elaborations and forecasts on UN DESA and WB data

If we separate our findings into North America and sub-Saharan Africa, we can see that the countries from which people move to the EU are likely to change as well. We think that over time, the role of the sub-Saharan African (SSA) component will grow compared to the role of the Northern African (NA) component. Even though, as we saw above, North Africa is only made up of five countries, which make up just over 15% of the population of all of Africa in 2019. From 1975 to 2005, an average of 75,000 people from both North Africa and Sub-Saharan Africa moved to Europe each year. This shows how important distance is when figuring out migration trends.

Fig. 8.10 - Comparison of forecasts of migration to the EU27, Using Total Population or Cohorts Aged 15-34

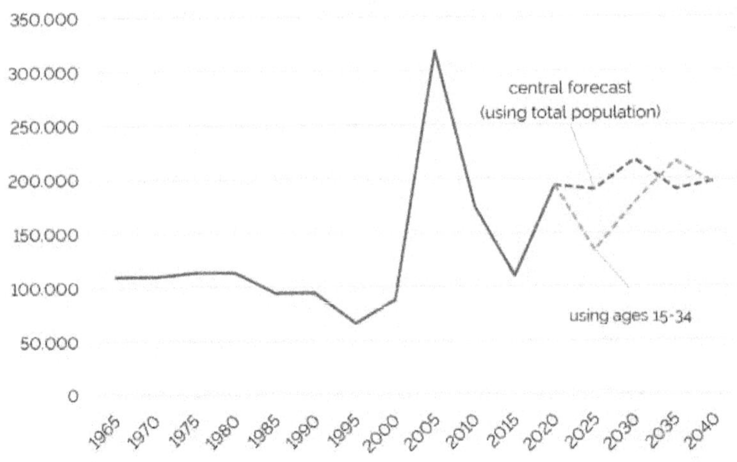

Source: authors' elaborations and forecasts on UN DESA and WB data

From 2005 to 2010, more people from sub-Saharan Africa (SSA) came to the EU than people from North America (NA). Around 60% of all migrants came from SSA. According to our predictions, this share will rise over the next 20 years and hit 77% of flows from Africa in 2040. This will slowly change the mix of African people living in the EU28 (see Figure 8.11). In 1975, about 70% of Africans living in the EU28 came from the five Northern African countries. This share had already dropped to 54% by 2020. Our main prediction is that expats from SSA will pass those from NA by 2030 and make up 55% of the total by 2040.

Lastly, because we use predictions for each country, we can rank the countries by how many people are likely to move to the EU27 each year over the next 20 years. Figure 8.12 shows both the center estimate of our forecast, which is based on the total number of people in each country, and the estimate based on the percentage of people in that age group.

First, it's important to know that our core forecast says Morocco and Algeria will still send the most people from Africa to the EU27 over the next twenty years. Senegal, Nigeria, and Somalia will come in second, third, and fourth, respectively. The UN says that in 2040, Nigeria will be by far the most populous country in Africa. Its population of 329 million people could be more than twice as big as that of Ethiopia, which is now the second most populous country in Africa. Still, Nigeria isn't thought to be the country with the most people moving to the EU. Simply put, this is because people from some countries are more likely to move than people from others. For example, Algerians and Gambians are much more likely to leave their countries than Nigerians and Ethiopians.

Fig. 8.11 - Regional composition of the total African population living in the EU28

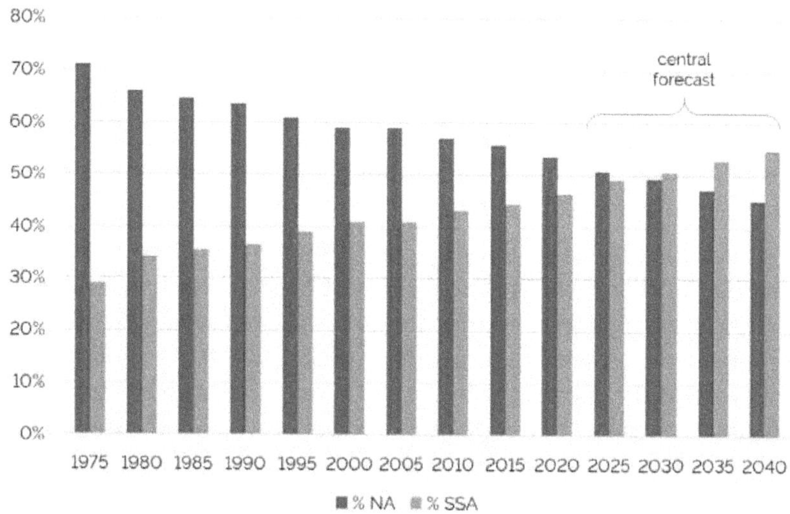

Source: authors' elaborations and forecasts on UN DESA and WB data

Fig. 8.12 - Country-level forecasts of net emigration to EU28

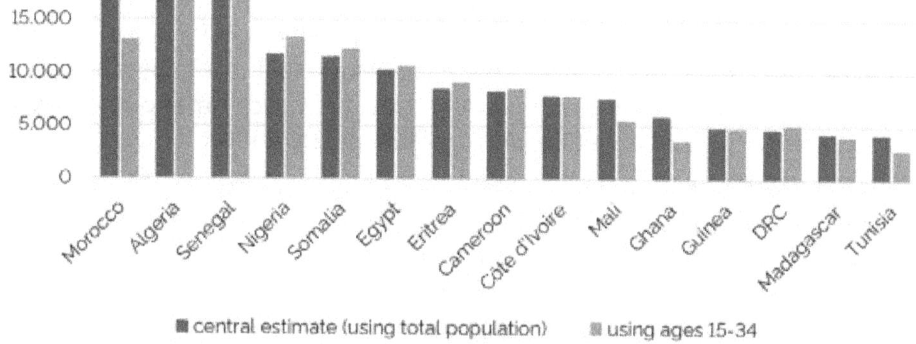

Source: authors' elaborations and forecasts on UN DESA and WB data

When we use the two different methods, the predictions of movement from Morocco to the EU27 are very different. This is something to keep in mind. This is very different from all other African countries, where central figures stay very stable (at least in absolute terms). This is because Morocco is one of the few countries in Africa where the number of people between 15 and 34 years old is not expected to grow much over the next 20 years. In 2040, there will be about 12 million people in this age group, compared to 11.6 million today. It remains to be seen if this will slow down net emigration to the EU, as predicted by migration models based on all the countries in the world, or if Morocco will be like other African countries, where changes in age distribution have little to no effect on future migration flows.

We don't think these country-by-country predictions are as solid as those for the whole continent of Africa, so we expect them to need more changes over the next few years. Still, EU and African policymakers may find them useful as a point of reference. In particular, they show which country or group of countries are likely to send the most people to the EU over the next 20 years. This helps everyone involved make better decisions about how to handle migrant policies.

Conclusion

Recent efforts to stop people from coming to Europe illegally by boat have been very successful. But these reductions were made possible by "externalizing" migrant control to transit countries through questionable bilateral deals. Also, their long-term viability is uncertain, especially if the incentives to move continue to be as structurally unfair as they have been over the past few decades.

In this chapter, we showed that the idea that it will be hard to control migration from Africa to Europe because of population growth is way off. Our predictions show that migration from Africa to Europe will continue to be a problem for EU policymakers, but it won't be a problem like this has never been before. As a result, it will be important to get ready for what could be large migration flows from Africa. This is a challenge that the EU as a whole can handle, especially if Member States plan ahead, help each other out, and work toward a better system for managing international migration.

We think that the number of people moving from Africa to Europe will be more than double the usual number from 1960 to 2000 (+116%), but will only go up by 7% from 2000 to 2020. This shows that the trend has changed a lot in the last 20 years, and it doesn't look like it will change a lot more in the near future. Between 2020 and 2040, we think the number of people moving from Africa to Europe will level off at about 260,000 per year. This means that by 2040, there should be between 14.9 and 16.6 million African people living in the EU28, up from 10.3 million in 2019. In terms of the EU28 population, this is the same as going from 2% today to somewhere between 2.9% and 3.3% by 2040, with 3.1% being the most likely number.

In addition to calming fears, better modeling of predicted migration flows from certain African countries can help EU policymakers decide what to do now and in the future. If we knew with enough accuracy which African countries will send the most people to Europe in the next 20 years, we could better focus our development aid and diplomatic efforts.

Our results show that leaders in Europe might not have as many options as people think. For example, the "migration plateau" says that the number of people leaving African countries won't change much even as their economies grow. At the same time, as African countries continue to grow, the EU's ability to use "carrots and sticks" to get reluctant partners to work together will become less effective, because each euro spent on the continent will be worth less and less.

On the other hand, there are still a lot of other policy tools that can be used to better control migration flows in the future. Customizing legal migration routes (especially for workers) to expected migration flows from certain countries can help the EU avoid the human suffering and economic losses that come from forcing migrants to move through illegal channels instead. Better regular channels could work better with programs that teach and train potential migrants while they are still in their home countries. This would save money and make it easier for them to fit in once they get to Europe. Lastly, spending money on integration policies that are right for people who are expected to come to Europe in the near future can help cut costs and put more attention on policies that work, like language classes or training for jobs in specific sectors.

In conclusion, knowing how people will move in the future is important if we want to move toward a way of governing movement that is based on realism instead of unfounded fears and myths. No matter what, there will always be some Africans who move to Europe. How governments choose to deal with this necessary change will determine how well everyone can use it.

Can Violent Conflicts Explain the Recent Increase in the Flow of Asylum Seekers From Africa Into Europe?

The big number of refugees and migrants coming to the European Union (EU) from other parts of the world is one of the most important things going on in Europe today. Between September 2013 and September 2015, four times as many people came to the EU each month seeking shelter. When asked about the most important problems facing the EU right now, Europeans were most worried about immigration by the middle of 2015. This problem has stayed at the top of their minds in the years since. People talk a lot about people from the Middle East, especially from Syria, which is in the middle of a civil war.

However, the number of people seeking protection from Africa tripled from 15,000 in the first quarter of 2008 to 44,000 in the first quarter of 2018. Since 2015, when the so-called refugee crisis was at its worst, the number of Syrians and Iraqis seeking asylum has gone down, but the number of Africans seeking protection has gone up. Most of the world's population growth is expected to happen in Sub-Saharan Africa in the 21st century. Because of this, experts and policymakers are paying more attention to African countries as places where people move to Europe.

In public conversations in Europe, war and political violence in people's home countries are often cited as major reasons why people seek protection in Europe. Many people think that wars and abuses of human rights in African countries are to blame for the rise in refugees. Between 2008 and 2018, there were more deadly fights in many African countries. The Armed Conflict Location and Event Data Project shows that the number of conflict-related deaths in Africa is going up. The number of deaths reached its highest point in the first quarter of 2015, when Boko Haram terror in Nigeria and nearby countries got worse. Later, the number of deaths went down again, but it was still a lot higher than the average of the previous years. On the other hand, many of these wars have been going on for years, but people from African war zones haven't been coming to Europe in large numbers over the past 10 years. Also, the overall trends don't have to show a link between violence and migration at the country (or person) level.

In this chapter, we try to answer the question of whether or not violent wars in African countries can explain the rise in people seeking asylum in Europe in recent years. Unlike most earlier studies on the subject, our quarterly measurement of conflicts and asylum emigration lets us study how political violence affects refugee flows in a more detailed way. For example, we can see how long it takes for a conflict to get worse before more people leave a country. We look into whether violent events and deaths have become more or less important in determining the number of refugees over the past few years. Lastly, unlike most other studies, we look at a lot of different control variables and modeling methods to show that the results are not affected by how the study was done.

Geographical Distribution of Asylum Seekers from Africa

It helps to start by looking at how people are spread out across the world. There are big differences between the countries of birth and the countries of destination. In Figure 8.13, the colors show how many African asylum seekers each European country took in. For African countries, the numbers show how many African asylum seekers moved to Europe. Between 2008 and the first quarter of 2018, most African refugees went to Italy (262,000 applications), France (238,000 applications), and Germany (219,000 applications). Central-eastern European countries, on the other hand, didn't get many asylum seekers. One exception was Hungary, where a lot of Africans came in mid-2015 before several countries along the so-called Balkan route closed their borders.

When the number of refugees coming in is compared to the total number of people living there, the picture is a little different (see the bottom panel of Figure 8.13). Between 2008 and 2018, 37 new protection requests came from African people for every 1,000 people living in Malta. This is by far the most number of refugees from across the Mediterranean for a country with such a small population. In Switzerland, there were 108,000 Africans who moved there in the last 10 years. This is 1.4% of the total population. Sweden and Norway are next, each with a population of 1%. Compared to this, less than 500 Africans asked for shelter in Poland (12 per million people) and 350 asked for asylum in the Czech Republic (35 per million). Spain was the target of a lot of refugee boats in the past, but between 2008 and 2018, it only took in 25,000 African refugees, or about 0.5 per 1,000 people.

Somalia has been the number one country of origin for asylum seekers, with more than 180,000 Somalis applying for asylum in Europe between 2008 and 2018. This translates to almost 2% of the population who fled to Europe within 10 years. 147,000 Eritreans, or 2.9% of the total population, sought refuge in Europe during this period. Even higher per capita outflows of asylum seekers were recorded in Gambia (31 refugees during 2008-2018 for every 1,000 inhabitants). In total numbers, Somalia and Eritrea are followed by Nigeria (132,000), Guinea (81,000), Algeria (72,000), and the Democratic Republic of the Congo (68,000). By contrast, citizens of southern African countries only rarely apply for asylum in Europe. This might be attributed to the fact that South Africa is a closer destination for refugees from, say, Zimbabwe, as are politically stable countries such as Botswana and Namibia.

Fig. 8.13 - African asylum applicants in inhabitants.

African asylum seekers, 2008-2018

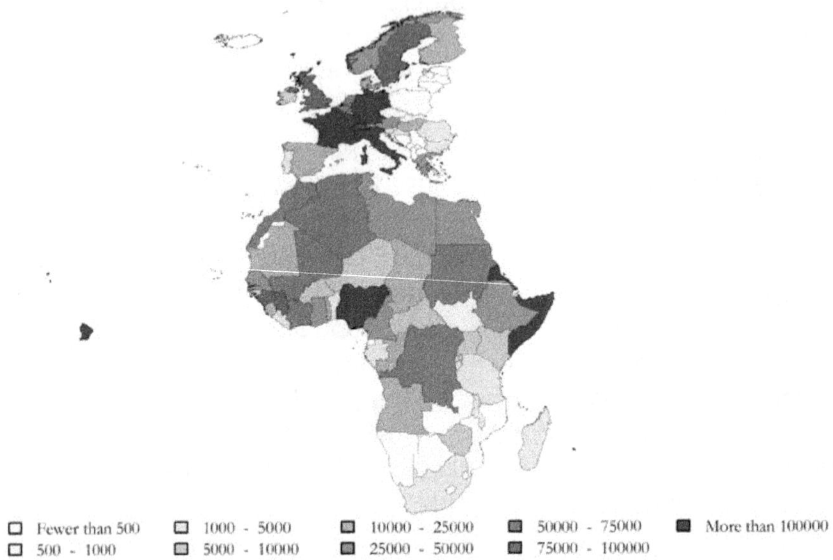

African asylum seekers per 1,000 inhabitants, 2008-2018

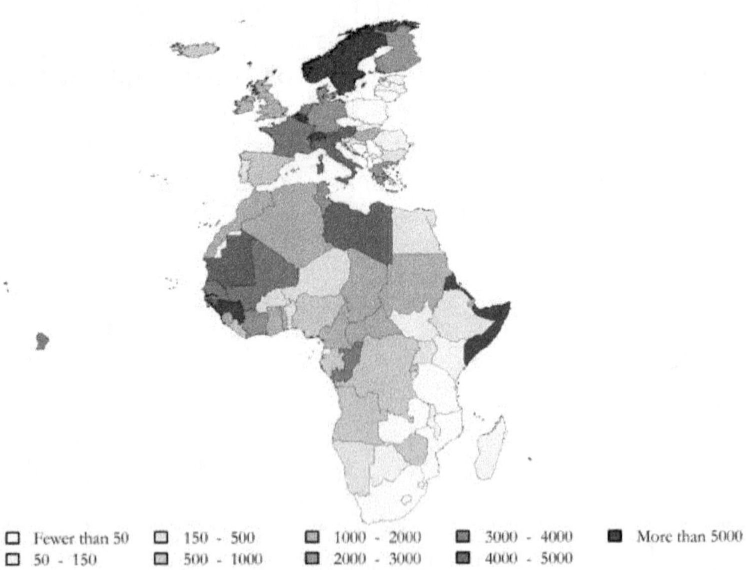

Disentangling these aggregate numbers, one can also look at trends in outflows from the most important sending countries in Africa and inflows into the most important receiving countries in Europe, respectively. Not all countries are responsible for the recent increase in refugee movements. Notably, numbers from Somalia have remained constant at a high level over the observed period of time, while a huge increase in inflows could be noted from Eritrea and Guinea, but also from Nigeria and Algeria. A similar pattern can be observed in the receiving countries. With the exception of a brief episode of "Arab Spring" refugee movements in mid-2011, levels were stable in the countries under study, with France attracting most African refugees. From 2013 on, however, the number of applications increased sharply, in particular in Italy and Germany. While some countries (e.g., Sweden) are receiving fewer refugees since the peak of the "refugee crisis" in 2015, the numbers have further increased in the most important destination countries (France, Italy, and Germany) since then. In the United Kingdom, by contrast, quarterly asylum applications from Africa in the first quarter of 2018 (2,500) remained constant compared with 10 years ago (2,100).

Since late 2013, the number of refugee seekers from several African countries has gone up a lot. This is around the same time that the Italian Navy started "Mare Nostrum," a search-and-rescue operation in the Mediterranean. Other countries joined, and the operation was replaced by a program run by Frontex, the border office of the European Union. In October 2013, more than 300 people died on a refugee boat off the coast of the Italian island of Lampedusa. This was one of the worst tragedies involving refugee boats that had ever happened. Since then, the Italian Navy and their partners have saved a lot of refugees, and a lot more people are now risking their lives in boats that shouldn't even be on the water. Cause and effect are hard to separate in a descriptive report, of course. It's possible that the number of refugees would have grown even if rescue missions hadn't been stepped up. Or, another way to look at it is that the fact that more people were saved and brought to Europe made more people risk the journey because they thought their chances of making it to the continent were higher. There's a good chance that at least some of the rise in migration is due to more search-and-rescue operations, more smugglers, and cheaper travel costs. It's hard to tell what will happen in this area in the future, especially since the right-wing Lega party took over Italy's ministry of interior in 2018 and closed the country's docks to private rescue groups.

Traditional models of movement at the microeconomic level assume that people move to improve their own lives. Migration happens when the expected benefit is greater than the cost of moving. Newer models of the rational choice paradigm are influenced by social psychology and look at both monetary and nonmonetary costs and rewards, such as how close you are to your family or how different you think other cultures are. This is true of the subjective expected utility (SEU) model, for example. People are thought to be logical actors who can figure out their own expected subjective utilities for different places. Personal goals like making as much money as possible, feeling safe, and being close to family and friends are given utilities, which are then multiplied by how likely it seems that each goal will be met at home or at possible migration places. The decision rule then says that players move if there is a place where the weighted sum of expected utilities minus the costs of moving is greater than the expected utility of staying where they are.

This concept works well with the general idea of "push factors" and "pull factors." The effects of violent battles on people's decisions about whether to leave or stay are clear: Many people think that violent battles make it less likely that they and their families will be safe where they live. This makes people more likely to want to leave their home country. So, violent battles have long been thought of as a major reason why people seek asylum.

But the question of how wars affect the prices of moving is not so easy to answer. For example, violent battles can wipe out savings or lower a person's income, making it harder to afford to move to Europe. In this situation, it's important to note that many refugees fleeing violent conflicts find shelter in other parts of their home country or in neighboring countries. Only a small number of them apply for asylum in Europe, even though many of them would probably benefit more from going there. This means that migration to Europe is often not possible, especially for poor countries, and that violent battles might make less people want to move to Europe instead of more. In the same way, there is consistent evidence that when wages and incomes grow in developing countries, emigration rates go up instead of down, or that there is an inverted U-shaped relationship between the two variables. Again, a likely reason for this is that higher incomes make it easier for people to pay for the costs of moving.

Because of this, many people who move to Europe come from countries with a medium level of economic growth, like North Africa. The poorest parts of the world have sent fewer people to Europe so far. When coming up with theories about how violent conflicts affect asylum movement, these results must be taken into account. Aside from the money needed to move to Europe, which can be affected by violent conflicts, moving to Europe usually takes time and planning, which may not be possible when a conflict starts. So, during civil wars or other disasters, there might be more reasons to leave, but fewer chances to do so. On the other hand, even if the amount of violence goes down again after a conflict, there may still be reasons to leave. Instead, people might wait to leave until, for example, they have the money to do so again. So, it's also important to think about the chance that a rise in violence could, after some time, lead to more people leaving their homes.

People have known for a long time that a number of other things can make people decide to move or not. Most of the time, economic reasons in the destination country are used to explain why people move from one country to another. For example, Ravenstein (1885) found in a well-known study that people tend to move to where there are jobs. Neoclassical theory believes that people will move between regions or countries as long as there are differences in wages, which are caused by different amounts of capital and labor on the market. So, since Africa's labor supply is growing a lot and there are still big gaps in income and quality of life between Africa and Europe, we should expect that many people will have strong reasons to move. Neoclassical theory's critics say that most people don't make decisions on their own. Instead, they say, decisions are made in the framework of family and other networks that need to be taken into account. For example, when people move to be with family again, economic factors like the number of jobs or income level are generally less important. As a result, many studies have found proof for migration networks. For example, "chain migration," which is less affected by economic factors or migration policies, is caused by family reunions and other factors.

Aside from the socioeconomic situation, people have known for a long time that geographic factors can help or hurt movement. Cohen, Roig, Reuman, and GoGwilt (2008) found that a model of only geographic and demographic factors can explain up to 64% of the changes in how people move around the world. Gross withdrawals are known to be affected by population size, growth, and age structure (Mayda, 2010): Most refugees are in their twenties, and if a country has a lot of young people, there are more people who could leave. It's particularly important to think about these demographic factors because Africa is the only continent where people are likely to keep growing at a very high rate into the 21st century. In the last 20 years, population estimates for Africa have always been changed up because, contrary to expectations, fertility has not gone down much in many countries. People have also talked about environmental issues and climate change as possible reasons why more people will leave Africa.

Lastly, laws about asylum and other things can affect the number of refugees who come to the European Union or a certain country in Europe. Even though asylum rules are becoming more similar across Europe, there are still differences between countries. So, countries with more open policies could be singled out or, on the other hand, countries could change their policies based on how many refugee requests they get. For example, Toshkov (2014) finds that when there are more asylum seekers, the rate of acceptance goes down, but when the rate of acceptance goes up, more asylum seekers come. But while the rate of official recognition can be seen, it is hard to measure administrative practice, such as deportations. Also, policy effects are complicated because they can affect many different countries and areas. For example, the Mediterranean routes to the shores of Spain, Malta, Greece, and especially Italy are the major ways that African refugees get into the European Union. This means that policy changes in these countries are very important for countries like Sweden and Germany that are taking in refugees. Also very important are the policies and actions of transit countries outside of the European Union. Events like a change in the government in Libya or political unrest in Mali can change the opportunities along the key routes to the Mediterranean. The eastern route from the Horn of Africa through the Gulf of Aden or the Red Sea is also important. During the height of the "refugee crisis" in 2015, many East African refugees joined Middle Eastern refugees on the Balkan path by going through the Arabian subcontinent. The last problem with modeling the effects of policy on asylum flows is that the way people in refugees' home countries think about asylum policies (for example, through stories spread on social media) might be different from the truth.

The following are the main points of our theoretical ideas. People move to Europe to apply for asylum if they think that doing so will benefit them more than any other choice they are considering. Physical security is one of the most important personal goals that need to be thought about before making this choice. We think that these goals and how important they are to us haven't changed much in the last ten years. With this assumption, there is no need to come up with a precise utility function that connects all of the personal goals that players could try to reach. This is because we want to know what caused the change in the number of refugees, not what caused the amount. We look at violent conflicts as one possible way that this rise in refugee migration might be happening. If everything else stays the same, a rise in violent conflicts makes it less likely that staying is better than going somewhere else. The expected chance of getting to Europe is also going down, though, because wars destroy wealth and can mess up transportation networks. So, other choices, like moving within the country or running away to a nearby African country, might be better for many. So, we think that violent battles will have an effect on the number of people leaving their home country, but we think that this effect will be small to moderate when it comes to people coming to Europe.

On the other hand, an increase in the amount of social capital might explain some of the rise in the number of refugees over time. If friends or family have already left the country and made it to Europe, they may be able to help with information and money that lowers the costs and increases the subjective benefits of moving to Europe, such as being close to family or people of the same ethnicity. The first movements might have started because of violent fights, among other things. Once a large group has settled in a new country, networks keep the migration going beyond the original reason for it.

Data and Methods

The number of refugee seekers from Africa (whose home country is called the "country of origin") in a European country ("country of destination") is the dependent variable we are interested in. It's important to remember that when we look at aggregate data, we can't make conclusions about individuals. For example, we can't say if it's "justified" for people from a certain country to flee to Europe, because that would be an ecological fallacy (even if violence and human rights violations are on the rise in a country, an individual asylum seeker might not have been affected, and if violence and human rights violations are on the rise in a stable country, an individual asylum seeker So, the things we look at are flows between two countries at a certain time, like the number of Algerians who asked for refuge in Austria in the first three months of 2008.

We look at quarterly data from 2008 to the first quarter of 2018, which is when the recent rise in African people seeking refuge in Europe could be seen. For the study, 48 African countries and 31 European countries were chosen, including all 28 EU Member States as of 2018 plus Norway, Switzerland, and Iceland. This choice gives us 1,488 pairs of 48 source countries and 31 target countries. Each pair is measured over 41 three-month periods, giving us a total of 61,008 observations. Eurostat (2018a) has information on how many refugee requests are made each quarter. Since the original measure has a very skewed distribution, we take the logarithm of bilateral flows. The level of violence in countries of origin is the major independent variable we are interested in. The Armed Conflict Location and Event Data Project has information about violent deaths and conflicts in the source countries. ACLED gathers geocoded, real-time information about violent protests and deaths in Africa that are linked to political violence. We put these numbers together to get quarterly counts of violent events and the number of people who died because of them. According to the ACLED definitions, violent incidents can be battles between two politically organized armed groups, as well as attacks on unarmed citizens by rebels or government forces, or riots. This definition rules out "normal" crime and limits the study to violence that is politically motivated. Both the number of events and the number of deaths from political violence have skewed distributions, so the log of both variables is also used.

Several other factors were added to the set of data. We figured out how many African refugee seekers each European country accepted every three months as a way to compare the policies of each country. This variable is the percentage of good decisions (i.e., recognition as a refugee under the Geneva Convention as well as subsidiary protection) on asylum applications from African citizens as a share of all decisions on Africans in the given quarter (calculated from Eurostat 2018b). On the other hand, we also figure out how many people from each African country were given asylum in Europe each quarter. Economic factors that change over time include unemployment rates and growth rates of gross domestic product (GDP) in the countries of destination. Several slow-changing or "sluggish" factors that don't change much over time are also taken into account. As bilateral time-constant factors, we use the distance between capitals (in 1,000 kilometers) and the number of years that a country was under colonial rule. We also figured out the size of the diaspora, or the number of people from the source country who were already living in the target country at the start of our time series. This number was based on citizenship. Other things that didn't change much over the 10-year time studied were the size and growth rate of the population, the level of socioeconomic development, and the degree of political freedom. All of these are important predictors of migration movements.

Due to the short amount of time that this study looked at, these effects (like socioeconomic growth in African countries) can't be seen in a unit fixed-effects model because there isn't much change that can be seen over time. But because these highly path-dependent factors haven't changed much in the past few years, they can't be to blame for the sharp rise in refugee seekers over the same time period, which is what we're trying to figure out. So, extending the time frame wouldn't help, since the fast rise in a short amount of time is our explanation, and past trends can't be the cause. Instead, we are focusing on a fine-grained study of things like violent conflict that can change quickly and did change quickly at the same time that a big rise in refugees was seen.

While all of the information is known about the main factors of interest, there are some pieces of information missing for several control variables. We filled in missing data using all of the information in the data set and Amelia II for R. Each statistical model was estimated separately in 10 multiple-imputation data sets, and the results (coefficients and standard errors) were combined using Rubin's (1987) rules.

Statistical Models

With T = 41 (quarters) and n = 1,488 (country dyads), our time-series cross-section (TSCS) data are a case of "medium-T, large-N". Three methods suitable for this type of data are considered: a fixed-effects (FE) model, a random-effects (RE) model, and a dynamic panel model including a lagged dependent variable (LDV). All of these models try to address the issue of unobserved heterogeneity in the data causing multiple measurements of the same unit to be usually similar to each other. In our case, wherein units are pairs of country of origin and country of destination, multiple observations of "Algeria-Austria" will likely be correlated and systematically differ from all observations of, say, "Nigeria-Italy." Most often, not all of these systematic differences can be explained by the observed variables, and it is usually suspected that historical, cultural, or other factors account for part of the autocorrelation among the errors.

The fixed-effects model alters the standard linear model by splitting up the error term into an idiosyncratic and a unit-specific time-constant term. It can be written as

$$yi,t=\beta Xi,t + ni + \mathcal{E}i,f$$

where yi,t is the outcome for country-pair i in quarter t, Xi,t is a vector of explanatory variables with regression weights β, ni is a time-constant error term varying across units only, and $\mathcal{E}i,t$ denotes the idiosyncratic error for each observation with mean zero and constant variance. In the FE model, ni may be correlated with the other predictors and is treated as "fixed" or equivalent to a set of n-1 dummy variables for each unit, thereby, eliminating all variance between units. Only differences within country-pairs are relevant in this model. For instance, if we look at all 41 observations for unit "Nigeria-Italy," are those observations with an above-average number of conflict deaths in Nigeria also the time periods for which asylum migration to Italy was higher? We cannot explain why migration from Nigeria to Italy has been generally higher than migration from Algeria to Austria, and all time-invariant predictors are disregarded by the analysis. But these consequences are in fact intended since we want to identify an effect responsible for the observed changes over time instead of some cross-sectional correlation . Moreover, both the dependent and the independent variable of interest show considerable variance over time, including sharp increases and abrupt decreases. Therefore, the problems associated with slowly changing path-dependent variables in FE models described by, for example, Plumper and Troeger (2007), do not apply here.

Since the aggregated time series are obviously nonstationary at least since around 2013, the danger of spurious regression exists since even two purely stochastic nonsta- tionary time series (random walks) are known to be significantly correlated more often than not . The shift in mean asylum flow over time might be attributed to "common shocks" (such as changes in European asylum policies in the Mediterranean) and can be captured by a time-specific error term 8t, which is equivalent to a set of dummy variables for each quarter (also denoted as time or period fixed- effects). We estimate a model with period effects and include seasonal dummies in all other models.

The random-effects (RE) model can also be expressed by Equation (1), but contrary to the FE model, in the RE model the time-constant error term g is uncorrelated with the other regressors. As a result, it only accounts for the serial correlation in the errors and there is still variance between units that can be explained by other unit-specific characteristics. The RE model (or random-intercept model in the terminology of multilevel models) can therefore take the effects of time-invariant variables such as geographic distance into account, which is not possible with FE. However, the central assumption that unit-specific errors are not correlated with the regressors is, as in most applications, not very plausible.

Finally, we add a lagged dependent variable (LDV) to the model. The LDV is included to capture all effects that led to a specific level of the dependent variable at the previous time point. Similar to the other approaches described above, the LDV model aims at capturing unobserved heterogeneity between the units under study—that is, the undisclosed reasons for why bilateral asylum flows are generally higher between one pair of countries compared with another pair . In the longer run, however, given sufficient variation over time and between units, different units might converge to different levels, which cannot be explained by the LDV . Therefore, unit fixed-effects might still be able to explain part of the variation between country pairs. A formal expression of this model can take the following form:

$$yi,t = \alpha + \gamma yi,\ t\text{-}1 + \beta Xi,t + ni + \mathcal{E}i,t$$

All models are estimated using the plm package for R . Since a sizeable number of potential control variables were suggested in the literature and compiled for this study , an important question concerns which of these to include in the respective model. A well-known issue with aggregate cross-country data is the usually high level of multicollinearity. For instance, level of socioeconomic development, political regime type, population growth rates, unemployment, and political violence might all be correlated in the countries of origin. Throwing all of these variables simultaneously into a multivariate model, we would likely not be able to figure out which of these variables is responsible for the observed differences in asylum emigration. A key issue with these "garbage-can models," as they are often referred to , is the fact that coefficients of independent variables of interest might be heavily sensitive to the inclusion or exclusion of one or two variables from the long list of controls without a plausible theoretical mechanism behind this finding. We attempt to tackle this issue by sampling only a few control variables at a time, estimating many different model specifications, and report the degree to which the main effects of interest change across these models.

Results

We start by looking at what makes people move from one country to another to get protection (see Figure 8.14). Figure 8.14 shows a plot of the standardized regression results from a random-effects panel model with factors that don't change over time, like the distance between countries. These results show which factors are usually causing more people to seek asylum between one pair of countries and another pair of countries. At this point, we can't say that a certain factor is the cause of the rise in refugee flows between two countries. Still, this study shows us a few interesting things. First, even though people can move around the world more easily now, distance is still one of the biggest problems with asylum travel. Also, the size of the diaspora is one of the best ways to predict refugee movements. This means that people who live in countries with small "expat communities" in Europe are less likely to try to get protection in Europe. There are more asylum requests when there are violent battles, but the effect isn't as big as it is when other things are taken into account. The analysis also shows that the amount of income in the country of destination is a more important pull factor than poverty in the country of origin.

Turning to within-country regressions, Table 8.2 shows that the only predictors of refugee moves from one country to another are those that change over time and change quickly. There are no near-static measures in the short run, such as GDP per capita. All models have fixed effects for country and time, as well as a dependent variable that is a bit behind the time. All of the other factors are also pushed back one quarter to deal with possible problems with endogeneity (or the direction of causality). Table 8.2, Model 1, shows that when the number of violent events goes up in the African source country, the number of asylum seekers in the European destination country goes up by a small amount. If the unemployment rate in the targeted country goes up, fewer refugees will go there, but the GDP has no effect on this. Changes in the number of refugees from a certain country are also linked to changes in the rate of acceptance of refugees from that country in Europe. This is an interesting finding, but the scope of this study doesn't allow for a more in-depth look at the direction of cause and effect and the mechanisms behind this correlation. Another important finding has to do with how long it takes for the number of refugees to rise after the number of violent events goes up. We find that violent conflicts are important predictors of refugee flows, both right now and one quarter later. After that, there is no longer any statistical meaning. This means that yearly measurements of asylum movement dynamics, which are most often used in the literature, may miss this relationship because the link has already gone away after a year, but it can be found with ease within a few months.

Fig. 8.14 - Predictors of quarterly bilateral asylum flows from Africa to Europe, 2008-2018 (random effects model).

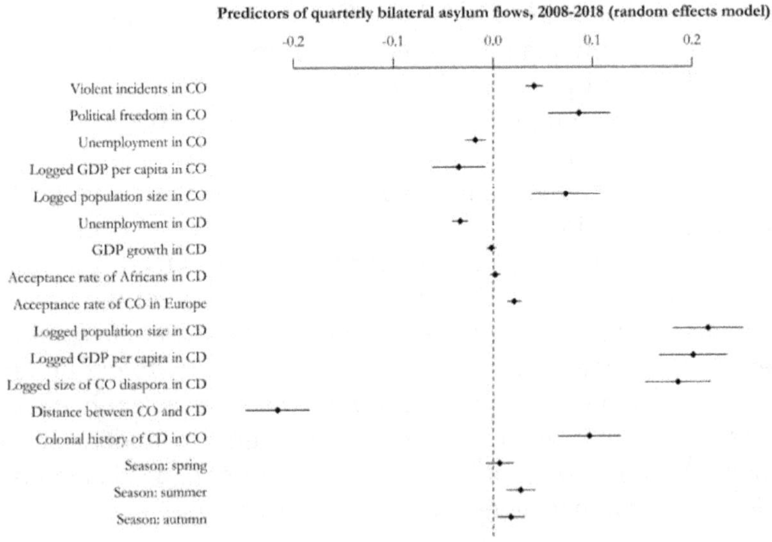

Note. CO = country of origin, CD = country of destination. Figure plots standardized regression coefficients and 95% confidence intervals (i.e., 1.96 times the standard error, which is scaled to conform to the standardized coefficients by the same scaling factor). N = 61,008 (48 countries of origin, 31 countries of destination, 1,488 country-dyads, 41 quarters).

Table 8.2 Time-Variant Predictors of Quarterly Bilateral Refugee Flows From Africa to Europe, 2008-2018

	Panel				
	All countries (1)	COs with high recognition rate (2)	COs with low recognition rate (3)	CDs with high recognition rate (4)	CDs with low recognition rate (5)
Log(Asylum flow, t-1)	.436*** (.007)	.444*** (.009)	.421*** (.011)	.435*** (.008)	.433*** (.010)
Log(Conflict incidents, t-1)	.010* (.004)	-.004 (.005)	.030*** (.005)	.005 (.005)	.014* (.006)

Unemployment rate in destination, t-1	-.008*** (.001)	-.005* (.002)	-.011*** (.002)	.009*** (.002)	-0.15*** (.002)
GDP growth in destination, t-1	-.001 (.003)	-.001 (.004)	-.001 (.003)	.008 (.004)	-.006 (.004)
Acceptance rate for asylum seekers from country of origin in Europe, t-1	.080*** (.024)	.144*** (.039)	.013 (.027)	.104*** (.031)	.059 (.034)
Country of destination's acceptance rate of African asylum seekers, t-1	-.007 (.015)	-.005 (.023)	-.010 (.017)	075*** (.016)	.097*** (.027)
Country-pair fixed-effects	Yes	Yes	Yes	Yes	Yes
Period fixed-effects	Yes	Yes	Yes	Yes	Yes
Observations	59,520	29,760	29,760	28,800	30,720
R^2	.202	.212	.190	.201	.209

Note: CO = country of origin, CD = country of destination. Panel models with country-pair and period fixed effects. Data sources: see text.

$^*p < .05$,

$^{**}p < .01$,

$^{***}p < .001$.

People leave their African countries for Europe for many different reasons, which shows that each African country is different. People often talk about whether or not many "refugees" are actually "migrants" who have little chance of getting protection under asylum rules but use the asylum system because they don't have any other way to get to Europe. Again, it's important to stress that we can't use our aggregate statistics to look at the reasons why each person seeks refuge. We also don't want to get into a conversation about "deservingness" or whether European authorities are too lenient or too strict in how they decide who gets asylum. But it might be interesting to make a distinction between countries in Africa from which a lot of people get help in Europe and other countries whose citizens are mostly turned away when they try to get asylum. Eritreans (81%) and Somalis (67%), on the other hand, are mostly accepted as refugees or given subsidiary protection under the Geneva Convention, while this is true for only a small number of Algerians (4%), Moroccans (8%), and Nigerians (17%). So, based on the overall acceptance rate, the group is split in half. This comparison is shown in models 2 and 3 of Table 8.2.

Strangely, this means that violent battles only cause refugees to move to countries in Europe with low acceptance rates. This finding could be taken in many different ways. It's possible that the present acceptance rates have little to do with what's going on in the countries of origin because European officials make their decisions based on wrong or old ideas about the countries of origin. On the other hand, high acceptance rates might be seen as a sign by people in the source country that going to Europe is possible, and this might be the case even when there is peace. On the other hand, people from other countries whose countrymen were mostly turned away from Europe only risk moving there if the security situation suddenly gets worse. Otherwise, they don't risk moving and being turned away. In the same way, refugees go to European countries that are known for being strict about deciding who gets asylum when there is a lot of conflict (Model 5 of Table 8.2), while countries that make decisions more leniently get applications no matter how violent things are in the country of origin (Model 4).

So, there is some evidence that violent conflicts cause people to seek refuge, but not in all sending and receiving countries. But how much of the huge rise in asylum seekers seen during the study period can be linked to violent conflicts getting worse? Conventional measures of model fit, like R2, show that this prediction doesn't do a very good job of explaining things in general. We also use a split-sample design by time period to see if the effect of violence has gotten worse during and after the so-called refugee crisis, when the number of people asking for protection went up by a lot.

Figure 8.15 shows how things turned out. The y-axis on the right shows the number of refugee requests from Africans in each European country every three months. This is shown by the gray line.

Fixed-effects panel models are estimated within three distinct periods: 2008-2011, 2012-2014, and 2015-2018. Regression coefficients are shown for the effect of violent conflicts on asylum flows and for the lagged dependent variable, indicating the degree to which asylum flows are self-reinforcing and driven by past flows (y-axis on the left). The findings suggest that as the number of refugees increased, violent conflicts became less important as a driver of asylum flows. Instead, refugee movements increased between countries that had already witnessed high bilateral flows in the previous quarter. This is evidence against the assumption that an increase in violent conflicts can by itself explain the rising number of African refugees coming to Europe during and after the peak of the refugee crises. Rather, violent conflicts seem to have played a role in the early phase during which events such as the "Arab Spring" took place, but the later development points more toward "cumulative causation."

This means that emerging diasporas in European countries attract more and more refugees beyond the initial cause(s) that prompted the earlier refugees to flee their countries.

Fig. 8.15 - Effects of lagged flows and violent incidents on current asylum flows, by period, and quarterly number of African asylum applications in Europe.

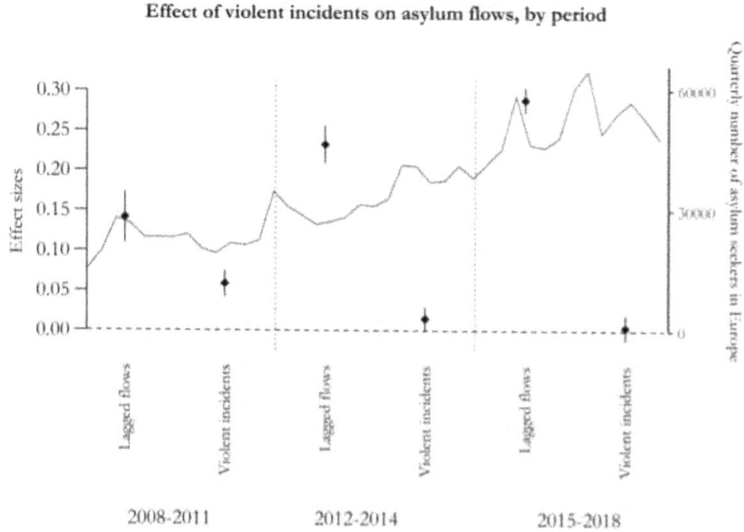

Note. Plot shows unstandardized regression coefficients and 95% confidence intervals from three separate models estimated within the different time periods. All models include country-dyad and time fixed effects, a lagged dependent variable and violent conflicts as the sole other predictor of quarterly bilateral refugee flows.

Checks

With this kind of data, there are a lot of different ways to describe it. For example, many different sets of control variables are equally plausible from the start, but they might lead to different results for the major effect that is being studied. One reason for this is that there is often a lot of multicollinearity at the country level when it comes to things like income, schooling, or war. This problem has been called "model dependency" by Ho, Imai, King, and Stuart (2007). Schrodt (2014) says that one of the biggest mistakes in research today is that academics often don't think about how their results would change if model and control variables were changed in small ways. Because of this, different researchers can look at the same data and come to different opinions. This has clear effects on study and policy that are based on unstable empirical evidence.

Table 8.3 Results from 1,000 models with different specifications for the effect of violent incidents on bilateral asylum flows, by time period.

Statistic	Time period		
	2008-2011	2012-2014	2015-2018
Average t-value for violent incidents	5.89	3.71	2.34
Percentage of models in which violent incidents was a significant predictor of asylum flows at $p < 0.05$	70.2%	56.2%	46.4%

To fix this problem, we repeated the results shown in Figure 8.15 using different statistical models. In the way of what is called the random subspace method in machine learning, we first pick at random from a list of 29 possible control variables. These include both time-variable and time-invariant or nearly time-invariant factors, such as geographic distance, past colonial experience, diaspora size, political freedom, sensitivity to climate change, and different economic and demographic indicators. We also use chance to decide if the model should include one or more of the following: fixed effects for the country of origin, fixed effects for the country of destination, fixed effects for time, lags of the independent variable (and, if so, how many time steps), and lags of the independent variable.

Table 8.3 shows the results of estimating 1,000 randomly adjusted models for each of the three different time periods shown in Figure 8.15. First, it's clear that models rely on each other over time: Changing the statistical significance of an effect can be done by picking a different set of control variables or a different estimator or time lag. In line with the results shown in Figure 8.14, we find that over time, there is less and less proof that violent conflicts cause people to seek asylum. During 2008–2011, a clear majority of all models showed a statistically significant effect. During and after the "refugee crisis" of 2015–2018, however, this was not the case. This backs up the idea that violent conflict is usually a reason why people flee to Europe. However, the recent sharp rise in asylum seekers is not likely to be caused by a worsening of conflict. Instead, it is more likely that migration is a self-reinforcing process.

Conclusion

Over the past 10 years, the number of Africans seeking protection in the European Union has tripled. Even though there were a lot of violent battles in many countries, this does not explain why there are so many more refugees now. On the other hand, we find that since the so-called "refugee crisis" of 2015, the statistical link between violent conflicts and asylum movement is actually weaker than it was in years past. This may show that the link between wars and refugee flows is more complicated than is usually thought. One possible explanation is that violent conflicts like the "Arab Spring" helped increase the number of people coming to Europe in the beginning, but that later changes were mostly caused by migratory networks, so that migration became a self-reinforcing process.

Lastly, a change in the way opportunities are set up could also be an ad hoc reason for this rise: Even though people had reasons to move in the past, they now think they are more likely to be successful. This could be because of the increase in sea rescue tasks and the fact that the "Dublin" rules are no longer being followed. These rules say that asylum requests must be made in the country where the person first set foot in the EU. However, how these rules are followed changes from country to country and over time. For example, while the total number of asylum requests in Germany went up from 48,000 in 2010 to 477,000 in 2015, the number of "Dublin transfers" to other European countries went down from 2,400 to 2,000, which is 0.4% of the total number of asylum requests. So, refugees who enter the European Union probably have a better chance of getting to and living in the country they want to go to (where relatives already live, for example). Also, many requests for asylum are turned down, but official rejections don't always lead to forced actions like deportations. There isn't a lot of good information about these problems, so it's hard to model in quantitative studies the opportunities created by laws, policies, and administrative practices, as well as how refugees see these issues through social media or second-hand accounts.

If you look into the future, it seems possible that migration from Africa to Europe will continue to be very important. The number of people living in Africa is expected to double by 2050. Also, everyone agrees that, at least in the short and medium term, future progress in socioeconomic growth will lead to more people leaving the country, not less. In many European countries where African immigration was low before the last decade, there are now large communities of people from different African countries. Based on our data, this is likely to make more people want to move to Europe in the coming years and decades. One of the biggest unknowns is, of course, where European immigration policies will go in the future. In many national parliaments, the number of right-wing parties has grown over the past few years. This could mean that European governments will take more restrictive steps. On the other hand, in the past, governments from different political groups were not very good at stopping or managing migration.

Chapter 9
Factors Influencing Asylum Seeking in Europe

Using the push/pull forces framework, this chapter looks at what makes people try to get asylum and how well this framework can explain asylum-seeking in European countries. Our analyses show that most pull and push factors give good reasons for why people seek asylum. There is a lot of power behind the different political push factors and proximity variables. But the business cycle, as measured by the unemployment rate in the country of birth and the country that takes in refugees, does not explain why people move from one country to another. In this way, migrations for asylum are different from migrations for work, which are based on job possibilities. Based on these results, it seems likely that some countries will get more refugee seekers because of their unique qualities. To solve this problem at the European level, host countries need to work together more. It is also important for the EU's asylum strategy to cover "push factors," or the real reasons why people want to come to the EU.

In 2015, there were more people from the Middle East than ever before coming to the EU. More than a million people travelled by boat and on land to get to different EU Member States. This wasn't something new. In the past, a lot of people from countries with problems moved to Europe to live in places that were safer and better off. European countries are the most popular places for refugees to go because of where they are and how well their policies for settling asylum seekers are set up.

Most refugees go to countries close to where they came from or that are entrances to Europe because it is easier to get there. During the Yugoslav refugee crisis in the early 1990s, about 400,000 people left their homes and went to live in other countries. During the height of the Arab Spring, a lot of people from Tunisia and Libya moved to the islands off the southern coast of Italy. The problem with the refugee crisis of 2015 was that a lot of refugees showed up all at once at the borders of a few EU Member States, mostly Greece, Italy, and Hungary, but these countries could only take in a limited number of refugees. The Dublin Regulation, which is the core of the Common European

Asylum System and says that the "first EU country of entry" is important, makes this fact even more complicated.

Both in the US and in the EU, people had different thoughts about the refugee situation. The media focused on how dangerous things were in the war-torn countries of the refugees and in the sea, which made people feel sorry for them. But the arrival of an unheard-of number of refugees at Europe's borders caused fear and gave political power to far-right parties who linked this disaster to feelings against immigration.

The Syrian war is getting worse, which is the immediate cause of the refugee problem. However, people have different ideas about what started this war in the first place. This suggests that the number of refugees going to Europe depends on political factors outside of the EU. Compared to the huge amount of work that has gone into improving border controls at both the national and EU levels, not much has been done to end the civil war that has made the country unstable. So, the EU is getting a shock from the outside because of the sudden changes in the area around Europe.

In this area, empirical studies aren't as far along as they could be, and political migration has become more important. There aren't many studies because it's hard to get complete data on asylum-related migration, and even when you do, macro-level statistics can only tell you so much about why people seek asylum. Real things, like migration flows, are often left out of aggregated statistics. Individual and case-specific factors are more important. But the refugee crisis of 2015 made it clear that some macro-level factors can explain how much migrant pressure there is on Europe. This study looks at what caused the flood of refugees into European countries from 2008 to 2014, before the unprecedented crisis. Based on migration studies that have already been done, we put the factors into three groups: (1) pull factors, (2) push factors, and (3) proximity factors. We then built a model based on the gravity model, which is often used in observational studies of international trade.

This is how the chapter is put together. In the next section, we'll talk about how big the refugee problem was and how it got worse, as well as how the EU and its member states dealt with it. The third one is about the causes of the refugee problem. In order to find these factors, it looks at the research literature about what makes people become refugees. The fourth is a scientific study to find out what causes the wave of refugees into Europe. The result gives the EU's policy on refugees a direction for the future.

A "refugee" is someone who has been forced to leave his or her country because of abuse, war, or violence and cannot safely go back. This is different from "economic migrants," who want better living conditions or higher incomes.

In fact, though, it's hard to tell the difference between refugees and economic migrants for two reasons. First, the reasons why both groups risk their lives to leave their homes are often very identical. Second, a person may be in both groups at the same time, because areas with a lot of crime are also often very poor. Still, it is possible to analyse the differences between refugees and other types of travellers.

Europe has always had to deal with pressure to move from North Africa and the Middle East. Both political and economic factors have pushed people to move. Stats can help people understand how bad the refugee situation in Europe is. Frontex, the European Border and Coast Guard Agency, says that between 2009 and 2013, the number of illegal aliens coming into the EU stayed the same, at around 100,000 per year. In 2014, the number jumped all of a sudden to 284,000, mostly because there were so many more Syrian refugees as the civil war there got worse. In 2015, more than a million people who had to leave their homes came to Europe. The unofficial number may be higher than what Frontex said because they only counted cases that were found and didn't count Syrian refugees in Turkey and other countries that are not EU members. Jordan, which has a population of 6.5 million, and Lebanon, which has a population of 4.5 million, both publicly took in more than 635 thousand Syrian refugees.

From 2009 to 2013, there were 323,000 asylum seekers and refugees. In 2014, that number almost doubled to 627,000. In 2015, there were more than a million. Most people who asked for asylum came from countries where wars were getting worse, but their home countries were very different. Up until 2012, most people seeking refuge came from Afghanistan. Since 2013, though, more people are coming from Syria.

Dilemmas for EU's Approach to Refugees

Since what happened in Yugoslavia in the early 1990s, the EU has made a strategy for asylum at the EU level. In the setting of the EU's institutions, "venue shopping" was used to explain how asylum policy changed over time. At first, it was between governments, but it was able to break free of these limits. It is now part of the Justice and Home Affairs (JHA) cooperation, which deals with things like the free movement of citizens and immigration problems that cross borders. Asylum policies, which are often thought of as part of the larger "EU migration and asylum policy," stayed mostly as guidelines and frameworks for how to deal with refugees and coordinate different practises between Member States, rather than as a set of shared rules. In the system of parallel powers, the issue of asylum has always been controversial and met with resistance from EU Member States. It has taken a long time and a lot of work for Europe to come up with a set of rules that everyone can agree on for asylum. But different talks about asylum problems at EU venues led to better protection for asylum seekers in a number of European countries, with a "judicialization" effect that grew over time.

Since the Arab Spring, the number of refugees and people looking for asylum has gone up, and countries' policies on refugees have reached the point where they can no longer work without more cooperation. The Syrian war getting worse and the huge number of refugees showing that the current policy structures are not enough.

Two questions sum up the main problems with the EU crisis structures. The first is about the Schengen Agreement, which made it so that most internal border checks were no longer needed in the Schengen Area. Once refugees enter the territory of one of the Schengen signatories, they can move to other countries without having to go through border checks, regardless of whether they are officially recognised as refugees or not. Most refugees prefer to settle in countries like Germany and Sweden where they can get better treatment and live in better conditions. Most North African illegal immigrants want to live in France or the UK because they speak the same language or have historical ties there. Based on the Schengen deal, the current EU border system has made it harder and harder for border countries to let refugees into their countries without looking bad. Countries that share land or sea borders with non-EU countries had to tighten their border controls, and some of them had to do this until they could no longer do so. This is especially true for places like Greece and Italy that have long coasts or borders and a lot of islands. Greece and Italy asked the EU for more money to help them control their maritime borders and run places where refugees can stay. Some countries put back limited border checks between themselves and other Schengen States. When it comes to illegal movement, one Schengen State with weak border controls can be used as a way in to the whole Area.

The second question is how to house and move refugees who are mostly living in certain countries. The 'first country' concept is written into the Dublin Convention, which 12 EU Member States signed in 1990. By EU Regulation 343/2003, the Convention became part of the EU law system. Based on the first country concept, it decides which Member State is in charge of looking into the asylum request. This is mostly to stop people from asking for refuge in any country they want (called "asylum shopping") and staying in the EU without any country taking responsibility for looking into their request (called "orbiting"). Most refugees get into the EU through countries like Italy and Greece, which are called "gateway countries." However, most refugees prefer to go to other

EU members that are known for having better living standards and being more welcoming to refugees. Under the Dublin Regulation, as more and more people move to the area, the refugees have to take on more and more responsibility.

Theoretical Perspectives

The push/pull theory has had a big impact on studies of labour migration, which in turn have had a big impact on studies in this area. The theory comes from neoclassical economics and explains why people move by looking at wage differences and models of the supply and demand of work. The push/pull theory believes that people are 'rational' economic agents who move because they want to improve their own lives, such as by getting higher wages and more job opportunities. This theory has been used to study different kinds of refugees, such as those who move within Europe and those who move to seek asylum. In this system, the things that make people decide to move are put into two groups: push factors and pull factors.

People leave their home countries because of many different push forces. Most of the time, violent battles and religious or political persecution push people to look for asylum. There are also things like poverty and unemployment that have an effect. Many people think that people who claim to be refugees but whose main goal is to make money are "fake refugees." But it's hard to tell the difference between purely political reasons and a mix of push forces. People usually think that economic goals make political goals stronger in the push factor framework.

Pull factors bring people to a different place. Because of their good qualities, some countries get more immigrants than others. Common reasons are higher wages, better living standards, more job prospects, and the chance of getting refugee status, such as the rate of recognition. This framework is highly influenced by the theory of labour migration, which says that migrants can follow their plans to move without major problems. However, this doesn't always match up with the reality of forced migrations.

When it comes to asylum, the push/pull model is different from that of voluntary labour movement. First, the choice to move for work is made by weighing the benefits of moving and the costs of leaving home. Theories of voluntary movement usually show how migration works in terms of costs and benefits. When people are looking for asylum, the costs of leaving are often not taken into account when making choices about migration. This is because migrations are not believed to be voluntary. Second, it's not clear that people who are looking for protection know everything there is to know about where they are going. Most people think that people who are looking for protection make smart decisions about where they want to go. But because they are in a hurry and are in unusual situations, asylum seekers may not know everything about the different conditions where they are going.

Recent studies have tried to give a full picture of these things. The first is that 'push' factors are specific to the home country and include both political and economic factors. Violence is the single best way to predict how many refugees will move to Europe and other places around the world. The results of these empirical studies that are based on macro-data are backed up by studies that are more focused and use surveys and interviews. Poverty is a second thing that pushes. Several studies have found that poverty is not the only reason people become refugees, and that most people who seek asylum are running away from violent battles or persecution. Since violence is not a control variable, there is no clear link between the economy and people looking for refuge. But violence goes hand in hand with unstable income and very high jobless rates. Poverty may push someone to decide to ask for protection.

The second is that "pull" factors have to do with how the location is received. Most of the pull factors that are specific to a country of destination are based on the idea that asylum seekers are logical and that information is pretty well spread. Economic theory said that people looking for refuge would apply in countries with higher incomes and high chances of settling down, like those with low unemployment and high growth rates. Some studies looked at how a generous welfare system is linked to people looking for protection. But some studies disagree on these pull factors, saying that economic indicators, like the amount of income in the country of destination, don't have much of an effect on asylum applications. Some studies also tried to figure out how things like the acceptance rate and visa policy affect the number of refugees coming in and what that means.

The gravity model has also been turned into an empirical tool that works well for foreign trade. The empirical model, which has been changed to work for both one-way and two-way asylum flows, includes measures of "proximity" between places of origin and destinations. They have to do with history (ties to former colonies), culture (language similarities), and geography (physical distance). They are also based on studies of labour movement. In the research, there are different ideas about how these factors affect movement between two countries. For example, some studies find that a common colonial past has an effect on the way people move from one country to another, while others don't find any effect once other factors are taken into account. The same difference is found in research on asylum migration. Some studies find that a colonial connection has a big effect, while others find that a shared colonial past doesn't change the way people seek asylum. But linguistic closeness and distance seem to have big effects on the flow of asylum seekers. This is clear when you look at the network effects that come from linguistic proximity.

Table 9.1 is a summary of these factors based on what empirical study has found. Both people agree and disagree. Most scholars agree that "violence" is a push factor and that "income level of destination" is a pull factor, but only to a lower extent. For the rest of the factors, the findings depend on how well the data is covered and how the different variables are put together. This could be because most studies believe that information is shared well between different asylum groups or use macro-level data without taking into account why each person is seeking asylum.

Methods

We construct an equation based on the standard gravity model that is widely used in empirical studies on international trade and investment. The gravity model derives from the supply/demand functions; countries with larger GDPs tend to export/import more than do others. The model has been used in empirical studies in migration with specific adaptation to each research purpose and is well suited to the push/pull framework of asylum-related migration as well. Our equation takes the number of asylum applicants from all countries to European countries as a dependent variable and includes push/pull factors as explanatory variables with country fixed effect. In the equation, R_{jt} means the number of refugee applicants to a host country '*i*' from origin country '*j*' in '*t*' year. X_{it} refers to explanatory variables of host countries (pull factors) and Y_{jt} are variables related to origin countries (push factors). Z_{ijt} represents variables indicating the combination of push and pull factors (time-variant) or geographical and cultural/historical proximity (time invariant). μ_{it} (or μ_{jt}), an error term, consists of p, (or pj), an error derived from lack of observable variable, and ε_{it} (or ε_{jt}), a disturbance term derived from individual country effect.

$$R_{ijt} = c_1 + c_2 \sum_{k=1}^{l} X_{it} + c_3 \sum_{k=1}^{m} Y_{jt} + c_4 \sum_{k=1}^{n} Z_{ij(t)} + \mu) \text{ (Pooled regression estimation)} \quad (1)$$

$$R_{ijt} = c_1 + c_2 \sum_{k=1}^{l} X_{it} + c_3 \sum_{k=1}^{m} Y_{jt} + c_4 \sum_{k=1}^{n} Z_{ij(t)} + \mu_{it}(\mu_{it} = \mu_i + \epsilon_{it}) \text{ (Fixed effect estimation – host country)} \quad (2)$$

$$R_{ijt} = c_1 + c_2 \sum_{k=1}^{l} X_{it} + c_3 \sum_{k=1}^{m} Y_{jt} + c_4 \sum_{k=1}^{n} Z_{ij(t)} + \mu_{jt}(\mu_{jt} = \mu_j + \epsilon_{jt}) \text{ (Fixed effect estimation – origin country)} \quad (3)$$

Table 9.1 Empirical studies on determinants of asylum seeking based on macro-level data

Categories	Factors	Assumption	Studies
Push factors	Violence (political stability)	Violence in homeland causes fleeing home for asylum seeking abroad.	Neumayer (2005), Hatton (2009) Davenport, Moore, and Poe (2003), Moore and Shellman (2004)
	Poverty (income level)	Asylum seeking is motivated by poor living condition in origin countries.	Schmeidl (1997), Davenport, Moore, and Poe (2003)
	Unemployment	Loss of job and extended long period of unemployment increase the possibility to choose fleeing home.	Hatton (2016)
Pull factors	Income level of destination Job opportunities (measured by unemployment)	Asylum seekers have same motivation as economic migrants have.	Peridy (2006), De Haas (2011)
	Level of welfare/ social atmosphere	Asylum seekers prefer to settle in countries with more generous system and they are relatively well informed about destination countries.	Neumayer (2004), Beenstock, Felsentein and Rubin (2015)
	Migration policy		Hatton (2004), Neumayer (2005), Barthel and Newmayer (2015)
Proximity	Recognition rate Past colonial ties Linguistic similarities	Countries with a shared colonial past and similar languages have similar institutions and culture. It is easier for asylum seekers to adapt themselves to destinations.	Hatton (2004), Keogh (2013), Toshkov (2014) Havinga and Bocker (1999) Neumayer (2004), Barthel and Neumayer (2015)
	Geographic distance	Relatively low cost of move from home countries.	Neumayer (2005), Yoo and Koo (2014)

Taking account of the motivation of political asylum or fleeing home countries, we develop three groups of variables for the determinants of asylum seeking. The first group, 'pull factors', works as a centripetal force, pulling asylum seekers to destinations. These variables are mainly associated with the status of destination countries, such as GDP, population, per capita GDP, and social expenditure. For example, asylum seekers may prefer to migrate to larger and higher income countries with generous social spending, because once admitted with official refugee status, they could more easily integrate into local society, taking advantage of social benefits. Larger GDPs or populations of destinations result in a larger absorptive capacity of refugees into these societies. The variables in the second group, are 'push factors', which causes people to flee their homes and seek asylum abroad. We divide these variables into political and economic variables. For political variables, we use governance indicators related to 'political stability' from the World Bank's World Governance Indicators (WGI), after transforming all values as positive number for log transformation purpose. The economic variables are per capita GDP and unemployment rates in origin countries. The basic assumption is that economic situations and political stability affect the motivation of seeking asylum abroad. The distinction between asylum seeking and economic migration is often unclear, given that the two motivations work in parallel. This is particularly true in the recent surge of migration into the EU. Inspired by models of labour migration, the difference in per capita GDP between countries of origin and destinations is also included. This variable captures the combining effect of push/pull factors in economic terms. For third groups of variables, our equation includes 'proximity' variables such as past colonial ties, shared language as well as geographical distance. Table 9.2 summarises the variables used in the empirical analysis.

The dataset covers seven European countries (Germany, France, the UK, Italy, Spain, the Netherlands, and Sweden) for the period 2008 to 2014. These countries received 2,556,770 applications for asylum seeking during this period, that is more than 70% of total application to EU Member countries. The number of non-EU origin countries is 145 and together provide 7,154 observations. Our dataset has methodological challenges from the fact that bilateral asylum flows have a number of zero values. This is mainly because our dataset includes many small countries that are geographically far from Europe. For instance, more than 70 countries have no asylum seekers to Germany in 2008. Log transformation that is widely used in gravity models does not capture observations with this zero value and reports them as a missing observation. However, dropping observations in the way that an ordinary least square (OLS) method may lead to sample selection bias, in the sense that mainly large countries are 'selected'. Another practical problem is that regular OLS estimates could be inconsistent in the presence of heteroscedasticity . On the other hand, the nonexistence of refugees may have important implications for the analysis; origin countries are too small in population and too far from the destination, or too 'peaceful'. Thus, there are no asylum seekers originating from these countries. In order to tackle with this problem, we use a non-linear gravity model based on Poisson pseudo-maximum likelihood (PPML) estimation that has been widely used in empirical studies.

Table 9.2 Variables and Data

Variables			**Contents or research assumptions**	**Source**
Dependent variables			Number of asylum applicants (from national origin to destination)	Eurostat
Independent variables			Research assumption	
Pull factors	GDP per capita		Economic easiness	Eurostat
	Population		Absorptive capacity of a country	Global Insight
	Unemployment rate		Chance of finding a job and ease of establishment	Eurostat
	Social expenditure (% of GDP)		Level of the general attitude of society towards humanitarian issues	OECD SOX
Pull and Push factors	Difference in GDP per capital between home and destination	Standard variable used in migration studies		
Push factors	Economic variables	GDP per capita Unemployment rate	Assumption: Economic situations of origin countries may affect the motivation of asylum seeking.	Global Insight
	Political variables	Political stability	Assumption: Political stability and good institution of origin countries tend to reduce asylum seeking abroad.	World Bank
		Government effectiveness		
		Rule of law Corruption		

Proximity variables		Geographic distance	Proximity variables	CEPII
		Common language	Standard dummy variables used in a gravity model	
		Colonial link		

Analysis

Depending on the goals of the study, we use different methods and settings for different variables when doing regression analysis. The findings are shown in Table 9.3. The results of regression are shown in the first three columns, which are based on pooled regression. Column 1 shows the result of the basic analysis, which looks at both pull and push factors and focuses on social spending (SOXd) and the difference in GDP per person between the host country and the country of origin. Column 2 shows the result of the model that takes into account both the unemployment rates of the country of birth and the country of destination. This common equation shows why people move to work in other countries. In column 3, there are proximity variables with different pull and push values. In columns (4) through (6), the results of a regression analysis with factors in the same settings and fixed effects of the host country are shown. In columns (7) through (9), the results are shown for the fixed effects of the country of origin. From column 10 to column 12, you can see the estimates with time fixed effects.

Here are our conclusions. First, most studies show that the number of asylum seekers is linked to the per capita GDP and population growth of the destination country, but not the per capita GDP of the country of origin. Most sets of studies from Column (1) to Column (12) show that their coefficients are statistically important. We got the same results when we used the GDPs of countries instead of their populations. When it comes to economy and people, bigger countries tend to have more refugees than smaller ones. Also, the gap in GDP per person between the country of origin and the country of destination seems to be linked to the number of asylum seekers in all tests. So, people who move to Europe for refuge are like people who move there for work. The number of refugees coming to Europe can be explained by the usual factors of labour movement. The number of refugees is also closely linked to the amount of money spent on social programmes. Second, unemployment doesn't seem to be a good way to explain things about refugees. The number of refugees coming into a country is linked to its unemployment rate. This means that countries with a lot of unemployed people tend to get more refugees. This is the opposite of what has been happening in Europe since the global financial crisis with labour movement. Also, the jobless rate in the countries where refugees come from does not have statistically significant coefficients or is linked to the number of refugees leaving. So, it is too soon to say that all refugees are looking for jobs abroad because of economic pull forces. Third, political security is one of the most important factors that explain why people leave their home countries as refugees. We used all six of the World Bank's governance factors, and most of the time the results were the same. Last but not least, distance gives statistically significant negative values that range from -1.31 to -0.83. In foreign trade, distance is seen as a cost of transport and is seen as a barrier to trade between two countries. (Krugman, 1991) says that distance may be linked to things like culture similarities and historical ties. Distance has a strong effect on migration linked to asylum. Given that the average coefficient of distance in gravity models of trade is -0.6, refugee migration is more sensitive to distance than trade flows. This is why a huge number of refugees went to just a few European countries in 2015. Shared languages and past colonial ties are two other indicators of closeness that give mixed results. Only one choice with origin country fixed effects (Column 9) shows positive and statistically significant coefficients for language, and the past colonial link does not show consistent and significant coefficients.

Table 9.3 Result of the regression analysis: PPML estimations

	Pooled regression			Fixed effect (host country)			Fixed effect (origin country)			Fixed effect (year)		
	(1)	(2)	(3)	(4)	(5)	(6)	(7)	(8)	(9)	(10)	(11)	(12)
$GDPPC_i$	4.12***	6.90***	4.04***	11.41***	12.69***	12.03***	4.05	6.36***	1.94	3.86***	5.86***	2.00
	(0.80)	(0.77)	(1.12)	(4.07)	(3.81)	(4.59)	(2.51)	(0.75)	(4.36)	(0.74)	(0.77)	(1.24)
$Population_i$	0.93***	1.11***	1.04***	11.60**	8.26	7.12	0.91***	1.07***	0.92***	0.89***	1.00***	0.75***
	(0.13)	(0.15)	(0.19)	(5.91)	(8.75)	(8.52)	(0.11)	(0.12)	(0.16)	(0.13)	(0.15)	(0.21)
Unemploy-ment$_i$		0.69***	0.44*		1.81***	1.33*		0.65***	0.24		0.27	-0.57*
		(0.20)	(0.24)		(0.66)	(0.78)		(0.21)	(0.30)		(0.22)	(0.32)
SOX_i	1.27***		0.57	5.87**		4.49	1.39***		1.15*	1.04***		1.70**
	(0.37)		(0.59)	(2.66)		(4.01)	(0.34)		(0.59)	(0.38)		(0.66)
$GDPPC_j$	-0.10	-0.26***	-0.06	-0.11*	-0.24***	(0.03)	-1.53**	-1.79*	-1.43	-0.12*	-0.24***	-0.05
	(0.07)	(0.05)	(0.09)	(0.06)	(0.05)	(0.09)	(0.75)	(1.00)	(1.11)	(0.06)	(0.05)	(0.09)
$Population_j$	0.21***	0.18***	0.15***	0.21***	0.19***	0.16***	2.30**	4.96**	5.11***	0.21***	0.20***	0.17***
	(0.03)	(0.04)	(0.04)	(0.03)	(0.04)	(0.04)	(1.00)	(1.95)	(1.96)	(0.03)	(0.04)	(0.04)
Unemploy-ment]		-0.20*	-0.21**		-0.15	-0.16		-0.34***	-0.36***		-0.17	-0.18
		(0.11)	(0.10)		(0.10)	(0.10)		(0.09)	(0.09)		(0.11)	(0.11)
Pol. Stabil-ity$_j$	-1.90***	-1.94***	-2.02***	-1.87***	-1.87***	-1.93***	-0.59	0.10	0.08	-1.83***	-1.82***	-1.88***
	(0.26)	(0.37)	(0.38)	(0.25)	(0.36)	(0.36)	(0.44)	(0.48)	(0.49)	(0.25)	(0.35)	(0.36)
$Difference_{ij}$	149***		2.18***	1 49***		2.23***	1.27		3.41	139***		2.12***

	(0.50)		(0.68)	(0.49)		(0.68)	(2.07)		(3.49)	(0.47)		(0.65)
$Distance_{ij}$	-1.31***	-1.30***	-1.2***	-1.27***	-1.26***	-1.18***	-1.15***	-1.01***	-0.83***	-1.29***	-1.28***	-1.20***
	(0.09)	(0.11)	(0.11)	(0.09)	(0.11)	(0.11)	(0.22)	(0.23)	(0.26)	(0.09)	(0.11)	(0.11)
Language			0.25			0.33			1.36***			0.28
			(0.24)			(0.23)			(0.32)			(0.23)
Colony			-0.32			-0.30			-0.79**			-0.35
			(0.23)			(0.22)			(0.33)			(0.22)
Constant	-49.47***	-59.83***	-55.35***	-167.45***	-141.32***	-171.17***	-44.53***	-61.18***	-56.93***	-4434***	-47.97***	-34.14***
	(6.05)	(8.15)	(9.40)	(48.32)	(36.04)	(55.45)	(5.34)	(9.40)	(9.84)	(5.27)	(8.39)	(10.40)
Observa-tions	6,854	3,799	3,630	6,854	3,799	3,630	6,372	3,484	3,381	6,854	3,799	3,630
R-squared	0.13	0.14	0.14	0.16	0.16	0.17	0.36	0.47	0.51	0.15	0.16	0.16

*Note: (1) Standard errors in parentheses: *** $p < 0.01$, ** $p < 0.05$, * $p < 0.1$. (2) All variables are log-transformed before conducting regression analysis except dependent variable (number of asylum seekers) and dummy variables.*

In the end, we think the following. First, push and pull forces are a good way to explain why people seek asylum in Europe. More people who want refuge come from countries with low incomes and unstable governments. More refugees tend to go to countries with more money and more people (or a higher GDP). The amount of money spent on social services could also help explain things. Distance from a place has a bad effect on how many people move there. This shows that, in general, the same factors that affect migration for work also affect migration for protection. But factors like shared language and colonial ties don't seem to explain why people move to seek refuge. Second, looking for work is not a good way to explain why so many refugees are coming to Europe. The unemployment rates of both the country of origin and the country of destination do not explain why refuge seekers choose to go to certain countries. Our results show that the generalised model based on labour migration does not fully describe how an asylum seeker makes decisions. It is not clear that people looking for protection know everything there is to know about where they are going. Images of the location that aren't too clear may be enough to decide where to go. So, forced migration is clearly different from movement that people choose to do. Under the "Dublin rule," people who want to seek asylum in Europe have to choose a way to get there. As long as this rule is being talked about, the effects of each variable on the flow of refugee seekers may change. Third, political push factors, like political security, have a strong ability to explain why people seek asylum and move. All factors that have to do with how stable a country's government is and how strong its institutions are are strongly linked to the number of refugees from that country. Most of these factors, which are caused by problems in the home countries of migrants, are out of the hands of the target countries. This will remain the biggest problem for asylum policies in wealthy countries. The problem of refugees in Europe is a clear sign of this.

Conclusion

With a push/pull factors framework, this chapter was supposed to look at what causes people to try to get shelter and see how well this framework can explain asylum-seeking to European countries from 2008 to 2014, before the refugee crisis in 2015. We have tried to connect each macro-level variable to a specific study assumption about asylum-related migration and tested each assumption against real-world data to see if it is true. Most of the real-world studies done in this area have been based on theories of labour migration, which assume that asylum seekers make decisions and take actions that make sense. Our study used a similar method, but we tried to add something new by making the following claim: Because they are "forced" to leave their home countries, asylum seekers may not know everything there is to know about where they are going. When political "push" factors are too strong, economic "pull" factors, which are especially important in labour movement, may not be enough to explain where someone chooses to seek asylum.

We have shown that most variables linked to push and pull factors explain well why people seek asylum in Europe. Countries with high incomes and lots of people are more appealing than countries with low incomes and few people. The level of income in a place seems to be a big factor in choosing to move there. This is shown by the good effects of differences in income between countries of birth and countries of destination. But the business cycle shown by the unemployment rate did not explain why people were looking for work because they were seeking refuge. As has been said in previous studies, this could be because the overall level of economic development in these countries has a bigger effect on how economically attractive target countries are than short-term changes like economic growth and unemployment rates. So, migrations for refuge should be handled differently than migrations for work, which are based on job openings. Our work shows that political push factors have a big effect on migrations related to asylum. Even more than for foreign trade and investment, the variables of proximity are important for this type of migration. Refugees tend to gather in countries that are close by, and the refugee crisis of 2015 showed this closeness effect.

In recent migrant history, the refugee crisis of 2015 was like nothing that had ever happened before. This made it important to do more research in this area. Several policy ideas have been put forward so far, both at the EU level and at the level of each individual country. This is shown by the European Agenda on Migration, which was presented by the European Commission in 2015.

What do you think this study means for policy? First, pull factors and proximity variables show clearly that some countries have more asylum seekers because of things like their level of economic growth, their social security systems, their location on the map, and their historical ties. So, a few countries would be the main places where people would move, which could get out of hand. Such migration trends could upset the Schengen agreement, which is important for the Single Market to work. In this way, the refugee problem is an issue for all of Europe. It is much bigger than what a few host countries can handle, so EU Member States need to work together more. Second, it's easy to see what we can learn from this situation. "Nice fences don't make for nice neighbours." "Good neighbours make good neighbours." This well-known saying is true about cross-border policies for refugees, and our results back it up. Strong border controls and strict recognition procedures in the "securitization" process, which is about making a "good fence," may stop refugees from coming into Europe in the short term. However, this won't stop a large number of refugees from close-by countries that are politically unstable and have a lot of people. This means that the EU's refugee policy should cover "push factors," or the real reasons why so many people are seeking asylum. In this way, preventive humanitarian measures, such as development aid to help build institutions, should be made in line with security policies from the outside. This would be another way that the refugee problem would affect other parts of policy.

Cross-Country Analysis and Recommendations

The size of the crisis in 2015 caused budget shortfalls for both the European Union and the case study countries of Germany, Sweden, and the Netherlands. These shortfalls were fixed by moving resources, raising overall budgets, and using emergency funds. In the case of the Netherlands, policymakers even took money from reserves for the future to help with growth. Even though this kind of response from governments and organizations is expected, fewer people know that these budget changes came at the cost of other humanitarian, development, and asylum programs that helped people before they thought about moving to Europe. During the crisis, it was also clear that EU and case study country officials thought their answers were not enough, given the size of the job and the political crisis that followed. European officials took part in almost constant changes to the budget to keep raising budget lines that dealt with migration, sometimes more than once in a short time. Adding euros or krona to the problem, on the other hand, did not always make it easier to deal with the situation.

Migration is now the main focus of European policymakers. Irregular migration and migration pressures are high on the list of goals for the next MFF by the European Commission, even when it comes to funding for external instruments. The focus of the European Union's development work on reducing poverty, strengthening the rule of law, promoting democracy, and fighting corruption is coming under more and more scrutiny. At the same time, border security, reforming the security sector, and trying to stop human trafficking are becoming more important in relations with key third countries. Of course, some of the things that can lower "push factors" for migration also help achieve traditional EU development goals, but a lot of work is done through the lens of migration, which can make it hard to focus on other goals.

Before the crisis, instruments and programs in key origin and transit countries were only used for development. Now, they are also used for a wide range of security operations, sometimes using the same funding streams (like IcSP). With more money going to security and stability measures in these countries, the budgets of more traditional European security projects, like disarmament and nonproliferation, have stayed the same.

Different countries and organizations have dealt with the migration problem in different ways when it comes to their budgets. Both the European Union and Germany have put the most money into development efforts and security missions abroad (mostly in the Sahel region and the Middle East), which means they are focusing on the outside of the problem. The Netherlands and Sweden, on the other hand, have focused more on the internal side by giving priority to the processing of refugee seekers, their returns, and the control of their own borders. In many ways, this may be a distinction without a difference, as the external and internal aspects of migration have become more and more intertwined. Development and security efforts in source and transit countries lower the number of migrants coming to Europe, which is seen as a more stable outcome. Controlling the borders and making it easier for people to leave also reduces the number of migrants who come. Actions inside and outside the person make the person more stable.

Because politics and budgets are so important, there are now a lot of EU and national departments and bodies in charge of a wide range of projects related to the outside of migration. Coordination between all of these different players is becoming more difficult, which makes an already difficult institutional and financial landscape even more complicated. Not only was it hard for national ministries to keep track of each other's work at first, but different countries gave different ministries responsibility for issues linked to migration. This made it very hard for European countries to work together.

European Union

Ironically, right after the Arab Spring in 2011, the European Union cut funding for internal security and the Common Foreign and Security Policy (i.e., crisis management operations, conflict prevention, nonproliferation measures, and special representatives) in 2012-2013. However, this was clearly reversed in 2015-2016, when the migration crisis was at its worst. The European Union is still trying hard to stop this from happening. At the start of the crisis, it had some of the worst budget problems, which are still going on today. Due to its requirement for a balanced budget and its seven-year budget cycle (which makes it less responsive to changes in policy), the European Union didn't have a lot of extra money it could use to deal with the problem. In 2016, its spending on migration went over the agreed-upon budget limit, which meant that other budget items had to be cut.

The crisis also caused the European Union to create new funding tools worth billions of euros. This is in addition to reallocating funds, raising budgets, and using up reserves (and the Contingency Margin, the last-resort fund when other reserves have been used up). The EU Emergency Trust Fund for Africa, the EU Regional Trust Fund in Response to the Syrian Crisis (the Madad Fund), and the Facility for Refugees in Turkey are all examples of new instruments. However, "new" is not the best word to use because many of them were "repackaged" versions of funds that had already been promised. The main reason for making these new tools was to avoid the normal, complicated EU procurement process and combine EU funds with funds from other countries. But the benefit of the sidestep may have been lost due to the difficult design of pooled and rebranded funds, which seems to confuse the bureaucratic designers themselves. Also, EU officials ran into another problem: the more new instruments the EU made, the less the member states wanted to give to them because they were afraid it would make it harder for them to control and decide how the money was spent in the end. Lastly, and this is important, there is a chance that budgets and programs that are focused on the short term and rely on contingency funds will make it harder to figure out how to spend money and set priorities over the long term, especially in third world countries.

Increases in EU funding for development, security, and stabilization efforts since 2015 have been welcomed by policymakers and some actors in priority countries. However, these changes have brought to light another problem: agencies and organizations that receive the new funds don't always have the capacity to process these funds and provide the related services quickly enough. For example, the amount of money the Commission gave Frontex went up by a huge 225 percent from 2015 to 2016. Frontex was told to grow its staff pool to 1,000 people by 2020, but its funding needs were lowered in 2017 because it was taking so long to hire new people. Implementers of development projects face similar problems, so a bigger budget is not the only thing that needs to be done to solve the migration problem. The quick scale up of resources has helped meet important needs, but it could make it harder to set clear goals and plans for how to use the money well.

In a broader sense, the crisis showed that the foreign policy tools created by the Lisbon Treaty have not united the outside policies of the European Union. On the contrary, the number of organizations, such as the High Representative of the Union for Foreign Affairs and Security Policy, the European Commissioner for Migration, Home Affairs, and Citizenship, and the Directorate General for Civil Protection and Humanitarian Aid Operations, added to the confusion by making it harder to figure out how decisions are made. There are also many different ways to pay for the different tools used to deal with the problem. Importantly, policymakers have made new types of partnerships with priority countries, such as migration compacts, which are a framework for cooperation with key countries. Sometimes, they do this instead of or in addition to the work done through the European Neighborhood Policy, the Instrument for Pre-Accession, and the Commissioner for Enlargement, whose focus is meant to be on more than just migration-related problems. Some instruments' work in areas of interest has sometimes shifted from reducing poverty to improving security and preventing conflicts. For example, the ENI's work in Mediterranean countries has shifted from reducing poverty to improving security and preventing conflicts. Since 2015, the European Union's foreign policy has focused on agreements with countries that send migrants that emphasize their returns and repatriation. It has also shifted the focus of development programs from Latin America and eastern Asia to Asia and Africa, and most security missions to the Middle East and Africa. In transit and origin countries like Libya, Niger, and Mali, where the EU is in charge of security operations, spending and responsibilities have grown.

Member States: Germany, The Netherlands, and Sweden

In 2015 and 2016, the national refugee and reception systems of all three EU members were filled to capacity. New budget lines and emergency funding tools were made and used. For example, development funds were used to pay for domestic costs related to the arrival of migrants. All three countries put back temporary border controls or mobile border units because they were overwhelmed by the number of people coming in 2015. Germany and Sweden used the emergency provisions of the Schengen Agreement and have been renewing these controls every six months for the past three years. This shows that a return to normal Schengen order is very unlikely. So, controlling the borders is very important for all three. All three countries still have military deployments in priority countries for the migrant crisis, mainly MINUSMA, and in the Mediterranean Sea for coast guard operations to stop human trafficking networks and, by extension, to keep control of arrivals at the European Union's external borders. Concerns about how migrant flows could affect security at home have made people pay more attention to counterterrorism. A lot of attention has also been paid to making it easier for people whose requests for asylum were rejected to go back home quickly. Overall, migration has become a clearer priority for budgets for development, humanitarian aid, and security. This has sometimes made it necessary to put other regions and problems lower on the list of priorities. But, and this is important, the crisis has forced better internal coordination between the different departments and portfolios that deal with migration.

These are the things that all three member states have in common, but Germany, the Netherlands, and Sweden have dealt with other parts of the problem in different ways.

Germany and the Netherlands have had to limit their total spending and budgets for development because their national budgets have to be balanced. Sweden has kept its development spending at about 1% of GDP, but since the crisis, the focus of development aid has moved from sub-Saharan Africa to the Middle East, North Africa, and Asia (MENA) region. Also, migration-related programs have gotten more attention than global education or health, and development funding has been used to pay for costs related to refugees already in Sweden. But the problem of people moving has also forced governments to find ways around their budgets. Sweden and the Netherlands had to use money from future budgets to pay for things now. Germany mostly used budget carryovers from earlier years because it had budget surpluses, which are rare in the rest of the EU. To pay for rising costs related to refugees living in their own countries, the Netherlands and Sweden used a mix of present and future development funding. Germany, on the other hand, put these costs in separate budget lines that included both past development spending and new spending.

The three countries also have different ideas about how movement affects the rest of the world. Since 2015, security-related actions in Sweden have not taken up a bigger share of the total budget. The Netherlands and Germany, on the other hand, are putting more and more emphasis on peace and stability actions in priority countries in the Sahel and the Middle East. They are mainly focused on reforming the security sector, keeping the peace, and stopping people from becoming radicalized. Sweden, on the other hand, has put action through multilateral platforms at the top of its list. This may show how different the countries' security cultures are. The Netherlands and Germany are members of NATO and can deal with security threats from the outside, while Sweden, which is not a part of NATO, has to rely on other multilateral forums.

Even though the three countries have different institutional structures, budgets, and ways of thinking about strategy, their overall approach has been pretty similar after the initial period of high arrivals. They have all tried to keep a balance between security-related activities to deal with the crisis and aid and development efforts to stop more people from moving.

Recommendations

When we look at what happened after the migrant crisis in 2015, in 2018, European officials seem to be happy that the crisis is over. Even though the number of arrivals may be down because of the agreement with Turkey and the greater cooperation with the Libyan Coast Guard, this likely won't be a sign of relief because the reasons people leave and the demographics of the countries where they come from aren't changing. The problem is still there, and the European Union and its member states need to stop responding to crises and start making long-term plans for how to handle and control migration. The word "crisis" is misleading and should be replaced with "Europe's vision for the future of chronic migration." In light of these facts, here's what we think you should do:

- Understand and properly assess the chronic nature of the migration challenge. Europe has typically underestimated the level and direction of migration flows. New estimates must be developed over the next de cade based on realistic arrivals, continuing crises, and demographic projections in Africa, the Middle East, and South Asia, as well as the Balkans and Eastern Europe.
- Relatedly, a better understanding of the impact of development and security eforts, as well as funding shifts between priorities, is necessary. There is an increasing potential for tension between the aims and objectives of the European Union's humanitarian, development, and stabilization efforts in third countries, particularly in light of recent research suggesting that rising incomes in developing countries (a positive indicator and objective for development assistance) can lead to increased emigration. On the other hand, shifting EU development objectives away from strengthening the rule of law, good governance, and civil society development toward border security and migration prevention may exacerbate migratory pressures. Shifts in funding imply trade-offs, and these must be understood.
- The European Union should undertake a "best practices" assessment of the most efective border security and law enforcement capacitybuilding programs in conflict zones. When undertaking more controversial types of activities (such as with the Libyan Coast Guard), training in rule-of-law princi ples should be strengthened and streamlined across each activity.
- The European Union, and member states separately, should map out the various ministries and agencies involved in migration-related policies, and establish productive linkages and communication channels across them.
    - The creation of migration "fusion centers" could bring a variety of agencies and actors together at both the country level and in

  - Brussels or capitals (in a format similar to the EU Emergency Response Coordination Centre).
- These fusion cells should also directly liaise and share bordercontrol information with officials at Europol, Eurojust, and Frontex at both the EU and member-state level.
- The European Union should open participation in the Trust Funds to non-EU countries as a way to harness more investment for recipient countries.

The European Union and its member states must improve clarity on funding pledges nationally and through the Trust Funds, as well as the rate of allocation and delivery of funds and activities.

  - Greater transparency related to the names of the organizations responsible for implementing migration-related funding and the amount of funds they receive for specific activities would be welcome. However, any public listing of these organizations should be mindful of the potential impact of transparency on their work in certain countries.
  - The European Union and member states should create an alert mechanism for migration-related instruments when large amounts of funds are disbursed over a relatively short period of time to a source or transit country.

Instead of relying on less-than-ideal funding reserves or emergency plans, the next MFF needs to have more freedom every year and go beyond a single midterm review. This flexibility should be based on assessments of migration and estimates of the future for the years 2021 to 2027.

Effects of the Crisis on Development and Humanitarian Aid

The EU and national policymakers were caught off guard by how quickly and how many people came to Europe. This put a lot of stress on the migration and asylum processes. Within the European Union, the costs of taking in large numbers of new asylum seekers and migrants put a huge strain on local services and forced cuts and reallocations from other parts of the EU and national budgets, such as development and humanitarian aid, to make up the difference. At the same time, policymakers increased their investments in key countries where migrants come from or go through on their way to Europe. This was done to cut down on illegal migration to Europe and avoid the next crisis.

In 2015 and 2016, EU and national policymakers made big promises to deal with the "drivers" of migration in the Middle East, North Africa, and sub-Saharan

Africa. They did this by openly linking development and humanitarian aid to the goals of managing migration. The European Union started three major funding programs with billions of euros: the Facility for Refugees in Turkey, the EU Regional Trust Fund in Response to the Syrian Crisis (Madad Fund), and the EU Emergency Trust Fund for Africa. The Facility for Refugees in Turkey and the EU Regional Trust Fund in Response to the Syrian Crisis (Madad Fund) are meant to help Syrian refugees and host communities. The EU Emergency Trust Fund for Africa is meant to address the root causes of irregular migration and displacement in Africa. At the national level, Germany, Sweden, and the Netherlands have all increased development and humanitarian aid for countries or areas sending migrants to Europe. Migration is becoming a bigger part of their operations.

EU and national leaders didn't have a lot of tools to deal with the problem as it happened. Budget limits are set a long time in advance, so there isn't much room to move money around quickly to meet new needs. Because of this, funds for migration in 2015 and 2016 were very tight. To pay for asylum and reception services in the European Union and for promises to help more key sending or transit countries, which is the focus of this monograph, officials had to get creative by using emergency funds and moving money from other places. And now that many of these emergency funding methods have run out, the EU and national policymakers have even less ability to deal with a future crisis.

This part looks at how the recent crisis changed how the European Union and individual countries spent money on the external side of migration. It does this by looking at the experiences of Germany, the Netherlands, and Sweden. It looks at how policymakers got more money, especially from development and humanitarian budgets, to deal with the crisis. It looks at both the promises made and the money that was actually given, and it looks at what these new investments in third countries mean for policy in general.

The migration problem showed how hard it is to deal with a situation that changes quickly. Most of the European Union's funds for migration were quickly used up by the crisis. This forced the EU to rush to get money from other sources, including emergency funding measures, to keep its promises and fill spending gaps. And where funds weren't completely gone, officials had to deal with two problems. First, they had to get money to people quickly enough to keep up with their rapidly changing needs. Second, they had to make sure that the people who got more money knew how to spend it well.

In 2015 and 2016, the European Union spent more money on migration in non-EU countries. They did this because they knew that if they wanted to stop people from coming to Europe illegally, they would have to invest in the countries from which people come or through which they pass. After talking about migration for months, African and European leaders released a Joint Action Plan at the Valletta Summit on Migration in November 2015. This plan set priorities in the areas of addressing the causes of migration, legal migration pathways, protection and asylum, tackling irregular migration, and returns. The EU Emergency Trust Fund for Africa was also created to help put this plan into action (see below). And in June 2016, the European Union launched the Migration Partnership Framework, which aims to make compacts with partner countries that help reduce irregular migration to Europe by making borders stronger, making it easier for illegal migrants to go back home, and addressing the reasons why people move. EU spending on migration has included efforts to manage migration (like making it easier for Libya to patrol its coastal waters), improve conditions for refugees and host communities (like expanding education and health services in countries that are taking in Syrian refugees), and give people jobs so they don't have to move. This all costs money.

Fig. 9.1 - Changes in Budget for Key Migration-Related Funds, 2015-2016

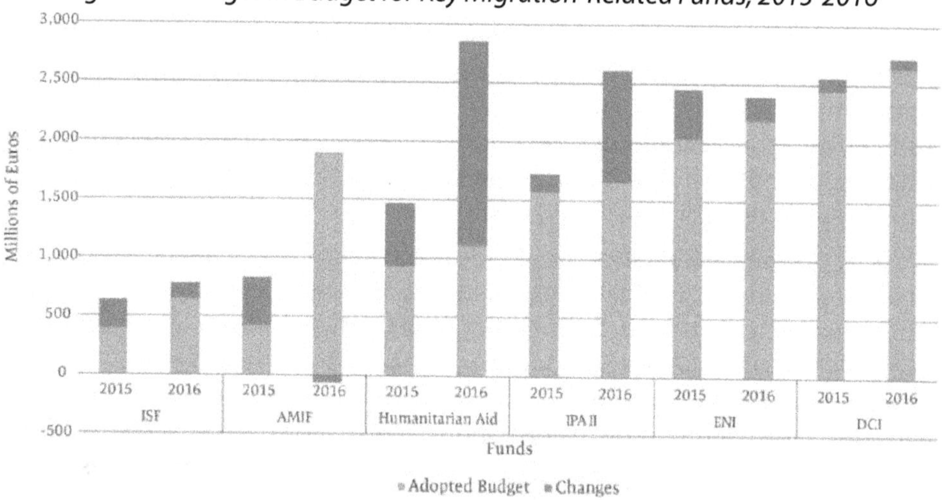

Note: This table compares the budgets adopted for each year with the actual budgets allocated by the end of the year (reflecting amending budgets, carryovers, transfers, and assigned revenue). It uses commitment appropriations.

Source: European Commission, Financial Year 2015: Report on Budgetary and Financial Management, 2016, http://ec.europa.eu/budget/library/biblio/documents/2015/2015 report budgetary financialmanagem ent.pdf; European Commission, Financial Year 2016: Report on Budgetary and Financial Management of the European Commission, 2017, http://ec.europa.eu/ budget/library/biblio/documents/2016/Report on budgetary and financial mana gement-2016 en.pdf.

Innovative Financing Approaches

First, during 2015 and 2016, the European Union raised the budgets for many of its funds that help with migrants. Figure 9.1 shows how much these budgets have changed over this time period by comparing the budgets that were passed at the beginning of each year to the amounts that were put into these funds at the end of the year. For example, the Asylum, Migration, and Integration Fund's budget more than doubled from 2015 to 2016 because it got more money to help with asylum and reception services and border control during the crisis. In the same way, the budget for humanitarian aid went up by €1.7 billion over the course of 2016 in reaction to the Syria crisis and other crises in Iraq, South Sudan, Yemen, Lake Chad, and other places.

The EU 2014-2020 Multi-annual Financial Framework set spending limits and funding goals years in advance, so the Commission relied heavily on several emergency funds to fill in budget gaps. But by the end of 2016, the Commission had used up all the money in the Emergency Aid Reserve and the Flexibility Instrument. It had to use the Contingency Margin, which is a "last resort" fund used when all other options have been used up, to pay for more migration-related costs. In the summer of 2017, the European Union made changes to its budget that added more money to the emergency funds and changed the rules so that the Commission could get more money in case of an emergency. But what happened in 2015 and 2016 shows that the European Union doesn't have many ways to react directly to big crises.

Policymakers were able to use funds from other parts of the budget as well as disaster funds. EU budget rules make it hard to move money from one part of the budget to another or for member states to share money with each other. Midway through 2017, the EU budget was changed to give an extra €3.9 billion for migration-related measures (both internally and externally) between 2017 and 2020. This was done by reallocating unused funds from other parts of the budget, but at the height of the crisis, policymakers ended up shifting resources between priorities within the same area of the budget as needs came up.

Even though this process freed up money that was badly needed, it raises questions about how it was done. It's hard to keep track of how money is moved around for two reasons. First, money that has been promised doesn't always come through because goals can change. One example is the money that was set aside for the EU relocation mechanism. As the scope of the relocation plan was scaled back, some of that money was moved to help resettle Syrians under the EU-Turkey deal. Second, when money is moved around, there is a chance that it will be counted more than once. Different promises could be talking about the same pot of money. When the Facility for Refugees in Turkey was set up in

November 2015, the Commission promised €1 billion to it. This money came from other funds for Turkey, like the Instrument for Pre-Accession Assistance, or IPA II. Then, when the Commission promised €1 billion at the Supporting Syria and the Region Conference in London in February 2016, the Facility offer was counted again. So, the same pot of €1 billion could be counted in three different ways. Both of these cases show that just adding up pledges is not a good way to figure out how much money is being spent.

A different problem is that some partner countries just don't have the resources to manage and spend the extra money that has been given to them. Scaling up operations takes time, and officials need to be realistic about what is possible, especially in fragile countries where the government's reach is limited and institutions are weak. To spend more on migration, budgets need to be bigger and the people who will get the money need to be able to use it well.

Innovative Financing Tools

The Commission's second strategy to step up spending on migration was to repurpose more of its external assistance (including development, neighborhood, and humanitarian funds) toward migration-related goals, in part through the creation of several new instruments:

- The Madad Fund. Launched in December 2014 as a five-year program, the Madad Fund was designed to coordinate nonhumanitarian assistance for Syrian refugees and host communities in Egypt, Iraq, Jordan, Lebanon, Turkey, and the western Balkans. It has pooled about €1.5 billion in funds, primarily from EU funds (the European Neighborhood Instrument [ENI], IPA II, and the Development Cooperation Instrument [DCI]), but including more than €150 million from 22 EU member states and Turkey. Projects have been funded in areas such as education and vocational training, health care, and municipal infrastructure.
- The EU Emergency Trust Fund for Africa. Launched in November 2015 as a five-year program, the EUTF for Africa is intended to address the factors driving irregular migration and displacement in key sending or transit countries in North Africa, the Horn of Africa, and the Sahel and Lake Chad region. The EUTF Africa was established with €1.8 billion from the European Commission (including the European Development Fund [EDF]), with the initial expectation that member states would match this contribution, which did not come to fruition. To date, it has pooled about €3.4 billion in funds, primarily from the European Development Fund (about €2.98 billion), but with other

funds pledged by other EU funding sources (including DCI, ENI, AMIF, and humanitarian aid [ECHO]), and €414 million combined from EU member states, Switzerland, and Norway. Most of its projects focus on economic development, with its other priority areas including migration management, governance, and basic service provision.

- The Facility for Refugees in Turkey. Launched in 2016 to accompany the EU-Turkey Statement, the Facility for Refugees in Turkey aims to coordinate humanitarian and non-humanitarian assistance for refugees and host communities in Turkey. The Facility covers the provision of basic services (e.g., health and education), municipal infrastructure, humanitarian assistance, migration management, and socioeconomic support. Between 2016 and 2017, it managed €3 billion in funds, €1 billion of which came from the European Union (including IPA II, ECHO, DCI, ENI, and the Instrument Contributing to Stability and Peace [IcSP]) and €2 billion from member states. The Facility is slated to be extended with another €3 billion in funds.

All three instruments were made to try to make sure that the money that different EU and national bodies spend in one or more countries is used in the best way possible. They provide a way to combine funds from different policy portfolios, such as development aid, pre-accession funds, and emergency aid, in order to try to get economies of scale. Both the Facility and Trust Funds have given out money much faster than the normal ways of getting money. Between 2016 and 2017, the Facil i ty, for example, planned to spend €2.9 billion, hired projects worth €1.7 billion, and paid out almost €900 million. This is a much faster rate than normal procurement processes, which can take years.

More generally, they show that migration is becoming a bigger focus of EU aid to key countries that send or receive migrants. The European Development Fund, for example, has given the EUTF Africa almost 90% of its total income. The Development Cooperation Instrument (DCI) has also given the EUTF Africa more money. More development and humanitarian aid, as well as funds from the neighborhood, are now going to projects in Asia and Africa. This is shown by the huge increase in humanitarian aid funding for Syria and other crises in 2016. The Migration Partnership Framework is another example. It was set up by the Commission in June 2016 as a way to work with Ethiopia, Mali, Niger, Nigeria, and Senegal on migration management and returns, solving the causes of migration, and making it easier to move legally. In January 2017, the budget was changed to give the Migration Partnership Framework more money. This included an extra €400 million for DCI's work on migration and asylum in Asia and sub-Saharan Africa, €100 million for cooperation with Asia, and €250 million for ENI's Mediterranean budget line.

But it can be hard to make sure that using development and humanitarian aid for migration-related reasons doesn't go against the goals, rules, and requirements of these sources of money. At the moment, 90 percent of EU aid must qualify as overseas development assistance (ODA). This limits both the countries that can get help and the kinds of help that can be paid for. For example, these rules limit how much can be spent on security, which has consequences for building up the ability to handle migration in places like Libya. In practice, though, spending from the Trust Funds, especially on activities related to managing migration, is said to push the limits of what is allowed under ODA spending, which says that the main goal must be economic development and that most spending can't go toward security forces or the "promotion of the donor's security interests." More generally, it's hard to see how using development aid, which is supposed to help reduce poverty, to try to stop migration makes sense, since migration is known to help sending countries grow.

These new tools have made the EU budget more flexible and responsive. They offer a way to combine the many different EU and non-EU funds that are available and get money to people much faster than through the normal procurement process. But they have to deal with a lot. First, it has been hard to get member states to contribute to the Trust Funds. So far, the European Union has given the most money. This may be due in part to the fact that this instrument is still fairly new, so member states are hesitant to give money straight to the Trust Fund or are waiting to see what happens while domestic budgets are under pressure. And when it came to the EUTF Africa, some member states thought they were already helping through the EDF, which is paid for by member states and provides most of the Trust Fund's money. Second, the Trust Funds rely on trusted implementing partners, which are mostly member state development agencies or international organizations (like the International Organization for Migration), to speed up the procurement process. However, this leaves out other civil society actors outside of Europe who may be better equipped to provide services. It also gives the impression that money is being reused. For example, Germany is one of the biggest donors to the EUTF Africa, giving €157.5 million. The German Agency for International Cooperation (GIZ), on the other hand, is one of its most important implementing partners, putting €211.6 million into EUTF-funded projects.

In the future, the European Union will need to come up with a clear, well-coordinated plan for all the foreign aid that is now being used to help migrants. Policymakers are under pressure to move quickly to stop migration flows, and since 2015, they have put together a lot of money for key countries that are sending or transiting migrants. But some of the projects don't have clear goals or even results that can be measured. In a way, "addressing the root causes of migration" could be a catch-all phrase for most development projects, since it can include investments in jobs and economic growth, government, education and vocational training, health services, and infrastructure. But what does success look like when you have such a wide range of goals?

Migration Related Spends by Germany, Sweden and The Netherlands

At the national level, as well as at the EU level, the migration problem had a big effect on budgets. The number and speed of arrivals far exceeded what national asylum and reception systems could handle. In a rush to increase services to meet demand, EU and national officials used other parts of their budgets and emergency funding tools. Figure 9.2 shows that the costs of taking care of refugees in their own countries started to eat up national ODA funds, leaving less money for developing countries.

During this time, migration became a top priority in development spending. As a result, member states increased their aid to key sending and transit countries and put more money toward figuring out why people move. This extra money for priority countries has come from emergency budget lines, often at the cost of other geographic or topical priorities, which shows that priorities are changing in the long term. And since there are now a lot of groups working on migration, coordinating these activities becomes more important and harder.

Germany

In reaction to the crisis, Germany increased its spending on migration in non-EU countries and put political relationships with Turkey, Afghanistan, and Tunisia, which are key countries of origin or transit for mi grants, at the top of its list. The German government thinks that development and humanitarian aid are important ways to deal with the migration problem, both in terms of stabilizing host countries and investing in education, jobs, and infrastructure to make it less appealing to leave.

Before the crisis, Germany was already spending more on development and humanitarian help. In 2013, the government signed a coalition agreement that said it would spend an extra €2 billion on aid until 2017. The Federal Ministry for Economic Cooperation and Development (BMZ) in Germany did some work related to migration, such as reintegrating refugees and internally displaced people, and promoting the development benefits of migration, such as through pilot programs that encourage the temporary migration of middle- or high-skilled migrants. But the main political goals of BMZ's work were to carry out the 2030 Agenda for Sustainable Development, deal with climate change, and, through a special project, help fight hunger.

Fig. 9.2 - In-Country Refugee Costs as Share of ODA

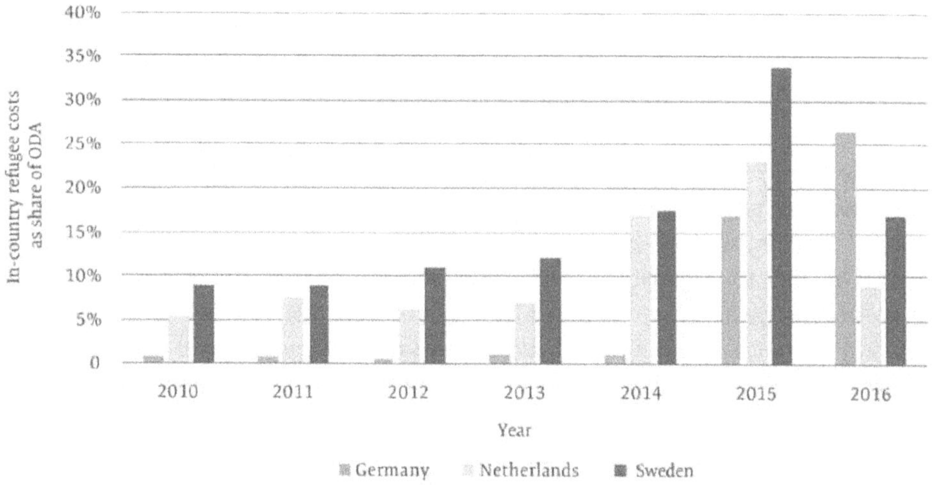

Note: DAC allows reporting in-refugee costs for a 12-month period as part of ODA spending. Methods of recording in-country refugee costs vary, which means that data are not necessarily comparable across countries. Germany adjusted its methodology for reporting in-country refugee costs in 2015 (e.g., including education costs), which partly accounts for the large increase between 2014 and 2015.

Source: OECD, "Query Wizard for International Development Statistics," http://stats.oecd.Org/qwids/#?x=1&y=6&f=4:36.2:1.3:51.5:3.7:3 &q=4:1.36+2:1+3:51+5:3+7:1.2.3+1:10.16.21+6:2010.2011.2012. 2013.2014.2015.2016.

BMZ was also taking steps to give more help to weak states, with a special focus on helping Africa. In 2014. BMZ set up three special programs to: 1) improve food security and fight malnutrition; 2) promote stability and economic growth in the Middle East and North Africa region; and 3) help people who have been displaced and the towns that are hosting them in the short term. with a focus on helping refugees get back into society and fixing the problems that cause people to move. The idea behind these projects was to provide extra money for key policy priorities that would go along with money given to each country, but could be spent faster and give policymakers more freedom.

As the situation got worse, more money from Germany's budgets for development and helping people went to migration. Each year, the funds for the three special projects grew from €160,000,000 in 2014 to €685,000,000 in 2017. The line in BMZ's budget for handling crises and rebuilding also went up, from €49 million in 2014 to €500 million in 2017. Between 2014 and 2017, the budget for humanitarian help and preventing crises at the Federal Foreign Office was cut in half from 303 million euros in 2014 to 1.2 billion euros in 2017. Germany also increased its budgets for both the Federal Foreign Office and the BMZ to help multilateral groups, mostly the United Nations. In the future, these buying habits are likely to stay the same. In June 2015, Chancellor Merkel promised to give an extra €8.3 billion to development cooperation between 2016 and 2019, with a focus on the things that make people move. And before the election in September 2017, Chancellor Merkel promised to raise the budget for growth by 1.7%.

Like the European Union and other countries in this book. Germany had to find a way to spend more on immigration while still staying within a fairly strict budget. The regular, top-down structure of Germany's budget and the fact that it is important to stay within the budget make it hard to move money around to meet new needs. Even though the government could meet some needs by moving money around in the budget or using money that was left over from the previous year, it could not meet all of its needs this way. This wasn't good enough. To pay for the rising costs of asylum and integration for the Lander, the federal government had to use supplementary funds, which are rare and can only be done after the Budget Committee of the Bundestag and the Ministry of Finance give their approval. But unlike the Netherlands and Sweden, Germany did not cut its development budget to cover the costs of housing refugees, which rose to €8.3 billion between 2015 and 2016 (see Figure 9.2). Germany doesn't add in-country refugee costs to its previous development spending. However, this rise in refugee costs, along with more money spent on development, has helped Germany reach its ODA spending goal of 0.7% of GNI in 2016.

Germany's development policy is putting more and more emphasis on migration. This has led to both more money being spent on migration and a change in how the work is done to put more emphasis on migration. In 2016, BMZ updated its Africa policy plan paper, which put a lot more emphasis on migration. The paper emphasized the role of economic development in addressing the causes of displacement and migration, especially in North Africa, through the special initiative for the MENA region, several expanded regional or national economic development initiatives, and a new project ("Skills Initiative for Africa") with the African Union on vocational education and jobs. The paper also said it would help Eritrea, Ethiopia, Kenya, Nigeria, Somalia, and Sudan, which send, house, or receive a lot of refugees, as well as the African Union's Open Fund for Policy Advice on Displacement and Migration and UNICEF. BMZ is also putting more attention on migration management. It is doing this through a number of capacity-building projects run by GIZ with money from BMZ and the EUTF Africa, as well as by doing more to help refugees and other migrants return home voluntarily or by force.

Germany is putting more and more emphasis on using economic and humanitarian aid to deal with the things that make people want to leave. One problem is that this has made people pay less attention to Latin America and Asia and more attention to key countries where people come from or go through. BMZ's investments are now mostly in Afghanistan, the Central African Republic, Pakistan, South Sudan, Syria, and Ukraine, as well as North Africa, West Africa, the Horn of Africa, and the Balkans, all of which send or house migrants on the main routes to Europe. There is a chance that migration will get more attention than other important development problems in other parts of the world, like climate change. Another problem is that the government focus on stopping people from coming to Europe doesn't fit well with some of Germany's goals for development and humanitarian aid. BMZ's main goal is to help people get out of poverty, and stopping migration, which helps both the people who move and the places they leave, can be at odds with this goal.

The Netherlands

In reaction to the migration crisis, the Dutch government increased its spending on migration in other countries. This included giving more money to the area around Syria and starting new projects, like the Addressing the Root Causes Fund (ARC), to help fix the problems that cause people to move. Because of this, more humanitarian and development funds went to places where migrants come from or go through, like the Syria area and North Africa. At the same time, the rising costs of taking in asylum seekers and refugees (see Figure 9.2) have eaten up a lot of the development budget, which could put long-term projects at risk.

As part of its austerity program, the coalition governments that ran the Netherlands from 2010 to 2012 and from 2012 to 2017 changed its growth program and made deep cuts to the budget. From 2010 to 2012, the government narrowed the focus of its development aid by putting more emphasis on economic development and putting less emphasis on some areas, like education. It also moved toward more thematic programs. From 2012 to 2017, the government combined aid, trade, and investment into a single portfolio. In reaction to the economic crisis, the Netherlands cut its budget for development by about €1 billion per year, or about 15 percent, starting in 2012. In 2012, the Netherlands also started including the costs of keeping refugees in the country as part of its ODA spending.

For a number of years, the Netherlands' top development priorities have been food stability, water, security and the rule of law, sexual and reproductive health and rights, and sexual and reproductive health and rights. However, migration is becoming a bigger issue, so it is still a priority. From 2013, the Netherlands started to put more money into emergency aid for refugees that was tied to longer-term help. In 2013, the Dutch government started increasing the amount of money it spent on emergency aid. In 2014, it set up a €570 million Emergency Relief Fund that would last for three years. The fund worked in addition to the existing budget for humanitarian aid. Its goal was to provide more money, make humanitarian aid more flexible (€120 million was set aside as an emergency reserve), and make it possible to finance crises over a longer period of time in places like Syria, South Sudan, and West Africa during the Ebola crisis. One of the fund's main goals was to improve conditions for refugees in their first countries of asylum, build disaster preparation, and encourage new ways of giving aid. The Netherlands also agreed to run the Regional Development and Protection Programme (RDPP) for the Horn of Africa. This program started in June 2015 and pools money to help refugees and host communities in Ethiopia, Kenya, Somalia, Sudan, and Uganda. Its Steering Committee gives advice on how to spend the money. It also gives money to the RDPP, which was set up in the Middle East the year before.

As the European migration problem got worse, the Netherlands spent more on migration and refugees, as well as in key sending or transit countries, like the Middle East. Humanitarian aid spending went up a lot from 2014 to 2015, thanks in part to the creation of the Emergency Relief Fund. In 2015, an extra €110 million that hadn't been given to Syria was sent there. In the spring of 2016, the Dutch government said it would spend an extra €260 million in 2016 and 2017 to help Syrian refugees and host towns in Iraq, Jordan, Lebanon, and Turkey build long-term resilience. After the Valletta Summit in November 2015 and the start of the EUTF Africa, the budget for the RDPP for the Horn of Africa grew dramatically. The Netherlands now manages a €150 million portfolio to help refugees and host communities, working closely with the EUTF Africa's Horn of Africa regional window.

The government also started to put a lot more money into figuring out what was causing people to move, especially by making the Local Employment in Africa for Development (LEAD) fund and the Addressing the Root Causes (ARC) fund. The LEAD fund was started in 2015 with a budget of €25 million to help Algeria, Egypt, Libya, Mali, Nigeria, Somalia, and Tunisia find jobs for young people who are unemployed. The ARC fund was set up in 2016 with a budget of €125 million to help countries like Afghanistan, Burundi, the Democratic Republic of the Congo, Ethiopia, Jordan, Lebanon, Mali, Pakistan, Somalia, South Sudan, Sudan, and Syria deal with war, instability, and other problems that cause people to move without permission. The government also gave another €25 million through the Dutch Good Growth Fund (DGGF) in the summer of 2015 to help with youth unemployment and migration.

But these gains in spending on development and humanitarian aid came at a time when costs for refugees living in the country ate up a big chunk of the development budget. Between 2015 and 2016, the cost of taking in refugees and people seeking asylum hit €1.6 billion. This was a big chunk of the Netherlands' overall budget for development (see Figure1.2).

The Dutch government had to use a number of clever budgeting tools to keep other development programs from being cut because of rising costs related to refugees. The Dutch budget for development cooperation has a fixed ceiling that is tied to GDP. A lot of the extra money came from planned budgets for the future that are tied to the predicted growth of GDP in the Netherlands until 2020. Some of the extra money came from the Dutch asylum account and money that wasn't used in other parts of the budget. But most of the budget's freedom was used up in the end. As of 2017, all of the expected growth in the economy up to and including 2020 had already been spent, leaving the government with little room to handle any future crises. In October 2017, the new coalition government said it would increase the ODA budget until 2021 to make up for cuts made in the past and bring it back up to 0.7 percent of GNI. It also said it would give €1 billion to make up for the drop in funding under the previous cabinet. If this hadn't happened, the Ministry of Foreign Affairs (MFA) might have had to cut some of its development projects by a lot.

Migration is now at the top of the Netherlands' list of priorities for economic cooperation. The 2017 coalition agreement said that more money would be spent on both "the causes and the effects of migration." This meant giving more help to refugees and making reception conditions better, such as giving refugee children access to education. It also made Iraq, Jordan, and Lebanon key aid countries. In addition to increasing the budget for development cooperation and making up for cuts made in the past, the government has promised to spend an extra €140 million on disaster aid in 2018. This will help make up for the fact that the disaster Relief Fund will close at the end of 2017. Focusing more on refugees and migration has led to better coordination within the Ministry of Foreign Affairs, between its development and humanitarian aid portfolios, and with other ministries, like the Ministry for Security and Justice.

Even though the Netherlands was able to get a lot of help to deal with the migration problem, this help came with some costs. As we've already talked about, these funds were taken from planned budgets for the future. This left lawmakers with a growing hole in their budget and not much room for maneuver if another crisis happened before the funds could be restored. Another thing to think about is that even though the creation of more funds made it easier to deal with the crisis, there are still questions about whether this extra freedom is worth the extra costs of managing budgets. And finally, it was sometimes hard to figure out how to spend this emergency money. A lot of emergency funding comes with a short amount of time to spend it, which can be hard to do when actions need to be stepped up a lot. For example, in May 2016, a promise of €260 million was made to help Syrian refugees and host towns. The plan was to spend €180 million in 2016 and €80 million in 2017. After talking with the Ministry of Finance, this deadline was pushed back to 2019. However, this shows how important it is to spend money quickly and see results in the short term, as well as how hard it is to increase capacity, even in a funding country.

Sweden

Sweden, like the Netherlands, uses its development budget to pay for some of the costs of hosting refugees. This meant that when the costs of hosting refugees in Sweden went up in 2015 and 2016 (see Figure 9.2), money was taken from the budgets for development and international aid. The crisis also changed funding and policy objectives. For example, money in the budget was taken away from other programs (like thematic cooperation and research) to help people in the Middle East and provide humanitarian aid.

Migration has been a part of Sweden's foreign aid for a long time, but only in the context of maximizing the benefits of migration for development by encouraging temporary mobility, involving diasporas, and making it easier for skilled workers to temporarily return home. Sweden's aid policy strategy for 2013 said that these attempts were part of the country's plan to help people get out of poverty. Since 2007, Sweden has paid more attention to subSaharan Africa when it comes to economic aid. But unlike the Netherlands and, to a smaller extent, Germany, which give most of their development aid based on a theme, Sweden still gives most of its aid on a bilateral basis.

Over the past 10 years, most of Sweden's development and humanitarian aid went to sub-Saharan Africa. However, as the migration problem got worse, more money went to the MENA and Asia regions. Sweden's development agency (Sida) said in February 2016 that it would be redistributing funds to work on peace and conflict resolution in the Middle East, especially in the Syria region, and increasing humanitarian aid. This would be at the expense of some global programs and research initiatives, such as global education and health programming. From 2015 to 2016, Sida's budget for the Middle East and North Africa went up by about 40%, from €75.5 million to €108.4 million, and its budget for emergency aid went up from €296.9 million to €380.4 million. Sweden also gave more money to international groups working on these problems. For example, a change to the budget in November 2015 moved about €212 million

(SEK 2 billion) from future years to help multilateral and international groups working on humanitarian and crisis prevention problems.

Between 2015 and 2016, there was a lot of pressure on Sweden's budget for growth. The Swedish government had to cut the development budget because the costs of taking care of refugees in Sweden hit an estimated €2.8 billion (SEK 27.2 billion) between 2015 and 2016. Sweden's budget for development is based on a three-year cycle, with yearly appropriations. This gives the country some flexibility to change allocations as needed while keeping total funding levels for programs at the same level. But the size of the costs for refugees in their home countries and new needs in key receiving and transit countries made it look like development programs would have to be cut. When the 2016 budget was released in September 2015, Sweden's total ODA budget would have to be cut by €1.4 billion (SEK 13 billion) to pay for these costs related to refugees living in Sweden. The government debated whether or not to use up to 60% of its budget for growth to pay for costs related to refugees living in the country. In the end, they decided to put a cap of 30%. In April 2016, the Swedish government suggested cutting the budget for development by another €435 million (SEK 4.1 billion) to help pay for costs related to refugees already living in Sweden. But because the number of asylum seekers coming in went down, the autumn budget of 2016 restored earlier cuts to development cooperation (with €413 million [SEK 3.9 billion] in funding) and outlined another €265 million [SEK 2.5 billion] in funding for refugee and mi grant children, which would be split between humanitarian organizations, investments in fragile states, and other development funding.

Since the start of the crisis, Sweden's development cooperation has put more emphasis on forced migration and figuring out why people move. In March 2016, Sida was told to work on migration and development problems in a more organized way. In its 2016 aid policy plan, Sweden said it would focus more on resolving conflicts and building states. It said it would do this by focusing on what causes conflicts and other types of vulnerability. Even though it still focused on migration and development, this goal now talks about solving the causes of forced migration (like humanitarian crises and environmental factors) and helping refugees and other mi grants find ways to make a living. Migration management was a bigger focus. In line with Sustainable Development Goal 10.7, it promised to promote conditions for safe, orderly, and legal migration and to build countries' ability to manage migration (including returns) while protecting the rights of migrants and refugees. The 2016 aid policy plan also stressed the need to coordinate humanitarian aid and long-term development aid more closely, especially in situations with long-term refugees.

The changes to Sweden's development budget from 2015 to 2016 show how long-term development goals can be affected by emergencies. Due to the rising costs of housing refugees and asylum seekers, the development budget had to be drastically cut. It wasn't put back together until 2016, when the number of arrivals started to go down. In the meantime, putting more attention on the Middle East and North Africa took money away from other places, like sub-Saharan Africa, and programs with specific goals, like human rights or education and health. When you look ahead, almost all development funds for 2017 and 2018 will be higher. But if there was another disaster with rising costs for refugees in the country, the Swedish ODA budget would face the same problems.

Case Study of Turkey

Late in 2015, when Europe wanted to stop people from coming by boat through the eastern Mediterranean, they turned their attention to Turkey. In the spring of 2015, more and more people started to cross the Aegean from Turkey to Greece. In August alone, there were more than 100,000 people, and in October, there were twice as many. By the end of 2015, 856,723 people arrived by sea, according to the UNHCR. Greece's small asylum and reception facilities were quickly filled to capacity, and many people went on through the western Balkans and into northern European countries like Germany and Sweden without being stopped. Germany, which got the most refugee requests in 2015, led talks with Turkey to try to stop people from coming by boat. As part of this reaction, EU and national policymakers began to use money from their development, humanitarian, and, in the case of the EU, neighborhood and pre-accession budgets.

Europe had deep historical, cultural, and economic ties with Turkey before the migration problem. As a country that wants to join the EU, Turkey has already been given EU money. In 2015, 20 different EU services gave Turkey a total of €487 million in funding. Most of this money went to education and research, but there was also some funding for security, the neighborhood, and pre-accession. Syrian refugees in Turkey were also getting help from the European Union and its member states. Most of the EU's non-humanitarian aid came through the Madad Fund, which was set up in December 2014 to pool €1.5 billion for long-term help for Syrian refugees and host communities in the area. Along with what they gave through the foreign donor community, EU member states also gave to the Madad Fund.

In the summer of 2015, when Europe started talking with Turkey, getting more money for Syrian refugees was the most important thing. Late in 2015, talks led to the Joint Action Plan, which went into effect on November 29, 2015.

Under this plan, the EU agreed to give Turkey €3 billion to help Syrian refugees through a new program called the Facility for Refugees in Turkey. This amount would come from the budget of the EU and the budgets of the individual states. But during the talks at the beginning of March, President Erdogan told European leaders that Turkey would need twice as much, or €6 billion.

Due to the chaos of the past few months, officials didn't have much choice but to agree. The EU-Turkey Statement, which was signed in March 2016, suggested splitting this payment into two €3 billion chunks. The result of the negotiations showed that the European Union and its member states were willing to pay almost anything to stop people from coming to Europe illegally. After the EU-Turkey Statement, it wasn't strange that other important sending or transit countries quickly asked for more money. For example, in May 2016, Niger told the leaders of Europe that it would need €1 billion, which is about 15% of its GDP, to stop illegal movement through its land.

The Facility for Refugees in Turkey was set up to pool and organize the resources of the EU and its member states and, most importantly, to get money to refugees in Turkey much faster. Even though Turkey gets a lot of money for pre-accession assistance, for example, this money has been slow to get to people. For example, the normal procurement process for IPA II can take months or even years. The Facility, on the other hand, was able to bring in €3 billion in just two years. With the Facility funds, the European Union was able to start two major programs: the Emergency Social Safety Net (ESSN) and the Conditional Cash Transfers for Education (CCTE). It also paid for a number of other projects, mostly in the health care and education sectors. The Facility has definitely made a difference. As of February 2018, the ESSN had helped nearly 1.2 million vulnerable refugees with social services, and as of January 2018, the CCTE had given cash payments to about 260,000 refugee families whose children were going to school. The Facility is a good example of how the EU has come up with new ways to help people get money when they need it.

At the same time, a closer look at the money Europe has promised to give to Turkey shows how limited their resources are. Member states spent months debating how to pay for their initial €2 billion payment. In the end, they decided on a distribution key based on their share of EU gross national income (GNI). The European Union used €310 million in humanitarian aid, €650 million in IPA II funds that were already set aside for Turkey, and €20 million each from DCI and IcSP funds to pay for its €1 billion share. Because of this, the €1 billion was not "new" money for Turkey. Instead, the European Union used money from other projects and, most importantly, found ways to get money to Turkey more quickly that had already been promised. In turn, about €300 million of the Facility's fund were routed through the Madad Fund. This kind of money movement makes it harder to figure out how much money Europe is spending in Turkey.

As Europe gets ready to give Turkey another €3 billion by the end of 2018, the conversation about how the EU and its member states should share costs has started up again. Late in 2017, several member states asked the European Union to pay all €3 billion. However, in March 2018, the European Union said that the second tranche would be paid for in the same way as the first. This caused a standstill. Now, the Commission has agreed to change this ratio. It will pay for €2 billion of the next payment, and member states will pay €1 billion more.

Some of this hesitation may have to do with how it looks to give money to Turkey when relations with some EU member states are getting worse. The Facility has to deal with the EU-Turkey relationship, which is getting more and more tense, and Turkey's demands about how quickly money can be sent and how the Facilty projects can be run directly (which the EU has mostly refused to do). How well the money was spent has also been called into question by how quickly it was spent. This year, the European Court of Auditors will do an audit of the Facility, focusing on how it is run and what effects it has had. This may answer questions about whether the European Union has enough control over the projects it is funding. But the heated nature of this argument makes people wonder if EU or national policymakers really have access to another €3 billion.

These questions show that EU and national leaders who want to invest "upstream" in managing migration are in a bigger bind. What does it mean for European policymakers to get "value for money" when they invest in Turkey or other important sending or passing countries? And if the European Union's investments in Turkey, a long-term partner with strong institutions, are being looked at so closely, what does that mean for European investments in other key transit or sending countries where government is weaker and corruption may be more common?

Chapter 10
Effects of the Crisis on Security and Defence Expenditures

The migration issue is one of the biggest problems for the long-term stability, cohesion, and political stability of the European Union and its member states. Only between 2014 and 2016, the 28 EU member states got a total of more than 3 million asylum requests, and neither their policies nor their budgets were ready to handle the disaster. This is true for funding for development and humanitarian aid, but it is also true for security and defence budgets, which have been used more and more to deal with the crisis as European leaders have tried to answer to calls from their own countries for more security.

Even though the EU's development and humanitarian agenda and asylum framework are well-known and are changing to reduce migration by a large amount, the EU's ability to handle migration has become a more important security issue. Since the end of the Cold War, the idea of security has changed to include more than just standard interstate conflict and military power as threats to stability. Uncontrolled migration is an example of a new problem that comes from unstable areas near the European Union and can threaten stability between EU member states, either by itself or because of bad management. So, Europe's actions on migration outside of Europe have had to get bigger so that it can work with more people and do more things well beyond Europe's borders.

Since 2015, Europe has had to rethink its policy and budget priorities when it comes to the external side of the crisis. It has also made it easier for foreign policy, security, and defence players to take part in its migration management policy. In fact, the European Union's foreign and security policy has always been centered on supporting peace and stability, human rights, democracy, good governance, and steady growth in countries outside of its borders. Today, European leaders react to the migration crisis by putting more emphasis on border security at home as well as in the countries where migrants come from and go through. This is done to stop people from leaving Europe. Also, the line between internal and external security is becoming less clear because there are more police and, in some cases, the military in states, there are more checks and controls at the borders, and there are more training and security sector reform missions in countries of origin and transit. More and more, European military actions in Africa, the Middle East, and South Asia are seen as a strong reaction to uncontrolled migration flows, which are now seen as security threats in and of themselves. Foreign policy decisions have also become more based on how safe European countries think their neighbors are and how they will deal with security concerns linked to migration in third countries.

In the European Union as a whole and in our three case study countries (Germany, Sweden, and the Netherlands), more money has been put into security and stabilization efforts in countries like Mali, Niger, and Libya that migrants come from or pass through on their way to the European Union. These funds have come from an increase in the general budget or have been moved from other budget lines. Border control has also been given more importance in terms of money and politics, and programs that were originally made to help with growth have been changed to make people safer. Disarmament and nonproliferation programs, which usually get a lot of money, haven't seen a similar increase. However, European NATO countries and non-NATO countries close to Russia have increased border security and collective defence measures. This shows a clear shift in international security priorities toward protecting borders from both state actors and uncontrolled migration flows. The European Union and Germany have increased their funding for security operations abroad the most, with a focus on Sahel and Middle East countries that are important. Repatriation has become a tool of security policy, so Sweden and the Netherlands have put more of their money toward making it faster to process and remove asylum seekers.

We looked at budget data for the European Union and our three case study countries from 2012 to 2017 to figure out what these budget choices and changes meant. We talk about a few instruments and missions that have to do with the external side of the migration problem. Some of these got big budget increases, even though the EU doesn't have a lot of power when it comes to external security and defence. We also looked at the tools of foreign policy that the European Union can use to help with managing migration. Lastly, our analysis looks at spending on border security at the EU level. This is because border management at the European Union's external borders has become more focused on the outside world in recent years, and our analysis focuses on the costs of this (as opposed to, for example, helping member states internally). The different structures and budget line items of national defence and security organizations make it hard to compare spending, so we have to figure out how to understand data that isn't standardized.

The European Union is known around the world as a rich aid and development organization. Ironically, there is proof that a rise in the median income caused by big steps forward in development can help a person move around more. So, it's possible that development measures that were too good may have made people move. Other experts have said that this increased mobility has made states even weaker because the most skilled and able people have left to find better jobs. Also, the slow progress in governance and rule of law has led to more mobility. After all, it is easier to change countries than governments, and EU efforts to improve this area of growth have lagged behind.

But the European Union's role as an actor in foreign policy and security has taken a longer and more winding path. This is partly because EU treaties spell out the legal aspects of security responsibilities and partly because member states don't want to give up their sovereignty in this area. But with the start of the 2010s and the Arab Spring, and even more so with the start of the 2015 migration crisis, it became clear that a Union-wide response was needed to deal with the severe instability in Europe's neighborhood (even though foreign and security policy responsibilities are still split between the European Union, its member states, and a number of institutions and agencies). After the Arab Spring, the EU's Neighborhood Policy focused on the so-called "3 Ms" (money, mobility, and markets) to help build "deep democracy" and respect for global values, as well as to start and keep economic growth going. But the mobility part has lost some steam and is now a problem for Europe, even though the original goals were good. The European Union should have been more flexible in how it handled the 2015 crisis, since it had already dealt with two waves of migration starting in the 1990s. In 1993 alone, 700,000 asylum seekers and refugees asked for help, and between 1989 and 1993, about 4 million Europeans moved, mostly from the east to the west, thanks to grants from post-Soviet states and the wars in Bosnia and Kosovo.

Far too long, the European Union focused on policies that fell under the responsibility of security ministries, which mostly dealt with asylum policies. Because the 2015 migration crisis happened so quickly, standard tools for managing migration were not enough to deal with the problems at hand. Instead, hastily negotiated border agreements and security tools were used right away to help. And since no one agreed on the level of acceptance of mi grants (for example, Germany's "Welcome" stance and Hungary's "zero acceptance of mi grants"), the European Union's structure for making decisions based on consensus broke down, and security measures seemed to be the only thing that could be agreed on as a way to deal with crises.

We looked at the instruments and agencies that we thought were most relevant to the external dimension of both security issues and the European Union's relationship with countries of interest (origin or transit) in the context of the migration crisis. This allowed us to measure the EU's security response to the migration crisis and the changes in funding that came with it. When it comes to migration, EU funding decisions and actions in the security and foreign policy fields in origin and transit countries can be grouped into three broad trends: (1) capacity building; (2) mandate expansion and adaptation (including a shift in geographic focus and the use of crisis management as a tool to control migration); and (3) border control as the externalization of security concerns. As we explain in this part, EU instruments that are important fall into one or more of these groups.

This part talks about how these changes in funding and policy are reflected in changes to the funding and goals of several EU instruments and programs. These instruments carry out EU priorities and put its foreign and security policy into action. We talk about how the EU's reaction to the crisis has changed over time and how the migration crisis is affecting Europe's long-term budget, foreign policy, and security as an actor in foreign and security policy. Overall, the European Union's security-related measures have tended to focus more on migration-related topics (like border management, anti-trafficking, and smuggling efforts) and areas (like cities or areas along migration routes). Even though some crisis management missions take place in unstable areas, their mandates don't always address the most urgent needs, and these choices have long-term effects on the European Union's role as an actor in foreign policy and security.

Capacity Development and Expansion

At the start of the crisis, the European Union didn't have the tools it needed to deal with the fast growing number of migrants and the increasingly busy migration routes in and around the EU and further away. In fact, EU foreign policy has long been based on "concentric circles" of priorities: structural reforms are most important in the immediate neighborhood (western Balkans) in preparation for future enlargement; economic ties and lighter reforms are encouraged in the "near abroad" (places like Belarus and Morocco); and the European Union used traditional development tools in places like sub-Saharan Africa and Latin America. This concentric method made sense when security was low and borders were well-run. But the 2015 crisis showed that the European Union's current tools weren't enough. They couldn't stop people from leaving their country and going to Europe, and they couldn't handle the number of people coming through the southern coastal borders of the European Union.

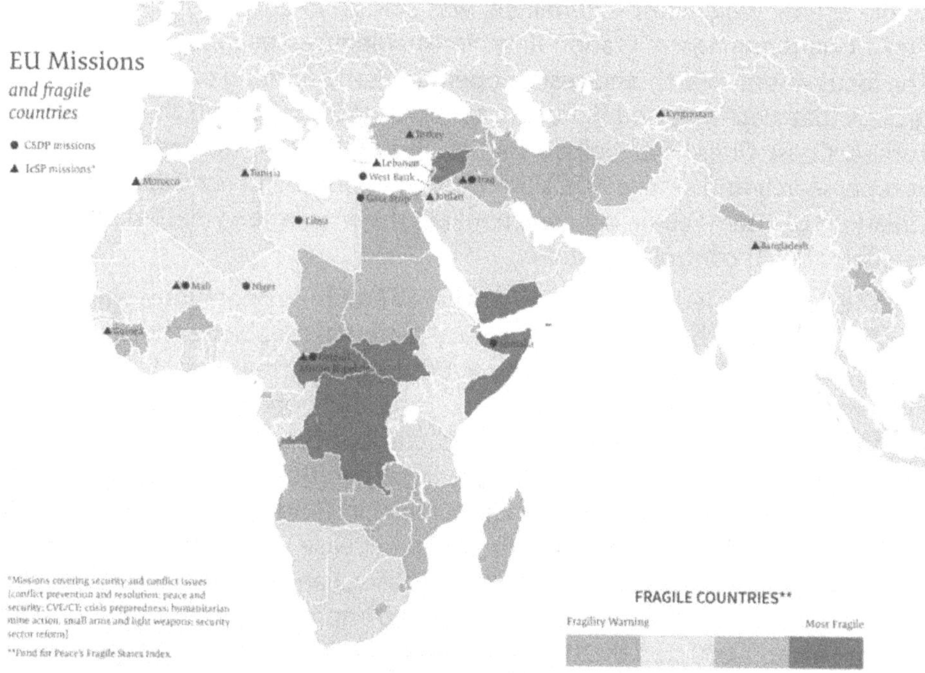

To fix these problems, EU policymakers came up with a plan to make some existing tools work on a larger scale or farther away (instruments that might be useful for migration) and to work directly with a few external actors who were seen as essential to control flows. This makes sense for some parts of the EU's response (like giving more money to programs in the Internal Security Fund that focus on managing borders), but giving more money to areas and actors that can't use it hurts the policy's overall effectiveness and leads to misdirection and public criticism of wasted taxpayer money. Also, the "go-to" and well-known tools may look good in the short term, but they may not be the best fit for a certain goal (for example, Frontex missions may not be the best fit for CSDP missions). Most dangerously, giving a lot of money to actors with a mixed record of rule of law and governance could make migration worse in the long run if governance and security don't get better or get worse.

This was especially clear for the Instrument for Stability and Peace (IcSP), Frontex (the European Border and Coast Guard Agency), and efforts to change the security sector in general. IcSP operations have been helping police and security forces in countries like Niger and Mali, which are important for migration, and training border police in Cameroon (a mission that costs almost €4 million) to improve border control and support border security. The mission in Mali goes beyond borders to help security forces and civil protection. The IcSP's biggest single action, which cost €20 million, was started in 2016 to help the Turkish Coast Guard manage migration flows in the Mediterranean and Aegean Seas. The focus was on search-and-rescue operations and fighting organized criminal groups that were involved in human trafficking. Even though the work of the Turkish Coast Guard has helped reduce the number of migrants coming to Europe, search-and-rescue NGOs are worried about the Coast Guard's possible violations of international law, which makes them question whether such deals can help the EU control migration.

The crisis also led to a huge expansion of Frontex's operations, which were mostly focused on building up the agency's internal capabilities but also on the agency's role in the security of external borders, its increased rights in returns, and, most importantly, its new ability to carry out operations on the territory of non-EU countries (under certain circumstances)—its externally facing competencies. It was changed into the European Border and Coast Guard in 2016. This was made possible by an increase in funding of €95 million (177 percent from 2015 to 2016) and a threefold increase in the funds set aside for return cooperation, even though some of these changes were made to be less generous in 2016. EU leaders have also tried to improve the agency by setting a goal of having 1,000 staff by 2020, up from 488 at the end of 2017. Even though Frontex's staff grew by a third from 2015 to 2016, it still can't find enough people to meet the goals set by EU officials. This means it may be hard for Frontex to do its job as it tries to balance national needs and EU responsibilities.

Broadening the Authority and Adaptation

The second change is in the way the European Union thinks about and spends money on the security aspect of migration from the outside. From the IcSP to the CSDP missions, the EU's tools for managing crises and promoting peace and stability have, for a long time, been based on needs, reacting to emergencies wherever they happen and being mostly unrelated to political goals. Since 2015, there has been more focus on missions or jobs that have to do with migration. Some of these started in 2011 after the Arab Spring caused trouble in the EU neighborhood. After the September 11 attacks, some civil and military crisis management and external action tools were changed to include counter-terrorism at the EU level. However, since 2015, the pace and scope of the change toward migration control and the geographic shift in certain instruments have been strong. This could threaten the European Union's good reputation as a development and foreign aid actor, as the long-term effectiveness of some missions is uncertain.

The European Neighborhood Instrument (ENI), which is one of the most important tools for EU action outside the EU, has been used to solve problems in the EU neighborhood for a long time. It's a good example of the kind of tools that the European Union has used in the past to do things related to migration, like broadening its original mission or changing where it focuses. Early on, the European Union showed that it was interested in using the ENI's partnerships and resources to help pay for crisis management in its neighborhood, such as with migration. The Arab Spring happened in 2011 and 2012, and it caused the European Union to rethink its relationship with its southern Mediterranean neighbors in the area of migration through partnerships that would fit with the goals of ENI and ENP. In the 2014-2020 Multiannual Financial Framework (MFF), the ENI got a lot more money, which shows how important it is becoming. In 2015, irregular migration and security threats were added to the ENP, and its budget was raised to show how important this tool is to the EU's approach to migration in third countries in its neighborhood. With a new focus on security, there is a greater need to coordinate and work together on activities related to conflict prevention, crisis management, and security-sector reform. All of these are important for the EU's efforts to stop migration and promote stability in some key neighboring countries, sometimes through security-related actions more than through traditional development means. More and more, the ENI is the tool of choice for EU efforts outside the EU to deal with migration pressures. This includes actions related to security and a shift from traditional goals (like rule of law and reducing poverty) to security goals. This increased focus on security and preventing conflicts, as well as the regional focus on important migration partners, shows that the European Union wants to use this tool, which requires a lot of money, to reduce migration.

The European Union has used its main foreign and security policy tool to activate its foreign policy apparatus in a broader way to address the causes of migration. Crisis management missions that are part of the Common Foreign and Security Policy (CFSP) are playing a bigger role and getting more money to deal with security problems that are thought to be driving migration. In recent years, CSDP missions have been focusing more on African and southern Mediterranean countries (such as Niger, Mali, and Libya, which are either countries of origin or transit). Notably, the goals of some CSDP tasks have changed to focus more on the need of the European Union to control migration. For example, the EU Capacity Building Mission in Support of the Malian Internal Security Forces (EUCAP Sahel Mali) was started in 2014 to help the national police, gendarmerie, and guard implement security reforms in Mali. This was done in response to the conflict in northern Mali in 2012, which caused the country to become unstable. After a strategy review in 2016, EUCAP Sahel Mali's mission was expanded to include strengthening domestic security forces in the fight against terrorism, as well as managing migration flows and border management. This review also extended the mission until January 2019. Its goal is to make it easier for the security forces of the G5 Sahel countries (Burkina Faso, Chad, Mali, Mauritania, and Niger) to work together and coordinate with each other. This is a French-led effort.

As crises got worse in 2015, IcSP missions stepped in more and more with actions linked to migration and counter-terrorism, including from a security point of view. Since 2015, the Instrument has grown from four security-sector reform missions to seventeen. All but two of these missions are in key countries of origin or transit, which are Yemen and Ukraine. However, Ukraine could become a country of origin if it becomes unstable again. More importantly, major EU funding actions since the 2015 crisis have focused on Libya (voluntary return of migrants or stranded migrants from sub-Saharan Africa), Tunisia (border management and fighting violent extremism), the western Balkans (actions related to migration, such as fighting organized crime in the context of migrant smuggling), and Chad and Nigeria (fighting the threat from Boko Haram). From CSDP missions and funds to using security-sector reform to control migration, these changes have made it clearer that security and defence forces are being used for migration goals. Also, they have led to a broader shift in EU foreign and security policy away from its focus on promoting peace and the rule of law and toward the goal of stopping migration. This is sometimes geographically at odds with where the most serious security crises are and where EU support would be more useful on its own, rather than in areas that are prioritized for migration (origin or transit). The risk that comes with these changes is that the European Union will start to see migration as a security or stability risk and won't look into how current foreign and security policies and tools may be causing more people to move there.

Managing Security Externally via Border Control

Based on the principle of subsidiarity, which says that national, regional, or local action is the best way to take action unless EU action is more effective, border control is mostly a matter for EU member states to deal with on their own. But the European Union has a role to play in protecting the outside borders and making sure that all member states handle their borders in the same way. This is a role that it has taken on with some urgency since 2015. Border control on the outside of the European Union is both a defence against real and imagined threats from outside the EU and a way to keep security worries as far away from EU borders as possible. This is especially true when it comes to the migration problem, because the European Union has been trying, through recent policy and funding decisions, to push threats away from its borders and toward the countries where people are coming from and going to. Increased border control seems to have a direct effect on the number of migrants arriving, especially since the EU-Turkey deal was signed. As a result, some policymakers see it as the only way to make sure that EU migration policy works.

Cross-border crime, especially smuggling, has also been linked to the problem of border control on the outside. Border control agents usually deal with the smuggling of illegal goods and products, but lawmakers are paying more attention to the smuggling of migrants because it feeds flows within Africa and to Europe. Migrant smuggling also seems to be talked about more and more as a security problem than as a humanitarian one, with the focus being on smuggling rather than on the people who move and why they do so. Because of this, border control is becoming more focused on security and operations to stop smuggling and crime in order to slow down migration. When border control efforts focus less on search and rescue and more on surveillance and smuggling, they miss out on an important part of keeping people safe.

Frontex shows how important border security is to the European Union. Even though a lot of its work still focuses on internal European borders and helping member states, it changed its structure, expanded its mission, and got more money in 2016 to focus on a stronger mission facing the outside world. For example, it put liaison officers in third countries, sent coast guard officers to help in emergencies, and gathered intelligence at the external borders and in Africa, including through the Africa-Frontex Intelligence Community. Frontex actions at external borders, especially in the Mediterranean Sea (like Joint Operation Triton), have put border control and surveillance ahead of search-and-rescue. Joint Operation Themis took the place of Triton in February 2018. It has a "enhanced law enforcement focus," which includes finding terrorist threats, and an operating area that stretches from Algeria to Turkey.

The IcSP has also added to this trend. Several projects that were classified as security-sector reform were linked to border control in countries like Niger, Tunisia, and Turkey that are important starting and stopping points and transit points. In fact, the EU's approach to security sector reform in countries of origin and transit puts more emphasis on the parts of law enforcement that deal with border control and anti-smuggling activities. For example, IcSP has helped police and border officials in third countries build their abilities to fight organized crime in the context of migrant smuggling. This was done in direct cooperation with Frontex, in part to improve border security and management.

Some CSDP operations that used to focus on training armed or police forces in professional methods, international law, or leadership skills now focus on migration. This is one way that border control is being extended well beyond EU borders. Another way is that some CSDP operations that used to focus on training armed or police forces in professional methods, international law, or leadership skills now focus on migration. EU officials in Mali have said that managing borders and borders in general have become an important part of their jobs.

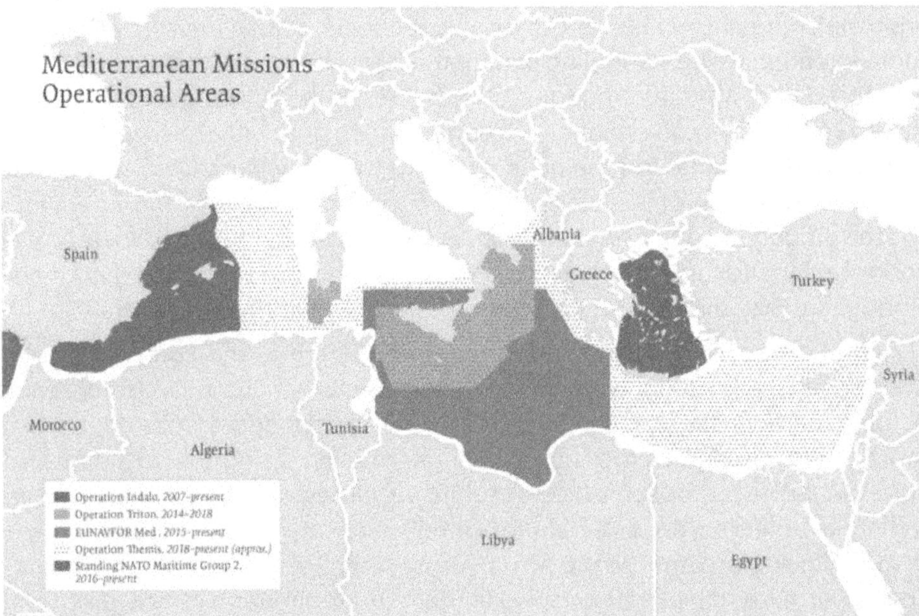

EU member states and Frontex have worked with third countries on border management for years, especially at sea through joint patrols. Since the 2015 crisis, efforts have been made to stop migrants from going further, including pushing boats back closer to the territorial waters of third countries, rather than just doing search-and-rescue missions. Earlier cooperation with third countries has become more ambitious, leading, for example, to CSDP missions like EUNAVFOR MED—Operation Sophia in the southern central Mediterranean (see below for more details) and the opening of the Sea horse Mediterranean network to third countries (Libya was the first), which is a satellite-based surveillance and communication infrastructure to share reports of maritime incidents among participating countries and strengthen border surveillance. The European Union is more and more ready to use security and military assets as well as money to reach its goals about migration.

From the EU's point of view, it makes sense to invest in border management (and stopping migration) at home and in third countries. However, focusing on border control along migration routes can take away resources that are required elsewhere. Cooperation with third countries can also be hard if their security and border systems can't handle the help that the EU gives them or if they don't actively back the rule of law. Restrictive and/or aggressive border management in places like the Sahel could also upset migration patterns that have been going on for hundreds of years and have helped the economy of the area. This could make unrest and conflict worse.

In the three countries looked at here—Germany, Sweden, and the Netherlands—the focus has been on making origin or transit countries along migration paths safer and more stable. They all still have military deployments in key countries, but the Netherlands and Germany have put more effort into reforming the security sector and keeping the peace, while Sweden has put more emphasis on taking action through multilateral forums. Border control at the borders of the European Union and along migration routes is a big part of how funding is decided. All three of these things help coast guard actions in the Mediterranean Sea to stop human trafficking networks and control who comes in at the borders of the European Union. Agreements with third countries about how to send people back have become an important part of foreign policy.

Germany has been a popular place to move to for a long time. More than 15% of its people were born somewhere else, and the country has eased restrictions on skilled migration in recent years. But the situation in 2015 caused a rush of people to come to Germany, which the country was not ready for. Angela Merkel surprised the people of Germany and Europe on August 31, 2015, when she told a press conference, "I'll put it simply: Germany is a strong country. We've done a lot of things, and we can do this." This was seen as a "open door" policy in response to the unexpected number of migrants coming through the eastern Mediterranean and Balkan routes. This announcement and the subsequent rise in the number of migrants coming to Germany put stress on the German government, civil society, and budget, especially since a balanced budget is still a key part of Germany's economic strategy.

The migrant crisis led to a lot of changes in international security and defence policy, mostly in the form of more deployments and a re-alignment of foreign policy through more money for preventing crises and resolving conflicts to deal with instability in countries of origin and transit. Germany has also put a lot of effort into securing its own and the EU's borders. It has worked to make sure that each EU member state will show unity and accept refugee quotas, and it has put in place temporary measures in transit or origin countries near the

EU. Even though Germans haven't been willing to put a lot of money into being ready or building a strong military, the country's military has sent troops to third countries that have a lot of migrants or send them to the European Union.

Some people have seen these changes in Germany's military deployments and foreign policy decisions as a shift in the way the country is responding to the problem from the outside. Over the past three years, there has been a clear rise in the defence budget. This is because the German military has been sending more troops abroad and taking on more missions linked to managing migration. Germany sends troops and military equipment to many different missions in countries of origin and transit. This includes helicopters in Mali, frigates for EUNAVFOR MED in the Mediterranean, and stabilization activities in Afghanistan and Kosovo. As approved by the Bundestag, Germany has sent more troops and combat helicopters to the UN Multidimensional Integrated Stabilization Mission in Mali (MINUSMA). The number of troops has gone from 650 to 1,000, which is the biggest military mission Germany has right now. In response to France's request to EU member states under Article 42.7 of the Lisbon Treaty after the Paris terrorist attacks in November 2015, this contribution was framed as a necessary effort to stabilize Mali and the Sahel region. This stabilization was linked to Europe because the Sahel region is a key migration route to Europe.

Fig. 10.1 - Evolution of Foreign Office Budget and Policy Priorities

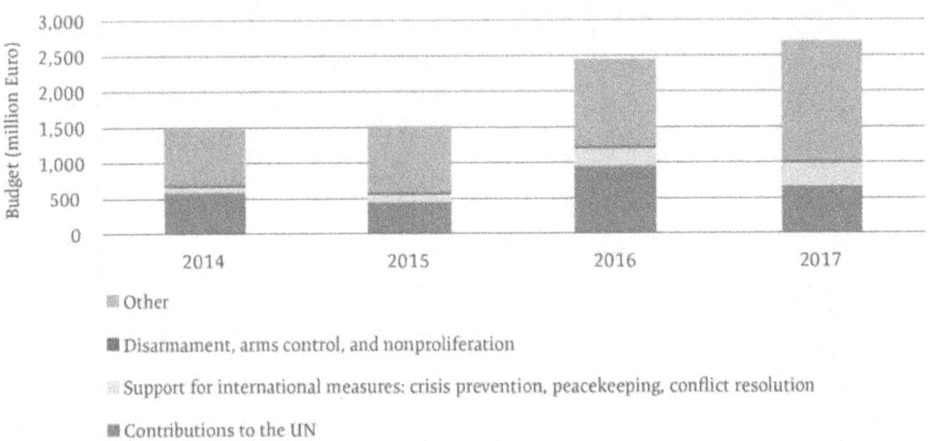

Outside of MINUSMA, there are between 150 and 350 German forces stationed in southern Mali as part of the EU training mission for the Malian army. The Bundeswehr has a base in Niamey, the capital of Niger. They have also given the police and troops in the country motorcycles and satellite phones as part of the bilateral help to stop the trafficking of migrants. Germany also strongly backs the G5 Sahel countries' efforts to work together on defence. This includes making it easier for the police and troops of Niger, Mali, Mauritania, Burkina Faso, and Chad to work together.

Even though the Bundeswehr has been active in other transit zones and origin countries (deployment in NATO's mission to stop illegal trafficking in the Aegean Sea; troop contribution to the anti-ISIL coalition to train the Iraqi Peshmerga and to the NATO-led Resolute Support Mission in Afghanistan), its efforts in the Sahel are the most direct sign of Germany's efforts to stop the flow of migrants by improving security in some of the biggest origin and transit countries. In line with EU efforts, Germany has focused on stabilizing key areas in Africa, but this has taken its attention away from more traditional security problems like arms control. In fact, the country's efforts to stabilize many of these countries are clear from the almost threefold increase in budget commitments in 2016 for contributions to international measures of crisis prevention, peacekeeping, and conflict resolution (like the police literacy training program in Afghanistan) and the almost doubling of spending for peace and stability efforts, which is a broader budget line that includes peacekeeping and crisis prevention measures. At the same time, the budget for disarmament and arms control has stayed the same for the past three years and has even gone down since 2012. This is partly because there isn't much international support behind arms control efforts right now. The 2018 government coalition agreement said that between 2018 and 2021, military spending and development aid would both go up by €2 billion. This was to keep Germany's commitment to its alliances and to peace and security.

In 2015, the Netherlands got almost twice as many refugee requests as they did in 2014. They got 44,970 requests, which is 2.7 per 1,000 people living there. When it started using mobile border guards in September 2015, it was one of the first countries in Europe to have some kind of border control. But the government has also been one of the biggest national contributors to EU efforts to deal with the problem outside of Europe and to development and humanitarian funding for countries of origin and transit. At the same time, the Netherlands has increased its funds for international cooperation and military missions and stepped up its security and stability efforts in countries in the south of Europe that are important for migration. In the country's most recent security plan, migration is mentioned as a possible threat (such as terrorists sneaking into migrant flows), but it also says that it can't be looked at only from the point of view of instability and danger.

The Dutch military has kept a small presence in tasks that it thinks are important to migration flows, like EUTM Mali, even though that presence is still small. Its largest mission is with MINUSMA, where the 11th Airmobile Brigade helps gather information and has flown seven attack and transport helicopters over the past three years. The German military has now taken over the mission of the helicopters. The Netherlands also sends troops to help with the Resolute Support Mission in Afghanistan, to train and advise in Iraq, to help with EUBAM in Libya, and to help with EUTM in Mali. Since 2015, countries have done more to help NATO and work together internationally. In 2016, a Dutch ship joined NATO's Standing Maritime Group 2 to map human trafficking networks in the Aegean Sea.

The Netherlands has also worked to improve peace and security in North Africa and Syria, which are important places for migration. More attention was also paid to efforts to stop illegal movement in North Africa and to improve how migration agencies work together. At the same time, funds for security and stability actions went up in 2016 to help with activities like reforming the security sector, building peace, and developing the rule of law. The new money added to the security and stability budget line in 2017 was said to be for migration cooperation and aid, especially in the form of security-sector reform in North Africa and Mali, help for the Lebanese border guard, and stopping radicalization in the Sahel. This is in line with the European Union's focus on security-sector change as a way to improve border security and security forces' ability to restore stability in countries of origin or transit. In a strange turn of events, Dutch investments in disarmament and arms control have gone down since 2014. At the same time, the Netherlands has reversed earlier decreases in military spending and promised to raise its defence spending to 2% of GDP by 2024 to help NATO reach its goals for collective defence.

Lastly, the Netherlands have put a lot of attention on border control, even at the border of the European Union. It has put more money into the Royal Marechaussee, the part of the military that is in charge of border control, and the navy, whose ships are used for border control duties. The country has given more money to Frontex tasks. For example, the Netherlands sends ships like the HNMLS Rotterdam to EUNAVFOR MED, as well as coast guard and military police officers to the Mediterranean.

In 2015, Sweden took in the second-most asylum seekers per person (16.7 per 1,000 residents, or about 163,000 people in total). This is more than double the number of refugees it took in during the Balkan wars in 1992. Sweden used to have a lot of good policies for Syrians, but now it has changed some of these policies to discourage refugee seekers and put some border controls back in place. The country has taken a number of steps to reduce the political and budgetary effects of the migration problem. In terms of security and defence, the country has taken a different approach than Germany. In fact, the security and defence budget for the external side of migration hasn't grown much since 2015. Instead, the Swedish government has been putting most of its attention on the internal side of migration control. Even though Sweden has spent more on defence, most of that money has been used to protect its territory from a possible attack by Russia.

Sweden has also worked to improve conditions in the countries of origin and transit for migrants who do not qualify for asylum. It has also worked to improve bilateral relations to encourage returns and repatriations, which is a tool that is being used more and more to reexternalize the burden of migration and deal with security concerns related to rejected asylum seekers who stay in Europe. Some choices about return and repatriation have made people wonder if migration pressures were affecting Sweden's foreign policy toward countries where people come from or go through. In fact, Sweden signed return agreements with Morocco and Afghanistan in 2016 to send back failed asylum seekers. This sparked debates in both cases: a week before the agreement with Morocco, Sweden decided not to recognize Western Sahara as an independent country, even though it is a disputed territory with Morocco. Some people think this decision was made because Sweden needed to reach an agreement with Rabat. In the case of Afghanistan, the Swedish Ministry of Foreign Affairs has a policy of sending back failed asylum seekers who have been in Sweden for more than

Part of Sweden's response to the migration crisis on the military side has been to focus on protecting the country's borders. For example, the Swedish Coast Guard has been given a little more money because it is still helping with Operations Triton and Poseidon (coastal patrol boats) in the Mediterranean, and the armed forces have sent staff to EUNAVFOR MED's headquarters in Rome. Sweden is also involved in missions in key countries of origin and transit, but not as much as Germany. It sends over 300 soldiers to MINUSMA to do intelligence, surveillance, and reconnaissance work. It also sends troops to EUTM Mali and has sent people to the anti-ISIL coalition (to train Iraqi armed forces) and Resolute Support Mission in Afghanistan.

At the same time, and as seen in Germany, Sweden's contribution to disarmament and non-proliferation efforts, which have generally been a focus of Swedish foreign policy, has decreased over the years, as have activities aimed at promoting peace and security. In 2017, funding for this area went back to where it was before the crisis. At the same time, internal migration management decreased, which led to budget cuts of over €70 million for the migration authority. This suggests that the sharp drop in migrant arrivals has freed up resources for Sweden to focus on peace and security activities again.

North Africans and people from sub-Saharan Africa have used the central Mediterranean migration path, which mostly goes from the Libyan coast to Italy (Lampedusa Island), for a long time. Nearly 40,000 crossings were found along the road in 2008 alone. In 2009, a deal between Italy and Libya that got a lot of bad press almost stopped these flows. But the Arab Spring and the way it shook up the region led to the fall of the Gaddafi regime. Since 2014, Libya hasn't had a central government and has been in a lot of trouble, so it's once again a major route for migrants. Between 2014 and 2016, more than 500,000 border crossings were recorded along the central Mediterranean route.

Due to a deal between the EU and Turkey in 2016, the eastern Mediterranean route has been mostly shut down. The European Union gave Turkey a promise of €6 billion to help the country's economy recover from taking in nearly 3 million refugees, to stop migrants from leaving Turkey, and to encourage Turkey to let migrants come back. Most of the migration to Europe went through the central Mediterranean route, but the people who went this way were different from those who went through the eastern Mediterranean route. For example, people from sub-Saharan or West African countries like Eritrea or Nigeria went this way instead of Syrians and Iraqis.

After Gaddafi was killed, Libya broke apart. This left large, ungoverned areas where smuggling and trafficking networks grew in size and power, leading tens of thousands of people to try to cross the Mediterranean, which is a very dangerous journey. On the sea, thousands of people died or went missing. Faced with a sharp rise in the number of people coming from Libya and a growing international focus on the deaths that happened when overcrowded, unseaworthy boats capsized in the Mediterranean, the European Union and its member states, led by Italy, looked for relief similar to what the EU-Turkey agreement gave. But the UN-backed Government of National Accord (GNA) in Libya didn't offer as many conditions as Turkey did in terms of safety, capacity, and control over its territory. Libya also didn't have a central authority with which to negotiate, so Italy made deals with different political and military groups in Libya to stop migrants from leaving Libyan territorial waters.

This is a good example of how Europe is trying to find short-term relief from migration flows and how its economic, foreign, and security policies are changing. These policies have effects on the people traveling through Libya, on the long-term stability of Libya, and on how well EU policies and funding choices work.

Before the increase in migrants crossing the central Mediterranean in 2014, the European Union started the EU Border Assistance Mission (EUBAM) in Libya in 2013. This was a civilian CSDP mission to help Libyan (GNA) border authorities improve border security and create a national integrated border management strategy. Due to rising tensions in Libya, the mission had to move its offices to Tunisia in 2014. However, it still helped the Libyan Naval Coast Guard and Customs. The goal of EUBAM Libya was changed in 2016 to make it more of a planning mission. Its plans include building up the capacity of border authorities and working with the Ministries of Interior and Justice on a full civilian security sector reform process.

EUBAM Libya has been extended five times since it started, and its resources have grown, even though things are still hard on the ground (the mission is still based in Tunis) and the Libyan forces can only absorb so much because they don't represent all of the clans and regions of the country. The mission's focus on border control is related to the European Union's desire to stop the flow of migrants through Libya, but it won't be very effective as long as Libya's political situation doesn't get better. Still, in February 2018, EUBAM Libya and the Libyan Ministry of Justice signed a deal to work together to improve Libya's criminal justice system. In March 2018, Prime Minister Fayez al-Sarraj and the GNA asked EUBAM in an official letter to write a white paper on reforming Libya's border security and management.

EUNAVFOR MED—Operation Sophia is another CSDP mission that started in 2015 to stop the business model of networks that smuggle and sell people in the southern and central Mediterranean. It was given a big, multi-step mission that included entry to Libyan territorial waters and, eventually, Libyan territory. To do this, it would have needed Libyan permission or a UN mission, neither of which the European Union was able to get. Part of the goal is also to find and save people. Operation Sophia was changed in 2016 to include training for the Libyan Coast Guard and Navy and enforcing the UN arms ban on the high seas off the coast of Libya. This was done in the same way that EUBAM Libya was changed. This change gave the European Union access to Libyan waters through proxies. The Libyan Coast Guard could then help Operation Sophia do some of the things it couldn't do in its small area of operation (see the map of military activities above for more information).

The mission has been extended twice, and each time, more money has been given to it by 27 of the 28 EU member states. Only Denmark has chosen not to contribute to CSDP tasks. But it hasn't been very good at stopping smuggling and crime networks, in part because its mission isn't clear. It hasn't done much to stop people from migrating, and the mission has been criticized for turning a blind eye to the Libyan Coast Guard and Navy's violations of human rights and work with smugglers and traffickers. However, EU officials support the training's strong screening process.

EU members also tried to stop the flow of people through the central Mediterranean. In October 2013, Italy started its own mission called Mare Nostrum. It was a humanitarian and military operation that focused on migration flows through the Strait of Sicily. The goal was to protect life at sea, stop human trafficking, and stop people from sneaking into Europe illegally. This operation finished in October 2014, but Italy's operation "Constant Vigilance" still patrols the Strait with ships and planes.

Frontex's action Triton took over the Italian efforts to patrol maritime borders, but it had a narrower mission and area of action. Triton also started out with few resources and money from partner states, which hurt its effectiveness. People didn't like that the operation didn't have a clear search-and-rescue mission and that it focused on stopping people from smuggling (EUNAVFOR MED was made to give this goal a military mission and worked with Operation Triton). Starting with a monthly budget of €2.9 million, EU leaders tripled Triton's spending in 2015 to bring it up to the same level as Operation Mare Nostrum and respond to the pressures of migration. Even though the budget went up, the operating area didn't get bigger. This led to people saying that EU leaders weren't doing enough to meet the search-and-rescue needs in the wider Mediterranean.

It's important to remember, though, that the EU has also been helping Libya since the Gaddafi regime fell. The European Union continues to work with the GNA to rebuild institutions and improve social and economic conditions. Its Stabilisation Facility has also budgeted €12 million from 2016 to 2019 to fix up schools and fix up public buildings. It has raised more than €180 million for projects related to migration, such as protecting vulnerable migrants across Libya. It has also given €120 million to the ENI and IcSP to support civil society, government, and mediation efforts, among other things.— The European Union's Action in Libya on Migration road map shows how these different efforts are coordinated in Brussels. The relevant offices meet once a week to talk about their plans.

After two CSDP missions, one Frontex mission, and a national mission that is still going on, the number of people coming through the central Mediterranean route dropped by 35 percent from 2016 to 2017. However, there is no sign that this will change soon. So far in 2018, more than 10,000 people have tried to cross the central Mediterranean to get to Italy. Even though this short-term cut is good, it has come at a cost in the long run. The European Union, and Italy in particular, have given a lot of money to Libyan institutions that can't use it and haven't been able to meet their goals so far. Also, unclear, broad, or overly ambitious mandates have had to be changed, clarified, and adapted many times over time. This is because the situation on the ground is hard and complicated, and overly ambitious goals may not have taken into account how complicated Libya's institutions and politics are right now. The European Union and Italy's focus on border control, trafficking networks, and stopping more people from coming to Europe—all of which are urgently needed in the short term—provides material support to different political or subnational factions and risks making the conflict last longer and making it more likely that more people will come to Europe in the future, if there isn't a political solution between the different groups soon. This unstable situation at home makes it hard to know how well European funding decisions will work, and these efforts could make it harder for institutions to get better at running themselves.

Aside from the human tragedy of migrants stuck in Libya and dying at sea, continued flows from Libya through the central Mediterranean continue to affect the cohesion of the European Union and the political stability in Italy (where the new government is clearly against immigration). This lack of cooperation will make it harder for Europe to find a political solution for Libya and stop people from moving there. There is no EU tool, fund, or national coast guard effort that can deal with this new reality. Without political will, measures taken by the EU and other countries in Libya risk being criticized and ineffective.

Chapter 11
Secure and Lawful Routes for Asylum Seekers

In 2018, 2.3 million more people were forced to move because of persecution, war, violence, or violations of human rights. This brought the total number of violently displaced people around the world to 70.8 million. The geography of the refugee problem shows that, contrary to what European media say, most refugees (85%) are hosted in low- and middle-income countries. In Europe, refugees only make up about 0.4% of the population, while non-EU migrants only make up about 4%.

Around the world, refugee situations have been going on for an average of 26 years because there are no long-term answers. Because of this, a greater number of refugees are going on dangerous journeys, even if they are doing it illegally. They are often at the mercy of human smugglers and traffickers, paying huge sums of money and risking detention and dangerous situations in transit countries, especially Libya. Even though everyone agrees that safe, orderly, and regular migration is important, the European reaction so far has mostly focused on managing migration from the outside, controlling borders, doing less search and rescue, and having strict visa policies. Not surprisingly, a number of experts think that this change from legal entry to illegal migration may be caused by stricter policies on visas and borders. Europe could learn a lot from studies done in the US over the last sixty years. These studies show that strict border controls have only led to a drop in illegal migration when they have been paired with a significant, long-lasting, and credible rise in visa opportunities and regular travel.

But in Europe, the question of safe and acceptable ways to get protection has become more important in recent years. This increased interest is due to a number of things, such as the need to protect Syrian refugees, a growing willingness to share responsibility, a desire to fix the dangerous route through the central Mediterranean, and growing pressure from a lot of people in Europe.

The system for protecting refugees all over the world is at a turning point. Most countries in the Global North have tight border controls, which makes it harder for refugees to get into their countries. However, some are trying out safe and legal routes that could become the main ways for refugees to get help in Europe and North America. This piece asks if and how the EU is making safe and legal ways for refugees to get to other countries. It will first look at the problems around the world with safe and legal routes, and then ask why resettlement and other routes to Europe are becoming more popular. Lastly, it will look at France and Italy to show how mobilizing citizens can be the future of protecting refugees in Europe.

A Toolkit for Refugee Protection

Safe and legal paths have been around for a long time. In fact, the global protection system has always given the international community the tools it needs to show support for countries that get a lot of people who need protection. People have been using resettlement and other paths for a long time. With all the problems the refugee situation is causing around the world, these tools are more important than ever.

Resettlement

Resettlement means "selecting and moving refugees from a state where they have sought protection to a third state that has agreed to accept them as refugees and give them permanent resident status." It is the most common solution used all over the world. About 8% of the world's refugees, or about 1.4 million people, will need to be resettled in 2019, according to figures from the UNHCR. This number is almost the same as it was in 2017, but it has gone up by 50% since 2012.

Even though resettlement is a tool with a lot of promise for integration, the international community has not done nearly enough to meet growing needs. Globally, the number of available quotas kept going up until 2016, when they reached a new high of 126,000 departures. In 2017, however, there was a sharp drop, and only 65,000 people were allowed to resettle.

Complementary Pathways

"Complementary pathways" has become the name for admissions programs that offer a way to help people. In addition to resettlement, they include non-humanitarian programs like family reunification, education (student visas), and job mobility, which can help refugees become more self-sufficient by helping them find a long-term solution. They also include humanitarian programs like community sponsorship programs.

Family reunification is an important way to make sure that society and culture are stable, and it is also one of the main ways that people legally move to the EU. In 2018, 359,724 people got a residence permit because they wanted to live with their family. This is about one-third of all new arrivals. But the process is complicated in a few ways that make it hard for people who are getting foreign protection to get in.

Several new research studies have shown that refugees should be able to get student visas and work permits, but this is still not the case in the EU or any other OECD country (0.4% for student visas and 0.1% for work permits among the main asylum-seeking nationalities).

Private or community funding started in Canada in 1978 and has been around since then. Canada is a very interesting case because, in addition to running government resettlement programs (GAR), it has been running private sponsorship programs for a long time, including in response to large-scale humanitarian crises like the one in Indochina in the 1970s. Since then, a number of other private sponsorship programs (PSRs, or Private Sponsorship for Refugees Programs) have been put in place, both for specific nationalities, like Afghans, Iraqis, or, more recently, Syrians, and through a system of quotas for this type of intervention that has grown over time. In fact, in the past few years, about 46% of all refugees who moved to Canada were funded by private groups.

Refugees can get into the country through three types of private sponsors:

- accredited organisations (the c.d. Sponsorship Agreement Holders, SAHs) that have formal agreements with the National Government Agency (Immigration, Refugees and Citizenship Canada - IRCC), to assist more refugees each year. Most of these organisations (SAH) are religious, ethnic, community or humanitarian, with previous sponsorship experience;
- groups composed of a minimum of five Canadian citizens or permanent residents over the age of 18 who can sponsor a person's entry to establish them in their local community or a recognised refugee. Through this modality the numbers of beneficiaries are more contained;
- community groups (Community Sponsors - CS), i.e. organisations and associations that operate in the same community where the refugees will settle.

The BVOR (Blended Visa Office Referred) program, which started in 2013, is a new semi-private sponsorship program. As we'll see in the next line, it's made up of closer cooperation between public institutions and private sponsors. When the above-mentioned mixed model and private funding were used together, the number of admissions in Canada went up by 125%.

Way Ahead

The future of safe and legal ways for refugees all over the world to move rests on what the international community has done over the past few years.

In fact, the New York Declaration for Refugees and Migrants backed the development and growth of Resettlement and Complementary pathways as a way to deal with this sensitive problem on a global scale. Building on this promise, the Global Compact on Refugees (GCR) recognized that making sure refugees have the right tools to be admitted can make it easier for them to get protection and show solidarity with countries and communities where there are a lot of immigrants. The countries that signed the agreement agreed to create a system to give refugees more chances in a more systematic, organized, and long-term way. They also agreed to put in place appropriate protection measures.

With the strengthening of the GCR and in the spirit of the Annual Tripartite Consultations on Resettlement (ATCR), a multi-stakeholder forum that brings together UNHCR, states, civil society, the private sector, and academia, a strategy has been made that includes a roadmap for the expansion of safe and legal channels over the next three years (2019-2021) and a blueprint for the further development of third-country solutions over the next 10 years (2019-2028) through an amb

This vision says that refugee solutions in third countries will grow so that by the end of 2028, 3 million refugees will have effective security and solutions through resettlement in 50 resettlement countries (1 million) and complementary pathways (2 million).

The Strategy's vision, which calls for more people to be involved, more places to be available, and better quality and safety measures, has three separate but similar goals and objectives:

1. Grow resettlement numbers with more countries initiating successful resettlement programmes. This means an increase in numbers of places in existing programmes, an expansion in the number of countries undertaking resettlement, but also an increase in the protection impact, efficiency and sustainability of programmes. The goal is supposed to be achieved through 60,000 annual resettlement departures in 2019 followed by an incremental increase of 10,000 departures per year to end with

150,000 in 2028, together with an expansion in the number of resettlement countries. In 2018, 29 countries were involved in resettlement, and through an incremental increase of 2-3 new resettlement countries per year it is estimated that 50 countries will receive resettled refugees in 2028.

2. Advance complementary pathways, improving access and developing more opportunities. The UNHCR- OECD study on complementary pathways finds a ratio of 2:1 when comparing first residence permits gained by foreigners with resettlement quotas. Using this ratio, the strategy states that by the end of 2028, 2 million refugees can be admitted to third countries through complementary pathways, based on the forecast for increasing complementary pathway numbers incrementally by 20,000 persons per year over a ten-year period, starting in 2019.
3. Build the foundation to promote welcoming and inclusive societies. The GCR is entirely non-political in nature but seeks to achieve its objectives through the mobilisation of political will, a broadened base of support, and arrangements that facilitate more equitable, sustained and predictable contributions among states and other relevant stakeholders. It is based on the fundamental principle of international solidarity, which can only be achieved if endorsed as a global public good by third countries receiving refugees. An environment that promotes solidarity, diversity and openness is essential for resettlement and complementary pathways to grow sustainably. Moreover, the arrival of refugees can trigger positive social and economic changes, transform civic culture and local institutions, and promote social cohesion, particularly when local communities are engaged in welcoming them.

So, UN Member States recognize, first, that a multi-stakeholder and partnership approach is the best way to increase the number of safe and legal channels, and, second, that this could become a sustainable policy approach that wouldn't need new measures to be made from scratch for each crisis. It would instead be a program that runs all the time and, over time, makes the international system for protecting refugees stronger. In the near future, we will find out if these statements of intent are just words or if they get enough support to make a real change in how refugee situations are handled around the world.

Secure and Lawful Pathways to EU

Since 2015, refugee resettlement programs in the European Union have grown a lot. They are now an important part of the European asylum policy. In Europe's past of helping refugees, there have been a lot of strange things. One of them is moving to a new place. Right after World War II, Europe was the first place this approach helped. In the 1970s, when South Asian refugees were in trouble, Western European countries did a lot to help them. But, with the exception of the Scandinavian countries, resettlement was left out of the protection tools that European countries could use. Instead, security worries drove asylum policies in the 1980s. Even though there was a small rise in resettlement in the middle of the 2000s, European countries are only taking it seriously after 2015. Considering how migration in Europe has changed over the past 70 years, we can question whether the current trends will last. In other words, it is still not clear if resettlement will become a "normal" way for people to get foreign protection in the EU. The sudden end of the oldest resettlement program in Europe, in Denmark in 2017, shows that no relocation program can be taken for granted. In the same way, not every EU member state has promised to take in refugees. Recent attempts to resettle refugees by the EU have been weak. This is because Europeans are becoming more suspicious of migration and there are more populist identity parties.

Resettlement vs Unauthorized Migration

The most recent wave of people moving to Europe happened during a time of crisis when the EU was trying to stop large numbers of refugees and migrants from coming to the continent's southern shores. Resettlement is one of the tools that the EU is pushing as part of a set of policies meant to deal with the so-called "migration crisis." Other tools include the hotspots in Greece and Italy, the relocation scheme, border controls, and partnerships with third countries. In line with UNHCR doctrine, this means that the rise of resettlement in Europe could be seen as a way to control migration rather than as a long-term answer for refugees.

Resettlement is an important part of a story. First, people who come in a safe and legal way are less likely to show up in a dangerous way. Second, resettlement shows that the EU is still open to refugees even though they are trying to close the borders. Third, resettlement is one of the things the EU promises to do when it talks with third countries about how to handle migrant flows. The point of this article is not to talk about these claims, but they do show that resettlement is a part of the new European refugee and immigration policy, and that one of its goals is to stop people from coming in illegally.

The EU-Turkey Declaration from March 2016 and the growing cooperation with the Libyan coast guard are both examples of how resettlement is used for things other than protecting refugees. In the first case, migration is an incentive for Turkey to work with the EU, along with 6 billion euros, easier visas, and a resumption of talks about joining the EU. Concerning the central Mediterranean route, refugees should get off their boats in Libya, then be sent to Niger, and as of October 2019, Rwanda, before being resettled in the EU.

Is it important? Even if we don't know why there are more resettlement programs, we should still be glad that more people are getting a chance to start over in Europe. After all, NGOs and the UNHCR have been pushing for European states to do more for a long time. But if resettlement is only a European problem, EU Member States won't be able to lay the groundwork for long-term programs that will be used after the crisis in Europe is over.

In this area, numbers are just as important, if not more important, than plans. Between 2015 and 2017, 24,800 refugees were placed in the EU through EU programs. Between September 2017 and October 2019, 39,000 refugees from the Middle East and the central Mediterranean route will be taken in as part of the European Commission's plan to take in 50,000 refugees. Since the South-East Asian refugee problem in the late 1970s, this is the most people who have come to Europe. But, as was said above, there have never been more people who need to move. Statistics show that Europe's help with resettling people around the world has been small, making up less than 6% of the total needs. And the rising involvement of Europeans hasn't been able to make up for the United States pulling out. Since 2017, the number of Americans coming has dropped by four times.

Also, European goals don't include people from the Democratic Republic of the Congo or South Sudan, who have a lot of needs but don't come to Europe illegally as often as people from other countries, so they don't get as much attention. The problem of resettlement is also a global one, but in Europe, it tends to be a reflection of the debate within Europe, and sometimes global concerns are lost sight of.

Private Sponsorship

Private sponsorship is a flexible idea in Europe, and it seems that three main methods have grown. The first is the extended family reunification-based approach in Germany, Ireland, and France, mostly for Syrian and Iraqi families. The second is the Humanitarian Corridors approach in Italy, France, and Belgium, which relies on agreements with receiving States to issue a certain number of humanitarian visas. The third is the Resettlement-based approach, which consists of welcoming refugees who are identified and referred by UNHCR to the UK, and more recently Germany and France.

The European Commission asked for a pilot study to look at how EU support for sponsorship programs would work legally and practically and what value it would add. The study looks at four different scenarios, ranging from building up people's skills and giving them money to new EU laws. It suggests that the European Commission help the spread of private sponsorship programs by giving states and civil society groups more ways to get money and by making tools for building up people's skills.

So, the time is right to accept resettlement and complementary pathways that have been shown to help protect refugees and that European states can continue to develop and grow. In this way, well-designed community sponsorship programs and a resettlement structure can help bring in a lot more refugees on a regular basis, help them integrate better, and make societies more tolerant and open. To make this happen, EU and national policymakers must take advantage of this chance and use the growing desire of people to help protect and integrate refugees.

Civic Empowerment in France and Italy: The Future of Refugee Protection?

The growing private funding programs in Europe show that people in Europe can take a more protective stance that balances out the fears that are common. Based on the number of resettlement and alternative routes, they are not yet an answer. However, the fact that people are getting involved to help refugees is a sign that they might be used to protect refugees and not just help them get to Europe. Numbers are important, but legal-channel pathways programs can also start a good and constructive chain reaction that can help all refugees and, in the long run, host communities as well.

Resettlement in Rural Areas of France

Integration of refugees is often used to judge how well resettlement plans work. No matter how big or small the idea of integration is, its political effects are important because governments are worried about how people will react to the fact that refugees are living among them. Even though states have full control over the selection and transfer processes, integration is a complicated process that includes a lot of different levels of decision-making and actors, such as the refugees themselves and the local people, since a big part of the process happens at the local level. Since resettlement involves an organized influx of refugees, it is possible to deal with problems like housing, health, education, and job training before they happen. This also means that resettlement can be a place to try out new ways for the different governmental, civil, and economic parts of society to work together.

This is what is going on right now in France with the way refugee programs are being run. Even though resettlement has been around for a long time in France, it has only become a key part of French refugee policy since 2015. In response to the EU Council's decision on July 20, 2015, and the "deal" between the EU and Turkey, France promised to take in 10,000 Middle Eastern refugees. France's promise was kept by the government that was put in place after the spring 2017 elections. In October 2017, President Macron said that 10,000 refugees would be resettled by the fall of 2019. This was in response to a new call from the European Commission in September 2017. The goals were for 7,000 Syrian refugees from the Middle East and 3,000 refugees who came through the central Mediterranean path. As of October 31, 2019, 9,233 refugees have come to this country because of this scheme. France is now the country in Europe that resettles the most people, and they plan to start a new program for 2020-2021.

The growing number of people moving to France has led the government to set up a program for placing refugees. Because of problems with how migrants were treated in big towns, France had to rethink and improve how they were spread out. This is how small towns have slowly become places where refugees can live.

This trend started when people living in camps in Calais and Paris moved away. In 2015, the government chose to quickly open around a hundred temporary housing centers. These centers were a key part of the final dismantling of the Calais camp in October 2016, which had been home to nearly 10,000 people. Most of these centers opened in small towns and country areas because there was cheap housing and free buildings there. Even though there were some signs of anger and political disagreement, they were mostly small. On the other hand, a lot of people came together to help these refugees, which was a strong sign of support. These service groups are still going strong. They made it possible for refugees to find new homes. The government figured out that small towns and rural areas in France would be safe havens for refugees and set up a way to spread out the large number of refugees who were being moved there.

In these places, refugees face unique problems. Even though housing is easy to find and can fit big families, refugees can feel lonely and have trouble getting around. There are also fewer health care services and no French classes for adults and teens. Even so, the lack of specific programs has been made up for in each of these areas by mobilizing local groups and having solidarity networks. In this way, the fact that refugees are visible has helped them become part of the community. It has also disproved the idea that people in small towns and rural areas are afraid of different cultures, conservative, and against globalization, which is often seen as a result of immigration.

This strong citizen solidarity and better contact between local stakeholders than in cities show that rural areas are good places for refugees to find work. In fact, they are a great way to bring people together. Strong social networks, for example, can make it easier to get a job. Volunteers often put refugees in touch with companies who are desperate for workers in areas where the local population is getting older and it's hard to bring in people from outside the area. So, refugees stay away from normal hiring practices, which can hurt them or be unfair to them.

Also, despite cultural, religious, and language gaps, refugees quickly become part of the local communities. Because volunteers are so involved in the lives of refugees, they help them learn the cultural and social norms of France. This is important because "these little things" can't be taught in a classroom as part of any welcome and integration program. Local communities help refugees feel like they fit in their new country and pave the way for them to stay in France for the long term.

Humanitarian Corridors in Italy

"Humanitarian Corridors" has won the 2019 Nansen Refugee Award, which is given by the UNCHCR to people or organizations that stand out for helping refugees around the world. Behind the "Corridors," which have helped more than 2,600 people get to Italy safely and legally, is a lot of work done by people in the area who want to help refugees. Integration happens at the local level, and according to research done by Caritas Italiana, there are three main factors that contribute to its success: the presence of a host community, families, and volunteers around the beneficiaries to help with social integration, housing, and work placement (an average of 12 people for each reception and 60% presence of tutor families are active alongside the beneficiaries within the Caritas network for Humanitarian Corrido).

The second thing is the people who are getting help. Most of them are families, which is how the vast majority of refugees around the world live. As a result, they fit in better with the local communities and help break the idea that most people who arrive by sea are single men because the trip is so hard. Even though most of the people who use humanitarian corridors are vulnerable, which is a requirement of the agreement with the government, the chance to have a personalized model of reception gives them a way to finally become independent.

Lastly, it's important for the success of neighborhood projects that national organizations help them out with tutoring and financial help.

Four parts of Italy's history can be used as models for other countries:

- Pre-departure preparation of the beneficiaries, which is provided directly by the organisations engaged in reception, and which helps level expectations; and pre-arriv- al orientation of the local communities who will host refugees.
- Communities that are willing to help can be activated if awareness-raising work is done before arrival, and this action normally results in solidarity and understanding. As regards the Caritas network involved in humanitarian corridors, training meetings were held before the arrival of the beneficiaries in over 85% of the areas involved.
- The Italian experience took care to find good matches between the beneficiaries of the programme and their host communities. Although the project in which beneficiaries are placed is the same throughout Italy and follows the same criteria, local peculiarities must be taken into account for a better integration. It is necessary to find the right match between the opportunities provided by the host community and the needs of the beneficiaries, and let the parties involved know the destination before departure.
- NGOs, public institutions and local organisations work closely together to select beneficiaries, sharing information and dividing responsibilities. This increases the complexity of the process, but in addition to ensuring its transparency, it allows the organisations that will be in charge of hosting the beneficiaries to be well aware of the contexts of the refugees' origin and to carry out a selection based the objective criteria of vulnerability and the possibility of reception. In this way the process as a whole acquires sustainability.

Way Forward with Citizen Mobilisation

Many people have shown that they can understand the boundaries that come with strict immigration policies and the opportunities that come with regular migration. Every selection process should involve citizens and the local community in order to come up with a new way to run the event.

The experiences of rural places in France and humanitarian corridors in Italy can teach us a lot. Integration of refugees through the help of citizens has been shown to work well. It could be a turning point for how European countries treat refugees and make them part of their communities. Since the 1990s, as asylum and social policies have become more complicated, only government servants, professional social workers, and lawyers have been able to help asylum seekers and refugees and take care of them. Citizens and local communities offer something extra that should be taken into account when policies are made and safe and legal routes are expanded in the future. With the help of the business sector, they are making the way for long-term integration to go well. Citizen involvement is also a chance to make society more open and friendly. In France, for example, people often worry about religion and, more specifically, the Islamic veil before refugees arrive, but those worries go away very quickly after they do. These worries give way to a desire to learn about the refugees' culture and, sometimes, to learn their languages.

Governments might be interested in a plan like "citizen mobilization." At first glance, it might seem like a way for the government to save money by letting volunteers and interested citizens help welcome and integrate newcomers. But countries should think carefully before going down this road. When people take part, they learn more about the real lives of refugees and the contradictions in Europe's asylum and immigration policies. Not only resettled or supported refugees will be given a warm welcome. Supporting hospitality might go against the growing attacks on people in civil society who help refugees on the water or at the border.

Lastly, the way refugees are treated when they move to rural areas raises questions about how problems faced by refugees and, to a greater extent, travelers are framed. In small towns and rural places, many of the problems that make it hard for refugees to settle in also affect the local people. French and Italian people who live in these places are also worried about their ability to move around and get to health and social services. In the same way, most people who live in big towns have trouble finding a place to live. Even though refugees have unique needs and are more likely to be in danger, many of these problems shouldn't be seen as "immigration problems" only. Instead, they give us a chance to stop thinking in terms of "us" and "them." And they make it hard for policymakers, who might find it easier to support policies that make it hard for people to come to Europe and that divide public opinion instead of trying to fix the social inequality in European countries.

Chapter12
Technology Solutions Centered on Migrants

Background

Integration of migrants and refugees in Europe is a complicated and difficult task right now. A few numbers can help you get a general idea of how big the task is...

As of January 1, 2018, there were 22.3 million people from outside the EU who were officially living in an EU Member State. This is 4.4% of the total population of the EU-28. 55% of these people were living in only Germany, Italy, and France. In 2018, almost 70% (230,000) of asylum requests given in the EU came from the same three countries. Figure 12.1 shows that in 2018 and in most EU Member States, the majority of non-nationals were from outside the EU. This gives you an idea of how non-nationals are spread out in each country.

Fig. 12.1 - Composition of non-national citizens per country

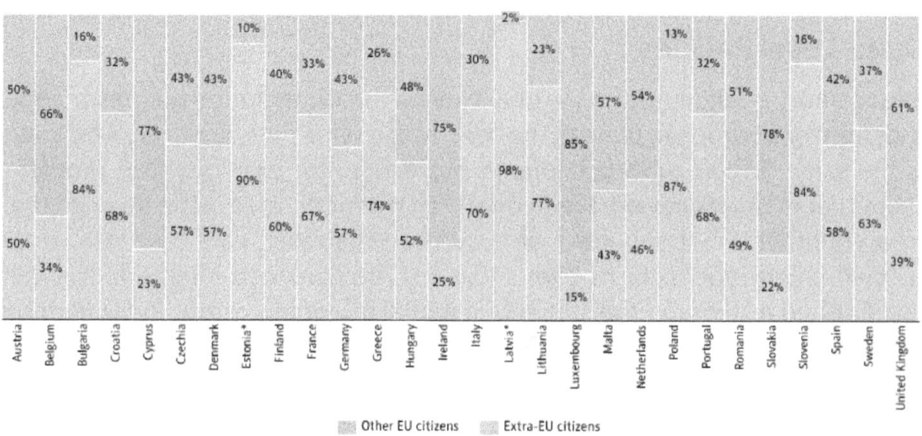

*In the case of Latvia and Estonia, the proportion of citizens from non-member countries is particularly large due to the high number of recognised non-citizens (mainly former Soviet Union citizens, who are permanently resident in these countries but have not acquired any other citizenship).

This number gives us a general idea of how big and hard the task of integrating migrants will be. In the area of migration, integration has been a hotly debated subject. Even though the word "integration" is usually used to describe how immigrants adjust to their new lives, experts still don't agree on what it means, how it works, or what its goals are. Most people agree, though, that integration that works helps people get better access to services and reduce differences in income, schooling, and health. Nobel Prize winner Amartya Sen says that "inequality of opportunity" is the kind of inequality that causes the most trouble.3. It happens when different people in the same society don't have the same chances. Then, it's clear that managing the integration process well is the most important thing to do to reduce these kinds of differences, strengthen social solidarity, and make the most of the political, social, and economic benefits that integration can bring to the EU as a whole.

It is not the point of this essay to do a literature study on how the process of integrating migrants and refugees is thought of. Integration is important to understand because it is a process that involves many different areas. To get a full picture of the process of integrating migrants and refugees, it is important to find and fully understand all the factors that are known to play a role. Integration can also be thought of as a process that involves more than one person. This means that integration needs a lot of different groups, like the government, the business sector, and civil society, to work together. No one person or group, no matter how skilled, can handle the task of integrating immigrants by itself. In the EU Common Basic Principles for Immigrants paper, it says that integration is a two-way process of migrants and people who live in EU Member States getting along with each other.

State-Level Policies

Each country is different, and the quality of national integration policies changes a lot from one European State to the next. At the same time, not every immigrant is the same. People who get foreign protection, for example, face problems that other migrants never have to deal with when trying to settle down in their new countries. So, it shouldn't be a surprise that each country has to make its own union process fit its own situation. The European Migration Network just finished a study on the status of national integration steps in EU Member States and Norway in 2018. As the map on the left shows, 18 Member States and Norway took steps to help third-country nationals improve their language skills; 19 Member States and Norway put in place legal measures, policies, and practices to help third-country nationals integrate into the labor market; and 15 Member States and Norway reported new steps to improve access to social security, social assistance, healthcare, housing, and a range of other services.

...while the European Union has only been able to offer guidelines and basic ideas that everyone agrees on...

As was already said, each country in the European Union is responsible for its own immigrant integration strategies. Still, since the Treaty of Amsterdam in 1999, the EU has set priorities and guidelines for EU Member States in this area, as shown by the Tampere Programme, which pointed out the need to set common goals for a stronger integration policy for people from outside the EU who live in the EU. The "Common basic principles" statement from 2004 is another step forward because it has guided and still guides most of what the EU does in the area of integration. With the signing of the Treaty of Lisbon in 2007, the EU and its institutions got the legal permission to offer incentives and help to EU Member States in order to make it easier for people from third countries to integrate. The 2016 EU Action Plan on the Integration of Third-Country Nationals is the most recent change in this area. It outlines key policy priorities and specific tools to help Member States create and improve their integration policies. In the past few years, a revised integration strategy has been set up in response to the need to focus on long-term solutions and combine the efforts of everyone concerned. The use of technology to help with merging is an important part of the new plan. The Commission said that the innovative use of technology, social media, and the internet needs to be encouraged at all steps of the integration process.

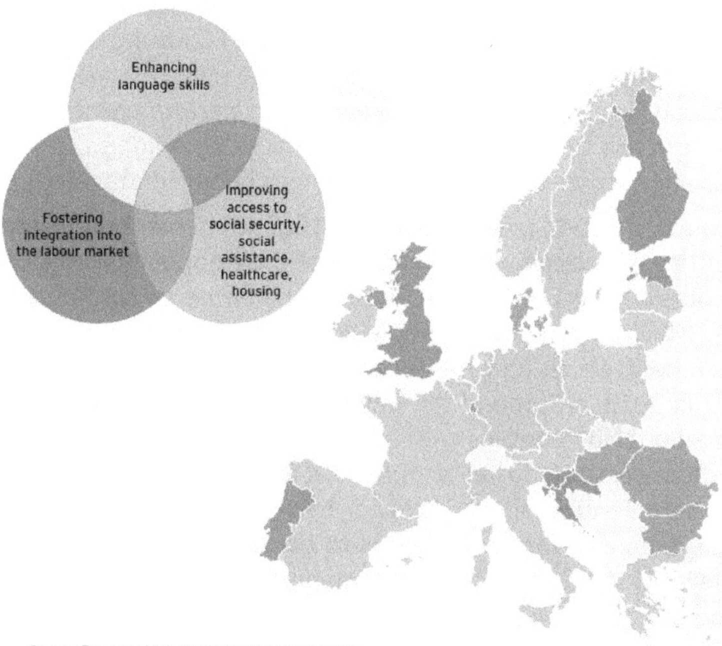

Source: European Migration Network; EY elaboration

People think that information and communication tools are the key to better managing the process of integration, but are European countries ready for this?

Using technology adds a new layer to the study of migration and how people adapt to new places. Technology has an obvious effect on migration because it makes the whole process easier, from preparing to move to getting settled in the new country. Migrants now use personal computers, cell phones, the Internet, and social media all the time. One important change is the rise of new technologies like Artificial Intelligence (AI), Big Data, and Blockchain, as well as the rise of "Fintech" companies that use phone apps instead of expensive real infrastructures. We're just starting to realize and use how these new tools could change the industry. Since the middle of the 2010s, these kinds of technologies have been used in most parts of the economies of rich countries. However, they are just now starting to be useful in the field of integrating migrants and refugees. Because ICT tools have a big effect on every part of the migration process, the EU sees digital technologies as a game-changer for migration and integration.

At the same time, though, EU countries don't all use and apply technology in the same way. In fact, the 2019 Digital Economy and Society Index (DESI), which is used in this paper as a proxy for technological readiness and, by extension, as a measure of the quality of integration services, shows that a number of EU countries do not do very well. The Index measures Europe's digital success and shows how the digital competitiveness of EU Member States has changed over time in five different ways. What becomes clear is that EU countries haven't all improved their digital performance at the same rate over the years. While Finland, Sweden, the Netherlands, and Denmark ("Top performers" cluster in the graph below) got the best scores in DESI 2019 and are among the world leaders in digitalization, other countries are a long way behind in this area.

There are groups of "Good performers" and "Urgent intervention needed" among the countries with between 4% and 8% of their population made up of people from outside the EU. This last group is made up of countries like Italy and Greece, which have a lot of people who are not from the EU and a low DESI number. Italy, which had the second-highest number of non-EU28 people in the EU in 2018, has one of the lowest DESI scores. We say that the level of digital readiness in countries with a lot of people from outside the EU ("Urgent intervention needed" cluster) should be at least close to what it is now. Countries in the "Intervention needed" cluster have a lower share of non-EU citizens, but their digital performance seems to be well below average. This means that the level of services related to integrating migrants and refugees is also below average.

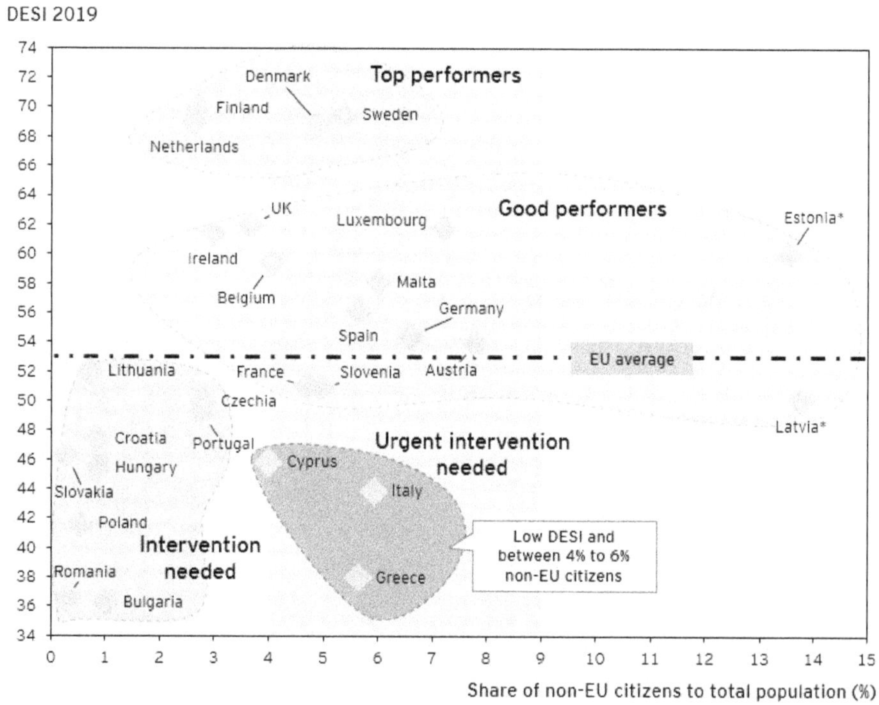

*In Estonia and Latvia, the proportion of citizens from non-member countries is particularly large due to the high number of recognised non-citizens (mainly former Soviet Union citizens, who are permanently resident in these countries but have not acquired any other citizenship).

If we combine these results with the most recent data from the European Quality of Government Index (EQI), which is one of the few ways to measure the quality of institutions at the regional level in the European Union, we can see that the quality of government services at the national level varies greatly. In this case, "institutional quality" is a multidimensional idea that includes high fairness, high standard of public services, and low corruption. According to the EQI, most places in Northern Europe, like Finland and the Netherlands, have stayed among the best in terms of government quality. However, many places in the south, like Italy (which is named second-worst), Greece, and Spain, have gotten worse over the past few years.

Even though new technologies may be the key to designing and applying better integration strategies, countries must also be ready to take advantage of what digital innovation has to offer. Better rules are a must if this is to happen. At the moment, it seems like there are a lot of EU-level projects that are successful but can't be linked together in a way that makes sense. This could be because of a bad policy framework that makes it hard for governments and the rest of society to work together toward a shared goal. So, it looks like the EU as a whole needs to get better not only to be able to compete on the global stage of digital competitiveness, but also to deal with its migration and integration problems in a more efficient and effective way. These problems are threatening the very idea of the European Union. Also, services for migrants are often universal services that help people become citizens. This means that a general improvement of public policies to help migrants become citizens would surely have good effects on the community as a whole.

Significance of Technology

The way ICTs are used in the merger process is not the same all over Europe...

Even though there isn't a clear policy framework, a number of grassroots initiatives have spread across Europe to deal with the problem of integration, especially during and after the refugee crisis of 2014-2015. We chose 60 of these projects that use technology in different ways to deal with the challenges and specifics of each part of the integration process in order to evaluate the current state of the art of the migrant integration process.

...there are several parts of the process of integrating migrants and refugees that need to be looked at.

As was said in earlier parts, integrating migrants and refugees is a complex process that involves many different areas. One way to look at it is through the framework that Strang and Ager (2010) made. This framework has shown to be a good way to explain what the criteria, methods, and contexts of integration are. The framework is built around four main key areas: means and markers, social links networks, facilitators, and foundation.

The fields of employment, education, housing, and health are the indicators in the first area of Means and Markers. The "public sphere" of integration is made up of these four areas. These areas are called "markers" because doing well in them is a sign of successful integration, and "means" because doing well in these areas is likely to have a positive effect on the integration process as a whole. Both of these four areas show success toward integration and help other areas reach their goals.

In the second section of Social Connections and Networks, the importance of ties in the process of integrating migrants and refugees is emphasized. The "private sphere" of integration is what these areas are talking about. The framework shows that social bonds, social bridges, and social links are the three most important types of interactions for the integration process. "Social bonds" are connections with people who share your sense of identity. "Social bridges" are connections with people from different backgrounds. "Social links" are connections with institutions, such as local and national government services. "Bonds" and "bridges" are words that describe connections between people in a society. These relationships can be thought of as "horizontal." "Vertical" ties between people and the institutions of the society in which they live are what social links are all about.

The third part of Facilitators is about the skills that people need to have in order to fit in well with the larger society. According to the theory by Strang and Ager (2010), these are "Language," "Cultural Knowledge," and "Safety and Security." Knowing the language and customs of the area is a key sign of integration. It's interesting to note that "cultural knowledge" can mean both that migrants and refugees learn about the local culture and that people in the area learn about the situations and culture of migrants.

Fig. 12.2 - The integration process framework

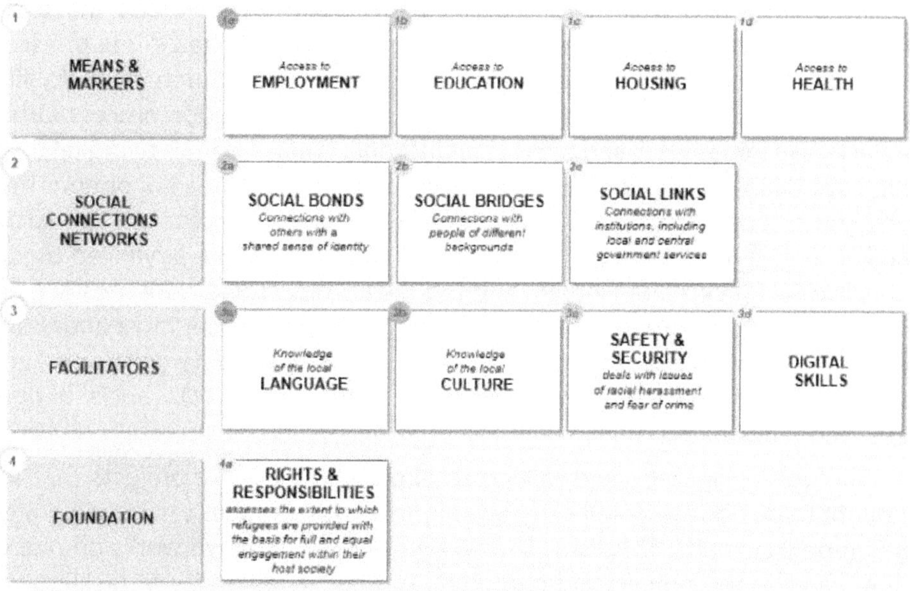

"Safety and security" is the field that deals with things like racial abuse and fear of crime. Research shows how important it is for people to feel safe and secure so that they can use services and interact with other people to build their lives and fit in. It is important to include "Digital skills" as a fourth sign in this group. The fact that digital skills were added to the model when they weren't there before shows how much new ICTs have changed since the original indicators were released. This shows how access to people, services, and rights is often made easier or even based on technology these days.

In the fourth area of Foundation, we look at how well migrants and refugees are given the tools they need to fully and equally participate in the society where they live. Citizenship and country, and the rights that come with them, are at the heart of what it means to be integrated in a given situation. Citizenship and the use of the rights and actions that come with it, such as voting, are important parts of how a person fits into a society as a whole.

...and there are hundreds of bottom-up projects that work on their own to solve the problems of integration by putting ICTs at the center of their business models.

Based on the framework we looked at in the last paragraph, we will find some of the most interesting projects that use the synergies created by the use of information and communication technologies to address the challenges of integrating migrants and refugees.

Index I shows that we were able to map 60 bottom-up efforts. Initiatives were found in every area of the integration structure described in the previous paragraphs. What comes out is a very different world. Some projects, like initiatives 3 and 11, try to cover several parts of the integration process. Other projects, like initiatives 5 and 6, focus on just one. When it comes to digital tools that have been put into place, there seems to be a wider spread of options that mostly use "apps and web-based platforms" as well as "websites and social media." Only a few of the projects in our sample used more advanced digital tools like AI, Blockchain, Fintech, and Big Data. These tools were mostly used to deal with Means, Markers, and Facilitators. Concerning the "most addressed domains," it looks like a lot of mapped efforts are using social media, apps, and web-based tools to try to solve problems in "Employment (1a)," "Social Bridges (2b)," and "Education (1b)."

Through desk study and talking to experts, a list of 12 projects that are thought to be good examples of how migrants and refugees can be integrated in Europe was made. This list is shown below. Each initiative works on one or more parts of the process of integration and has its own way of tackling the problem at hand.

Some projects use artificial intelligence to find the best place to move to.

Our research shows that getting entry to the job market is one of the most difficult parts of integrating migrants and refugees. We put together a map of two projects that made software that uses big data and machine learning to find the country where a migrant is most likely to find a job, making it easier for them to integrate. The IPL algorithm (Initiative 5) was made by the Immigration Policy Lab at Stanford and Zurich universities. It correctly predicts where a migrant is more likely to find a job. The formula has been tried out in both the U.S. and

Switzerland, where it greatly improved the chances of migrants and refugees getting jobs. The second project, Initiative 6, was named after Annie Moore, a well-known Irish immigrant to the United States. It is a software powered by artificial intelligence that was made by the universities of Oxford and Lind. It can match refugees to specific locations based on their needs, skills, and the number of resources and opportunities available in that country. It can also match migrants and refugees to opportunities that will help them integrate faster.

Rafiqi (Initiative 13) is an online platform that has won multiple awards. It uses artificial intelligence to help migrants and refugees find chances that will help them integrate faster. The author is a Middle Easterner who moved to Europe 10 years ago and now lives in the UK. He or she has found some of the problems that are making it hard for refugees to integrate into society. "First, there doesn't seem to be a single place where newcomers can find out about all the opportunities available to them and where NGOs, universities, employers, and volunteer mentors can find and sort refugee talent," the report says. Second, newcomers are often unemployed or overqualified for the jobs they have because they don't know about the right opportunities. Third, there are big efforts by governments and NGOs to match refugees with jobs in places like Germany and the Netherlands, but these efforts can't be scaled up by hand because there are so many refugees and so many different jobs. So, the Rafiqi platform aims to solve these problems by letting users find and use government services on their own and by matching them in real time and based on their traits and needs to the services that are best for them. A small group of refugees in London and Berlin are currently using the product as a trial test. They have access to jobs, job coaching programs, technical training, language and culture training, mentors, accredited certifications, and university degrees.

Others rely on face-to-face contact by pairing young immigrants with experienced local mentors to help them find a job...

DUO for a JOB (Initiative 20) is a non-profit organization that was started because of two things: on the one hand, Belgium has one of the lowest rates of activity for people over 50 in Europe, and on the other hand, young people with a migrant background have trouble getting into the job market. Since 2013, DUO for a JOB has been working to solve this double problem by getting these two groups of people in touch with each other. They do this by using software that matches young migrants with mentors who have more experience. The association has a cultural and intergenerational mentoring program. It pairs young job seekers with a migrant background with people over 50, ideally from the same professional sector, so that the mentors can help their mentees find jobs. DUO for a JOB has offices in Brussels, Liege, and Ghent. With the help of more than 750 teachers, they have put together more than 2,200 teams. According to Advocacy Director Julie Bodson, 73% of mentees have had a positive result (such as a short-term permanent contract, a traineeship, or a training program) in the 12 months after their coaching. The goal of the group is to get rid of differences in how migrants can access the job market and to fight discrimination by bringing back social cohesion, understanding, and local solidarity....and others help them make a personalized skills profile.

Skilllab (Initiative 1) is a skill assessment tool that helps job seekers quickly and in any language find out what their professional skills are and write them down. Ulrich Scharf, the company's Managing Director, said,

> our experience is mostly in the areas of employment and adult education since we specifically work with organisations to support refugees and migrants find pathways to sustainable careers. We believe that in the long-term, employment itself is perhaps the most important domain of the integration process because of its outsized impact on other domains.

Skilllab uses Artificial intelligence to interview users (in their native language) about the skills and knowledge that they acquired over the course of their lives. A mobile application enables users to capture past experiences of any kind and perform a skill assessment for all those past experiences. The resulting skill profiles are automatically generated and professionally translated into the language of the user's choice, producing detailed, professionally formatted documentation to be used with career counselling services and employment and education providers. Scharf continues by stating that although employment of migrants does receive much attention from the public sector, many authorities with significant migrant and refugee populations are focusing on a

> one-size-fits all approach to service provision that, by failing to provide highly personalised services to the individual, is at best ineffective and at worst counter-productive, leading to longer unemployment periods, and the shoe-horning of migrants into low-skilled, low-wage positions that neither provide the migrant with growth opportunity, nor take advantage of their skills on the labour market.

Some focus on giving migrants and refugees useful and high-quality material...

Refugee.Info (Initiative 11) is a digital and interactive tool that uses social media and social networks to connect directly with refugees and people seeking asylum in Italy. The main goal of the project is to help refugees and people looking for asylum get correct information about their rights and safety, such as how to apply for asylum, sign up for school, get health care, and find work. Refugee.Info (RI) is the European version of Signpost, which was started by the International Rescue Committee and Mercy Corps at the height of the refugee crisis in Europe in 2015. This program was made to help refugees who came to Greece with "nothing but their cell phones" "Since then," says RI Project Officer Elena Caracciolo, "we have spread our work across Europe and have already helped almost 1.4 million refugees and asylum seekers in Bulgaria, Greece, Hungary, Italy, and Serbia." Thanks to its partners, free Wi-Fi stations have been set up in places like Ventimiglia, Como, Rome, Foggia, and Milan where there are a lot of refugees. This makes sure that people can connect to the internet and use the platform. Caracciolo says that refugees and people looking for protection get most of their information from social media. Using social media lets us talk to people in real time and help them in a way that is unique to them. For example, from March 2018 to October 2019, we got about 30,000 messages on Messenger from more than 4,000 unique users, and 96% of them were answered within 15 hours (Facebook Analytics). The Project Officers continue by sharing some of the results of the recently completed internal impact report. They say that "76% of respondents believe that they are better informed after using Refugee.Info and that the information provided is reliable." This is important because the people they want to reach don't believe information on social media that doesn't come from their peers. "...while others help them make complex bureaucracy easier to understand and improve their digital skills.

Bureaucrazy (Initiative 2) is an app that was made by two Syrian refugee seekers who want to make German bureaucracy easier for everyone, not just people who have asked for asylum there since 2013. The app has three main functions: a translation service that turns official German papers into Arabic and English, a multiple-choice decision tree for common problems, and a mapping service that sends applicants to the right council office. The company's owners want their product to help people who just moved to Germany do things like open a bank account, rent an apartment, apply for a college course, or sign up at a job center. The app was made at ReDI School (Initiative 56), a non-profit "school for digital integration" in Berlin that teaches refugees and newbies how to use technology and code. It gives people the chance to get good training and work with the German start-up and digital industries. The goal is to give students valuable digital skills and a strong network of tech leaders, students, and graduates to help make new opportunities for everyone. Since it started, the School has grown to include Munich and Copenhagen, and its partners, Microsoft and Cisco Networking Academy, make it possible for the School to offer free online classes.

...or learn the local language and customs.

Mariana Brilhante, co-founder and chief marketing officer at SPEAK, says that language hurdles, being away from racial and religious discrimination, and complicated bureaucratic processes are the biggest problems that migrants face as they try to settle in their new countries. This is what the Portuguese startup SPEAK (Initiative 17) works on when it comes to the integration process. Through community-led language groups and cultural exchange events, SPEAK brings together people who are new to a place and people who have lived there for a long time. Participants learn from each other, find shared interests, and make new friends through these activities. Along the way, they break down barriers and deal with prejudice in their own cities. As people work together to learn new languages, they also break down barriers and build strong, deep ties. Participants use these new connections to get help with things like editing a CV, finding a babysitter, renting a house, or even getting a job. Relationships that are made and experienced in person have a much bigger effect on people's lives than those that are made online. SPEAK's experience is based on a model called "Online2Offline." Most of its processes are run online through a platform that was built in-house to make the company more efficient, reduce fixed costs, and make it easier to grow. Face-to-face learning and sharing of experiences gives people the chance to get to know each other well and form close bonds. The fact that the project can grow seems to make it even more interesting. In the past five years, SPEAK has grown into a group of more than 30,000 people from 160 different countries who live in 30 places around the world.

Lastly, some don't make solutions themselves; instead, they bring together experts and businesses to make solutions...

Techfugees (Initiative 3) is an international non-profit organization that acts as a global platform to find answers to the migrant crisis. It does this because it knows how important technology is as a tool for dealing with the problem of integrating migrants. The organization describes itself as "not a platform that creates solutions directly, but rather one that builds bridges and links between experts to implement high-tech solutions to the migrant crisis and help displaced people meet their needs in terms of access to rights information, access to employment, access to education, health, and social inclusion." Techfugees does this by setting up meetups and hackathons, and it now has a group of nearly 18,000 innovators from all over the world. Techfugees helped fund projects like Integreat (Initiative 10), which is one of the biggest local information apps for newcomers in Germany, and Antura and the Letters (Initiative 60), which is a free and open source smartphone game made in Germany to help Syrian refugee children learn to read, even when they aren't connected to the Internet.

These few examples show that there are a lot of separate projects with strong know-how, high potential, and new ideas that, if put together and put into a coherent and holistic policy framework, could be used on a bigger scale and help the whole of Europe.

The Increased Role of the State in the Digital Era

Technology is important, so why do states find it so hard to use? What do they need to do?

As was shown in the last part, there are a lot of interesting projects and solutions that use digital and innovative tools to help immigrants integrate. Even though these bottom-up events can have a lot of good effects on the community, the State needs to drive and encourage them as soon as possible. In fact, the digital revolution has changed the world in ways that have never been seen before. It has had a big effect on how public and social services are given to people. Also, digitalization is expected to play a big part in the transformation of the public sector as a whole, since it has the potential to make service production and delivery in public aid areas more productive and open to more people. Also, e-Services cut down on the time people have to spend in government offices, which makes people more likely to use them.

Fig. 12.3 - e-Government users between 2013 and 2018 (% of total EU citizens)

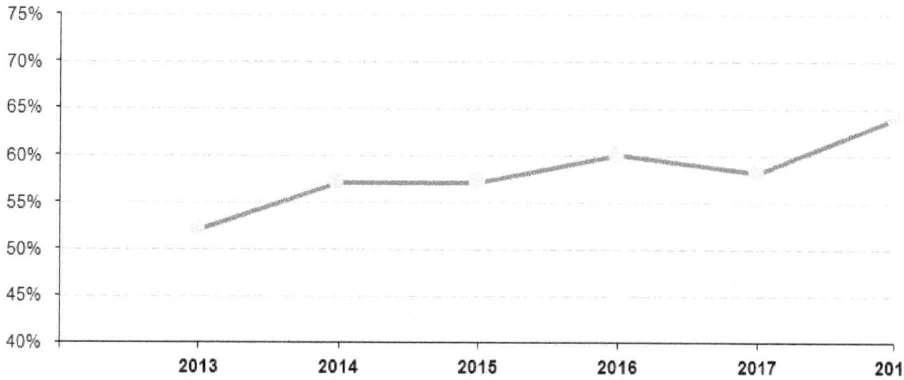

In this way, the digital success of every EU country has gotten better over the past year. For example, Finland, Sweden, the Netherlands, and Denmark got the best scores in DESI 2019 and are among the world's leaders in digitalization. Some other countries, on the other hand, still have a long way to go, and the EU as a whole needs to get better in order to be able to fight on the world stage.

Figure 12.4 shows that even though digital tools have come a long way, the public sector in some countries still doesn't understand how digital transformation works.

Fig. 12.4 - The Digital Economy and Society Index (2019)

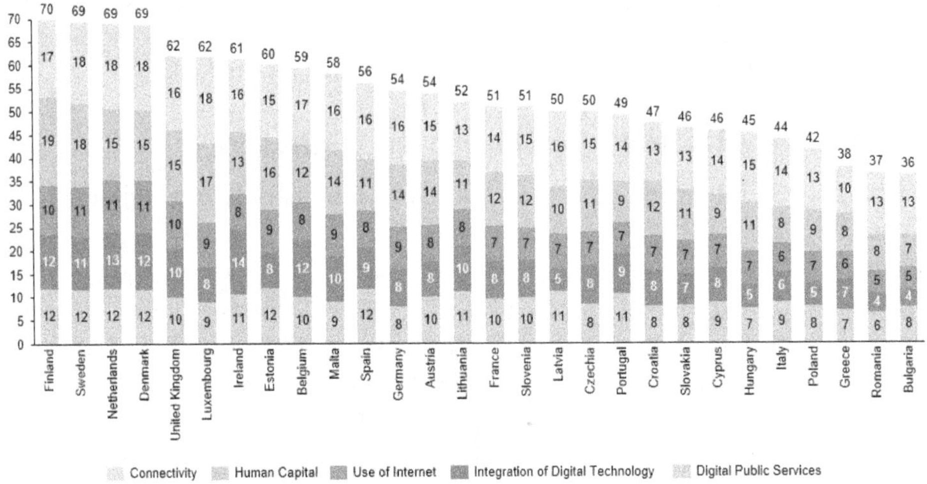

The low rate of digital innovation in some countries suggests that there are deeper structural barriers and challenges to overcome. These are related to the conservative and risk-averse traditions of the public sector, as shown by an INSEAD/EY study that looked at the "black box" of digital transformation in governments. Along with the lack of sound policy logic and the difficulty of introducing new technologies, the "black box" in technology implementation is closely tied to the public service culture, which can be a major barrier to digital innovation because it rarely involves innovation, experimentation, and taking risks.

All of this shows that when it comes to building the digitally-enabled public sector of the future, governments need to think about a few important things. First of all, technology has the ability to help governments make the world a safer place for all of their citizens while keeping strategic and important interests safe. It is very important to find a balance between the ideals and rights that are necessary for a democratic society to work and the protection of personal privacy. Using Big Data applications, Artificial Intelligence (AI), and machine learning to keep a closer eye on citizens puts a lot of limits on private life and the security of personal data. This could be especially true for people from other countries who live in a host country, since technology can be used to better identify them for security reasons, record them in specific databases, and keep track of their movements and personal lives.

Second, governments should keep in mind that many of the world's biggest problems can be solved more effectively by using smart infrastructures. This is because smart infrastructures let us use the latest technologies to get the most out of them and find more long-term solutions to problems like urbanization, climate change, and managing migration. When it comes to the integration of people from third countries in particular, smart infrastructures can shorten the distance between migrants and service providers, encourage the creation of new models for managing diversity, and make better use of resources through smarter spending and investment in programs and services that help people integrate in a way that is long-lasting and stable. In this way, projects for "smart cities" become very important. They use technology to find community-based answers to the most urgent problems caused by globalization that are driven by a vision. With a focus on technology, the cities of the future will help change governments so they can successfully carry out their economic visions. They will also build stronger networks of participation and better communication tools for more inclusive societies.

Third, the public sector should improve its skills and rethink how work is done to make it more efficient, put the customer first, and make sure that everyone is included. This means that states should spend more time and money helping their people improve their digital skills. Because of this, it is very important to speed up the upskilling or reskilling of people to meet the needs of the digital revolution. In this way, citizens and people from other countries can be put on the same educational tracks to learn and improve their digital skills and build high-quality training networks that open up new possibilities for everyone.

Even though technology can have some downsides, like limits on personal data and private life, it also has a lot to give the public sector, and its role is becoming more and more important in our daily lives. So, governments should think about how they could use ICTs to rethink how they provide services to the public, with the goal of putting citizens at the center of what they do and making it easier for citizens to get involved by making models and platforms that are open to everyone.

Here's the answer: Rethinking unity by putting immigrants first

When it comes to integrating people from third countries, results from Section 2 show that bottom-up approaches are great examples of how technologies can be used to help with different parts of the process, such as making it easier to access rights and information, education, and the job market, as well as making it easier to learn a language and making it easier for people to connect with each other. But bottom-up efforts aren't enough to help immigrants integrate on their own, so the states should back them up with well-structured policy strategies. Taking into account the needs that come from the challenges of integrating migrants, EU governments and public administrations are being asked to support bottom-up initiatives more and more. They do this not only by creating platforms and ecosystems where resources, means, and good practices can be shared, but also by creating a policy framework that encourages innovation and digitalization.

In a remodeled and digitally enabled public sector, citizens and people from third countries could be seen as customers and included in decision-making processes, programs, and services that touch and involve everyone. To renew their focus on citizen engagement, governments need to give their citizens the tools they need to learn digital skills and have meaningful conversations about how to improve how they serve their citizens and how to make the most money from putting citizen-friendly solutions into place. Fully involved citizens can make big changes to policies and programs that affect every part of city life and government services. They can also help come up with new ways to solve public policy problems more quickly.

In terms of integrating migrants, digital innovation and multi-stakeholder methods could put migrants and their needs at the center of public policy strategies. So, migrants will be able to show their preferences, advocate for their needs and interests, and choose the best solutions for social inclusion, such as access to the job market, help with language, co-housing, financial support, welfare, and health care systems. Within this new framework, EU governments and public administrations are told to make it easier for people to use public and social services by creating specific tools and platforms to help with integration. These tools and platforms will be able to incorporate the good practices that have been shown by bottom-up initiatives all over Europe.

Way Forward

Integration of migrants and refugees in the EU is still a problem for both central and local governments. As we've seen, there isn't yet a single, all-encompassing plan for integrating migrants. Instead, Member States have put in place plans that focus on different parts of the process. EU state administrations will have to take into account the key role that technology can play if they want to help set up well-structured and effective integration policies. These tools may make it easier for public administrations and local governments to do their jobs while also making it easier to handle integration actions and giving migrants more freedom and a better chance of being accepted.

Technology is an important tool for helping people find jobs and become part of society. ICTs can help immigrants find jobs, get their qualifications recognized, learn the language and culture of the host country, make friends, learn new skills, and find out about available education, health, and other services, as well as information about the host country's laws and administration. Given that ICT can help make better integration plans, EU Member States need to be ready to use what digital innovation has to offer. In this way, EU governments and administrations need to make new efforts to understand how digitalization is changing how social services should be organized and delivered. This will help them put citizens at the center of their actions and find practical solutions to social problems.

For policy actions to last in the so-called "digital era," it is important to make sure they are focused on migrants. EU governments and public administrations can reclaim their power to solve complex problems, like the integration of migrants, by letting citizens help them decide what to do and how to do it. To do this, they should be able to implement a multi-stakeholder approach that includes public and private actors as well as third-sector organizations and use ICT to promote social inclusion. In particular, EU governments must make sure that solutions are made with the needs of the people who are facing the problems in mind. This means that migrants and refugees should be at the center of the activities. Also, public players in the EU can come up with strategies that can be scaled from the national to the local level, used in other places, and changed to meet the changing needs of society.

In conclusion, digital solutions can pave the way for better customized services that can help both people from third countries and EU societies. They can also encourage the implementation of concrete action plans to ensure the long-term sustainability of migrant integration processes, with public actors setting standards and guidelines while keeping migrants at the center of their policy strategy.

Chapter 13
Migration Patterns, Advancement, and the 2030 Blueprint

Migration is one of the most important things about the twenty-first century. Even though people have always moved and always will, there is no doubt that the so-called "crisis" of 2015 brought migration to the attention of the international community, and there is no doubt that migration is now a major political concern in many countries. Importantly, while a lot of attention is paid to the growing flows between low-income and high-income countries, like between Africa and Europe or between South/Central and North America, most people move within their own country or between neighboring countries. In other words, movement is mostly a local thing that happens in both rich and poor countries.

International movement is both a problem and an opportunity for economic and social growth all over the world. Even though economic growth, development opportunities, security, and political instability can be reasons for migration from some countries, migration journeys are likely to be affected by key problems that countries and people everywhere face, such as resource scarcity and climate breakdown, gender and wealth inequality, quality livelihoods, the eradication of poverty, and the right to healthy and fulfilling lives in sustainable societies.

This chapter will talk about how migration and the 2030 Agenda affect each other, what that means for growth in different countries, and what the main policy areas of the 2030 Agenda are that will affect the future of migration to Europe. It will come up with key questions and themes and suggest policy solutions that will affect the way people move to Europe in the next few decades. It will also try to figure out what their effects will be on the future shape and size of migration to Europe in the context of the Sustainable Development Goals.

Migration has a big impact on all parts of economic and social growth around the world. Because of this, it will be important to reach the Sustainable growth Goals (SDGs). Even though the link between migration and growth is becoming more clear, it is still not well understood. We know that people leave their home countries because there aren't enough jobs and investments there. But we also know that migration can help with development and investment in the country of origin, fill labor gaps and encourage new ideas in the country of destination, and help with development in "transit countries" along the way. It is a good way to help people get out of poverty, not just for migrants but also for their families and the places they live in.

Migration can help achieve the goals of the 2030 Agenda for Sustainable Development (the "2030 Agenda") and lead to good development outcomes. To do this, we need to know how migration affects the success of all SDGs, as well as how the achievement of SDGs affects migration in the future. As Member States and International Institutions start talking about how to apply the Global Compact for Migration (GCM), it is more important than ever to understand these connections and what they mean for policy.

Three things make the 2030 Agenda a good place to look at and use the links between movement and development. First, the 2030 Agenda is the first worldwide framework for development that includes migration and recognizes it as a development dimension. The Agenda has goals about migration and recognizes how important it is to sustainable development. It also takes into account the unique risks that migrants may face.

Second, migration has an effect on every part of growth. The fact that the 2030 Agenda is multidisciplinary and crosses sectors makes it a good place to look at how migration and human mobility affect a wide range of development problems. This is important not only for figuring out what the problem is, but also for coming up with policy answers.

Lastly, and most importantly, the 2030 Agenda has the political "traction" it needs in the different Member States and in the international system. Migration has effects at every step of the way, especially in the country of origin and the country of destination. Because of this, migration interacts with many different sectors and requires coordination between many different players and more coherence across policies. This kind of cooperation can only happen if people at the highest levels agree, which the SDGs have already done. The SDGs are also multidisciplinary, which makes it easier for people from different groups to work together.

There are a number of goals in the 2030 Agenda that recognize the economic importance of migrants. These goals are SDGs 4, 5, 8, 10, 16, and 17. In particular, goal 10.7 of the 2030 Agenda, which is the most important part of migration, calls for "safe, regular, and responsible migration" to be made easier and "well-managed migration policies" to be put into place.

Outside of these goals, however, the Agenda says nothing about how migration affects growth as a whole. The main focus of our work is on these "indirect" links between migration and growth that have been left out. If countries want to reach the SDGs, they need to think about how migration affects them on every level and in every way, not just the goals in "to be solved," but a mechanism or plan that can help them reach many of the goals. To do this, governments and other players need to figure out the many ways in which migration is linked to different goals and targets. They also need to recognize that migrants can be vulnerable and should be taken into account under the general principle of "leaving no one behind."

Poverty Alleviation and Migration

Migration is a strong way to reduce poverty, and it can help reach all of the SDGs.

Migration for work can help lower poverty for migrants, their families, and the countries where they come from and where they live. Migrants and their families get more money and knowledge, which lets them spend more on basic needs, get more dependable and modern energy services, get access to education and health services, and make investments. For female refugees, having more money can give them more freedom and a better place in society. Migration can lead to higher wages and more economic growth in the country of origin through higher incomes, spending, the transfer of knowledge and technology, and investments made by migrant families. In the countries where they live, migrants can take jobs that aren't being filled, help with services, and pay taxes and social security that add to the government's budget.

But moving does not always work out as well as it could. According to our research on migration and sustainable cities, poor people who move to cities often work in the informal sector, where the benefits of moving are smaller. In the same way, it is very hard for low-skilled and semi-skilled newcomers to get good jobs. In terms of poverty, our study shows that the high costs of the different stages of migration reduce the financial benefits, and that those who would gain the most from migration can't do it in a regular and orderly way because of restrictions on mobility. Migration would be more beneficial for migrants, their families, and the places they move to if the process was more organized, predictable, and open to everyone. New Zealand's "recognised seasonal employer" program is a good example of how migration can be used to fight poverty. It is described in the ODI paper "Poverty migration and the 2030 Agenda for sustainable development" and is reprinted below with permission.

Jobs, Stable Livelihoods, and Migration in the 2030 Agenda

As the share of informal and risky jobs continues to grow in low-income countries, where they are more common than unemployment, the desire for good work is likely to drive a lot of migration to Europe in the coming years. ILO (International Labour Organization) numbers show that the number of people with "vulnerable employment" is higher than the number of people who are unemployed by a fair amount. Vulnerable employment in this case means that people have a lot of uncertainty at work, are more likely to have informal jobs, and are less likely to have job stability, social protections, or steady incomes. In 2017, it was thought that there were 1.4 billion people in these groups. In 2018, that number grew by 17 million. About 300 million people around the world work and live on less than $1.90 a day. Most people who move to better countries likely do so because they want to find good jobs. Figure 13.1 shows how many vulnerable jobs there are around the world. This shows how likely it is that people will move to find good work, often to high-income countries. The main thing that drives people to move for good work is the interaction between push and pull factors. Push factors include not having a secure way to make a living and being poor. Pull factors include higher wages and real or imagined better social protections. "Transit countries" that are housing migrants who are still looking to move somewhere else have the chance to put migrant populations to work and boost their own development, as has been seen with the Jordanian and Ethiopian compact approach to refugee employment.

Fig 13.1 - Share of the global labour supply in paid employment, vulnerable employment and unemployment

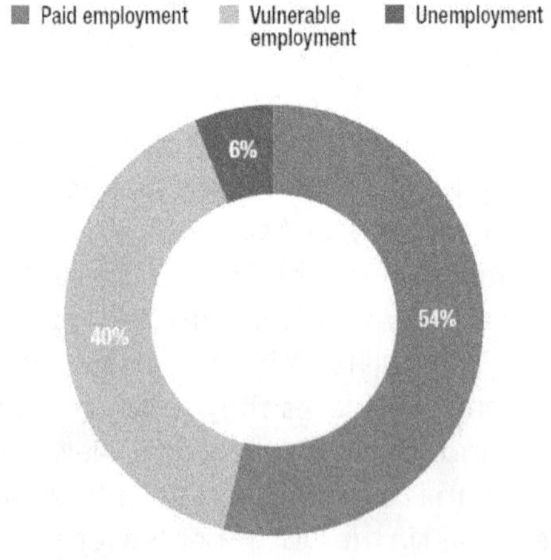

Source: ILO, 2018a.

Education, Healthcare and Migration

Migrants help make services better and are very important to the countries they live in as workers and customers. When access to basic services is denied or limited, these possible benefits are stifled, which makes it harder for migrants to help in a good way.

It is important to give refugees access to health care and health services to make sure they stay healthy and can continue to work. But it also helps the people in the countries where they live in important ways. For example, when migrant children are vaccinated, the chance of diseases that can spread is lower for everyone. Importantly, migrants often help directly with health and care services, which depend more and more on foreign labor in many countries. This also applies to social safety, where migrants can make important contributions to the fiscal balance of their host countries because the taxes and other payments they make are more than the benefits and services they get.

Still, giving migrants access to these services isn't always easy, especially when movement is sudden or wasn't planned for. Large, unexpected migration flows can throw off education systems, hurt migrant and refugee children, and cause conflict in the communities that are hosting them.

Importantly, the problems that make it hard for migrants to get basic services aren't technical and often aren't even financial. For example, giving migrants access to water and sanitation is often a problem of good government.

SDG 4, which is about education (see Table 2.2), is important for managing migration because it creates chances in sending countries and helps development by training and educating migrants, who are then better able to help the societies they move to. Research shows that levels of education help make societies more stable and democratic, and that countries that spend in this area get a good return on their money. If a lot of people come to a country all at once, as happened in Jordan and Lebanon, this can be bad for the school system, where fast refugee influxes made schools hard to manage because they were too full. But when migration is handled well, it can help education by bringing more people to schools with few students. It has also been linked to better student performance in some cases. Quality education is important for integration and building societies that are better because of migration. It is also important for growth. Figure 13.2 shows how a good education for second-generation migrants can make it easier for them to speak the languages of their new homes. This can help both migrants and their new countries grow and develop.

Fig. 13.2 - Percentage of immigrant students who do not speak the language of assessment at home

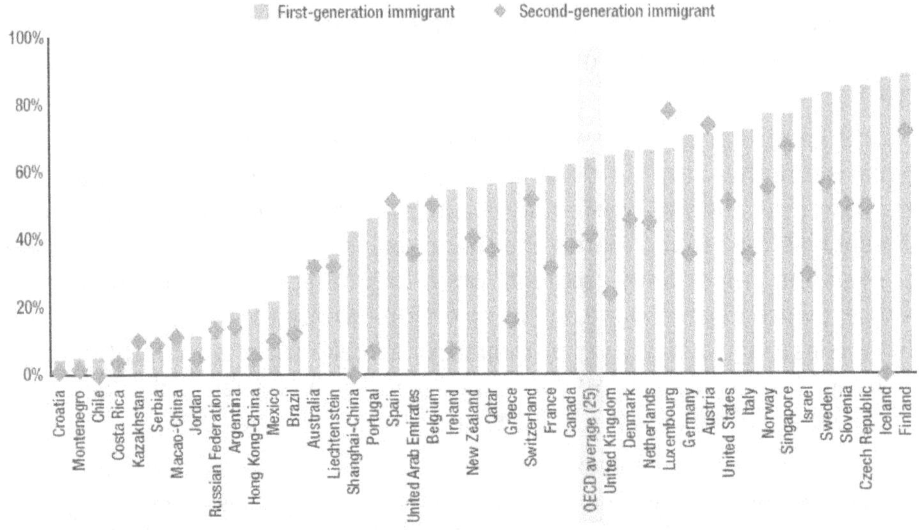

Source: S. Nicolai, J. Wales and E. Aiazzi, Education, migration and the 2030 Agenda for Sustainable Development. ODI Briefing Note, 2017

Lifelong learning for all (SDG4) is a key part of engaging migrant communities and giving them the tools they need to live happy, productive lives. Making sure people can get the education they need and don't have to move because they don't have enough chances is also important for development. By giving migrants and their children access to education and training, they will be better able to help meet the needs of the labor market. This will increase their addition to the local market, their ability to make money, and the money they can send back home. More generally, access to education helps meet a wide range of SDGs by bringing about economic and social benefits like better jobs, better health, less inequality between men and women, and more political participation.

Water and Energy Resources

Access to basic services like energy and water might not be the main reason why people move, but not having access to either is likely to make people's lives worse and create regional disparities. This can cause more people to move from areas and countries with poor access to these services to those with better and more reliable access.

Lack of access to water and sewage isn't always a reason why people move, but having these services can make migration safer and easier. But the difficulties refugees face in getting to them will make it harder to reach the

SDGs. SDG 6, which says to "ensure availability and sustainable management of water and sanitation for all", is hard to reach for people who are in transit or whose immigration status is uncertain because they might not be able to get these services. Access to water and sanitation may play a role in a person's choice to move, but it's not always true that lack of water is the main reason people move. If people don't have access to water, they might change their jobs from agricultural, which uses a lot of water, to service work, or they might move away. Even though there are times when moving might be a way to adapt to a lack of water or poor sanitation, water is likely to be a secondary factor that is hard to separate from other things like land degradation or fewer economic possibilities.

Fig. 13.3 - Distribution of migrants by level of education

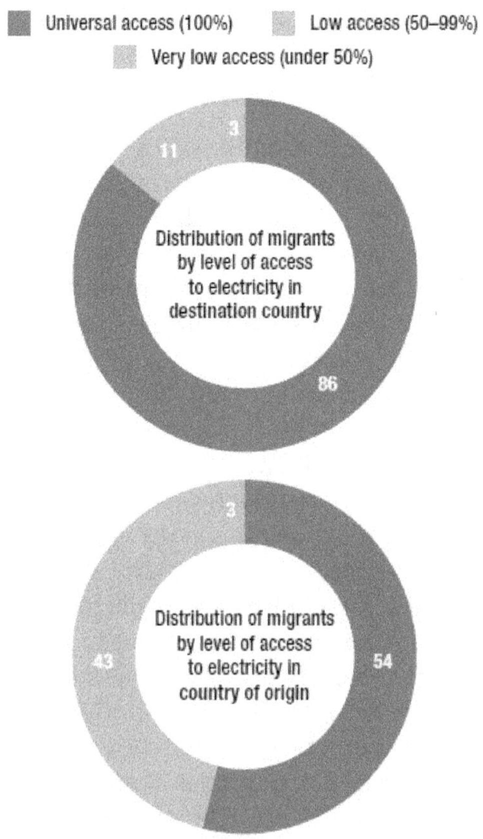

Source: UNDESA, 2015; IEA et al., 2018.

Access to energy is a key part of development, and a stable energy supply is needed for good jobs and strong development. Not only is it important for providing food, clean water, and a good quality of life, but it also makes it possible to provide services that help social and economic growth. SDG7 wants to make sure that everyone has access to reliable and affordable energy, but most of the people who don't have it yet live in rural parts of sub-Saharan Africa and South Asia. Access to energy has a big effect on people's ability to make a living, and people's choices to move for a better future are likely to be affected in part by how easy it is to get energy in the place they are leaving and where they are going. Figure 13.3 shows how access to power is different in countries that send and countries that receive migrants. The difference shows that there are high-quality ways to make a living, access to basic needs, and chances for productive work in the countries where people move to. All of these things depend on having access to good quality energy. Even though it might not be the main reason why people decide to move, having less access to the chances that come with having secure and reliable energy is often a factor.

Climate Change and Environment

Climate change is likely to hurt places like Africa and the Middle East and North Africa (MENA) countries by putting stress on resources, agriculture production, and water supplies, as well as making people feel less safe and possibly causing wars. Even though there is no one clear meaning of climate-induced migration, Wilkinson et al. (2016) drew a picture of what it means. Disaster-related movement has been a problem for a long time, especially within countries. From 2008 to 2015, disasters forced an average of 25.4 million people to move each year, both within and across borders. About 85% of these disasters were caused by the climate. The long-term changes in climate in different parts of the world and the turmoil they will cause may be more important for the future of migration to Europe. As climate-driven short-term migration becomes more common and adds to long-term changes in the climate of regions, parts of the global south, especially in Africa and the Middle East and North Africa (MENA) countries, will become less hospitable, which will lower the quality of life and change people's decisions about whether or not to move. In the even longer term, the rise in sea level and other existential threats to communities will help wipe out coastal and low-lying places. Importantly, a lot of the world's most fertile arable land is in low-lying places, which puts food supplies at even more long-term risk. Climate-induced migration is hard to describe and find because climate change has many effects on different time scales. People may move because of a disaster or because they want to stay alive in the face of more gradual climate change. As a result of these changes, many people will have to move, with estimates ranging from 25 million to 300 million by 2050. Figure 13.4 shows the recent trends in migration from countries that are vulnerable to climate change. However, it is important to keep in mind that climate-induced migration is not likely to be the main reason why a person moves. Instead, it is likely to be a catalyst that makes common reasons why people move worse. The international community needs to recognize that migration is a way to react to a changing climate (ODI brief). More and more, people in charge of making decisions will have to choose between making places that are under threat more resilient and making it easier for people to move out of those areas. Many of the steps that need to be taken to help people adapt to climate change and move away from it will require acts from developed states to make sure they meet the goals of the 2030 Agenda and "leave no one behind." Building up everyone's ability to take care of themselves is key to this, and helping people do this will help lessen the harmful effects of climate change and its effects on migration to Europe in the 21st century.

Integration of Migration

Policies and programs for development can be part of a larger plan to better handle migration and take advantage of its economic and social benefits. To do this, migration needs to be better merged into all of the goals of the 2030 Agenda. To "mainstream" migration into the 2030 Agenda, the links, opportunities, and challenges linked to migration under specific goals and targets need to be found, highlighted (like we do in our briefings), and taken into account when making policy.

Fig. 13.4 - Migration flows from countries vulnerable to climate change

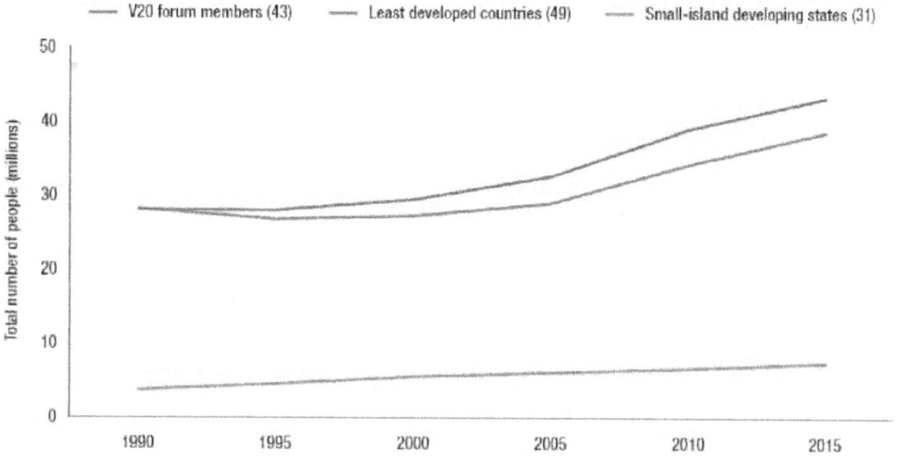

Source E. Wilkinson, L. Schipper, C. Simonet, and Z. Kubik, Climate change, migration and the 2030 Agenda for Sustainable Development, ODI Briefing Note, 2016

In this case, it is important that Member States' voluntary national reviews (VNRs) take into account the role of migration. Member states are already making progress in this area. In 2017, 29 of 43 national reviews included the words "migration" or "migrant," "refugee," "human trafficking" or "traffic in," "internally displaced persons (IDPs)" and/or "remittances" (CDP Subgroup on Voluntary National Reviews, 2018). At the same time, we need to keep in mind that refugees may be vulnerable in certain ways and may have certain needs. These things should be taken into account to make sure that no one is left behind. In 2017, only 25 of the 43 VNRs named migrants and refugees as a "left behind" group, though not always with specific actions or strategies.

Also, policymakers need to think about, measure, and account for migration in order to take advantage of its benefits and lower its potential problems. Migration should be a part of regional, national, and local plans and strategies for growth, from the first assessments of the situation to setting goals and planning to monitoring and evaluating. More and more countries are doing this. For example, "migration for development" is part of Bangladesh's 7th five-year plan for development. The many different parts of the relationship between migration and development offer concrete policy entry points that go beyond state participation. For example, the International Labour Organization's (ILO) focus on decent work has a lot to do with migration. As part of this agenda, any programming should take into account how vulnerable migrants are in the workplace and how hard it is for them to get to social safety programs at work.

Conclusion

The connections between migration and development also affect migration policy and practice, especially how the Global Compact for Migration (GCM) is put into place. Migration policy and practice and global development policy and practice haven't talked to each other or worked together much so far. The GCM, which is an attempt by states to find a common way to deal with global migration while taking into account its effect on development, is a chance to fix this and make real progress. The GCM says in its text that:

> Is rooted in the 2030 Agenda for Sustainable Development, and builds upon its recognition that migration is a multidimensional reality of major relevance for the sustainable development of countries of origin, transit and destination, which requires coherent and comprehensive responses.

The text also goes beyond the specific migration goals. It says that the GCM "aims to use the potential of migration to reach all Sustainable Development Goals." Also, in Objective 23, Member States agree to make sure that the GCM, the 2030 Agenda, and the Addis Ababa Action Agenda are all implemented in the same way. This is because migration and sustainable development are multifaceted and rely on each other.

From January 2019, Member States will work to put this Compact into action. This is where real change could happen. Even though the framework and goals are global, actions need to be led at the local level and be rooted in specific contexts, countries, regions, and markets where there are unique possibilities and challenges for growth. A lot of different groups must work together in unique alliances to get these things done. Businesses, city leaders, academics, journalists, and other people who can help find and try new ideas will need to play a more central role, along with Member States and the UN system. This is because businesses have a natural interest in labor mobility. Strategies should be flexible, and ways to help should be able to change to meet different needs and possibilities. It will be important to avoid "blueprint" methods and promises that can't be kept if we want to get the most out of combining these two related plans to make real changes.

Lastly, from the point of view of putting development into action, how to do development is just as important as what to do. When you look at migration through the lens of development, you run the risk of reinforcing or re-creating unhelpful dichotomies of giver and recipient or home country and new country. For example, the fact that in some host countries (especially in Europe), development aid is used as part of a larger strategy to discourage migration raises many concerns. Not only is it ineffective (there is no evidence that aid can change migration patterns), but it also risks misleading the public about the positive relationship between development and migration. Instead, the SDGs are a chance for countries to talk about migration and growth in a way that is mutual and based on a global framework.

Chapter 14
The Ukrainian Crisis Underscores the Necessity for Improved Coordination in European Asylum Policy

A few weeks after it started on February 24, 2022, the Russian attack of Ukraine caused the most people to flee their homes in Europe since the end of World War II. By March 29, 4,019,287 people were looking for refuge in the countries that near Ukraine. This number is already higher than the 4 million that the UNHCR expected at the start of the war, and some estimates say that the number of forced migrants could reach 9.9 million if the war keeps going and spreads to the west of Ukraine.

Europe's reaction to the influx of refugees is different from what it did in 2015, when more than a million refugees, mostly from Syria, came to Europe. On March 4, the Council of the European Union used the Temporary security Directive for the first time. This gave Ukrainian citizens who lived in Ukraine but were forced to leave after their country was invaded temporary security. This protection also goes to stateless people or people from countries other than Ukraine who have been forced to leave Ukraine under certain situations. This strategy is meant to help EU countries deal with large numbers of displaced people, since giving immediate protection makes the asylum process easier and faster.

The size of the recent Ukrainian flows is going to make people worry about how they will affect the countries where they end up. We take a quick look at the available research, which mostly calms fears about the bad effects of large numbers of refugees. But we think that the best way to deal with the present situation is for European countries to share responsibility. This, in turn, leads us to make rough estimates of how many refugees could be sent to each EU27 country based on their ability to take them in.

The economics literature has shown that, at least in the medium term, big migration flows don't hurt state finances or the job market. Immigrants often help a big part of the population by taking jobs where there aren't enough people to do them, creating jobs for the people who already live there, or just spending money or investing there. In the same way, foreigners do not add to the cost of running the government. Beyond the numbers, a lot of refugees have complementary skills and knowledge that allow them to stay connected to their home country. This, in turn, helps the economy, trade, and new ideas grow.

But these effects don't show up right away in the receiving country, and short-term problems can be big. This is especially true for immigrants who have been through terrible things. Also, refugees are often less prepared than economic migrants because they don't speak the language of their target country or don't have the skills they need to work there. Refugees may also have to take jobs for which they are overqualified because of the problems they face. This can make it harder for some people to get jobs in the host country, especially those with less education and foreigners who are already there.

Also, the process of integrating outsiders may take longer in some countries where there are a lot of migrants. Even though there is a lot of unity, the number of refugees in Greece has caused tensions, which may explain why support for the far right has grown. Germany, Austria, and Denmark have also seen things like this. Literature doesn't give a clear answer, but it does show how the location of migrants plays a complicated role in their integration. On the one hand, having networks makes it easier for refugees to get jobs, but if there are too many arrivals, this positive effect may be lessened. The network's make-up is also important. On the other hand, the benefits of networks may not last long for newcomers because people with big networks may have less reason to learn skills that are useful in their surroundings.

For short-term costs to be kept to a minimum and medium-term gains to be maximised, Ukrainian refugees must be welcomed and integrated well. Europeans have shown a lot of support for Ukrainians who are looking for refuge, but it will be hard to keep this support going in the long run. In the current emergency situation, governments must set up proper shelters and make sure everyone has access to basic services and medical care. Children are especially fragile, so their well-being needs to be given extra care. Ukrainians have direct access to the job market because of a programme that gives them short-term safety. This has been shown to help refugees get jobs and become part of the economy. The distribution of refugees within and across space, which rests on the ability of countries and regions to take them in, could make it harder for these measures to work and make them less likely to work. This shows how important it is for European countries to work together and how much better and more consistent planning is needed between them.

Unbalanced Distribution of Refugees

At this point, we still don't know how many people will go to each country. In the short term, most of them will probably choose a place that is easy to get to, like a neighbouring country, except for Russia and Belarus. More refugees are likely to move to other countries that don't touch Ukraine. As of March 29, more than a million applications for temporary protection had been made in these countries that don't touch Ukraine. This is more than 23% of the outflows that had been recorded at Ukraine's borders. In a second phase, countries like the United States, Kazakhstan, Canada, and Israel, where there are a lot of Ukrainians who have moved away, could also become important locations.

Below, we show different ways that Ukrainian refugees could be spread out among the 27 EU countries. We make distribution keys based on five different factors, which show how many refugees each country could take in based on five different situations. The first two take into account the networks that will be in place in 2020 and how appealing each destination has been to Ukrainians in the past few years. This is for the time from 2015 to 2020. Ukrainian refugees are free to choose where they want to stay for a while, which makes their networks abroad more important. Also, each country's ability to take in refugees, which can be estimated by the size of its people and its GDI, should affect where Ukrainian refugees go and be used as a criterion for the rest of the keys.

Our method, which is based on simple criteria, means that we leave out other important factors that could affect the number of Ukrainian refugees in each place. For example, we ignore limits on how many people can stay in a place. Also, we focus on the flow of refugees from Ukraine without thinking about how this might affect other flows or how war might affect the flow of refugees from other countries (like Russia). Overall, we want to come up with a reasonable order of magnitude for Ukrainian flows instead of making exact (and technically risky) predictions about where refugees will go.

In Table 14.1, the difference between the distributions of the total stock (column 1) and the recent arrivals of Ukrainian immigrants (column 2) shows how popular a place has been in the past and how it is now. The United Nations thinks that there will be 1,471 Ukrainians living in Luxembourg in 2020. This is 0.1% of the total Ukrainian population in the EU27. In contrast, between 2015 and 2020, 1,296 people came to the country, which is 0.4% of the total number of people who came to the EU27 during that time. The fact that Luxembourg has a bigger share of recent flows than it did in the past shows that this place has become more popular in recent years. Over the last five years, Ukraine has also become more appealing to people who want to move to places with a long history, like Poland or Germany. On the other hand, countries like Italy, Portugal, and France have lost some of their charm in recent years.

A population-based distribution key (column 3 of Table 14.1) would mean that all European countries have the same "number of refugees per person." Luxembourg has 0.14 percent of the population of the EU27, which is a bit more than the 0.10 percent of Ukrainian newcomers in 2020. Some countries have more Ukrainian immigrants than would be expected based on the number of people living there. This is especially true for places like Poland and Hungary that are close to Ukraine, as well as Germany, the Czech Republic, Italy, and Portugal. On the other hand, some places have a smaller Ukrainian community than their population size would suggest. This is the case for France, which has 15.1% of the population of the EU27 but will only house 1.3% of Ukrainian migrants in 2020. Another example is Belgium. Its people make up 2.6% of the EU27's total population, but only 0.2% of Ukrainians will live there in 2020.

A different kind of sharing takes into account how much money each place can make. For this, we use each country's share of the total GDP of the EU27. This would cut down on the amount of land that the four EU countries that near Ukraine (Hungary, Poland, Romania, and Slovakia) have. Col. 4 of Table 14.1 shows that people from Ukraine would be more likely to move to countries in Western Europe. For example, Germany's share would be 22.7%, which is more than its share based on the number of Ukrainians living abroad in 2020. In the same way, 15.7% would be France's share. Belgium and Luxembourg would each get 3% and Luxembourg would get 0.4%.

Lastly, keys with more parts can have more than one dimension. For example, a distribution key based on the German model (with a weight of one-third for population and two-thirds for GDP) gives Eastern European countries a little more weight than a key based only on GDI and makes Western European countries a little less important. In this case, Col. 5 of Table 14.1 shows that Luxembourg would take in 0.3% of refugees from Ukraine.

Table 14.1 Estimates of the distribution (shares in %) of Ukrainian refugees in the EU27

	(1) Key = Stock	(2) Key = Flow	(3) Key = Pop.	(4) Key = GDP	(5) Key = Mix	(6) Obs. Ref.
Luxembourg and bordering countries						
Luxembourg	0.1	0.4	0.1	0.4	0.3	0.1
Belgium	0.2	0.4	2.6	3.0	2.9	0.7
France	1.3	0.5	15.1	15.7	15.5	0.8
Germany	20.5	22.2	18.7	22.7	21.4	7.7

Bordering countries of Ukraine						
Hungary	5.0	9.5	2.2	1.6	1.8	7.2
Poland	19.3	20.6	8.5	6.5	7.2	46.1
Romania	3.1	9.5	4.3	3.1	3.5	12.0
Slovakia	0.8	0.4	1.2	0.9	1.0	5.5
Other destinations						
Austria	1.0	1.1	2.0	2.5	2.3	1.1
Bulgaria	0.8	1.5	1.6	0.9	1.1	1.6
Croatia	0.1	0.0	0.9	0.6	0.7	0.4
Cyprus	0.2	0.0	0.2	0.2	0.2	0.3
Czechia	9.3	9.2	2.4	2.2	2.3	8.5
Denmark	0.8	1.2	1.3	1.8	1.6	0.7
Estonia	1.7	0.7	0.3	0.3	0.3	0.3
Finland	0.2	0.4	1.2	1.4	1.3	0.4
Greece	1.4	0.1	2.3	1.5	1.8	0.4
Ireland	0.4	0.2	1.1	2.3	1.9	0.4
Italy	17.6	7.9	13.5	12.6	12.9	2.2
Latvia	2.3	0.0	0.4	0.3	0.3	0.2
Lithuania	1.5	2.5	0.6	0.5	0.6	1.0
Malta	0.1	0.1	0.1	0.1	0.1	0.0
Netherlands	0.2	0.5	3.8	5.1	4.7	0.5
Portugal	3.8	2.1	2.3	1.7	1.9	0.7
Slovenia	0.2	0.3	0.5	0.4	0.4	0.2
Spain	7.5	7.4	10.5	8.9	9.5	0.7
Sweden	0.7	1.1	2.3	2.8	2.6	0.4

Note: Table 1 shows the percentage of Ukrainian refugees that would be hosted in EU27 countries based on 5 different criteria and the observed distribution as of March, 29 (column 6). "Key = Stock", "Key = Flow", "Key = Pop", "Key = GDP", "Key = Mix", "Obs. Ref.______refer to distribution keys based on (1) Ukrainian migrant stocks in 2020, (2) Ukrainian flows over the last five years, (3) population share, (4) GDP share, (5) a mix of population and GDP, and (6) the distribution of Ukrainian refugee flows observed as of March 29, respectively.

The present distribution of refugees, shown in column 6 of Table 14.1, is very different from these five distribution keys. We think that more than 2.9 million refugees (73%) are currently living in neighbouring countries. Poland alone is home to more than 1.6 million of these refugees. On the other hand, as of March 29, 2022, more than 1 million temporary applications had been filed in countries that are not border countries.

These division keys can also be used to figure out how many Ukrainian refugees are in each of the different countries they are going to. To do this, a distribution key must be multiplied by the overall number of refugees who are expected to come to the EU27. In Figure 14.1, we show the estimates for Luxembourg and its neighbouring countries based on three different scenarios: one with 4 million refugees, one with 7 million refugees, and one with 10 million Ukrainian refugees in the EU27, which is currently thought to be the upper limit.

Fig. 14.1 - Distribution of Ukrainian refugees under different scenarios and distribution keys

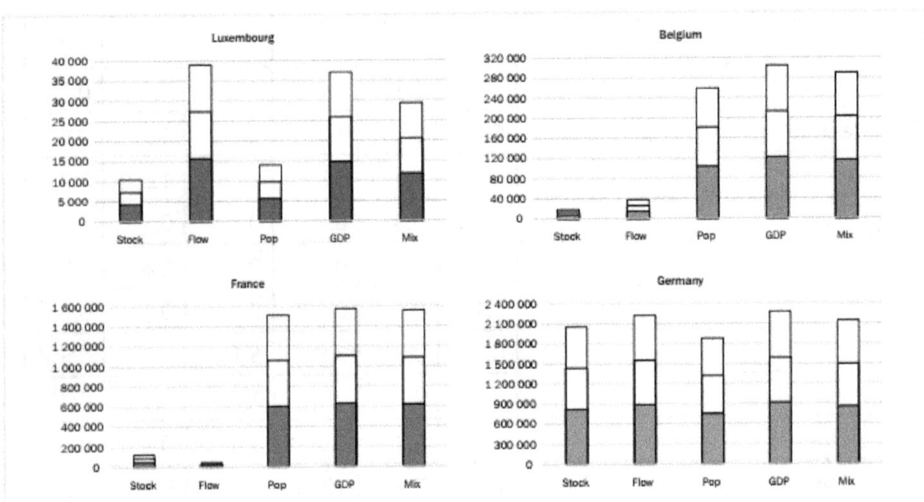

Note: Scenarios = 4 million refugees (colored), 7 million (thick frame), or 10 million (thin frame)
Note: See Table 14.1 for more information

With a population-based distribution, the number of refugees in Luxembourg could range from 5,600 to 14,000. This would depend on the situation. Belgium would take in between 103,000 and 260,000 Ukrainian refugees, France would take in between 603,000 and 1.5 million, and Germany would take in between 749,000 and 1.9 million. If all countries used a key that was based on the German model, these figures would be slightly raised. Based on current networks, the lower numbers that can be predicted are close to the ones that have already been seen in Luxembourg and Belgium. This trend shows that these countries were pretty popular places to go during the early stages of the war. Before the war, a lot of Ukrainians who had left their home country moved to Germany. Its distribution based on networks is even better than the one that would be seen if it were based on the people. In comparison, even though France is a fairly large country, it only had a small Ukrainian diaspora. Its population and GDP-based distribution keys are much more important than those based on networks.

Sharing Responsibility and Coordination

Even though the Temporary Protection Directive is now in place, Ukraine's neighbouring countries (Poland, Romania, Hungary, and Slovakia) are paying most of the costs and dealing with most of the logistical problems caused by the flood of refugees from Ukraine. If European countries worked together, people who were forced to leave their homes could be spread out more evenly, based on how many people each country could take in. By making quotas that can be traded, more complex systems could better take into account the preferences of immigrants and the needs of each host country. These ideas have the potential to make EU migration policies more coordinated, which is especially important in emergency situations like the one we are in now. It's a shame that the EU hasn't been able to come up with a way to coordinate in the past, especially since Europeans seem to want a way to distribute refugee seekers based on how many people each country can take in.

Long-term, it's possible that the influx of refugees from Ukraine won't have much of an effect on the economy, but it's very important to make sure that the refugees are managed and integrated well. Giving them refugee status, a temporary work permit, and access to health services will help them learn the skills they need, but the process of integration will take time, even though Ukrainian networks in the host countries play an important part. To be successful, it seems important to plan how people move between and within European countries so that there aren't too many Ukrainians in one place. We shouldn't forget about other refugee flows, because war and political pressures are still important in other parts of the world and are likely to cause more forced migrations.

Bibliography

Bansak, K., J. Hainmueller, and D. Hangartner (2017). Europeans Support a Proportional Allocation of Asylum Seekers. Nature Human Behaviour 1 (7), 0133.

Battisti, M., G. Peri, and A. Romiti (2022). Dynamic Effects of Co-Ethnic Networks on Immigrants' Economic Success. Economic Journal 132, 58-88.

Dagnelie, O., Mayda, A.M., and J.-F. Maystadt (2019). The Labor Market Integration of Refugees to the United States: Do Entrepreneurs in the Network Help? European Economic Review 111, 257-272.

De la Croix, D. and F. Docquier (2015). An Incentive Mechanism to Break the Low-Skill Immigration Deadlock. Review of Economic Dynamics 18, 593-618.

Dustmann, C., Vasiljeva, K., and A.P Damm (2022). Refugee Migration and Electoral Outcomes. Review of Economic Studies, forthcoming.

Duvell, F. and I. Lapshyna. (2022). The Russian Invasion of Ukraine: Scope, Patterns and Future Development of Displacement. IMIS Working Paper 14, IMIS. Osnabruck: IMIS.

Edo, A., Ragot, L., Rapoport, H., Sardoschau, S., and A. Sweetman (2020). An Introduction to the Economics of Immigration in OECD Countries: Insights from Recent Research. Canadian Journal of Economics 53(4), 1365-1403.

Fasani, F., Frattini, T., and L. Minale (2021). Lift the Ban? Initial Employment Restrictions and Refugee Labour Market Outcomes. Journal of the European Economic Association, 19(5), 2803-2854.

Fernandez-Huertas Moraga, J. and H. Rapoport (2014) Tradable Immigration Quotas. Journal of Public Economics 115, 94-108.

Hangartner, D., Dinas, E., Marbach, M., Matakos, K., and D. Xefteris (2019). Does Exposure to the Refugee Crisis Make Natives More Hostile? American Political Science Review 113(2), 442-455.

Mayda, A-M, Ch. Parsons, H. Pham, and PL. Vezina (2021). Refugees and Foreign Direct Investment: Quasi- Experimental Evidence from US Resettlements. Journal of Development Economics, forthcoming.

UNHCR (2022). Ukraine situation flash update #1. UNHCR Regional Bureau for Europe. 8 March 2022.

Adhikari, P. (2012). 'The plight of the forgotten ones: civil war and forced migration', International Studies Quarterly, 56, 590-606.

Alvarado, S.E. and D.S. Massey. (2010). 'In search of peace: structural adjustment, violence, and international migration', Annals of the American Academy of Political and Social Science, 630, 137-61.

Angelucci, M. (2012). 'US border enforcement and the net flow of Mexican illegal migration', Economic Development and Cultural Change, 60, 311-7.

Armigeon, K. and B. Ceka. (2014). 'The loss of trust in the European Union during the great recession since 2007: the role of heuristics from the national political system', European Union Politics, 15, 82-107.

Aziz, N.A., P. Monzini, and F. Pastore. (2015). Changing Dynamics of Cross-border Human Smuggling and Trafficking in the Mediterranean, Instituto Affari Internazionale, Rome.

Bansak, K., J. Hainmueller, and D. Hangartner. (2016). 'How economic, humanitarian, and religious concerns shape European attitudes toward asylum seekers', Science, 354, 217-22. Barthel, F. and E. Neumayer. (2015). 'Spatial dependence in asylum migration', Journal of Ethnic and Migration Studies, 41, 1131-51.

Bertoli, S. and J. Fernandez-Huertas Moraga. (2013). 'Multilateral resistance to migration', Journal of Development Economics, 102, 79-100.

Besley, T. and M. Reynal-Querol. (2014). 'The legacy of historical conflict: evidence from Africa', American Political Science Review, 108, 319-36.

Betts, A. (2003). 'Public goods theory and the provision of refugee protection: the role of the joint-product model in burden-sharing theory', Journal of Refugee Studies, 16, 274-96.

____(2006). 'Comprehensive plans of action: insights from CIREFCA and the Indochinese CPA', UNHCR, New Issues in Refugee Research, Paper No. 120.

Bruns, S. (2011). 'Operation ATALANTA at three: a success or failure?', Strategic Insights, 36, 8-12.

Cassarino, J.-P. (2010). Readmission Policy in the European Union, Committee on Civil Liberties, Justice and Home Affairs, European Parliament, Brussels.

_____(2014). 'A reappraisal of the EU's expanding readmission system', International Spectator, 49, 130-45.

Ceobanu, A.M. and X. Escandell (2010).'Comparative analyses of public attitudes toward immigrants and immigration using multinational survey data: a review of theories and research', Annual Review of Sociology, 36, 309-28.

Cuttitta, P. (2010).'Readmission in the relations between Italy and North African Mediterranean countries', in J-P. Cassarino (ed.), Unbalanced Reciprocities: Cooperation on Readmission in the Euro-Mediterranean Area, Middle East Institute, Washington DC.

Czaika, M. and H. de Haas. (2013). 'The effectiveness of immigration policies', Population and Development Review, 39, 487-508.

Davenport, C.A., W.H. Moore and S.C. Poe (2003). 'Sometimes you just have to leave: domestic threats and forced migration, 1964-1989', International Interactions, 29, 27-55.

Del Carpio, X.V. and M. Wagner (2015). 'The impact of Syrian refugees on the Turkish labor market', World Bank Policy Research, Working Paper 7402.

Docquier, F. and A. Marfouk. (2006). 'International migration by educational attainment (1990-2000)', in C. Ozden and M. Schiff (eds), International Migration, Remittances and the Brain Drain, Palgrave-Macmillan, London.

Engel, S. and A.M. Ibanez (2007). 'Displacement due to violence in Colombia: a householdlevel analysis', Economic Development and Cultural Change, 55, 335-65.

Erdogan, M. (2014). 'Syrians in Turkey: social acceptance and integration research', Migration and Politics Research Centre, Haceteppe University.

European Commission and Council. (2016). 'Towards a reform of the common European asylum system and enhancing legal avenues to Europe', at: http://ec.europa.eu/dgs/home-af fairs/what-we-do/policies/european-agenda-migration/proposal-implementation-package/ docs/20160406/towards_a_reform_of_the_common_european_asylum_system_and_enhan cing_legal_avenues_to_europe_-_20160406_en.pdf.

European Union Parliament and Council. (2012). Decision No 281/2012/EU at: http://eur- lex.europa.eu/LexUriServ/LexUriServ.do?uri=OJ:L:2012:092:0001:0003:EN:PDF.

Eurostat. (2015). 'Asylum applicants and first instance decisions on asylum applications: 2014', at: http://ec.europa.eu/eurostat/en/web/products-data-in-focus/-/KS-QA-15-003.

Facchini, G., A.M. Mayda, and R. Puglisi. (2009). 'Illegal immigration and media exposure: evidence on individual attitudes', CEPR Discussion Paper 7593.

Fearon, J.D. and D.D. Laitin (2013). 'How persistent is armed conflict?' unpublished paper at: https://esoc.princeton.edu/files/how-persistent-armed-conflict.

Fernandez-Huertas Moraga, J. and H. Rapoport (2015a). 'Tradable refugee-admission quotas and EU asylum policy', CESfo Economic Studies, 61, 638-72.

____(2015b). 'Tradable refugee-admission quotas (TRAQs), the Syrian crisis and the new European agenda on migration', IJA Journal of European Labor Studies, 4, 1-13.

Fink, M. (2012). 'Frontex working arrangements: Legitimacy and human rights concerns regarding 'technical relationships'', Merkourios, 28, 20-35.

Ford, R., W. Jennings, and W. Somerville (2015). 'Public opinion, responsiveness and constraint: Britain's three immigration policy regimes', Journal of Ethnic and Migration Studies, 41, 1391-411.

Freeman, G. (1994). 'Britain, the deviant case', in W. Cornelius, P.L. Martin, and J.F. Hollifield, (eds) Controlling Immigration: A Global Perspective, Stanford University Press, Palo Alto.

Gathmann, C. (2008). 'Effects of enforcement on illegal markets: evidence from migrant smuggling along the southwestern border', Journal of Public Economics, 98, 1926-41.

Gorinas, C. and M. Pytlikova (2016). 'The influence of attitudes toward immigrants on international migration', International Migration Review (forthcoming).

Haake, C.-J., T. Krieger, and S. Minter. (2010). 'External border enforcement, public goods and burden-sharing mechanisms in the EU', in R. Zapata-Barrero (ed.), Shaping the Normative Contours of the European Union: A Migration-Border Framework, Barcelona: UPF Centre for International Affairs.

Hainmueller, J., and D. Hopkins (2014). 'Public attitudes toward immigration', Annual Review of Political Science, 17,225-49.

Hanson, G.H. (2006). 'Illegal migration from Mexico to the United States', Journal of Economic Literature, 44, 869-924.

Hatton, T.J. (2004). 'Seeking asylum in Europe', Economic Policy, 38, 5-62.

_____(2009). 'The rise and fall of asylum: what happened and why?', Economic Journal, 119, F183-213.

Hatton, T. J. (2015a). 'Asylum policy in the EU: The case for deeper integration', CESifo Economic Studies, 61, 605-37.

Hatton, T.J. (2015b). 'Public opinion on immigration in Europe: Preference versus salience', Unpublished paper.

_____(2016). 'Immigration, public opinion and the recession in Europe', Economic Policy, 86, 205-46.

Hatton, TJ. and J. Moloney (2015). Applications for asylum in the developed world: modelling asylum claims by origin and destination, CEPR Discussion Paper 10678, London.

Humphris, R. (2013). 'Refugees and the Rashaida: human smuggling and trafficking from Eritrea to Sudan and Egypt', UNHCR: New Issues in Refugee Research, Paper No. 254.

Koser, K. and K. Kuschminder (2016). 'Understanding irregular migrants' decision making factors in transit', Australia Department of Immigration and Border Protection, Occasional Paper 21.

Luedtke, A. (2005). 'European integration, public opinion and immigration policy: testing the impact of national identity', European Union Politics, 6, 83-112.

Massey, D.S., J. Durand, and K.A. Pren (2016). 'Why border enforcement backfired', American Journal of Sociology, 121, 1557-600.

Melander, E. and M. Oberg (2006). 'Time to go? Duration dependence in forced migration', International Interactions, 32, 129-52.

_____(2007). 'The threat of violence and forced migration: geographical scope trumps intensity offighting', Civil Wars, 9, 156-73.

Moore, W.H. and S.M. Shellman (2004). 'Fear of persecution: forced migration, 1952-1995', Journal of Conflict Resolution, 48, 727-53.

Moore, W.H., and S.M. Shellman (2006). 'Refugee or internally displaced person? To where should one flee?', Comparative Political Studies, 39, 599-622.

Moore, W.H. and S.M. Shellman (2007). 'Whither will they go? A global study of refugees' destinations, 1965-1995', International Studies Quarterly, 51, 811-34.

Neumayer, E. (2004). 'Asylum destination choice: what makes some', west European countries more attractive than others? European Union Politics, 5, 155-80.

____(2005). 'Bogus refugees? The determinants of asylum migration to Western Europe', International Studies Quarterly, 49, 389-409.

Perez, A. (2010). 'The externalization of migration control in Spain and its impact on Moroccan and Ecuadorian migration', in R. Zapata-Barrero (ed.), Shaping the Normative Contours of the European Union: A Migration-Border Framework, UPF Centre for International Affairs, Barcelona. Phillips, J. (2015). 'Boat arrivals and boat "turnbacks" in Australia since 1976: a quick guide to the statistics', Australian Parliamentary Library at: http://apo.org.au/files/Resource/parlia mentarylibrary_boatarrivalsandboatturnbacksinaustraliasince1976_sep_2015.pdf.

Piper, M., P. Power, and G. Thom (2013). 'Refugee resettlement: 2012 and beyond', UNHCR, New Issues in Refugee Research Paper 253.

Rawlence, B. (2016). City of Thorns:.Nine Lives in the World's Largest Refugee Camp, Portobello Books, London.

Roberts, B., E. Alden, and J. Whitley. (2013). Managing Illegal Immigration to the United States:How Effective is Enforcement? Council on Foreign Relations, Washington, DC.

Roper, S.D. and L.A. Barria (2010). 'Burden-sharing in the UNHCR: refugee protection as an impure public good', Journal of Conflict Resolution, 54, 616-37.

Schmeidl, S. (1997). 'Exploring the causes of forced migration: a pooled time series analysis', Social Science Quarterly, 78, 284-308.

Steele, A. (2009). 'Seeking safety: avoiding displacement and choosing destinations in civil wars', Journal of Peace Research, 46, 419-29.

Suhrke, A. (1998). 'Burden-sharing during refugee emergencies: the logic of collective versus national action', Journal of Refugee Studies, 11, 396-415.

Thielemann, E. (2006). 'The effectiveness of governments' attempts to control unwanted migration', in C.A. Parsons and T.M. Smeeding (eds), Immigration and the Transformation of Europe, Cambridge University Press, Cambridge, 442-472.

Tumen, S. (2016). 'The economic impact of Syrian refugees on host countries: quasi- experimental evidence from Turkey', American Economic Review (P & P), 106, 456-60.

UK Home Office. (2016). 'Immigration statistics' at: https://www.gov.uk/government/publica tions/immigration-statistics-january-to-march-2016/asylum.

UNHCR. (2000). The State of The World's Refugees 2000: Fifty Years of Humanitarian Action, UNHCR, Geneva.

____(2001). Asylum Applications in Industrialized Countries, 1980-1999, UNHCR, Geneva.

____(2015a). Global Trends:Forced Displacement in 2014, UNHCR, Geneva.

____(2015b). Projected Global Resettlement Needs, 2016, UNHCR, Geneva.

____(2016). Global Trends:ForcedDisplacementin2015, UNHCR, Geneva.

UNHCR (Various Issues), "Asylum Trends: Levels and Trends in Industrialized Countries, UNHCR, Geneva.

Wlezien, C. (2005). 'On the salience of political issues: the problem with "most important problem"', Electoral Studies, 24, 555-79.

Akkerman, Tjitske. 2015. "Immigration Policy and Electoral Competition: A Fine-grained Analysis of Party Positions over the Past Two Decades." Party Politics 21 (1): 54-67.

Alonso, Sonia, and Sara Claro da Fonseca. 2012. "Immigration, Left and Right." Party Politics 18 (6): 865-884.

Bale, Tim. 2008. "Politics Matter: A Conclusion." Journal of European Public Policy 15 (3): 453-464. Barbou des Places, Segolene. 2004. "Taking Legal Rules into Consideration: EU Asylum Policy and Regulatory Competition." Journal of Public Policy 24 (1): 75-98.

Barthel, Fabian, and Eric Neumayer. 2015. "Spatial Dependence in Asylum Migration." Journal of Ethnic and Migration Studies 41 (7): 1131-1151.

Beine, Michel, Anna Boucher, Brian Burgoon, Mary Crock, Justin Gest, Michael Hiscox, Patrick McGovern, Hillel Rapoport, Joep Schaper, and Eiko Thielemann. 2016. "Comparing Immigration Policies: An Overview from the IMPALA Database." International Migration Review 50 (4): 827-863.

Bernhard, Laurent. 2012. Campaign Strategy in Direct Democracy. Basingstoke: Palgrave Macmillan.

Bloch, Alice, and Liza Schuster. 2005. "At the Extremes of Exclusion: Deportation, Detention and Dispersal." Ethnic and Racial Studies 28 (3): 491-512.

Bornschier, Simon. 2010. Cleavage Politics and the Populist Right: The New Cultural Conflict in Western Europe. Philadelphia, PA: Temple University Press.

Brunsson, Nils. 2009. Reform as Routine: Organizational Change in the Modern World. Oxford: Oxford University Press.

Byrne, Rosemary. 2002. "Future Perspectives: Accession and Asylum in an Expanded European Union." In New Asylum Countries? Migration Control and Refugee Protection in an Enlarged European Union, edited by Rosemary Byrne, Gregor Noll, and Jens Vested-Hansen, 383-391. The Hague: Kluwer.

Cooper, Robert, and Gibson Burrell. 1988. "Modernism, Postmodernism and Organizational Analysis: An Introduction." Organization Studies 9 (1): 91-112.

Cornelius, Wayne A., Takeyuki Tsuda, Philip L. Martin, and James F. Hollifield, eds. 2004. Controlling Immigration: A Global Perspective. Stanford, CA: Stanford University Press.

Costello, Cathryn. 2015. "Immigration Detention: The Grounds Beneath Our Feet." Current Legal Problems 68 (1): 143-177.

Costello, Cathryn, and Emily Hancox. 2016. "The Recast Asylum Procedures Directive 2013/32/EU: Caught Between the Stereotypes of the Abusive Asylum-seeker and the Vulnerable Refugee." In

Reforming the Common European Asylum System: The New European Refugee Law, edited by

Vincent Chetail, Philippe De Bruycker, and Francesco Maiani, 377-445. Leiden: Koninklijke Brill. Crawley, Heaven, and Dimitris Skleparis. 2018. "Refugees, Migrants, Neither, Both: Categorical

Fetishism and the Politics of Bounding in Europe's 'Migration Crisis'." Journal of Ethnic and Migration Studies 44 (1): 48-64.

Czaika, Mathias, and Hein De Haas. 2013. "The Effectiveness of Immigration Policies." Population and Development Review 39 (3): 487-508.

Czaika, Matthias, and Mogens Hobolth. 2016. "Do Restrictive Asylum and Visa Policies Increase Irregular Migration into Europe?" European Union Politics 17 (3): 345-365.

De Haas, Hein, Katharina Natter, and Simona Vezzoli. Forthcoming. "Growing Restrictiveness or Changing Selection? The Nature and Evolution of Migration Policies." International Migration Review. doi:10.1111/imre.12288.

Duncan, Fraser, and Steven Van Hecke. 2008. "Immigration and the Transnational European Centreright: A Common Programmatic Response?" Journal of European Public Policy 15 (3): 432-452.

El-Enany, Nadine, and Eiko Thielemann. 2011. "The Impact of the EU on National Asylum Policies." In The Area of Freedom, Security and Justice: Myth or Reality? Taking Stock of the Lisbon Treaty and the Stockholm Programme, edited by Sarah Wolff, Flora Goudappel, and Japp de Zwaan, 97-116. The Hague: TMC Asser Press.

Eule, Tobias. 2014. Inside Immigration Law: Migration Management and Policy Application in Germany. Farnham: Ashgate.

Eurostat. 2018. "Asylum and First Time Asylum Applicants [migr_asyappctza]." Accessed January 31. http://appsso.eurostat.ec.europa.eu/nui/show.do?dataset=migr_asyappctza&lang=en.

Freeman, Gary P. 2006. "National Models, Policy Types, and the Politics of Immigration in Liberal Democracies." West European Politics 29 (2): 227-247.

Hainmueller, Jens, Dominik Hangartner, and Duncan Lawrence. 2016. "When Lives Are Put On Hold: Lengthy Asylum Processes Decrease Employment among Refugees." Science Advances 2 (8): 1-7. Hatton, Timothy J. 2009. "The Rise and Fall of Asylum: What Happened and Why?" The Economic Journal 119 (535): F183-F213.

Hatton, Timothy J. 2012. Seeking Asylum: Trends and Policies in the OECD. London: Centre for Economic Policy Research (CEPR).

Havinga, Tetty, and Anita Bocker. 1999. "Country of Asylum by Choice or by Chance: Asylum-seekers in Belgium, the Netherlands and the UK." Journal of Ethnic and Migration Studies 25 (1): 43-61. Helbling, Marc, and Dorina Kalkum. Forthcoming. "Migration Policy Trends in OECD Countries." Journal of European Public Policy. doi:10.1080/13501763.2017.1361466.

Hooghe, Lisbet, Gary Marks, and Carole J. Wilson. 2002. "Does Left/Right Structure Party Positions on European Integration?" Comparative Political Studies 35 (8): 965-989.

Kaunert, Christian, and Sarah Leonard. 2012. "The Development of the EU Asylum Policy: Venueshopping in Perspective." Journal of European Public Policy 19 (9): 1396-1413.

Keogh, Gerard. 2013. "Modelling Asylum Migration Pull-force Factors in the EU-15." The Economic and Social Review 44 (3): 371-399.

Kitschelt, Herbert, and Anthony J. McGann. 1997. The Radical Right in Western Europe: A Comparative Analysis. Ann Arbor: University of Michigan Press.

Kriesi, Hanspeter, Edgar Grande, Romain Lachat, Martin Dolezal, Simon Bornschier, and Timotheos Frei. 2008. West European Politics in the Age of Globalization. Cambridge: Cambridge University Press.

Neumayer, Eric. 2004. "Asylum Destination Choice What Makes Some West European Countries More Attractive Than Others?" European Union Politics 5 (2): 155-180.

Oakley, Sharon. 2007. Accelerated Procedures for Asylum in the European Union: Fairness Versus Efficiency, Sussex Migration Working Paper No. 43.

OECD. Several annual editions. International Migration Outlook. Paris: Organisation for Economic Co-operation an Development.

Reneman, Marcelle. 2013. "Speedy Asylum Procedures in the EU: Striking a Fair Balance Between the Need to Process Asylum Cases Efficiently and the Asylum Applicant's EU Right to an Effective Remedy." International Journal of Refugee Law, 25 (4): 717-748.

Schmeidl, Susanne. 1997. "Exploring the Causes of Forced Migration: A Pooled Time-series Analysis, 1971-1990." Social Science Quarterly 78 (2): 284-308.

Scipioni, Marco. Forthcoming. "Failing Forward in EU Migration Policy? EU Integration After the

2015 Asylum and Migration Crisis." Journal of European Public Policy. doi:10.1080/13501763. 2017.1325920.

Sniderman, Paul M., Louk Hagendoorn, and Markus Prior. 2004. "Predispositional Factors and Situational Triggers: Exclusionary Reactions to Immigrant Minorities." American Political Science Review 98 (1): 35-49.

Statham, Paul, and Andre Geddes. 2006. "Elites and the 'Organised Public': Who Drives British Immigration Politics and in Which Direction?" West European Politics 29 (2): 248-269.

Thielemann, Eiko. 2006. "The Effectiveness of Governments' Attempts to Control Unwanted

Migration." In Immigration and the Transformation of Europe, edited by Craig A. Parsons and Timothy M. Smeeding, 442-472. Cambridge: Cambridge University Press.

Thielemann, Eiko. 2012. "How Effective Are National and EU Policies in the Area of Forced Migration?" Refugee Survey Quarterly 31 (4): 21-37.

Thielemann, Eiko, and Mogens Hobolth. 2016. "Trading Numbers vs. Rights? Accounting for Liberal and Restrictive Dynamics in the Evolution of Asylum and Refugee Policies." Journal of Ethnic and Migration Studies 42 (4): 643-664.

Toshkov, Dimiter, and Laura de Haan. 2013. "The Europeanization of Asylum Policy: An Assessment of the EU Impact on Asylum Applications and Recognitions Rates." Journal of European Public Policy 20 (5): 661-683.

Triandafyllidou, Anna. 2003. "Immigration Policy Implementation in Italy: Organisational Culture,

Identity Processes and Labour Market Control." Journal of Ethnic and Migration Studies 29 (2): 257-297.

UNHCR. 2016. Global Trends: Forced Displacement in 2015. Geneva: United Nations High Commissioner for Refugees.

Zaun, Natascha. 2017. EU Asylum Policies: The Power of Strong Regulating States. Cham: Springer.

Agence Europe. 2020. "New framework on asylum, management of external borders and fight against organised crime are priorities of Croatian EU Council Presidency." Bulletin Quotidien Europe, No. 12397. https://agenceurope.eu/en/bulletin/article/12397/12

Amnesty International. 2015. "EU: Action not words needed to end suffering of thousands". Amnesty International, July 14, 2015. https://www.amnesty.org/en/latest/news/2015/09/eu-action-not-words-needed-at-jha-to-end-suffering-of-thousands/

Amnesty International. 2016a. "Turkey: Illegal mass returns of Syrian refugees expose fatal flaws in EU-Turkey Statement". Amnesty International, April 1, 2016. https://www.amnesty.org/en/press-releases/2016/04/turkey-illegal-mass-returns-of-syrian- refugees-expose-fatal-flaws-in-eu-turkey-deal/

Amnesty International. 2016b. "EU's reckless refugee returns to Turkey illegal". Amnesty International, 3 June 2016. https://www.amnesty.org/en/latest/news/2016/06/eus-reckless- refugee-returns-to-turkey-illegal/

Amnesty International. 2017. "Libya: European governments complicit in horrific abuse of refugees and migrants". Amnesty International, December 12, 2017. https://www.amnesty.org/en/latest/news/2017/12/libya-european-governments-complicit- in-horrific-abuse-of-refugees-and-migrants/

Atak, Idil. 2015. "A look at the EU-Turkey Action Plan". Frangois Crepeau [Weblog], October 17, 2015. http://francoiscrepeau.com/a-look-at-the-eu-turkey-action-plan/

Borzel, Tanja A. 2016. "From EU governance of crisis to crisis of EU governance". Journal of Common Market Studies, 54, annual review: 8-31.

Campbell, Zach. 2017. "Europe's plan to close its sea borders relies on Libya's coast guard doing its dirty work, abusing migrants". The Intercept, November 25, 2017. https://theintercept.com/2017/11/25/libya-coast-guard-europe-refugees/

Carrera, Sergio and Leonhard den Hertog. 2016. "A European Border and Coast Guard: What's in a name?". CEPS Paper in Liberty and Security in Europe, No.88.

Carrera, Sergio, Leonhard den Hertog and Marco Stefan. 2017. "It wasn't me! The Luxembourg Court Orders on the EU-Turkey Refugee Deal". CEPS Policy Insights No. 15. https://www.ceps.eu/system/files/EU-Turkey%20Deal.pdf

Christides, Giorgos, Juliane von Mittelstaedt, Peter Muller und Maximilian Popp.

2016__„Closing the Balkan Route: Will Greece Become a Refugee Bottleneck?". Der Spiegel, 9 February 2016. <<http://www.spiegel.de/international/ europe/closing-balkan-route-means- migrant-crisis-for-greece-a- 1076232. html».

CNN. n.d. "Migrants accuse Libyan coast guard". CNN [Video]. https://edition. cnn.com/videos/world/2018/02/19/cfp-libya-migrants-rescue.cnn

Collett, Elizabeth. 2016. "The Paradox of the EU-Turkey Refugee Deal". Migration Policy Institute, July 9, 2018, http://www.migrationpolicy.org/news/ paradox-eu-turkey-refugee- deal

CONCORD (European NGO confederation for relief and development). 2018. "Partnership or Conditionality?", https://concordeurope.org/2018/01/24/ monitoring-eu-trust-fund-africa-publication/

Costello, Costello, Elspeth Guild and Violeta Moreno-Lax. 2017. "Implementation of the 2015 Council Decisions Establishing Provisional Measures in the Area of International Protection 26 for the Benefit of Italy and Greece". Study for the LIBE committee. http://www.europarl.europa.eu/RegData/etudes/ STUD/2017/583132/IPOL_STU(2017)583132_EN.pdf

Council of the European Union. 2015a. "Conclusions of the representatives of the governments of the Member States meeting with the Council on resettling through multilateral and national schemes 20 000 persons in clear need of international protection." http://data.consilium.europa.eu/doc/document/ ST-11130-2015-INIT/en/pdf

Council of the European Union. 2015b. "Council decision (EU) 2015/1523 of 14 September 2015 establishing provisional measures in the area of international protection for the benefit of Italy and Greece". Official Journal of the European Union, L 239/146. http://eur- lex.europa.eu/legal-content/ EN/TXT/?uri=OJ:JOL_2015_239_R_0011

Council of the European Union. 2015c. "Council decision (EU) 2015/1601 of 22 September 2015 establishing provisional measures in the area of international protection for the benefit of Italy and Greece". Official Journal of the European Union, L 248/80. http://eur- lex.europa.eu/legal-content/ EN/TXT/PDF/?uri=CELEX:32015D1601&from=EN

Council of the European Union. 2016. "EUNAVFOR MED Operation Sophia authorized to start two additional supporting tasks". Council of the European Union, August 30, 2016. http://www.consilium.europa.eu/en/press/press-releases/2016/08/30/eunavfor-med-sophia- op-add-supporting-tasks/

Council of the European Union. 2018a. "Note from the Presidency to the Council regarding the reform of the Common European Asylum System and Resettlement." ST 9520 2018 INIT. May 30, 2018a. https://eur-lex.europa.eu/legal-content/EN/ALL/?uri=consil :ST_9520_2018_INIT

Council of the European Union. 2018b. "Migration response. Saving lives at sea and targeting criminal networks". Council of the European Union, http://www.consilium.europa.eu/en/policies/migratory-pressures/sea-criminal-networks/

Council of the European Union. 2018c. "Migration response. How the EU manages migration flows". Council of the European Union, http://www.consilium.europa.eu/en/policies/migratory-pressures/managing-migration-flows/

Council of the European Union. 2018d. "Migration response. Central Mediterranean route". Council of the European Union, http://www.consilium.europa.eu/en/policies/migratory- pressures/central-mediterranean-route/

Council of the European Union. 2019a. "Proposal for a Directive of the European Parliament and of the Council on common standards and procedures in Member States for returning illegally staying third-country nationals (recast) - Partial general approach." May 23, 2019. 2018/0329(COD). https:// data.consilium.europa.eu/doc/document/ST-9620-2019-INIT/en/pdf

Council of the European Union. 2019b. "Way forward for EU Migration and Asylum policy - outcome of discussions - Presidency report." November 22, 2019. 14364/19. https://data.consilium.europa.eu/doc/document/ST-14364-2019-INIT/en/pdf.

de Bruycker, Philippe. 2016. "The European Border and Coast Guard". European Papers, Vol.1, No. 2: 559-569.

de Marcilly, Charles and Angeline Garde. 2016. "The EU-Turkey Agreement and its implications". European issues, no. 396. http://www.robert-schuman.eu/en/doc/questions- d-europe/qe-396-en.pdf

den Hertog, Leonhard. 2016. "EU budgetary responses to the 'refugee crisis'". CEPS Paper in Liberty and Security in Europe, 93. https://www.ceps.eu/system/files/LSE%20No%2093%20LdH%20on%20EU%20Budgetary%20Resp onses%20to%20the%20Refugee%20Crisis.pdf

Den Heijer, Marten, Jorrit Rijpma and Thomas Spijkerboer. 2016. "Coercion, prohibition and great expectations". Common Market Law Review, Vol. 53, No.3: 607-642.

Deutsche Welle. 2018. "Frontex launches new EU border control mission Operation Themis". Deutsche Welle, February 1, 2018. https://www.dw.com/en/frontex-launches-new-eu- border-control-mission-operation-themis/a-42417610

ECRE et al. (2016). "The implementation of the hotspots in Italy and Greece". http://www.ecre.org/wp-content/uploads/2016/12/HOTSPOTS-Report-5.12.2016..pdf

Ekathimerini. 2015. "EUs refugee relocation scheme 'not enough,' says UNHCR chief'. Ekathimerini, August 12, 2015. http://www.ekathimerini.com/202427/article/ekathimerini/news/eus-refugee-relocation- scheme-not-enough-says-unhcr-chief

Euractiv. 2015. "Germany suspends Dublin Agreement for Syrian Refugees". Euractiv, August 26, 2015. https://www.euractiv.com/section/economy-jobs/news/germany-suspends-dublin-agreement-for-syrian-refugees/

Euractiv. 2016. "Alarm over effectiveness of EU-Turkey refugee deal grows in Brussels". Euractiv, November 2, 2016. http://www.euractiv.com/section/justice-home-affairs/news/alarm-over-eu-turkey-refugee-deal-grows-in-brussels/.

European Commission. 2015a. "Communication from the Commission to the European Parliament, the Council, the European Economic and Social Committee and the Committee of the Regions. A European Agenda on Migration". 13 May 2015. https://ec.europa.eu/home-affairs/sites/homeaffairs/files/what-we-do/policies/european- agenda-migration/background- information/docs/communication_on_the_european_agenda_on_migration_en.pdf

European Commission. 2015b. "European Commission makes progress on Agenda on Migration. Press release" 27 May 2015. http://europa.eu/rapid/press-release_IP-15- 5039_en.htm

European Commission. 2015c. "Managing the refugee crisis". 23 September 2015. http://europa.eu/rapid/press-release_IP-15-5700_en.htm

European Commission. 2015d. "Proposal for a regulation ... establishing a crisis relocation mechanism and amending Regulation (EU) No 604/2013 of the European Parliament and of the Council of 26 June 2013 establishing the criteria and mechanisms for determining the Member State responsible for examining an application for international protection lodged in one of the Member States by a third country national or a stateless person". http://eur-lex.europa.eu/legal-content/en/ALL/?uri=CELEX:52015PC0450

European Commission. 2016a. "Progress report on the implementation of the hotspot approach in Greece". 4 March 2016. https://ec.europa.eu/ home- affairs/ sites/ homeaffairs/ files/ what - we- do/policies/ european - agenda-migration/proposal-implementation-package/docs/ communication_20160304_progress_report_on_the_implementation_of_the_hots pots_in_greece_en.pdf

European Commission. 2016b. "Proposal for a Regulation ... establishing the criteria and mechanisms for determining the Member State responsible for examining an application for international protection lodged in one of the Member States by a third-country national or a stateless person (recast)". 4 May 2016. http://eurlex.europa.eu/legal-content/EN/TXT/?qid=1465212426716&uri=CELEX:52016PC0270

European Commission. 2016c. "Managing the refugee crisis. A new partnership framework. Factsheet". 07 June 2016. https://ec.europa.eu/home-affairs/sites/homeaffairs/files/what- we-do/policies/european-agenda-migration/background-information/docs/20160607/factsheet_managing_refugee_crisis_new_partnership_framew ork_en.pdf

European Commission. 2016d. "Proposal for a Regulation ... establishing a Union Resettlement Framework and amending Regulation (EU) No 516/2014 of the European Parliament and the Council." Brussels, 13 July 2016. https:// ec.europa.eu/home- affairs/sites/homeaffairs/files/what-we-do/policies/ european-agenda-migration/proposal- implementation-package/docs/20160713/resettlement_system_en.pdf

European Commission. 2017a. "EU Emergency Trust Fund for Africa". https://ec.europa.eu/europeaid/regions/africa/eu-emergency-trust-fund-africa_en

European Commission. 2017b. "Relocation: Commission launches infringement procedures against the Czech Republic, Hungary and Poland". 14 June 2017. http://europa.eu/rapid/press-release_IP-17-1607_en.htm

European Commission. 2017c. "Fifteenth report on relocation and resettlement. COM(2017) 465 final". Brussels, 06 September 2017. https://eur-lex.europa.eu/legal-content/EN/TXT/PDF/?uri=CELEX:52017DC0465&from=EN

European Commission. 2017d. "Commission recommendation of 27.9.2017 on enhancing legal pathways for persons in need of international protection. C(2017) 6504". https://ec.europa.eu/home-affairs/sites/homeaffairs/files/what-we-do/policies/european- agenda-migration/20170927_recommendation_on_enhancing_legal_pathways_for_persons_in_need_of_international_protection_en.pdf

European Commission. 2017e. "Towards a more efficient EU return policy. Factsheet". November. https://ec.europa.eu/home-affairs/sites/homeaffairs/files/what-we-do/policies/european-agenda-migration/201 71114_factsheet_towards_an_efficient_and_credible_eu_return_policy_en.p df

European Commission. 2017f. "Communication: Commission contribution to the EU Leaders' thematic debate on a way forward on the external and internal dimension of migration policy". https://ec.europa.eu/home-affairs/sites/homeaffairs/files/what-we-do/policies/european-agenda-migration/20171207_communication_on_commission_contribution_to_the_eu_leaders_themati c_debate_on_way_forward_on_external_and_internal_dimension_migration_policy_en.pdf

European Commission. 2017g. "EU action in Libya on migration. The Commission's contribution to the leaders' agenda. Factsheet". 07 December 2017. https://ec.europa.eu/home-affairs/sites/homeaffairs/files/what-we-do/policies/european- agenda-migration/20171207_eu_action_in_libya_on_migration_en.pdf

European Commission. 2017h. "The EU's key partnership with Africa. The Commission's contribution to the Leaders' agenda. Factsheet". 07 December

2017___https://ec.europa.eu/home-affairs/sites/homeaffairs/files/what-we-do/policies/european- agenda-migration/20171207_the-eu_key_partnership_with_africa_en.pdf

European Commission. 2017i. "Working with partner countries. The Commission's contribution to the leaders' agenda. Factsheet". 07 December

2017___https://ec.europa.eu/home-affairs/sites/homeaffairs/files/what- we-do / policies /european- agenda-migration/20171207_working_with_partner_countries_en.pdf

European Commission. 2017j. "Rapport Annuel d'Activites et de Resultats. Fonds fiduciaire de l'Union europeenne pour la Republique Centrafricaine Fonds Bekou https://europa.eu/capacity4dev/trust-fund-bekou/documents/rapport-annuel-2017-du-fonds- fiduciaire-bekou

European Commission. 2018a. "EU Trust Fund for Africa. Support to Libya. Factsheet"08 May 2018. https://ec.europa.eu/neighbourhood-enlargement/sites/near/files/eutf-noa-ly- 08052018.pdf

European Commission. 2018b. "Progress report on the implementation of the European Agenda on Migration. COM(2018) 301 final". Brussels, 16 May 2018. https://ec.europa.eu/home- affairs/sites/homeaffairs/files/what-we-do/policies/european-agenda-migration/20180516_progress-report-european-agenda-migration_en.pdf

European Commission. 2018c.______Migration Management. EU crisis management tools. Factsheet". 16 May 2018. https://ec.europa.eu/home-affairs/ sites/homeaffairs/files/what- we-do/policies/european-agenda-migration/20180516_migration-management-eu-crisis- management-tools_en.pdf

European Commission. 2018d. "Proposal for a Regulation ... establishing the Asylum and Migration Fund. COM(2018) 471 final, 2018/0248(COD)". https://eur-lex.europa.eu/legal- content/EN/TXT/?qid=1530262451165&uri=CELEX%3A52018PC0471

European Commission. 2018e. "Europe's support to refugees and their host countries. EU regional trust fund in response to the Syrian crisis. Factsheet" updated in June", https://ec.europa.eu/neighbourhood-enlargement/sites/near/files/eutf_syria_factsheet- english.pdf

European Commission. 2018f. "The legal and practical feasibility of disembarkation options. Follow-up to the informal working meeting of 24 June 2018." 29 June 2018. https://ec.europa.eu/commission/sites/beta-political/files/migration-disembarkation- june2018_en.pdf

European Commission. 2018g. "Migration: Regional Disembarkation Arrangements. Followup to the European Council Conclusions of 28 June

2018.______July 2018. https://ec.europa.eu/home-affairs/sites/homeaffairs/files/ what-we-do/policies/european-agenda-migration/20180724_factsheet- regional-disembarkation-arrangements_en.pdf.

European Commission. 2018h. „Enhancing safe and legal pathways to Europe" September 12, https://ec.europa.eu/commission/sites/beta-political/files/soteu2018-factsheet-legal- pathways_en.pdf.

European Commission. 2018i."Proposal for a Directive of the European Parliament and of the Council on common standards and procedures in Member States for returning illegally staying third-country nationals (recast)". Brussels, September 12, 2018. COM(2018) 634 final 2018/0329 (COD). https://ec.europa.eu/commission/sites/beta-political/files/soteu2018-returning-illegally-staying-third-country-nationals-directive- 634_en.pdf

European Commission. 2019a. "Migration. Immediate measures needed" March 2019. https://ec.europa.eu/home-affairs/sites/homeaffairs/files/what-we-do/policies/european- agenda-migration/20190306_managing-migration-factsheet-immediate-measures- needed_en.pdf.

European Commission. 2019b. "A step-change in migration management and border security." March, 2019. https://ec.europa.eu/home-affairs/sites/homeaffairs/files/what-we-do/policies/european-agenda-migration/20190306_managing-migration-factsheet-step- change-migration-management-border-security-timeline_en.pdf.

European Commission. 2019c. "EU-Turkey Statement. Three years on" March 2019. https://ec.europa.eu/home-affairs/sites/homeaffairs/files/what-we- do/policies/european- agenda-migration/20190318_eu-turkey-three-years-on_en.pdf.

European Commission. 2019d. "A Reinforced European Border and Coast Guard" November https://ec.europa.eu/home-affairs/sites/homeaffairs/files/what-we- do/policies/european-agenda-migration/20191108_managing-migration-factsheet- european-border-and-coast-guard_en.pdf.

European Commission. 2019e. "Delivering on resettlement." December 2019. https://ec.europa.eu/home-affairs/sites/homeaffairs/files/what-we-do/policies/european- agenda-migration/201912_delivering-on-resettlement.pdf.

European Commission. 2019f. "A Europe that protects our borders and delivers on a comprehensive migration policy", https://op.europa.eu/en/publication-detail/- /publication/b3d12be1-8d84-11e9-9369-01aa75ed71a1/language-en/format-PDF/source- 104286965.

European Commission. 2019g. "Progress report on the implementation of the

European Agenda on Migration." COM(2019) 481 final. Brussels, 16 October, file:///C:/Users/anieman/AppData/Local/Microsoft/Windows/INetCache/Content.Outlook/MWXXUP4O/20191016_com-2019-481 -report_en.pdf

European Commission. 2020. "Managing Migration. EU Financial Support to Greece" January https://ec.europa.eu/home-affairs/sites/homeaffairs/files/what-we- do/policies/european-agenda-migration/202001_managing-migration-eu-financial-support- to-greece_en.pdf.

European Commission (n.d.) "Full list of Member States' notifications of the temporary reintroduction of border control at internal borders pursuant to Article 25 et seq. of the Schengen Borders Code", http://ec.europa.eu/ dgs/home-affairs/what-we-do/policies/borders-andvisas/schengen/reintroduction-border-control/docs/ms_notifications_-_reintroduction_of_border_control_en.pdf

European Council (2015). "Meeting of heads of state or government with Turkey - EU-Turkey statement". 29 November 2015. http://www.consilium.europa.eu/en/press/press-releases/2015/11/29-eu-turkey-meeting-statement/

European Council. 2016."EU-Turkey statement". European Council, March 18, 2016. http://www.consilium.europa.eu/en/press/press-releases/2016/03/18/eu-turkey-statement/

European Council. 2017. "Malta Declaration by the members of the European Council on the external aspects of migration: addressing the Central Mediterranean route". European Council, February 2, 2016. http://www.consilium.europa.eu/en/press/press-releases/2017/02/03/malta-declaration/

European Council. 2018a. "European Council conclusions, 28 June 2018". European Council, 421/18, June 29, 2018. http://www.consilium.europa.eu/en/press/press-releases/2018/06/29/20180628-euco-conclusions-final/

European Council. 2018b. "European Council conclusions, 18 October 2018." European Council, October 18, 2018. https://www.consilium.europa.eu/en/press/press-releases/2018/10/18/20181018-european-council-conslusions/.

European Court of Human Rights. 2014. "CASE OF TARAKHEL v. SWITZERLAND (Application no. 29217/12)". 4 November 2014. http://hudoc.echr.coe.int/eng?i=001- 148070».

European Court of Justice. 2011. "Joined Cases C-411/10 and C-493/10 N. S. v Secretary of State for the Home Department and M. E. and Others v Refugee Applications Commissioner and Minister for Justice, Equality and Law Reform". 21 December 2011. http://eur- lex.europa.eu/legal-content/EN/ALL/?uri=CELEX:62010CJ0411

European Parliament. 2019. "Regulation of the European Parliament and of the Council amending Regulation (EC) No 810/2009 establishing a Community Code on Visas (Visa Code)" May 15, 2019. 2018/0061 (COD). https://data.consilium.europa.eu/doc/document/PE-29-2019-INIT/en/pdf.

Eurostat. 2015. "Asylum applicants and first instance decisions on asylum applications: 2014, March". http://ec.europa.eu/eurostat/documents/4168041/6742650/KS-QA-15-003-EN-N.pdf/b7786ec9-1ad6-4720-8a1d-430fcfc55018

Eurostat. 2017a. "1.2 million first time asylum seekers registered in 2016, 16 March". http://ec.europa.eu/eurostat/documents/2995521/7921609/3-16032017-BP-EN.pdf/e5fa98bb- 5d9d-4297-9168-d07c67d1c9e1

Eurostat. 2017b. "Countries of origin of (non-EU) asylum seekers in the EU-28 Member States, 2015 and 2016, 15 March". http://ec.europa.eu/eurostat/statistics-explained/index.php/File:Countries_of_origin_of_(non-EU)_asylum_seekers_in_the_EU-28_Member_States,_2015_and_2016_(thousands_of_first_time_applicants)_YB17.png

Forensic Oceanography. 2018."Mare Clausum. A report by Forensic Oceanography (Charles Heller and Lorenzo Pezzani), affiliated to the Forensic Architecture agency, Goldsmiths, University of London", www.forensic-architecture.org/wp-content/uploads/2018/05/2018- 05-07-FO-Mare-Clausum-full-EN.pdf

Hanewinkel, Vera. 2015. „Kurzdossiers Zuwanderung, Flucht und Asyl" Bundeszentrale fur politische Bildung, December 15, 2015.http://www.bpb.de/gesellschaft/migration/kurzdossiers/217369/fluchtmigration-hintergruende?p=all

Human Rights Watch. 2016a. "Greece: Refugee "Hotspots" Unsafe, Unsanitary". Human Rights Watch, May 19, 2016. https://www.hrw.org/news/2016/05/19/greece-refugee- hotspots-unsafe-unsanitary

Human Rights Watch. 2016b. "Turkey: Border Guards Kill and Injure Asylum Seekers". Human Rights Watch, May 10, 2016. https://www.hrw.org/news/2016/05/10/turkey-border- guards-kill-and-injure-asylum-seekers

Human Rights Watch. 2016c. "Q&A: Why the EU-Turkey Migration Deal is No Blueprint". Human Rights Watch, November 14, 2016. https://www.hrw.org/news/2016/11/14/qa-why- eu-turkey-migration-deal-no-blueprint.

Karageorgiou, Eleni. 2016. "Solidarity and sharing in the Common European Asylum System". European Politics and Society, 17(2), 196-214. doi: 10.1080/23745118.2016.1121007

Koenig, Nicole and Marie Walter-Franke. 2017. "One year on: What lessons from the EU- Turkey 'deal'?". Jacques Delors Institut, March 17, 2017. http://www.delorsinstitut.de/2015/wp-content/uploads/2017/03/20170317_EU-Turkey-deal- one-year-on-NK-MW.pdf

Menendez, Agustin Jose. 2016. "The refugee crisis". European Law Journal, Vo.22, No.4: 388416.

Metcafle-Hough, Victoria. 2015. The migration crisis?. London: Overseas Development Institute, UK. https://www.odi.org/sites/odi.org.uk/files/odi-assets/publications-opinion- files/9913.pdf

Ministry of the Interior of the Republic of Poland. 2016. "Joint Statement of Ministers on establishment of the Migration Crisis Response Mechanism". 21 November 2016. http://www.msz.gov.pl/resource/12d5f115-0fe9-42b6-b73d-8deeea23983dJCR

Nielsen, Nikolaj. 2017a. "EU monitoring of Libyan coastguard done by Libyans". EU Observer, November 21,2017. https://euobserver.com/migration/139962

Nielsen, Nikolaj. 2017b. "EU and Italy put aside €258m to boost Libyan coast guard". EU Observer, November 29, 2017. https://euobserver.com/migration/140067

Nielsen, Nikolaj. 2019a. "EU migrant boat plan fails to get extra support". EU Observer, October 9, 2019. https://euobserver.com/migration/146214.

Nielsen, Nikolaj. 2019b. "Greek migrant hotspot now EU's 'worst rights issue'". EU Observer, November 7, 2019. https://euobserver.com/migration/146541.

Nielsen, Nikolaj. 2019c. "Erdogan: refugees will enter Europe unless EU does more." EU Observer, November 8, 2019. https://euobserver.com/migration/146566.

Nielsen, Nikolaj. 2019d. "EU states fell short on sharing refugees, say auditors." EU Observer, November 14, 2019. https://euobserver.com/migration/146610.

Nielsen, Nikolaj. 2019e. „Finnish EU presidency brief broadly offshores migration." EU Observer, November 29, 2019. https://euobserver.com/migration/146763.

Nielsen, Nikolaj & Fotiadis, Apostolis. 2019. "'Inhumane' Frontex forced returns going unreported". EU Observer, September 30, 2019. https://euobserver.com/migration/146090.

Niemann, Arne, and Johanna Speyer. 2017. "A Neofunctionalist Perspective on the 'European Refugee Crisis". Journal of Common Market Studies, 56(1): 23-43.

Niemann, Arne and Natascha Zaun. 2018. "EU refugee Policies and Politics in times of Crisis". Journal of Common Market Studies, Vol. 56., No. 1: 3-22.

Pastore, Ferruccio and Giulia Henry. 2016. "Explaining the crisis of the European migration and asylum regime". The International Spectator, Vol.51; No.1: 44-57.

Pauly, Svenja, Bank, Katrin, Julia Bloser, Arne Niemann and Natascha Zaun. 2016. "The EU's response to the so-called refugee "crisis"'. Political Science Applied, Vol. 7: 14-20.

Peers, Steve. 2016. 18 March. "The final EU/Turkey refugee deal". EU Law Analysis [Weblog], March 18, 2016. http://eulawanalysis.blogspot.de/2016/03/the-final-euturkey-refugee-deal- legal.html

Rankin, Jennifer. 2017. "EU court dismisses complaints by Hungary and Slovakia over refugee quotas". The Guardian, September 6, 2017. https://www.theguardian.com/world/2017/sep/06/eu-court-dismisses- complaints-by-hungary- and-slovakia-over-refugees

Ripoll Servent, Ariadne and Florian Trauner. 2014. "Do supranational EU institutions make a difference?". Journal of European Public Policy Vol.21, No.8: 1142-62.

Shaun, Walker. 2019. "Croatian police use violence to push back migrants, president admits." The Guardian, July 16, 2019. https://www.theguardian.com/world/2019/jul/16/croatian- police-use-violence-to-push-back-migrants-says-president.

Slominski, Peter. and Florian Trauner. 2017. "How do Member States Return Unwanted Migrants?". Journal of Common Market Studies, 56(1): 101-118.

Spijkerboer, Thomas. 2016. "Fact Check: Did the EU-Turkey Statement Bring Down the Number of Migrants and Border Deaths?" Oxford Border Criminologies Blog, September 28 2016. https://www.law.ox.ac.uk/research-subject-groups/centre-criminology/centreborder- criminologies/blog/2016/09/fact-check-did-eu

Statewatch (2015) "Explanatory note on the "Hotspot" approach", www.statewatch.org/news/2015/jul/eu-com-hotsposts.pdf

Stefanov, Daniel. 2018. "The hazards of haste". European Council on Foreign Relations, June 27, 2018. https://www.ecfr.eu/article/commentary_eu_migration_policy_under_pressure

The Guardian. 2016. "EU officials finalise common asylum system to resettle refugees". The Guardian, July 13, 2016. https://www.theguardian.com/world/2016/jul/13/eu-officials-finalise- common-asylum-system-resettle-refugees

Trauner, Florian. 2016. "Asylum policy". Journal of European Integration, 38(3): 311-325.

Ulusoy, Orgun. 2016. Turkey as a Safe Third Country? Oxford Border Criminologies Blog, March 29; 2016. https://www.law.ox.ac.uk/research-subject-groups/centre-criminology/centreborder-criminologies/blog/2016/03/turkey-safe-third

UNHCR. 2017. "Syria Regional Refugee Response". 2 July 2017. <<http://data.unhcr.org/syrianrefugees/regional.php>>.

UNHCR. n.d. UNHCR Global Appeal 2015 Update. Turkey. http://www.unhcr.org/publications/fundraising/5461 e60c52/unhcr-global-appeal-2015- update-turkey.html

Vataman, D. 2016. "Migration and refugee crisis". "Challenges of the Knowledge Society", 2021 May 2016, Bucharest, Vol. 10: 544-549.

Wagner, Martin, et al. 2016. The implementation of the Common European Asylum System. Study PE 556.953, published by the Directorate-General for Internal Policies of the European Parliament.

www.europarl.europa.eu/RegData/etudes/STUD/2016/556953/IPOL_STU(2016)556953_EN.pdf

Weber, Bodo. 2016. Time for a Plan B. Democratic Policy Council, Working Paper,

September. <http://www.democratizationpolicy.org/pdf/DPC_Policy_Paper_Europ_refugee_crisis_EU _Turkey_deal.pdf».

Zaun, Natascha. 2017. "States as Gatekeepers in EU Asylum Politics". Journal of Common Market Studies, 56(1): 44-62.

Beck, N., & Katz, J. N. (2011). Modeling dynamics in time-series-cross-section political economy data. Annual Review of Political Science, 14(1), 331-352.

Borang, F. (2015). Large-scale solidarity? Effects of welfare state institutions on the admission of forced migrants. European Journal of Political Research, 54(2), 216-231.

Borjas, G. J. (1989). Economic theory and international migration. International Migration Review, 23(3), 457-485.

Cohen, J. E., Roig, M., Reuman, D. C., & GoGwilt, C. (2008). International migration beyond gravity: A statistical model for use in population projections. Proceedings of the National Academy of Sciences of the USA, 105(40), 15269-15274.

Croissant, Y., & Millo, G. (2008). Panel data econometrics in R: The plm package. Journal of Statistical Software, 27(2), 1-43.

De Haas, H. (2007). Turning the tide? Why development will not stop migration. Development and Change, 38(5), 819-841.

De Jong, G. F., Abad, R. G., Arnold, F., Carino, B. V., Fawcett, J. T., & Gardner, R. W. (1983). International and internal migration decision making: A value-expectancy based analytical framework of intentions to move from a rural Philippine province. International Migration Review, 17(3), 470-484.

Die Zeit. (2015). Fluchtlingsprognose: Sechs Grunde fur die steigenden Fluchtlingszahlen. Retrieved from http://www.zeit.de/politik/deutschland/2015-08/fluechtlinge-prognose-deutsch- land-europa/komplettansicht

European Commission. (2018). Standard Eurobarometer 89 - Wave EB89.1. TNS opinion & social at the request of the European Commission, doi:10.2775/00.

sEurostat. (2018a). Asylum and new asylum applicants: monthly data [tps00189]. Retrieved from http://ec.europa.eu/eurostat/tgm/table. do?tab=table&init=1&language=en&pcode=tps00189&plugin= 1

Eurostat. (2018b). First instance decisions on applications by citizenship, age and sex Quarterly data (rounded) [migr_asydcfstq]. Retrieved from http// ec.europa.eu/eurostat/web/asylum-and- managed-migration/data/ database

Eurostat. (2018c). Outgoing 'Dublin' transfers by receiving country (PARTNER), legal provision and duration of transfer [migr_dubto]. Retrieved from http//ec.europa.eu/eurostat/web/asylum- and-managed-migration/data/ database

Eurostat. (2018d). Population on 1 January by age group, sex and citizenship [migr_pop1ctz]. Retrieved from http://appsso.eurostat.ec.europa.eu/nui/ show.do?dataset=migr_pop1ctz&lang=en

Eurostat (2018e). Quarterly national accounts [namq_10]. Retrieved from http:// ec.europa.eu/ eurostat/web/national-accounts/data/database

Fargue, P., & Bonfanti, S. (2014). When the best option is a leaky boat: why migrants risk their lives crossing the Mediterranean and what Europe is doing about it, Migration Policy Center

Arpaia, A., A. Kiss, B. Palvolgyi, and A. Turrini. 2014. "Labour Mobility and Labour Market Adjustment in the EU." European Economy Economic Papers No. 539. Brussels: European Commission.

Avdan, N. 2014. "Do Asylum Recognition Rates in Europe Respond to Transnational Terrorism? the Migration-security Nexus Revisited." European Union Politics 15 (4): 445-471. doi:10.1177/ 1465116514534908.

Barslund, M., M. Busse, and J. Schwarzwalder (2015) "Labour Mobility in Europe: An Untapped Resource?" CEPS Policy Brief No. 327. Brussels: Centre for European Policy Studies.

Barthel, F., and E. Neumayer. 2015. "Spatial Dependence in Asylum Migration." Journal of Ethnic and Migration Studies 41 (7): 1131-1151. doi:10.1080/136 9183X.2014.967756.

Beenstock, M., D. Felsenstein, and Z. Rubin. 2015. "Immigration to the European Union from Its Neighborhoods: Testing Welfare-chasing and Related Hypotheses by Spatial Gravity." International Journal of Manpower 36 (4): 491 -517. doi:10.1108/IJM-01-2014-0010.

Brekke, J.-P., M. Roed, and P. Schone. 2017. "Reduction or Deflection? the Effect of Asylum Policy on Interconnected Asylum Flows." Migration Studies 5 (1): 1-32. doi:10.1093/migration/mnw028.

Collyer, M. 2004. "The Dublin Regulations Influences on Asylum Destinations and the Exception of Algerians in the UK." Journal of Refugee Studies 17 (4): 375-400. doi:10.1093/jrs/17.4.375.

Crawley, H. 2010. Chance or Choice? Understanding Why Asylum Seekers Come to the UK. London: Refugee Council.

Cummings, C., J. Pacitto, D. Lauro, and M. Foresti. 2015. "Why People Move: Understanding the Drivers and Trends of Migration to Europe." ODI Working Paper 430. London: Overseas Development Institute.

Czaika, M., and M. Hobolth. 2016. "Do Restrictive Asylum and Visa Policies Increase Irregular Migration into Europe?" European Union Politics 17 (3): 345-365. doi:10.1177/1465116516633299. Davenport, C., W. Moore, and S. Poe. 2003. "'Sometimes You Just Have to Leave: Domestic Threats and Forced Migration, 1964-1989'." International Interactions 29 (1): 27-55. doi:10.1080/03050620304597.

De Haas, H. 2011. "Mediterranean Migration Futures: Patterns, Drivers and Scenarios." Global Environmental Change 21 (1): S59-S69. doi:10.1016/j.gloenvcha.2011.09.003.

Eisele, K. 2014. The External Dimension of the EU's Migration Policy - Different Legal Positions of Third- country Nationals in the EU: A Comparative Perspective. Leiden: Martnus Nijhoff Publishers.

European Asylum Support Office. 2016. "The Push and Pull Factors of Asylum-related Migration: A Literature Review." EASO Report. Luxembourg: Publications Office of the European Union. Funk, M., and R. Parkes. 2016. "Syrian Refugee Flows and Ebbs." Alert Issue 2016-5. Paris: European Union Institute for Security Studies (EUISS).

Garces-Mascarenas, B. 2015. "Why Dublin Doesn't Work." Notes Internationals No. 135. Barcelona: Barcelona Centre for International Affairs (CIDOB).

Grogger, J., and G. H. Hanson. 2011. "Income Maximization and the Selection and Sorting of International Migrants." Journal of Development Economics 95 (1): 42-57. doi:10.1016/j.jdeveco.2010.06.003.

Guiraudon, V. 2000. "European Integration and Migration Policy: Vertical

Policymaking as Venue Shopping." Journal of Common Market Studies 38 (2): 251-271. doi:10.1111/1468-5965.00219. Hatton, T. 2004. "Seeking Asylum in Europe." Economic Policy 19 (38): 6-62. doi:10.1111/j.1468-0327.2004.00118.x.

Hatton, T. 2009. "The Rise and Fall of Asylum: What Happened and Why?" The Economic Journal Volume 119 (535): F183-F213. doi:10.1111/j.1468-0297.2008.02228.x.

Hatton, T. 2016. "Refugees, Asylum Seekers, and Policy in OECD Countries." American Economic Review: Papers & Proceedings 106 (5): 441 -445. doi:10.1257/aer.p20161062.

Havinga, T., and A. Bocker. 1999. "Country of Asylum by Choice or by Chance: Asylum-seekers in Belgium, the Netherlands and the UK." Journal of Ethnic and Migration Studies 25 (1): 43-61. doi:10.1080/1369183X.1999.9976671.

James, P., and L. Mayblin 2016. "Factor Influencing Asylum Destination Choice: A Review of the Evidence." Asylum.welfare.work Working paper: 04/16.1. Sheffield: University of Sheffield.

Kamm, H. 1992. "Yugoslav Refugee Crisis Europe's Worst since 40's."The New York Times, 24 July. Kaunert, C., and S. Leonard. 2012. "The Development of the EU Asylum Policy: Venue-shopping in Perspective." Journal of European Public Policy 19 (9): 1396-1413. doi:10.1080/13501763.2012.677191.

Keogh, G. 2013. "'Modelling Asylum Migration Pull-force Factors in the EU-15.'" The Economic and Social Review 44 (3): 371 -399.

Krugman, P. 1991. "The Move toward Free Trade Zones." In Proceedings from Economic Policy Symposium, Federal Reserve Bank of Kansas City, 22-24 August. Jackson Hole (Wyoming).

Leamer, E. E., and J. Levinsohn 1994. "International Trade Theory: The Evidence." NBER Working Paper No. 4940. Cambridge: National Bureau of Economic Research. doi:10.3168/jds.S0022-0302(94) 77044-2.

Leonard, S., and C. Kaunert. 2019. Refugees, Security and the European Union. New York: Routledge. Liebling, H., S. Burke, S. Goodman, and D. Zasada. 2014. "Understanding the Experiences of Asylum Seekers." International Journal of Migration, Health and Social Care 10 (4): 207-219. doi:10.1108/IJMHSC-06-2013-0016.

Mayda, A. M. 2010. "International Migration: A Panel Data Analysis of the Determinants of Bilateral Flows." Journal of Population Economics 23 (4): 1249-1274. doi:10.1007/s00148-009-0251-x. Moore, W. H. and Shellman, S. M. 2004. 'Fear of persecution: A global study of forced migration, 1952-95', Journal of Conflict Resolution 48(5): 723-745

Neumayer, E. 2004. "Asylum Destination Choice: What Makes Some West European Countries More Attractive than Others." European Union Politics 5 (2): 155-180. doi:10.1177/1465116504042444. Neumayer, E. 2005. "Bogus Refugees? the Determinants of Asylum Migration to Western Europe." International Studies Quarterly 49 (3): 389-409. doi:10.1111/isqu.2005.49.issue-3.

Pedersen, P. J., M. Pytlikova, and N. Smith. 2004. "Selection or Networks Effects? Migration Flows into 27 OECD Countries', 1990-2000." IZA Discussion Paper No. 1104. Bonn: Institute of Labor Economics (IZA).

Peridy, N. 2006. "Welfare Magnets, Border Effects or Policy Regulations: What Determinants Drive Migration Flows into the EU?" Global Economy Journal 6(4): 14-39. doi:10.2202/1524-5861.1186. Radu, D., and T. Straubhaar. 2012. "Beyond 'Push-pull': The Economic Approach to Modelling Migration." In An Introduction to International Migration Studies: European Perspectives, edited by M. Martiniello and J. Rath, 25-56. Amsterdam: Amsterdam University Press.

Robinson, V., and J. Seagrott. 2002. "Understanding the Decision-making of Asylum Seekers." Home Office Research Study No. 245. London: Home Office.

Santos Silva, J. M. C., and S. Tenreyro. 2006. "The Log of Gravity." Review of Economics and Statistics 88 (4): 641 -658. doi:10.1162/rest.88.4.641.

Schmeidl, S. 1997. "'Exploring the Causes of Forced Migration: A Pooled Time-series Analysis, 1971-1990."' Social Science Quarterly 78: 284-308.

Toshkov, D. (2014) 'The dynamic relationship between asylum applications and recognition rates in Europe (1987-2010)', European Union Politics 15(2): 192-214.

Valenta, M., and K. Thorshaug. 2012. "Asylum-seekers' Perspectives on Work and Proof of Identity: The Norwegian Experience." Refugee Survey Quarterly 31 (2): 76-97. doi:10.1093/rsq/hds002.

Yoo, E., and J. W. Koo. 2014. "'Love Thy Neighbor: Explaining Asylum Seeking and

Hosting, 19822008." International Journal of Comparative Sociology 55n(1): 45-72. doi:10.1177/0020715214525431.

Policy Brief, October 2014. Florence: European University Institute.

Freedom House (2015). Freedom in the World 1972-2014. Washington, DC: Freedom House. Granger, C. W., & Newbold, P. (1974). Spurious regressions in econometrics. Journal of Econometrics, 2(2), 111-120.

Halaby, C. N. (2004). Panel models in sociological research: Theory into practice. Annual Review of Sociology, 30(1), 507-544.

Hatton, T. J. (2009). The rise and fall of asylum: What happened and why? The Economic Journal, 119 (535), F183-F213.

Ho, D. E., Imai, K., King, G., & Stuart, E. A. (2007). Matching as nonparametric preprocessing for reducing model dependence in parametric causal inference. Political Analysis, 15(03), 199-236.

Holzer, T., Schneider, G., & Widmer, T. (2000). The impact of legislative deterrence measures on the number of asylum applications in Switzerland (1986-1995). International Migration Review, 34(4), 1182-1216.

Honaker, J., King, G., & Blackwell, M. (2011). Amelia II: A program for missing data. Journal of Statistical Software, 45(7), 1-47.

Kahle, D., & Wickham, H. (2011). ggmap: Spatial Visualization with ggplot2. The R Journal, 5(1), 144-161.

Kalter, F. (2011). Social capital and the dynamics of temporary labour migration from Poland to Germany. European Sociological Review, 27(5), 555-569.

Keogh, G. (2013). Modeling asylum migration pull-force factors in the EU-15. The Economic and Social Review, 44(3), 371-399.

Kim, K., & Cohen, J. E. (2010). Determinants of international migration flows to and from industrialized countries: A panel data approach beyond gravity. International Migration Review, 44(4), 899-932.

Kreft, S., Eckstein, D., Junghans, L., Kerestan, C., & Hagen, U. (2014). Global climate risk index 2015. Bonn/Berlin: Germanwatch.

Le Monde. (2014). Naufrages en Mediterranee: « La croissance de l'Afrique peut accentuer l'envie d'emigration. Retrieved from http://www.lemonde.fr/

societe/article/2014/09/17/pourquoi-2014-est-une-annee-noire-pour-l-immigration-en-mediterranee_4489230_3224.html

Lee, E. S. (1966). A Theory of Migration. Demography, 3(1), 47-57.

Massey, D. S., Arango, J., Hugo, G., Kouaouci, A., Pellegrino, A., & Taylor, J. E. (1993). Theories of International Migration: A Review and Appraisal. Population and Development Review, 19(3), 431-466.

Mayda, A. M. (2010). International migration: A panel data analysis of the determinants of bilateral flows. Journal of Population Economics, 23(4), 1249-1274.

Mitchell, J., Pain, N., & Riley, R. (2011). The drivers of international migration to the UK: A panel-based Bayesian model averaging approach. The Economic Journal, 121(557), 1398-1444.

Moore, W. H., & Shellman, S. (2011). Whither will they go? A global study of refugees destinations, 1965-1995. International Studies Quarterly, 51(4), 811-834.

Neumayer, E. (2004). Asylum destination choice: What makes some West European countries more attractive than others?'. European Union Politics, 5(2), 155-180.

Neumayer, E. (2005). 'Bogus refugees? The determinants of asylum migration to Western Europe'. International Studies Quarterly, 49(3), 389-410.

NY Times. (2015). More War, Less Cash, New Routes Drive Migrant Push to EU. Retrieved from http://www.nytimes.com/aponline/2015/09/12/world/europe/ap-eu-eu-migrants-why-now.html

OECD. (2018). Quarterly National Accounts. Retrieved from https://stats.oecd.org/index. aspx?queryid=350#

Ortega, F., & Peri, G. (2013). The effect of income and immigration policies on international migration. Migration Studies, 1(1), 47-74.

Pedersen, P. J., Pytlikova, M., & Smith, N. (2008). Selection and network effects: Migration flows into OECD Countries, 1990-2000. European Economic Review, 52(7), 1160-1186.

Piguet, E. (2013). From 'primitive migration' to 'climate refugees': The curious fate of the natural environment in migration studies. Annals of the Association of American Geographers, 103(1), 148-162.

Plumper, T., & Troeger, V. E. (2007). Efficient estimation of time-invariant and rarely changing variables in finite sample panel analyses with unit fixed effects. Political Analysis, 15(2), 124-139.

R Core Team (2013). R: A language and environment for statistical computing. Vienna, Austria: R Foundation for Statistical Computing. Retrieved from http://www.R-project.org

Raleigh, C., Linke, A., Hegre, H., & Karlsen, J. (2010). Introducing acled: An armed conflict location and event dataset special data feature. Journal of Peace Research, 47(5), 651-660.

Ravenstein, E. G. (1885). The laws of migration. Journal of the Statistical Society of London, 48 (2), 167-235.

Rubin, D. B. (1987). Multiple imputation for nonresponse in surveys. Hoboken, NJ: Wiley. Ruyssen, I., Everaert, G., & Rayp, G. (2014). Determinants and dynamics of migration to OECD countries in a three-dimensional panel framework. Empirical Economics, 46(1), 175-197.

Schmeidl, S. (1997). Exploring the causes of forced migration: A pooled time-series analysis, 1971-1990'. Social Science Quarterly, 78(2), 284-308.

Schrodt, P. A. (2014). Seven deadly sins of contemporary quantitative political analysis. Journal of Peace Research, 51(2), 287-300.

Sjaastad, L. A. (1962). The costs and returns of human migration. Journal of Political Economy, 70(5, Part 2), 80-93.

Stark, O., & Bloom, D. E. (1985). The new economics of labor migration. American Economic Review, 75(2), 173-178.

Toshkov, D. D. (2014). The dynamic relationship between asylum applications and recognition rates in Europe (1987-2010). European Union Politics, 15(2), 192-214.

Toshkov, D., & de Haan, L. (2013). The Europeanization of asylum policy: An assessment of the EU impact on asylum applications and recognitions rates. Journal of European Public Policy, 20(5), 661-683.

UN [United Nations]. (2016). Demographic yearbook. New York: United Nations.

Vogler, M., & Rotte, R. (2000). The Effects of development on migration: Theoretical issues and new empirical evidence. Journal of Population Economics, 13(3), 485-508.

Wilson, S. E., & Butler, D. M. (2007). A lot more to do: The sensitivity of time-series cross-section analyses to simple alternative specifications. Political Analysis, 15(2), 101-123.

World Bank. (2015). World Development Indicators. Retrieved from http://data.worldbank.org/ data-catalog/world-development-indicators

Zipf, G. K. (1946). The P1*P2/D hypothesis: On the intercity movement of persons. American Sociological Review, 11(6), 677-686.

Index

U

V

W

www.ingramcontent.com/pod-product-compliance
Lightning Source LLC
Chambersburg PA
CBHW070251260926
51849CB00001BA/154
* 9 7 8 9 3 9 5 5 2 2 9 2 2 *